REMARKABLE ENCOUNTERS

REMARKABLE ENCOUNTERS

Men and Women Who Have Shaped Our World

VAGIF GUSEYNOV

UNICORN

First published by Unicorn
an imprint of the Unicorn Publishing Group LLP, 2018
101 Wardour Street
London W1F 0UG

www.unicornpublishing.org

10 9 8 7 6 5 4 3 2 1

ISBN 978-1-911604-33-4

Editor: John Parker
Project Manager: Rena Lavery
Cover Design: Unicorn Publishing Group
Typeset by: Vivian@Bookscribe

Printed in China on behalf of Latitude Press

CONTENTS

Alessandro, Sofia and Massimo

INTRODUCTION

Dedicated to my darling grandchildren
Alessandro, Sofia and Massimo

When my daughter proposed that I write a book based on my meetings and conversations with famous people from Russia and several other countries, needless to say it seemed an excellent idea.

The first thing I did was to take a piece of paper and start jotting down names, individuals I had met during my work and travels around the world covering a period of almost thirty years. These names came purely from memory. It is indeed true that when experience is retained in your heart and soul then nothing is lost.

Why had the people I was listing on my piece of paper made such an impression on me? Many were famous of course, or were destined to become so. Some became lifelong friends. I realised that meeting these individuals had been among the most memorable experiences of my life, and that to do justice to them I must make it my goal to recall them, and the circumstances in which I met them, as accurately as possible.

The list grew longer. At one point I had over fifty names. Finally I selected thirty-nine to go in the book. I assumed that some would be well known to virtually everyone – Leonid Brezhnev, Boris Yeltsin, Mikhail Gorbachev, Yuri Gagarin, Fidel Castro, Che Guevara, Henry Kissinger and Pope John Paul II. Other outstanding figures such as Kerim Kerimov, had worked for many years behind the scenes, far from the public gaze, but had nonetheless played a vital role in Soviet history and on the international stage.

The heroes and heroines you will find in these true-life accounts are diverse in their characters and achievements, but they share the distinction of having left an indelible footprint in the pages of history. The other element that binds them together is the appearance of the author at some point in their lives, in some cases with just a few lines of conversation, in others as a recurring player or a lifelong friend.

Momentous events and ideas are portrayed here. History and politics are by nature controversial, and according to national and personal perspective and the intellectual climate of time and place, opinions on thirty-nine people at the heart of those events and ideas will inevitably vary. My aim above all, dear reader, weaving my own recollections with the life stories of these remarkable individuals, is to bring each of them to life in your imagination. I hope you find the results not only thought-provoking but also enjoyable.

Vagif Guseynov

YURI ANDROPOV

'Asia, what a disquieting reservoir of men! The safety of Europe will not be assured until we have driven Asia back behind the Urals. No organised Russian state must be allowed to exist west of that line.'

Adolf Hitler

Well before 1941 this was the Führer's grand plan, the intended culmination of Operation Barbarossa, to forcibly relocate the entire Russian population east of the Ural Mountains, annexing huge swathes of territory, including the great cities of Moscow and Leningrad, for the German people, fulfilling his dream of *lebensraum*, living space for the Aryan race to procreate and prosper: *'Increase (of) our peasant population is the only effective defence against the influx of the Slav working class masses from the East.'*

(Hitler quoted in *The Devil's Disciple* by Anthony Read)

In the Great Patriotic War which ensued, the Soviet Union had to contend not only with the might of the German fascists but also with their Axis allies in Scandinavia and Europe: Finland, Italy Bulgaria, Romania and Hungary. In 1941, the Hungarians took part in the invasion of Russia, but when repulsed by advancing Soviet troops, they turned to the Allies to seek peace. Before a deal could be brokered, however, the Germans had poured into their country and installed the fascist Arrow Cross Party as the new government. In the summer of 1944 Arrow Cross Party members and Hungarian police are thought to have collaborated with the Nazis in the deportation of over 400,000 Jews, most of whom it is believed were killed in Auschwitz. By the end of 1944 Soviet troops had reached Budapest and two months later the city surrendered.

In the post-war rearrangement Bulgaria, Romania and Hungary swiftly became socialist republics and in 1955 would be among the founding signatories to the Treaty of Friendship, Co-operation and Mutual Assistance – the Warsaw Pact. In Hungary, the Soviet Union had approved Matyas Rakosi to lead the Communist government, and in carrying out its programme of Stalinisation the regime imposed strict rules on conduct, instigating purges of Titoists and Trotskyists, backed up by the repressive tactics of the Hungarian State Security Police, the AVH, including imprisonment and alleged torture of political opponents. Between 1948 and 1956 an estimated 350,000 people deemed to be undesirables were either jailed or executed, while over half a million are said to have been sent to labour camps in the Soviet Union.

The death of Stalin in 1953 and the appointment of the moderate Imre Nagy as Hungary's prime minister, curbed the activities of the AVH to some extent and brought a degree of political openness in parallel with Khrushchev's thaw in the Soviet Union. However, Nagy's liberalism, extending to acceptance of free market economics, marked him out as a revisionist. Soon the pendulum had swung back and a new and far more conservative Communist, Erno Gero was in place. The reversal was not well received among Hungary's intelligentsia, particularly the students, and on 23 October 1956, emboldened by concessions recently won by Polish workers, they began to make their feelings clear.

At a gathering of some 20,000 people by the statue of Polish and Hungarian hero Jozsef Bem, a manifesto calling for democracy and independence from foreign powers was read out and, in a symbolic gesture of defiance to Moscow, protesters cut the Communist coat of arms from their Hungarian flags. At approximately 21.00 hrs, after Gero had spoken on the radio denouncing the manifesto, a large statue of Stalin was toppled. Meanwhile, outside the radio station events took a turn for the worse as AVH officers fired tear gas followed by bullets into a crowd, killing several. The story quickly reached the West:

> *'Tens of thousands of people have taken to the streets in Hungary to demand an end to Soviet rule. There are believed to have been many casualties in a day which started as a peaceful rally, and ended with running battles between police and demonstrators in which shots are said to have been fired. The demonstrators are demanding that the former Prime Minister, Imre Nagy, be returned to power.'*
>
> (BBC On This Day)

As I have described in the chapter on Mikhail Suslov, he was in Budapest at the time, and on 27 October reported back to Moscow his impression that the proposed new government was 'reliable.' With Khrushchev wary of a Suez-type debacle, on 30 October after lengthy discussions in the Presidium the following statement was issued by Moscow:

> *'The Soviet Government is prepared to enter into the appropriate negotiations with the government of the Hungarian People's Republic and other members of the Warsaw Treaty on the question of the presence of Soviet troops on the territory of Hungary.'*
>
> (Russian Department of State Bulletin no. 907)

Just twenty-four hours later, however, concerned by talk of Hungary adopting neutrality and leaving the Warsaw Pact, and that multi-party democracy would open the door to capitalism, the decision was reversed. Khrushchev launched Operation Whirlwind, mobilising Soviet planes and armour towards Budapest, and throwing those inside the city into further confusion, uncertainty and fear.

'On Nov. 1, 1956, with the streets of Budapest blackened from battle, with Soviet forces pouring into the country despite their agreed withdrawal from the capital, Imre Nagy, the leader of the Government, who sought to bring about change, found himself under pressure from all sides. He called Mr. Andropov to his office and denounced the troop movements.' (R.W. Apple Jr., Special Correspondent to

The New York Times; interviewed Hungarians and Westerners in Budapest, Geneva and elsewhere who knew Yuri V. Andropov during his years in Hungary, on their expectations for the new Soviet leader. December 28th 1982)

Forty-two-year-old Yuri Andropov was the Soviet Union's Ambassador to Hungary, a posting that had suddenly become anything but dull. As in many a revolution, the thirst for revenge had been stronger than for reconciliation, and the obvious targets were the State Police officers who had profited from the ill-treatment of their fellow Hungarians:

> '*The hated men and women of the AVO faced the wrath of the people in whose name they had murdered and maimed. Hundreds were kicked and beaten to death or shot in the streets. Many hung from trees and lamp posts, head downwards to be spat at by the passing crowds.*'
>
> (Clare Doyle *Socialist World*, 21 October 2006)

From his office in the centre of Budapest, Andropov was among those witnessing the mob violence and lynching. The shocking scenes were to have a scarring effect on him and would influence his decision-making in matters of Soviet policy for the rest of his career. But what did he tell Imre Nagy that day about reports that the Russian military were approaching the city?

> '*The Soviet Ambassador said he knew nothing of this but promised to find out. Some time later, after what Hungarians close to the situation have described as a heated telephone conversation, he gave his word that the influx of Soviet troops would be halted.*' (Ibid)

That same afternoon, however, Nagy's cabinet announced they would indeed be leaving the Warsaw Pact. The following day, Andropov, alarmed that Hungarians were sacking the Soviet Embassy, tried to calm the situation, assuring the new head of the National Guard, Bela Kiraly: '*Believe me, general, the Soviet people are Hungary's best friends*' (Ibid) and that the withdrawal of Soviet troops could be discussed.

Decades later, however, Kiraly looked back on Andropov's assurance with scepticism, '*Here was this man Andropov who clearly understood what was going on ... yet he pretended until the last moment to me and to the Prime Minister and to others that everything was business as usual. Even pirates, before they attack another ship, hoist a black flag. He was absolutely calculating.*'

A number of Hungarians concur with the view that Andropov played a key part in steering events in Hungary from November 1956. According to Nagy's press aide, later jailed for four years, '*...it was Andropov who persuaded Kadar to go over to the Soviet viewpoint.*' (Ibid) Kadar was to be Nagy's replacement and, again according to several Hungarians, it was Andropov who helped persuade Khrushchev to accept him. Andropov was also believed to have been a shrewd judge of the party leaders and the Hungarian people, and that '*...when Tito opted for Kadar, Andropov was in a position to support him.*' (Ibid)

As for Nagy, following the Soviet invasion Andropov told the former Prime Minister, who had taken refuge with the other discredited leaders in the Yugoslav Embassy, that he could expect safe conduct if he left the building. Watching from his window, Andropov allegedly waved to Nagy before seeing him arrested and taken off in a van. Two years later, after a secretly held trial, Nagy would be executed and buried in an unmarked grave.

To take back control of Hungary an additional 150,000 Soviet troops and 2,500 tanks were deployed. The resistance numbered around 3,000, and although armed with only automatic pistols and homemade Molotov cocktails it fought fiercely. Some 20,000 of them died, and while the borders remained open an estimated quarter of a million people fled the country. Thousands more were imprisoned or interned and there were over 200 executions. For his part in restoring law and order Andropov would earn the unofficial title among Hungarians as the 'Butcher of Budapest'.

The Hungarian Revolution is also generally regarded as the making of Andropov. In 1957 he was back in Moscow running the Department for Liaison with Communist and Workers' Parties in Socialist Countries, a full member of the Central Committee of the Communist Party of the Soviet Union by 1961, and in 1967, through Suslov's influence he became head of the KGB. The timing seemed fated, in a sense even propitious, when the following January in Czechoslovakia the reformist Alexander Dubcek became First Secretary of the Communist Party.

Dubcek's reforms extended to greater freedom of speech, the relaxation of travel restrictions, a degree of decentralisation and democratisation and separating the country into the Czech Republic and Slovenia. In Hungary, Kadar expressed support for Dubcek, but Moscow feared an erosion of Communism, which NATO and the West could exploit. After several months of discussions between the Warsaw Pact countries they failed to find a compromise. The Soviet Union saw no other option than to enact the 'Brezhnev Doctrine' – the right to intervene when a socialist country seemed in danger of veering towards capitalism.

The invasion on 21 August 1968 was not on the scale of Hungary a decade earlier and caused far less bloodshed. It also differed in being a combined Warsaw Pact operation, comprising troops from the Soviet Union, Bulgaria, Poland and Hungary. Since the event, however, theories have emerged suggesting that Andropov exaggerated the threat from NATO, or even suppressed evidence in order to strengthen the case for invasion. Oleg Kalugin, a Soviet agent in Washington, claimed to have knowledge of *'absolutely reliable documents proving that neither the CIA nor any other agency was manipulating the Czechoslovak reform movement'.* (Christopher Andrew and Vasili Mitrokhin, *The KGB in Europe and the West*)

If this were true, it might underline what some observers have referred to as Andropov's 'Hungary Complex', the horrific events he witnessed in Budapest colouring his reactions whenever any revisionist or reformist elements manifested themselves within the Soviet sphere: *'Andropov*

Vagif Guseynov's first meeting with Andropov, 1 May 1978

remained haunted for the rest of his life by the speed with which an apparently all-powerful Communist one-party state had begun to topple.' (Ibid)

Similar situations would arise with Afghanistan in 1979 and Poland in 1981, though the decision not to step in against Lech Walesa and Solidarity signalled that the Brezhnev Doctrine of intervention was no longer considered feasible or appropriate.

My own first meeting with Andropov was on the annual International Workers Day, 1 May 1978. According to protocol, in the large Colonnade Hall in the Kremlin, a symposium of Moscow Workers had assembled, and being by now the deputy secretary of the youth division of the All-Union Communist Party, according to protocol I had come along to represent the young people of the Soviet Union. With me was one of the army generals that I knew. When the symposium was over we proceeded out to Red Square where, at the top of the Lenin Mausoleum, members of the

Politburo were now assembled to watch the May Day parade, while others lined the route below.

After the parade my friend the general met with Andropov and said, '*I would like to introduce you to my compatriot.*' Very aware of his status as long-serving chief of the KGB, I found he also had a sense of humour as he joked with my friend about being '*late as usual.*' He and the general sat on a committee together and were well acquainted.

Considering all that he had experienced during the previous few decades, I imagined that Andropov's sense of humour must have proved invaluable to him at times. I was told that when Brezhnev had asked him to run the KGB he replied, '*You are burying me now.*' His Stalinist predecessor in the post had been shot dead. Apparently when Andropov went home and told his wife Tatyana about the appointment the first thing she said was, '*Yuri, what did you do?*'

A few years later I would experience a similar kind of emotion when asked to become Azerbaijan's KGB chief. Things had loosened up a bit by then, but all the same there was a faintly ominous feeling donning the mantle of the KGB, compounded by a sense that one could not refuse.

When Brezhnev died in November 1982, Andropov became the first ex-KGB chief to be elected General Secretary of the Communist Party. In commenting on the appointment, Janos Berecz, editor of the Hungarian party newspaper *Nepszabadsag*, gave his impression of Andropov's role in 1956, '*When the Government changed, he stopped being Comrade Andropov and started being Mr. Andropov. He learned from that experience. He knows perfectly well that the crisis here, and similar crises elsewhere in Eastern Europe, have nothing to do with Western imperialists arriving here and manufacturing difficulties. He knows that crises arise from within and have to be solved from within. That counts for a lot.*' (*The New York Times*, 28 December 1982)

Western observers seemed to know little about Andropov, other than that his recent KGB role made them nervous. In 1983 Ronald Reagan referred to the Soviet Union as the '*evil empire*', a phrase hardly expected to improve East–West relations. Reagan was also the proponent of the American Strategic Defence Initiative, the so-called Star Wars programme to position anti-missile systems in space, a move that could potentially provoke a re-escalation of the arms race.

Reagan must have been as surprised as anyone by the news that in 1982 Samantha Smith, a ten-year-old girl from Maine, had written a letter to the new General Secretary of the Communist Party, congratulating him on his appointment and expressing her concerns about nuclear war. '*...I would like to know why*,' she said in conclusion, '*you want to conquer the world or at least our country. God made the world for us to live together in peace and not to fight.*'

The text was published in *Pravda*, and when prompted by a second letter from Samantha, Andropov eventually wrote her a long reply, assuring her of his commitment to peace and inviting her and her family to visit the Soviet Union.

American schoolgirl Samantha Smith in Moscow, 1982

'...No one in our country – neither workers, peasants, writers nor doctors, neither grown-ups nor children, nor members of the government – want either a big or 'little' war. We want peace – there is something that we are occupied with: growing wheat, building and inventing, writing books and flying into space. We want peace for ourselves and for all peoples of the planet. For our children and for you, Samantha.'

Three months later Samantha travelled with her parents to Moscow, where at a press conference she observed that 'the Russians are just like us.' Andropov spoke to her on the telephone but did not come out to meet her. It later transpired he was seriously unwell and had been admitted to hospital. Suffering from renal failure, Yuri Andropov died on 9 February 1985 aged sixty-nine.

On the 23 April that year Samantha Smith and her father were killed in an aircraft accident over Maine.

Andropov's style when dealing with regional or any other issues was to listen very carefully to the person that was on the spot, and where appropriate incorporate what they said into an action plan. Taking local knowledge on board was definitely in evidence in his dealings with the Caucasus. As well as being extremely analytical he was also very proactive and believed that people should use their initiative. I remember at one meeting when someone produced a litany of complaints he asked straight out why on earth they didn't make some effort to improve things themselves.

The willingness to roll up his sleeves in circumstances that would defeat lesser men was observed by a Western diplomat who had been in Budapest during Andropov's time:

'When he came to Hungary, he was forty years old, a junior functionary, not even a member of the Central Committee ... then he became Ambassador, which was in itself unusual, because few diplomats are ever promoted

without changing posts. Then the country fell apart, which should have marked him for oblivion.'

(*The New York Times*)

Instead of oblivion, it marked Andropov for the highest office in the Soviet Union, albeit for little more than two years. Yet Hungary in 1956, which caused his wife Tatyana to suffer a nervous breakdown, must have been an immensely difficult and dangerous predicament for him. In that kind of violent, volatile situation you can either shoot yourself, side with the opposition or keep faith with your country. Andropov chose the latter. Despite many negative accounts of him I believe he was at heart a man of integrity, his campaign against corruption as zealous as his pursuit of dissidents. Until his death he believed in the idea of Communism when so many had abandoned it.

For a public figure Andropov led a very ascetic and inconspicuous life, and despite great efforts the FBI and the US State Department had very little information on him. B. L. Prozorov in his book *Declassified* says that the CIA did not even know his wife's name. Andropov remembered names, and people. At the end of the 1970s, whilst working as the Secretary of the Central Committee of the Komsomol on international issues, I was invited regularly to public events. At these seated gatherings the senior party officials sat at the front, while Komsomol secretaries, trade union and military leaders and the general public took the rows behind. Andropov, carrying himself well, was always courteous, attentive and friendly, the first to stretch out his hand and say hello. At one such event organised by the Moscow authorities, Semyon Kuzmich Tsvigun introduced me to Andropov as his fellow countryman and a friend. Yuri Vladimirovich Andropov smiled, '*Semyon Kuzmich*,' he said, '*you are about three years too late. Comrade Guseynov and I have both been coming here at least that long!*'

LEONID BREZHNEV

From the outside the Kremlin building in Moscow seems vast. As you enter and get your bearings however, the dimensions become less overwhelming and you begin to study what is around you. From an architectural point of view the interior is stunning. Through the magnificent rooms designed by Italian Renaissance architects, emanates 600 years of Russian history and the aura of power exercised by a succession of rulers good and evil – Ivan the Terrible, the Romanovs, Stalin.

In 1974 we had Brezhnev, by then in his tenth year as leader of the Soviet Union. I was in my second year as First Secretary of the Lenin Komsomol (Youth Communist League) of Azerbaijan Central Committee (Baku), and in Moscow for the reunion of the republics. It was a feature of the Soviet government that every four years the leaders and representative delegates of all the republics would be summoned to Moscow, where for a period of eight consecutive days they would sit together in the Kremlim with the members of the Politburo and the Presidium including Brezhnev. These gatherings were an opportunity for the republics' leaders, who lived hundreds if not thousands of miles away, to speak face to face with the leaders of the USSR about their problems and concerns. The subjects under discussion might range from the building and repair of houses, schools, public spaces and transport facilities, to the state funding and support of the arts; grants for young composers, painters and writers and the development and maintenance of art galleries.

Over the eight days the central government leaders would listen patiently to the comments and requests from each republic, learning about their problems and often their criticisms of say the Ministry of Culture or of Education. For example, a Komsomol representative from Siberia might describe how for the last couple of years he had been writing to the Minister

President Gerald Ford and Soviet General Secretary Leonid Brezhnev sign a Joint Communiqué following talks on the limitation of strategic offensive arms. The document was signed in the conference hall of the Okeansky Sanitarium, Vladivostok, USSR in 1974

for Urbanisation requesting repairs to the local concert hall, school or nursery, or that a road be built to provide better access to these facilities. His letters, however, have gone unanswered he says, or there have been promises but no action. Now, on behalf of those people in Siberia he would like to share this information with the Presidium and ask if something can be done. Hearing such a request Brezhnev might then say, '*Wait a second, is the Minister for Urbanisation here?*' Everyone would then look around the room and the minister would reply, '*Yes I am here.*' Brezhnev would ask him directly, '*Why don't you build this road?*' The minister might then say it would be built, to which Brezhnev might reply, '*How long will it take?*' If the Minister replied three months Brezhnev was likely to say no it should be done in two.

Brezhnev speaking at the opening ceremony of the 18th Soviet Young Communist League Congress at the Kremlin Palace in Moscow, 1978

Andrei Gromyko once referred to Brezhnev's weekly Politburo meetings as 'quiet, orderly and methodical' (Arkady Shevchenko *Breaking with Moscow* 1985, pp 207–208). These four-yearly gatherings of the republics on the other hand were certainly orderly but they could also be confrontational and Brezhnev was quite forceful when he judged that there was a legitimate need that had been overlooked or ignored. He also took steps to ensure that commitments were fulfilled; after a minister had given an assurance on a new school say, or the provision of funds for a young painter, he would turn to the head of the Committee of the National Control Union – a voluntary group comprised of workers, professors and artists from all parts of the Soviet Union – and ask them to discuss the details with the minister and see that the necessary plans were formalised. Of course this was a totalitarian state but these meetings demonstrate, I think, that within that system there was a democratic process at work, a channel of communication for listening to what individual representatives of the people had to say, taking on board their concerns and acting on them. This process of communication and feedback took place at a local level too and in a moment I will describe how Brezhnev supported me in this respect.

Leonid Brezhnev was born in the Ukraine on 19 December 1906. At fifteen years old he followed his father into the local steel mill while studying at night and later attending a Land Surveying and Reclamation school in Kursk. A member of Komsomol, he joined the Communist Party at the age of twenty-five and subsequently took a degree in steel engineering. His first entry into politics was election to deputy mayor of his home province of Dneprodzerzhinsk in 1937, followed by swift promotion to the post of local party secretary. The party leader there at the time was Nikita Khrushchev and this is believed to be when the men's friendship began. During the Great Patriotic War, Brezhnev was made a political commissar and served in the Crimea and the Battle of the Caucasus on the Black Sea as well as in Ukraine. These experiences gave him an affinity with the armed services that would help him to forge strong friendships among the military in peacetime.

In the aftermath of the war the Communist Party assigned Brezhnev to various supervisory roles in the reconstruction of Ukraine. In 1950, the Central Committee summoned him to Moscow where he was promptly elevated to Party Leader of Moldavia for the next two years. In 1953, Stalin died and in 1955 his successor Khrushchev appointed Brezhnev as Party Leader of Kazakhstan. His particular brief was to implement the Virgin Lands programme in the republic. To the surprise of many observers Brezhnev achieved encouraging results at the beginning, cultivating some 85,000 acres of land and with it a reputation as a determined and skilful manager. The success of the Virgin Lands programme was short-lived, but fortunately for Brezhnev he had by then been recalled to Moscow with his good name intact, and in May 1960 was appointed Chairman of the Presidium of the Supreme Soviet.

Nominally Brezhnev was now the Soviet head of state although Khrushchev as First Secretary held the actual power. Khrushchev's days were numbered, however. A poor manager, who had exported food while Russia went hungry, Khrushchev had sold off large amounts of the country's gold reserves to pay for his mistakes. Now he would pay again as some 600 members of the Presidium stood up to declare their disapproval and lack of confidence in him. Brezhnev, though regarded as Khrushchev's long time protégé, is thought by some to have worked behind the scenes to have him removed. Khrushchev's opponents claimed that his tendency to act autonomously was *'in contempt of the party's political ideals.'*

Thus by 1964 Brezhnev became General Secretary of the Communist Party and effectively the leader of the Soviet Union and to begin with at least his emphasis was on government by consultation. At the same time the relative freedom of cultural expression allowed during Khrushchev's 'thaw' years was to a large extent withdrawn. Brezhnev himself made the position clear in a statement of zero tolerance of perceived disloyalty to the Soviet ideal:

Greeting Brezhnev on his official party visit in September 1982

'People who fall for self-publicity, ready to make a name for themselves not through work for the homeland but by any politically dubious means – and not disdaining to praise our ideological opponents – sometimes fall into their net. The Soviet public harshly denounces the abominable deeds of these double-dealers 'Renegades should not expect to get away unpunished. The country's enemies clutch with great tenacity at any manifestations of ideological immaturity or hesitation among the intellectuals.'

Whilst there were no apparent purges, nor any return to outright Stalinist practices, numerous writers, artists and intellectuals who through their public utterances or works were deemed to be enemies of the state, were placed in mental institutions. Under Brezhnev's management, however, during the rest of the decade and into the 1970s agricultural output increased steadily most years although broader economic growth was less impressive. What was to be applauded was his focus on improving the living conditions of the Russian people.

I would see Brezhnev's personal commitment to this policy in action between 1980 and 1983, when during my time as *First Secretary of the Baku City Committee of the Communist Party of Azerbaijan, every Saturday the twenty or so mayoral officials would sit in a bus and take a ride around the town. Baku being the fourth largest city in the Soviet Union these inspections would take at least all morning. Making their way slowly along the twenty-eight kilometre promenade, the shoreline of the Caspian Sea on which Baku is situated, the mayors would observe the state of the properties, roads, parks, beaches and public amenities and check out what needed doing: which houses needed repairing, the roofs with missing tiles, where paint was peeling or mouldy piles of unsightly rubbish or abandoned cars.

---

*The First Secretary of the City's function was to oversee the entire social and political day-to-day running of the city, and no decision was taken, even by the city mayors, without the First Secretary of the City's approval. The First Secretary of Baku City Committee of the Communist Party of Azerbaijan reported directly to the Head of the Republic.

Left: September 1982. Breznev in Baku on an official party visit, when Vagif Guseynov was the First Secretary of the Baku City Committee of the Communist Party of Azerbaijan

Wherever something required attention the mayor for that area would have to make a note and see that it was fixed. The relevant mayor would then return later to check that the job had been done satisfactorily, and they would then phone me with a report. Managing this regular maintenence and upgrading work was a small part of my overall duties as First Secretary of the City Committee but nonetheless an important one. This was totalitarianism but good totalitarianism, in the sense that it was about improving people's environment, encouraging pride in the community. In the West they were doing the same thing but they called it democracy.

On one of the weekly inspections of Baku in 1982, as the bus drove slowly along the promenade the mayors were rather more keen-eyed than usual, and for good reason: the town was expecting a visitor by the name of Leonid Illyich Brezhnev, leader of the Soviet Union. As First Secretary of the City Committee I was responsible for arranging the official reception, and the various ceremonies, meetings and events that were to take place throughout the visit. This came at a tense time for me, as my relations with the central government of Azerbaijan were very strained. Three months earlier I had uncovered a huge corruption case in Baku involving about thirty people. Officials had been stealing building materials, furniture and other supplies as well as taking bribes. In local construction projects the cement had mysteriously gone missing and the houses were being put up using sand, making the buildings unsafe and putting people's lives at risk. When the scandal came to light the main culprits were kicked out of the party and some went to jail. Heydar Aliyev the First Secretary of the Communist Party of Azerbaijan did not like it because some of his people were allegedly involved.

My concern was that in the light of this affair the Azerbaijan leadership would report negatively on me to Moscow, or at least try to claim credit for uncovering the corruption while tarnishing my name by implication. With all the practical preparations for Brezhnev's visit, however, I did not have time to dwell too much on these worries. The main event to welcome our visitor was to be held in the Palace of Lenin. There were to be around 5,000 people in attendance including City Committee First Secretaries from other parts of the Soviet Union. Whilst there was great excitement, everything was conducted according to protocol and there were certain rituals that had to be observed, such as the band playing the national anthems of each of the republics represented. It was a great honour when Brezhnev presented Baku with the Medal of Friendship and gave medals to the military veterans and a number of our local workers, a very democratic affair.

To my surprise and great relief Brezhnev's speech included many words of support for me as First Secretary of the City Committee, and one could tell that he really enjoyed his visit, which included a tour of Baku. I had a personal meeting with him for twenty minutes during which he complemented me on the new buildings. 'You have done a great deal for the city in a short space of time,' he told me. He also advised me quietly, 'Do not make mistakes with the government.'

It transpired that Brezhnev, who had numerous sources of information at his disposal, had known everything about the corruption scandal in Baku and precisely who had done what. I could guess that Aliyev would not like the public expressions of support I had received from Brezhnev and I could surmise his thoughts: who is this young man gaining such a good reputation with the central government in Moscow, etc. I was seen now as a threat, a potential competitor for the leadership of Azerbaijan and this made the republic's government very suspicious of me.

This feeling seemed to be confirmed when I was invited to Moscow for a symposium of the First Secretaries of the thirty largest cities in the Soviet Union; even though Baku was the fourth largest city, Aliyev refused permission for me to attend. But by now the people in Moscow were really looking after me, and I received a phone call from a party official there telling me that I was definitely going. Aliyev then asked to see me and repeated this information and told me that I was in trouble.

Shortly after his visit to Baku in 1982 Brezhnev died. The next day I

Leonid Brezhnev speaking in Baku on an official party visit

was sacked as First Secretary of the Baku City Committee and made Azerbaijan's Minister of Sport instead, pushed by the republic's government to the sidelines, and in their eyes out of the running for political leadership.

I remember Brezhnev, of course, for the help and guidance he extended to me during the beginning of what would prove a very difficult time in my life. But I also remember him as a funny and above all kind and decent person. When speaking, one could hear he was from Ukraine where people speak differently to the Russians, southern, very genial and outgoing rather like the Italians. Brezhnev's early political career began in Moldovia, then a part of Ukraine where eighty per cent of trade was wine making, and perhaps where he discovered his penchant for drinking and the anecdotes of multiple cognacs or straight vodkas that he would down at parties began. His fondness for good food was equally well known, along with fast cars, hunting and cigarettes. Through over-indulgence he put on weight and the cigarettes could not have helped his health problems in the latter years.

Yet these were the things he enjoyed and while recognising the need for moderation he saw the humorous side to it all. Referring to his cigarette box fitted with a time lock designed to limit his smoking, he would then admit jokingly to having a spare pack of Philip Morris Multifilters in his pocket. Alongside the indulgences, Brezhnev lived in many ways a simple life. As General Secretary of the Communist Party he could have moved to a better house but remained in his old apartment on Kutuzov Prospekt, in the house next to ours. The personal, down-to-earth side of Brezhnev was more likely to be observed away from the Kremlin.

In 1963 on a trip to Iran he had reportedly curtailed a long series of earnest toasts by raising his vodka glass with the words, *'Down with protocol! Long live freedom!'* The same year, in a conversation with Glenn T. Seaborg the Chairman of the United States Atomic Energy Commission, he allegedly confided that he found the majority of Soviet buildings ugly and that Russian architectural students could learn a lot from time spent abroad. There was no standing on ceremony one night at the circus either, when he had insisted on kissing every one of the female performers in their skimpy costumes as they brought him bouquets. The story suggests he enjoyed the circus's bravura and simplicity, with its sawdust and spectacle, as much if not more than the more formal and 'high brow' entertainments of the ballet or opera.

Brezhnev's heartiness and love of pleasure did not seem to diminish the clarity of his thought, his attention to detail or the seriousness with which he took the responsibilities of government. During three and a half years as First Secretary of the Baku City Committee of the Communist Party of Azerbaijan I received four personal letters from Brezhnev concerning requests he had received from citizens, one I remember was about housing and in another case someone had been kicked out of their job. The gist of each letter was '*Comrade Guseynov, I have been informed of the following issue … it seems like the local authorities did not pay attention … please look into the matter and find out what really happened…*'

Considering the massive size of the Soviet Union, where some 265 million people inhabited a sixth of the world's landmass, responding to letters like this on a personal basis alongside all his other governmental duties, even in a relatively calm period for the Soviet Union, shows an impressive dedication to the people that saw him as their leader.

In literature the Soviet Union is represented as a very strict totalitarian society and of course in comparison to Britain or France, for example, that is true. At the same time it is not entirely correct. Democracy was being practised in Russia and this applied in foreign as well as domestic policy. A key example was the intervention in Czechoslovakia in 1968, of which as Brezhnev says in his memoirs, he did not approve. All the other members of the Politburo voted for sending the troops in.

My autobiography contains extracts of conversations in which Vladimir Kryuchkov, the former KGB leader, asked Andropov how he could have voted for the invasion knowing that many people might die. Andropov replied that he could not have done otherwise because he felt he must support the Minister of Defence, who had been put in place by Stalin at the age of thirty-two and was involved in the development of the atomic bomb. Andropov was very aware of the threat posed if Czechoslovakia fell into NATO hands. Western nations had been on the borders of Russia for centuries and always exerting pressure to push further. The Russian people had been involved in numerous wars over those years to defend their homeland on all fronts. The Minister of Defence and Andropov had concurred on the seriousness of the threat to Russia and the rest of the Politburo had agreed. Whether Brezhnev was right or wrong to take the opposite view is a matter of debate and opinion. The point is that he could and did act freely and democratically and that the Soviet Union was not the monolithic entity so often perceived in the popular imagination.

Another common image in Western media was of Brezhnev as a slow and stolid figure, one by implication ineffectual. It is not an accurate picture of the man even in his later years. During the Great Patriotic War against fascism he had not stayed at home or taken a desk job but done his bit leading his troops from the front and putting himself in the line of fire. This sense of loyalty and purpose demonstrated in his youth was a quality he carried with him into government.

Most of all I remember his humour. In Komsomol we had come up with an idea to raise money for overseas famine relief. On a specified Saturday, workers in various industries from bakers to builders to factory staff would donate any wages they earned on that day to the fund. Brezhnev was very approving and sent us his good wishes adding, *'Tell them not to put the money in their pockets and spend it on vodka!'*

FIDEL CASTRO

Almost as soon as I had moved to Moscow in 1978 in the capacity of Secretary of International Affairs of the All-Union Komsomol Central Committee of the USSR Communist Party, just after the 1 May celebrations, I began working on preparations for the 11th World Festival of Youth and Students. The host city that year was to be Havana, and it was the first time since the 1960 revolution that Cuba had held an international event on this scale. At a meeting with Boris Pastukhov, the First Secretary of the Central Committee of Komsomol, he brought me up to speed on the mood: *'You are getting involved in international affairs at a very difficult time.'* What was new? Soviet diplomacy and international relations were always conducted in combat conditions.

In terms of Cuba's position internationally, what was happening right now? Since the Bay of Pigs invasion to remove Castro and then the missile crisis, relations with the United States had been frozen. In 1977, however, newly elected President, Jimmy Carter, had made diplomatic overtures towards Castro, including indicating a willingness to negotiate on fishing rights within the ninety miles of the Caribbean that lay between the two countries. Restrictions on visiting Cuba were reviewed, while Castro released a number of political prisoners. There had even been talk of re-establishing the countries' embassies in Washington and Havana. The vocal anti-Castro lobby within the US, which included a substantial Cuban expatriate community, remained strong. The Soviet Union's close fraternal relationship with Cuba also continued to provoke fear and suspicion among America's hawks.

Meanwhile, sat in Moscow, for the next hour Pastukhov went over the most painful areas of current concern to the Soviet youth movement. I was urged to listen to the opinions of Gennady Yanayev and Viktor Grigoriev on these issues, and most importantly to visit the international department of the Central Committee of CPSU more often. Pastukhov said, '*Vagif, bear in mind – what we have here is the focus of the best experts in the country, who have information on the state of the international communist movement – that's a fact.*'

Facts, facts and more facts, we examined them all. After several days of negotiations, discussions and clarifications, talking about who should go to Havana, how many we could take and from where, and how to get them there, we had reached agreement on most of the key points. One month ahead of the festival I was to fly out to Havana for a few days to meet our Cuban colleagues and have preliminary talks about the arrangements – the logistics of the whole three-week programme – the staging of the numerous concerts, parades, talks, performances and conferences. There were also the practicalities of providing accommodation and catering for the artists, public speakers, performers, support staff and delegates to sort out. Later on, a number of documents would also have to be signed, resolutions from the youth organisations of the participating countries for submission to the United Nations. The most important of these resolutions was a call to curb the arms race, and another to find ways of dealing with famine throughout the world.

At the end of the week I flew back to Moscow to assist in the travelling arrangements for the attendees. In response to our request, Alexei Nikolaevich Kosygin, Chairman of the Council of Ministers of the USSR, had instructed the Ministry of the USSR Navy to allocate four large passenger ships. These vessels would transport our Soviet delegation of over a thousand people to Cuba, together with youth representatives and visitors from European, Asian, African and South American countries. Boarding at Odessa and a series of ports en route, more than 12,000 passengers would be making the voyage.

The Central Committee of the Komsomol announced that Viktor would be commander of our flotilla, and on the day of departure a celebratory gathering was held in Odessa in honour of the delegates. As the ships departed there was loud cheering on the docks from the crowds of friends and associates who had come to see everyone off. We would now sail down through the Black Sea into the Mediterranean then out through the Straits of Gibraltar into the Atlantic Ocean. After eighteen days the flotilla anchored in Havana to receive a warm welcome from thousands of Cubans.

As soon as we came ashore a telegram was sent to Alexei Kosygin on behalf of all the students and delegates, confirming our safe arrival and thanking him for his help in making our trip possible. Kosygin responded with warm wishes for a successful and enjoyable time at the festival. Young people from over 130 countries were on their way by air and sea to join us on the 'Island of Freedom.' Our Soviet delegation was among the largest, comprising students, people from the working and rural communities, young writers, musicians, painters and poets – the *crème de la crème* of Soviet youth. The combined Latin American contingent would number around 70,000 and Europeans 25,000. Socialist states being a minority, most attendees were from the capitalist and developing parts of the world. Some countries had just a handful of delegates, and while the totalitarian and right wing governments such as Guatemala and Franco's Spain had sent no official parties, their citizens managed to travel in as independent tourists. North Korea was there, though not the Chinese. Since Mao's death in 1976, China's government was in transition and relations with the Soviet Union were still very tenuous. I think all but seven or eight countries were represented in Havana that year. It really was a huge event; even the Americans came.

At the time we arrived President Castro was not available, so after meeting the Soviet Ambassador to Havana, Fidel's brother Raul was the first person from the Cuban government to greet me. Raul was closely involved with the festival and talked through the programme of events with me. Our friends in Cuba had contacted us earlier with a number of requests, for which I had prepared a checklist of replies. The requests included practical items – asking if we could supply particular musical instruments or technical equipment for example – and updated information about what accommodation and catering arrangements the delegates would require. The Cubans were amazing at organising these big events – the carnivals and processions featuring huge colourful floats, hundreds of lavish costumes, six or seven hours of singing and dancing, all choreographed and synchronised to happen at the right time and place. It was clear they had already put a great deal of time and effort into creating what promised to be a spectacular affair.

Another part of my job here was discussing agreements to developing countries on health, infrastructure and in particular education. During the festival I would be meeting representatives from a whole range of countries to receive requests for their students to attend courses in the Soviet Union. This added up to a tremendous number of people looking for places across the seventy or more courses available at Soviet universities and specialist colleges.

Each day I would report to Raul on what was happening with the different delegations – which countries had arrived, which were yet to come and any difficulties or delays. Meanwhile the joint petitions from the youth organisations of the world against nuclear arms had been drawn up, and one by one each country's representatives had added their signatures to the document to be presented to the United Nations. When it came to the French, the Yugoslavians and the Romanians, however, all three were for some reason reluctant to sign. In the end they wrote out their own versions and signed them, but on examination these were found to be word for word identical to the original. It was just one more thing to add to the huge workload of fifteen-hour days, each filled with meetings, problems and more meetings.

The day before the start of the festival the leaders of the Cuban organisations assembled in the centre of Havana. President Fidel Castro, accompanied by other senior members of the government now made his appearance. A final rehearsal for the grand opening ceremony was performed, at the end of which my Cuban colleague Rafael Arufe came up to me and said that Castro wanted to speak with me. I walked over to where the President was standing with his cabinet. Fidel greeted me and asked what I thought about the rehearsal we had just seen and the overall preparations. I expressed the opinion of my colleagues that the opening promised to be colourful, dynamic and fully in keeping with the chosen motto of the world youth forum – For Anti-Imperialist, Solidarity, Peace and Friendship. As for the technical side of things, I emphasised that it was beyond all praise.

Fidel thanked me for my contribution and told me Raul had been keeping him closely informed. He then asked, '*When will Boris Pastukhov arrive?*' I gave him the intended date of Boris' arrival, adding that the previous day the First Secretary of the Central Committee of Komsomol had been working with the Politburo of the Central Committee of the Communist Party of the Soviet Union, discussing a large construction scheme in Siberia, and that enquiries had been made about the involvement of Komsomol in the project. Perhaps prompted by the mention of construction work, Fidel then told me that he had a request for the Soviet government, which he would like me to relay. Cuba needed to improve its infrastructure by building roads and houses, but the people needed equipment – cranes, earth moving vehicles and trucks, that kind of thing. I said I would be glad to do what I could to assist in the matter. With that Fidel said goodbye, and wished me fruitful work at the festival.

Fidel Castro had never been afraid to ask for things, but then he had not become President of Cuba by being shy. His upbringing had not been one of poverty, his father, originally from Spain, having done well as a sugar cane farmer in Cuba's Oriente Province. One of seven siblings, for much of his early childhood Fidel lived with his teacher and attended the Catholic La Salle School in Santiago de Cuba. A rebellious streak was perhaps already emerging: for alleged misbehaviour he was taken out and sent instead to the Dolores private school followed by the El Colegio de Belen, both run by the strict Jesuits.

Although keener on sport than studying, Fidel embarked on a Law degree at Havana University. Engaged in the macho rough and tumble of student politics he was vocally anti-imperialist and anti-corruption, his public denunciation of the Cuban regime bringing him for the first time to the attention of the media. Political activism in Latin America was a dangerous game, and his championing of Eduardo Chibas' Party of the Cuban People brought death threats. Defiant, Fidel armed himself with a weapon and a posse of supporters. While still at university he took part in a plan to depose the right-wing government of the Dominican Republic, but America intervened and the Cuban military swooped on the conspirators. Later at a demonstration against witch-hunts of alleged communist sympathisers, Fidel suffered severe injuries at the hands of government security officers. 1948 saw more involvement in direct action, this time in Bogata, commandeering police weapons during a street protest after the assassination of Columbia's left-wing leader Ayala. It was also the year of Fidel's wedding to Mirta Diaz Balart. Although an unarranged marriage and the cause of some disquiet among their traditionalist families, Mirta's father provided the couple with a lavish three-month honeymoon in New York.

The taste of luxury did not lure Fidel from radicalism. More significant was the assassination of his friend Justo Fuentes, a committed socialist. He had also begun to engage with political theory, turning to Marx and Engels for an understanding of the problems besetting Cuba – poverty, corruption, racism and division. Gang violence remained endemic even on the campuses, and the newly elected Cuban leader Carlos Prio Socarras seemed unable or unwilling to tackle the issue. Fidel decided to go public and name names. Predictably the names wanted his blood and he was forced to lie low until completing his studies.

Now a qualified lawyer, Fidel chose his clients on the basis of their need, people from the more deprived sections of the community of whom there were all too many. Working often pro bono it was hard to pay the bills, and Mirta would be dismayed to find that the electricity had been disconnected or their furniture taken away by creditors. Fidel's priority was the political struggle. When Chibas committed suicide he felt the call more strongly than ever, and in the 1952 election put himself forward as a candidate in the poor part of Havana. Democracy was not to prevail, however, as before the election could be held General Fulgencio Batista instigated a military coup

Fidel Castro arrives MATS Terminal, Washington, D.C., 15 April 1959

and declared himself President of Cuba. After several attempts to challenge Batista's power through the courts, Fidel the lawyer found that the law was useless. It was time for Fidel the revolutionary.

But Fidel was not a bloodthirsty revolutionary. In planning the storming of the Macondo Barracks in July 1953, he counselled his followers not to use violence unless they were met with armed opposition. He also warned them that the revolution might not come immediately, or without sacrifice. '*In a few hours you will be victorious or defeated, but regardless of the outcome – listen well, friends – this Movement will triumph... If we fail, our action will nevertheless set an example for the Cuban people, and from the people will arise fresh new men willing to die for Cuba. They will pick up our banner and move forward...*'

Batista's forces repelled the attack, torturing and executing prisoners without trial. Fidel and a handful of comrades retreated into the Sierra Maestra Mountains. Martial law was imposed, while propaganda claiming that the attackers had killed patients in a hospital was disseminated among the populace. Over the next few days more of the Movement were apprehended, among them Fidel. At his trial at the Palace of Justice on 21 September he conducted his own defence, stating that Batista had seized power unlawfully and that his presidency was therefore unconstitutional. On this basis, the charge against him and his co-defendants of 'organising an uprising of armed persons against the Constitutional Powers of the State' was rendered invalid. Revelations of torture by the army bolstered the defendants' case, and when the trial ended over half of the 122 accused were released. Fidel, however, was sentenced to fifteen years imprisonment and his brother Raul to thirteen. Before being led away to the Island of the Pines, Fidel delivered what would become a famous address. 'History Will Absolve Me,' written on matchboxes while awaiting trial, in eloquent and impassioned tones and reportedly lasting several hours, described the poverty and illiteracy of Cuba's poor, the shameful lack of schooling and healthcare, and the iniquitousness of the Batista regime that perpetuated this state of misery.

Fidel Castro, president of Cuba, at a meeting of the United Nations General Assembly, 22 September 1960

Conditions in the prison were relatively humane, until, after singing anti-Batista songs, Fidel was placed in solitary confinement. A far greater ignominy was the discovery that his wife Mirta had taken employment in a government department, causing a rift that would lead the couple to divorce and Mirta to gain custody of their son Fedelito. In 1954, Batista allowed an election to take place, but with no opposition candidates in evidence

5 March 1960: A memorial service march for victims of the La Coubre explosion. On the far left is Fidel Castro while in the centre is Che Guevara

the legitimacy of the procedure was given little credence. Believing it might enhance his image, he also bowed to pressure for an amnesty for Fidel and his comrades. Aware of being monitored, Fidel and Raul kept a low profile for several months until a renewed hard line on radicals prompted them in 1955 to set sail for Mexico: '*All doors of peaceful struggle have been closed to me*' wrote Fidel, '*... I believe the hour has come to take our rights and not beg for them, to fight instead of pleading for them.*' It was in Mexico that the Castro brothers met Che Guevara, and between them they would now turn the tide of Cuban history.

Observing them both over the three weeks of the Havana festival, one had the clear impression that Fidel, whom I understood regularly worked a fifteen-hour day, was the engine of ideas, while Raul's great strength was

The Hotel Nacional de Cuba Havana, Cuba, 21 May 1978. During the Cuban missile crisis Fidel Castro and Che used the hotel as their headquarters

in implementing them. Raul seemed on the whole more family orientated, but I believe both brothers adored their mother. As united in their politics and beliefs as in their personal feelings towards one another, there was no rivalry and one could see the love between them. Neither had they forgotten their commitment to the poor and illiterate, and educational issues were high on the agenda throughout the festival, with debates and seminars focusing intently on how they could most effectively improve schooling for disadvantaged children everywhere. There was also an important declaration calling for amnesty for political prisoners around the world, another for an international day of youth each year.

It was now approaching the end of the festival and we would soon be packing up to leave. Fidel came up to have a few words. As we were discussing all the heavy equipment that had to be loaded back on to the ships, he made a suggestion: to save time and effort why did we not just leave it all here for the Cuban people – we were talking about tools, vehicles,

Vice-president General Raul Castro and his brother president Fidel Castro attend the 11th world festival of youth and students, in August 1978 in Havana.

cranes, fork lift trucks, as well as a large number of musical instruments, lighting rigs, amplifiers and portable stages – thousands of dollars worth of gear. Some of these items were what Fidel had requested from the Soviet Union when he spoke to me on my arrival. I sent another telegram to Suslov asking what we should do. Suslov replied that it would destroy the Soviet economy. A couple of days later a second telegram arrived giving consent to leave everything for our hosts.

The 11th Festival of Youth and Students had been an exhausting yet exhilarating experience. As well as having the huge honour of meeting Fidel and Raul Castro and so many of their amazing fellow Cubans, I had encountered another pair of brothers. They were still in the process of stepping onto the world political stage and their surname was Ortega. Fidel had introduced us. The Ortegas were very keen to come to Moscow, and Fidel was very much in favour of them going. I said I would see what I could do and contacted the Soviet Embassy in Havana. The Soviet ambassador called me back later and said there was a telegram from Kosygin inviting the Ortegas to the Kremlin and specifying the date. Kosygin was very efficient. When I gave the brothers this news they thought I must be a very important person. Fidel's voice had of course entirely swayed the decision.

Leaving the Ortegas to celebrate I said a fond farewell to everyone and boarded the ship, my two suitcases crammed with applications to Soviet universities. When I got back to Moscow, Suslov would read every one of them.

NICU CEAUŞESCU

We are in Bucharest. I have arrived with my colleagues to represent our Soviet youth organisation. I am a Secretary of International Affairs of the All-Union Komsomol Central Committee of the USSR Communist Party. It is a familiar scenario, and today we are scheduled to see a number of different delegations. We are presently with people from our host country, members of the Romanian Communist Party. What is more unusual is that our opposite number as it were, the representative of Romania's youth community and the person we are here especially to talk with, is not present. We are given to understand that he is on his way. So we begin to discuss the items on the agenda and make some small talk until he arrives. The clock ticks. A quarter of an hour goes by, half an hour. Ten minutes later the person we have all been waiting for turns up. A lean young man with aquiline features, close-cropped dark hair and sideburns, and wearing tinted glasses, he strides over and sits down. He is not only forty minutes late, but judging by his unsteady demeanour and slurred speech, quite drunk. Will anyone from his delegation reprimand him, comment on his behaviour, or just ask where he has been?

No. This is Nicu Ceauşescu, the son of Romania's feared autocratic leader, and his heir apparent. We exchange a few words, Ceauşescu's remarks barely coherent, after which his complexion turns pale and he leaps from his chair and runs out of the room. I wait for him to return, turning meanwhile to a colleague from our department to continue the conversation. Five more minutes tick by and the young Ceauşescu does not come back. It is now almost time for our next appointment, with a delegation from the Democratic People's Republic of Korea. We expect none of them to be late.

The following morning I am at a meeting of the International Preparatory Committee. Nicu Ceauşescu is there. He comes up to me and apologises

Nicu Ceauşescu (1981)

for what happened the day before. I reassure him, observing that all of us are only human and that no one is immune from sickness at some time or another. He nods his head in agreement. As we say goodbye I take the liberty of offering him some advice in confidence, saying quietly in his ear that it is important not only to drink well, but to eat properly too.

Let us consider this young man's heritage, the place from which he had come. Once part of the Ottoman Empire, in the late 1930s Romania had been taken over by the fascist government of Antonescu. Killing thousands of Jews and Gypsies, the regime had supplied oil and huge military support to the Nazis, and remained an enemy of Russia in the Great Patriotic War right up until 1944, when the armed forces switched sides and Soviet forces arrived. After the war, Romania became a socialist republic and a member of the Warsaw Pact. In 1965, Nicolae Ceauşescu, a former cobbler, became general secretary of the Romanian Communist Party, and in 1968 rose to head of state. After a relatively liberal honeymoon period Ceauşescu's rule became increasingly hard-line and more Stalinist in its approach to censorship and its reaction to dissent. There was talk of Ceauşescu building a 'cult of personality' around his leadership, while not creating much else in terms of the material or cultural well being of his people. Relations with other countries, including the Soviet Union, were either distant or strained. Maybe it was concern over this reputation that had prompted him to appoint his son Nicu first as Youth Minister, and then Secretary of the Communist Party Central Committee on International Issues.

Nicu was Ceauşescu's youngest child, and his promotion suggested that his father was grooming him to succeed as leader. Further evidence of such preparation was the appointment of Romania's Foreign Affairs Minister, Stefan Andrei, as Nicu's mentor. It was believed that Andrei, who came from the same remote village as Nicolae Ceaucescu, and was reportedly a literate, bookish man, had been trying to steer Romania's foreign relations more towards far eastern and African countries, and away from the Soviet Union. In the West, this apparent willingness on the part of Romania's leadership to 'stand up to Russia' was received favourably for obvious reasons. In terms of improving his personality, Stefan Andrei's tutelage seemed to have little effect on his pupil, as from what I saw of Nicu Ceauşescu at close hand he seemed a consistently rude and insolent young man who looked down on everyone he met.

The fact that he apologised to me that day seems remarkable given his reputation, for as well as a fondness for alcohol, Nicu was notorious for his wild parties, lavish jewellery, glamorous women and expensive cars, several of which he had crashed around Bucharest while drunk. He was also said to have lost huge amounts of money gambling. Many of the stories that would emerge about him were extreme, possibly exaggerated or even made up, including the rumour that while still in his teens he had raped a

Vagif Guseynov meeting with Nicu Ceauşescu in Romania, 1977

classmate. Among the more colourful allegations were those that appeared in the memoirs of Ion Pacepa, a defector from the Romanian intelligence services, who claimed that on one occasion over dinner Nicu had poured whiskey over a government minister, urinated on a dish of oysters and tried to rape a waitress.

In 1977, Bucharest suffered a terrible natural disaster, an earthquake that killed 1,500 people and reduced large parts of the city to rubble. Ceauşescu, inspired by a visit he had made to North Korea in 1972, turned the calamity into an opportunity, announcing a competition to create a new civic centre at the heart of the capital, a seat of government that all Romanians could be proud of, a 'House of the People,' as it was called. A young female architect called Anca Petrescu, recently qualified with the state design institute, submitted her drawings along with numerous other entrants, and by 1981 she had met with Ceauşescu, who was still undecided about the kind of look he wanted for the building. Petrescu later claimed to recall that the dictator, '*...was a good listener, a very patient man... He was not a vampire.*' Though excluded from the shortlist, Petrescu persisted, making an elaborate scale model of her design and writing to Ceauşescu with a request to present it to him. Several other architects had made models, which were set out for the leader to view. One story has it that he was immediately enchanted with Petruscu's gilt encrusted vision, another that he was swayed by the charms of its creator.

Whatever the reason, Petrusca's design was chosen and in 1983 the project swung into action. A particularly important requirement was that an expansive avenue should be built leading up to the new building, that this avenue should be called the 'Victory of Socialism Boulevard' and that it must be wider than Paris's Champs Elysees by precisely one metre and longer by six. To make way for the grandiose structure and avenue, Ceauşescu ordered the tearing down of large parts of historic Bucharest, including in one district some 40,000 homes, many of whose residents, given only two days notice, were obliged to flee leaving their furniture and

The extravagant House of the People in Bucharest

other possessions to be destroyed in the demolition. Also flattened were six synagogues and Jewish temples, nineteen churches of Orthodox Christian denomination and three Protestant churches.

At twelve storeys high with additional underground levels and comprising over 1,000 rooms, on completion the House of the People would be the second largest public administration building in the world after the Pentagon. According to Ceaușescu everything used in the construction was sourced from within the country, though local people later refuted this claim. Accounts of the materials refer to 700,000 tonnes of bronze and steel, 900,000 cubic metres of wood and 200,000 square metres of bespoke woven carpets. The design is also said to have incorporated a staggering one million cubic metres of Transylvanian marble, while the luxurious fittings included almost 500 chandeliers made from 3,500 tonnes of crystal. The largest of the chandeliers incorporated 1,000 light bulbs and reportedly weighed five tonnes, while the massive doors carved from cherry, oak and elm left whole forests decimated.

Ceauşescu took a meticulous interest in the programme, often changing his mind about details of the design and turning up unexpectedly to inspect progress. According to Anca Petruscu he once ordered a number of large columns to be completely remade on the grounds that their carved flowers were unequal by one centimetre. There were other idiosyncratic demands; Ceauşescu having unusually small feet ordered the stonemasons to cut the massive marble staircases with exceptionally narrow steps, while advice to install air conditioning was ignored due to his fear of a chemical attack on the government.

As the monstrosity grew, so did Ceauşescu's vanity and delusions of grandeur. Adopting the titles *Conducator* (Leader) and *Geniui din Carpati* (Genius of the Carpathians), he had a unique personal sceptre fashioned, indicating what could only be a surreal conception of himself as royalty. In constructing the House of the People some one million Romanian citizens were employed, including soldiers and political prisoners, with different shifts toiling night and day. Nuns were even brought in to embroider gold thread into hundreds of metres of curtains. Accidents on site were frequent and sometimes fatal. Over five years of work the House of the People is estimated to have consumed up to forty per cent of Romania's GDP. Meanwhile the enterprise had saddled the country with massive foreign debts, which Ceauşescu was attempting to pay off through wholesale export of the country's agricultural and industrial produce. This disastrous strategy caused widespread food shortages, leaving ordinary citizens living off nettle soup and scraps, while basic medical supplies were becoming almost non-existent. Ceauşescu tried to mask this reality by appearing on television entering shops bulging with provisions. Many thought him genuinely unaware of the problems and organised petitions.

In November 1971, the seventy-one-year-old was re-elected for a further five years as leader of the Romanian Communist Party. On 21 December, however, a mass meeting intended to reassure the nation went seriously wrong as hecklers began chanting and jeering. Following attempts to quell the demonstrators by force, Ceauşescu and his wife Elena fled from Bucharest by helicopter, but with the army capitulating, the couple were soon caught and handed over. After a brief trial they were executed on Christmas Day. The House of the People stood unfinished.

The Romanian people had come to hate the whole Ceauşescu family. In his time Stalin had been a tyrant undeniably, but in his defence he had faced huge challenges of modernisation and achieved a great deal in economic terms for his country, quite apart from helping to defeat the Nazis in the Great Patriotic War. Under Ceauşescu the ordinary people had been oppressed but had nothing to show for it. The ruling family did tremendous harm, the idea of governing being all about themselves; they gave nothing and achieved nothing, and treated the populace like dirt. When news came out of the emaciated children chained to their beds in the state orphanages, it was no wonder people were angry. The only way the authorities could maintain power was through murder and intimidation, and from everything I have heard the Gestapo were like kindergarten teachers compared to Ceauşescu's secret police. Just walking the streets of Bucharest in the 1980s and looking at people's faces it was obvious; no one was smiling, ninety-nine per cent of the population seemed depressed, not wanting or daring to look at one another. The only good I remember in Romania was the wine, which was excellent.

With the fall of Ceauşescu, Anca Petrescu, architect of the building project that had financially crippled Romania, was held to have been complicit in the corruption and neglect that characterised the regime. A campaign led by a group of architects for her to be charged with misusing public assets did not succeed, but she was effectively barred from her profession, her home was set on fire and she was subjected to death threats. Asked about how she could justify her role in the House of the People when so many Romanians were suffering, Petrescu is quoted to have replied, '*That is a question originating from someone who can only understand a system based on profit as motivation.*' In the meantime she had moved to Paris to design apartments for a holiday company.

Over the next four years the House of the People remained a white elephant, and the subject of controversial debate within Romania. Should it be demolished, turned into a museum of communism, or even a Dracula theme park? While these options were argued over, the expensive marble interior, wooden doors and carpets began disappearing in the hands of looters. Finally, by 1994, the building was renamed the 'Parliament Palace' and adapted to house the government chambers, courts and an international conference centre and art gallery. In 2002, Anca Petrescu was invited to return and design a special cupola. In 2004, she stood for election as mayor of Bucharest, but apparently garnered just four per cent of the votes. Perhaps it was too soon, the unpopularity of her building, chiefly its association with the Ceauşescu regime, together with its awkward staircases, stifling lack of air-conditioning and gross proportions still earned it the title in travel guides of one of the world's worst eyesores.

With the passage of time, however, the Parliament Palace has come to be viewed less critically, and some Romanians even claim to like it. It is the grandiose monument that Nicolai Ceauşescu presumably expected his son Nicu to preside over as his successor. That dream of succession, which some, satirically paraphrasing Stalin's theory, referred to as the dictator's idea of 'socialism in one family', was never achieved. Nicu had been arrested around the time of his parents' execution. It was alleged he had ordered shots to be fired on a crowd of demonstrators in Sibu, killing over one hundred people. At his trial in 1990 he joked with the prosecutors, claiming he had been drunk at the time and could not remember anything of the events. A charge of genocide was reduced to instigation of aggravated murder, and a sentence of twenty years imprisonment imposed. Two years later the charge was changed again, to illegal ownership of firearms, dropping to a five year sentence, and shortly afterwards he was released on grounds of ill health. The ordeal, along with years of smoking and heavy drinking had taken its toll. Nicu had been diagnosed with cirrhosis of the liver in 1989, and friends believe that it was being denied access to treatment that hastened his condition, resulting in his death in a Vienna hospital in 1996 at the age of forty-five. He was survived by his brother Valentin, a nuclear physicist, and sister Zoe, a mathematician.

If Ceauşescu's youngest son had ever taken up residence in the building in which his father had invested so much hope, and squandered so much of his people's resources, one can only assume he would have perpetuated the legacy of repression and neglect. Looking for something positive to say about Nicu Ceauşescu is difficult, but perhaps it should be mentioned that he claimed to have strongly opposed his father's destruction of the old parts of Bucharest when the House of the People was being planned. That, and the fact that he once apologised to me for being drunk, can hardly be called redeeming features.

Nicu Ceauşescu (1990)

STEPHEN COHEN

It was over sandwiches and coffee in Berlin that I first met Stephen Cohen. The coffee was good, the conversation even better. It was the mid 1970s, the time of Gerald Ford and Brezhnev and high hopes for détente with the Helsinki Accords. This was also an intriguing time for Stephen, as we shall see. Our meeting took place while we were attending a conference of the Council on Foreign and Defence Policy, and his first book, *Bukharin and the Bolshevik Revolution* had been published a couple of years earlier to wide critical acclaim.

Since his execution as a traitor by Stalin in 1938, Nikolai Bukharin had remained a pariah figure in official Soviet history. Stephen's account charted Bukharin's rise to prominence from the time of Lenin's death in 1924, when he became Stalin's right hand man, working with him on the 'socialism in one country' plan and the ejection of Zinoviev, Kamanev and Trotsky at the 1927 fifteenth party conference. Stalin had initially opposed the rapid industrialisation plan favoured by the ousted triumvirate, believing instead in the New Economic Policy (NEP) put forward by Lenin and Bukharin, but a severe shortage of grain in the harvest of 1928 changed his mind. Thus followed the enforced agricultural collectivisation programme and the terror.

Bukharin, however, demurred, promoting instead the merits of 'socialism at a snail's pace' and arguing that higher agricultural yields, providing surplus grain for export, could be achieved if the peasants were given the opportunity to enrich themselves. Stalin, intransigent, forced Bukarin to recant his 'capitalist' views, which he did, pleading for reinstatement. Privately, however, Bukharin maintained his position, confirming as much in telephone conversations with Stalin's enemies, in which he condemned the widespread killing of men, women and children in the name of

collectivisation and referred to Stalin as 'not a man but a devil'. Through phone taps Stalin was listening to every word. In February 1937 Bukharin was arrested and in March the following year, after a drawn out show trial, was shot. His confession obtained under duress closed with the statement: '*The monstrousness of my crime is immeasurable especially in the new stage of struggle of the USSR. May this trial be the last severe lesson, and may the great might of the USSR become clear to all.*'

According to Stephen Cohen, however, Bukharin's confession may have been anything but sincere. Stephen's 1973 book was the first major study of Bukharin, and important in highlighting that there had been a real alternative to Stalin's policy of intense industrialisation, collectivisation and the mass killings in the name of socialist purity. At the same time the author pulled no punches in analysing Bukharin's shortcomings, including the missed opportunities to out-flank Stalin. '*Mr. Cohen makes this clear... By collaborating wholeheartedly with Stalin until 1928 (despite some twists and turns), he (Bukharin) made possible Stalin's victories over all other rivals.*' (Harrison B. Salisbury *New York Times* 25 November 1973)

Stephen reminded readers that Bukharin was himself a prolific author, whose works including *Imperialism and World Economy* and *The Economics of the Transition Period*, written around the time of World War One had become largely forgotten. The re-examination of this important figure, for so long consigned to apparent oblivion, had been undertaken with '*... brilliance and dogged determination. One must read this work to realize the extent to which Bukharin the man has been obliterated by the operation of the Soviet "memory hole" and the extermination of almost all those who knew him. (Ibid) Bukharin talked of 'militaristic state capitalism' and described Stalin's regime as 'the present day monster, the modem Leviathan,' which in Stephen's words, 'mercilessly crushes all resistance.*' (Ibid)

Bukharin and the Bolshevik Revolution also examined what Stephen saw as Bukharin's attempt to condemn Stalin by subtly investing his final confession with a double meaning: '*Mr. Cohen demonstrates rather conclusively that Bukharin did not testify as did his prototype, Rubashov, in Arthur Koestler's Darkness at Noon as a last service to the party. His testimony almost certainly was compelled in his effort to save the lives of his young wife and son... Bukharin then sought by means of Aesopian language to turn the trial into an "anti-trial" in which he would place Stalin under indictment. This manoeuvre was only partially successful. It was clearly understood in a brilliant analysis written for the State Department at the time by George Kennan*. A few of the Western correspondents present suspected what was going on, though the tactic was too subtle for United States Ambassador Joseph Davies and most of the*

*More about George Kennan can be found in the chapter on Angela Stent, see p.386

world. They heard Bukharin's plea of guilty but did not penetrate the meaning of his brilliant duel with the prosecutor, Andrei Vishinsky.' (Ibid)

The promise to spare Bulkarin's family was partially kept, in that his widow Anna Larina, twenty-five years his junior, was not executed but separated from their young son and held in a series of gulags until Stalin's death in 1953. On her release she was suffering from tuberculosis, and even then was not allowed to return to Moscow until 1959. Now remarried to a man she had met in the gulags and with whom she bore two more children, she wrote repeatedly and at length to Khrushchev demanding that Bulkarin be rehabilitated – the Soviet term for the positive reinstatement of an individual's legacy – but to no avail. Meanwhile, in secret, Anna began writing her memoirs: *This I Cannot Forget.*

It was in May 1975, seventeen months after the publication of his work on Nikolai Bulkarin, that Stephen Cohen received a communication from Anna and Nikolai's son Yuri, with whom she had been reunited in 1956 when he was eighteen. *'A copy of my book had slowly found its way to the family,'* said Stephen. Three months later Stephen had a clandestine meeting with Anna in Moscow, a dangerous undertaking for her and Yuri, as she was still under surveillance. Anna told Stephen about her memoirs, which she was convinced would not be published in her lifetime. Stephen felt otherwise, and while he had certain criticisms of her portrayal of Bulkarin, encouraged her to persevere with the writing. Understanding her fear of the manuscript and carbon copies being discovered and destroyed by the authorities – random searches were still carried out against families of dissidents – he began smuggling chapters out of the Soviet Union. The smuggling continued for more than seven years, while Yuri, yearning to learn more about the father he had never known, began, said Stephen, *'the huge work of translating my long book on Bukharin into Russian... helped by a remarkable family friend, Yevgeny Aleksandrovich Gnedid.'*

Gorbachev came to power and *This I Cannot Forget* was published in journal form in the Soviet Union in 1988. It became a bestseller and a central feature of Bulkarin's rehabilitation. Stephen Cohen, by now a close friend of Anna's, in 1992 wrote an introduction to an English edition. Detailed and providing a comprehensive historical overview, the introduction was judged by Robert Conquest, author of numerous works on Soviet Russia, to be '*a model of its kind, giving not only the political and human background, but also describing his own relations with Larina and the Bukharin family.*' Stephen opened with Lavrentiy Beria's advice to Larina in 1938: '*If you want to live, then shut up about Bukharin!*' Describing the gulags as '*a debased world, "covered in the shame of unbridled terror, awash in the blood of the innocent… the tears of women…torn from their children and husbands"…*' Anna's book was, said Stephen, '*…different, indeed unique…not primarily the story of her twenty years of suffering and survival in the Gulag – that, too would make an astonishing volume – but of her previous life as a daughter and wife among the founding fathers of the Soviet Union.*'

Stephen also managed to find and give to Anna the last love letter that Bukharin had written to her from prison on 15 January 1938. In the introduction to her memoirs he reiterated his view that Bukharin had remained true to his beliefs: '*Already condemned…Bukharin's last struggle was to indict Stalin's regime by showing that its criminal accusations were political falsifications and that the original Bolsheviks had never been a "counterrevolutionary organisation" but the revolution's true leaders with different visions of the Soviet future.*' This view was backed up by Larina describing how she had committed to memory a statement recited by her husband, confirming his true beliefs, for her to pass on to future generations.

Following Anna Larina's death in 1996 at the age of eighty-two, Stephen described her as a remarkable personality and having been '*…the last living link to the generation that made the revolution… she lost everything… but she showed no bitterness. She endured this horrible experience but it didn't deform her psychologically. In 1988, she was able to resume public life in a way that astonished people.*' (Article by Alessandra Stanley, *New York Times*, 26 February 1996)

Stephen Cohen is a man who searches for the truth in any debate, whether over the past or the present. Just as he was unwilling to produce a mere hagiography of Bukharin, a figure he clearly admires, so he has abstained from the chorus of approval at the dissolution of the Soviet Union, whose faults he would readily concede. '*For most western commentators the Soviet break up was an unambiguously positive turning point in Russian and world history.*' (*Guardian*, 13 December 2006) He also points out that this apparent consensus was not limited to the political sphere: '*American academics reacted similarly, most reverting to pre-Gorbachev axioms that the system had always been unreformable and doomed. The opposing view that there had been other possibilities in Soviet history, "roads not taken", was dismissed as a "dubious", if not disloyal, notion.... Such certitudes are now, of course, the only politically correct ones in US (and most European) policy, media and academic circles.*' (Ibid) This reaction, equating the Soviet break up with a breakthrough to democracy, '*was based mainly on anti-communist ideology and hopeful myths.*' (Ibid)

Stephen's claim backed up by research has been that the Russian people did not share the outsiders' perception of their country: '*A large majority of Russians... as they have regularly made clear in opinion surveys, regret the end of the Soviet Union, not because they pine for 'communism' but because they lost a secure way of life. They do not share the nearly unanimous western view that the Soviet Union's 'collapse' was 'inevitable' because of inherent fatal defects.*' (Ibid) In the same article Stephen cites the manner of Gorbachev's reforms, the power struggle that moved Yeltsin to overthrow the state in order to get rid of Gorbachev, and the asset grabbing by elites, as reasons in most Russians' minds for the demise. He suggests that any initial euphoria among the intelligentsia gave way to more sober reflection, and the sense that a wrong turning had been taken: '*...a growing number of Russian intellectuals have come to believe that something essential was lost – a historic opportunity to democratise and modernise Russia by methods more gradualist, consensual and less traumatic, and thus more fruitful and less costly, than those adopted after 1991.*' (Ibid)

Stephen Cohen's understanding of Nikolai Bulkarin grew through meticulous research and an enduring friendship with his widow. Mikhail Gorbachev he knows in person. Bulkarin and Gorbachev were perhaps both well intentioned and defeated by a combination of circumstances and their own weaknesses and mistakes, and in Gorbachev's case, in my opinion, failure to govern with a sufficiently firm hand. Stephen has tended to the view that it was chiefly Boris Yeltsin who dealt the coup de gras to the Soviet Union: '*Yeltsin abolished the Soviet Union with the backing of the nomenklatura elites – pursuing the "smell of property like a beast after prey", as Yeltsin's chief minister put it – and an avowedly pro-democracy wing of the intelligentsia.*' (Ibid, 13 December 2006)

In 2008 on the occasion of Stephen's seventieth birthday the publishing house of the Russian State University of Trade and Economics and the

From left to right: Stephen F. Cohen, Katrina vanden Heuvel, Hendrik Hertzberg and Virginia Cannon attend Time Warner's Conversations On The Circle at Time Warner Headquarters on 27 November 2007 in New York City.

Association of Researchers of Russian Society (AIRO–XXI) produced *Stephen Cohen and the Soviet Union/Russia*, a special book compiled in his honour. Thirty-five of Stephen's Russian friends contributed to the volume, including Mikhail Gorbachev, Sergey Baburin, Yevgeny Yevtushenko, Gennady Zuiganov, Viktor Kuvaldin, Roy Medvedev, Pavel Palazhchenko, Leonid Parfionov, Yevgeny Primakov, Vitaly Tretiakov, Anatoly Utkin, Mikhail Shatrov and myself. In a long tribute Gorbachev praised Stephen as a '*courageous and objective scholar*,' observing that '*Today's world, as never before, needs a new democratic and humanistic vision of the future. I think that with his knowledge and his bold and original research Steve Cohen has contributed to the formation of such a vision*.'

From that first meeting in Berlin in the 1970s Stephen and I have kept in touch ever since. Like me he attended and spoke at a lot of conferences including those of the Council on Foreign and Defence Policy, at which delegates exchanged scientific and political information for the benefit of the world community. Both in the business of writing and broadcasting, the fact was that Stephen and I needed one another in helping to assess and understand the situations in each other's countries. Not politically active in the sense of being aligned or holding positions in government, we were part of a wide group of people from the Soviet Union, America, Europe and elsewhere, all intent on achieving common goals focused on disarmament and the furtherance of détente.

To this end Stephen and I have published a number of books and papers together, and helped to promote each other's work. Several of his articles have been published in my magazine *Vestnik Analytik*, invariably stirring interest and considerable debate among political scientists, historians and the readership in general. When he came to Russia my colleagues and I would help him to appear on state TV, and when I visited the States he would do likewise, whatever the specific story, trying to get our broad message of international unity out to the wider public. Stephen himself has featured frequently in the American media. One time in Los Angeles we were having dinner in the restaurant and a couple came up to us and said excitedly, '*Hey we saw you on TV and we really agree with your views.*' It was totally unplanned and very gratifying. LA was a fantastic place, and a highlight of one trip there for me was when the mayor of the city invited Stephen and myself on a tour of the Paramount Studios.

In 2011, Columbia University Press published Stephen's *Soviet Fates and Lost Alternatives: From Stalinism to the New Cold War,* in which he brought together his ideas about Bukharin, Khrushchev and Gorbachev. According to the cover notes the book '*challenges conventional wisdom about the course of Soviet and Post-Soviet history.*'

Amy Knight in the *New York Review of Books* found it '*Provocative and insightful*' while for William W. Finan Jr. in *Current History,* the book prompted comparison with the early insights of George Kennan, '*Kennan's understanding of the Russian state... has proved to have enormous currency over time. Cohen's views should be given similar credence.*'

For Rehanna Jones-Boutaleb of *Foreign Policy In Focus,* the final chapter – the epilogue – was the most perceptive: '*Cohen... raises the question of "who lost the post-Soviet peace," i.e., what happened to the promised "strategic partnership and friendship" between Moscow and Washington, assured by leaders on both sides after 1991? He explains that the story line put forward by a majority of American political and media establishments was that friendly state relations, cultivated by former presidents Bill Clinton and Boris Yeltsin in the 1990s, were destroyed by the "antidemocratic" agenda of Vladimir Putin. Refuting these charges, Cohen argues that the opportunity for a constructive post cold-war partnership between both states was lost long before Putin took office: the Clinton administration effectively contributed to the dissolution of positive relations by promoting a false triumphalist vision of Cold War history.*'

One can appreciate that the notion of Russia having 'lost' the Cold War and being seen and treated by the Americans as a defeated nation would hardly

Stephen Cohen campaigning on behalf of the Kremlin

be conducive to constructive dialogue. But as Rehanna Jones-Boutaleb pointed out, the suggestion that the US and not Russia should therefore be blamed for the unsatisfactory relationship between the two countries after 1991 was not well received by mainstream Western politicians and historians. In an appearance on CNN Stephen described the incursion into Crimea as protecting *'Russia's traditional zones of national security.'* (Reported by Cathy Young in the Daily Beast) In *The Nation* magazine of which he is a contributing editor, he also castigated America's media for 'toxic' reporting about Putin. For these and other statements about Russia that contradicted conventional wisdom among democrats as well as republicans, Stephen Cohen was referred to in *Newsweek* as *'the man who dared make Putin's case.'* Less courteous commentators dubbed him *'Putin's ally'.*

Accused of naïve idealism, Stephen has stood his ground, showing an independence of mind and spirit that has been appreciated and applauded even by those who take issue with some of his arguments. Writing in *Russia Today* in June 2015, Dr. Leonid Gold warned that the West should in fact be on its guard lest the situation under Putin deteriorate and a more draconian leadership take over, '*and Putin will seem like a democrat and a peacemaker in comparison… I think Cohen doesn't quite factor into the equation the long-term objectives of American foreign policy. It's not so much about prejudice and Cold War inertia as it is about fear of the future. Nevertheless the role that Cohen plays in the modern political discourse is vitally important, because the existing rhetoric – along the lines of* "You're either with us or you're against us" *– is not helping at all. Cohen is not only a brilliant scholar and speaker, he's also a prime example showing that an intellectual can actively influence decision-making and situation development, and that it's possible to remain independent at the time when ideas serve those who can pay more.*'

Stephen was born in Kentucky but has roots close to Russia, his grandfather having migrated to the USA from Lithuania. I was also surprised to learn that he had a relative in my home city of Baku, whom I was pleased to be able to assist over a difficulty with the government. Married twice, Stephen's second wife Katrina vanden Hueval is twenty-one years his junior, not quite the age difference between Bukharin and Anna Larina. As editor of *The Nation* Katrina has worked closely with her husband and assisted in the progressive magazine's financial survival.

The poet Yevtushenko's eulogy for Stephen's seventieth birthday was written in verse form, describing him as '*A rarity in politics, no two-faced Janus.*' I wholeheartedly agree. In all the years I have known him, I have never heard Stephen speak sarcastically or acerbically about anyone. Professional and diplomatic, his criticisms are always at a political level, never personal. At the same time he is adept at building relationships and is a very good listener. I have never known him to interrupt anyone or be impatient to push an agenda in a conversation. Intelligent and highly educated academically, Stephen also has a tremendous breadth of knowledge about people and the world. Charming and easy to talk to, he is a naturally gregarious person who loves to socialise yet he also maintains a depth and reserve, and is respectful of other people and their space.

Stephen Cohen is a most interesting person, an outstanding political scientist who rightly commands huge authority. In illuminating the world of the past and of the present he is rigorous in his use of facts. His very special quality, however, lies in bringing those facts alive, infusing historical events with imagination and humanity:

> *'Among the many strengths of Soviet Fates is not just Stephen Cohen's long time depth of expertise but his unrivalled storytelling ability and, perhaps above all, his razor-sharp insider observations based on personal exchanges, interviews, and experiences with key actors.'*
>
> (Nanci Adler *Journal of Modern History*)

LE DUAN

In January 1961, John F. Kennedy was elected President of the United States, while Nikita Khrushchev was issuing a pledge of Soviet support for wars of national liberation around the world. Large numbers of Vietnamese people had fought a war of this kind during the early 1950s against their French colonisers. The conflict had, however, resulted in a divided country with a Communist dominated administration in Hanoi running North Vietnam while the South was declared a republic. When attempts to reunify the country through elections failed, Kennedy, still then a senator, had reiterated Eisenhower's domino theory, warning of the implications of Communist led governments taking hold in South East Asia: *'Burma, Thailand, India, Japan, the Philippines and obviously Laos and Cambodia are among those whose security would be threatened if the Red Tide of Communism overflowed into Vietnam.'*

A 'Red Tide' from the direction of Latin America had now come within one hundred miles of US soil on the island of Cuba. The failure of the Bay of Pigs invasion to depose Castro's government could only intensify American fears of a worldwide ideological takeover. As Honecker's wall went up in Berlin, the Viet Cong and North Vietnamese forces were gaining increasing control of rural South Vietnam, with US General Edward Lansdale reporting that the country was in a critical condition and should be treated as a combat area of the Cold War. It was felt in Washington that something had to be done. On the 11 May 1961 a 'Presidential Program for Vietnam' was drawn up, its objectives being: *'to prevent communist domination of South Vietnam; to create in that country a viable and increasingly democratic society, and to initiate, on an accelerated basis, a series of mutually supporting actions of a military, political, economic, psychological, and covert character designed to achieve this objective.'*

Le Duan on the right, with his translator

Some suggest that had Kennedy lived to see what came about as a result of this mission statement, he might have been appalled. Yet under his watch some highly questionable acts of war were already being carried out, notably the use of the defoliant Agent Orange. Under the euphemistically named 'Operation Ranch Hand' the powerful herbicide was sprayed from the air onto areas of suspected Viet Cong infiltration. An estimated four million Vietnamese were exposed to the chemical, which apart from its long-term damage to the environment, left up to one million people with serious health disorders including leukaemia, Hodgkin's Lymphoma and other types of cancer.

Regular bombing raids against the Viet Cong were also flown, while on the ground the CIA and US military advisors trained South Vietnamese in counter-insurgency tactics. The North Vietnamese government had meanwhile set up a version of its Politburo – the Central Office for South Vietnam – to assist in uniting the military and political struggle. The Americans later dubbed the COSV the 'Communist Pentagon' and vowed to destroy it, but the organisation being essentially a mobile network with no fixed location, this was almost impossible.

American money was provided for South Vietnam's Prime Minister Diem to increase his army, but so far there had been no actual US ground troops deployed. As the Viet Cong continued to make gains, however, direct intervention was now under discussion, with some advisors adamant that the insurgents could not otherwise be defeated. Responding to the hawks, a note of caution was sounded by Senator Mike Mansfield: '*We cannot hope to substitute armed power for the kind of political and economic social changes that offer the best resistance to communism.*' Questioning why such an evolution had not already come about, Mansfield said, '*I do not see how American combat troops can do it today.*' Those who still wanted to 'go in' were also reminded of America's long and costly involvement in the Korean War less than a decade earlier. Whilst stopping short of wholesale 'boots on the ground', Kennedy did however increase the supply of equipment to the South Vietnamese government, including helicopters and aircraft. A small number of US special forces were also deployed to train South Vietnamese self defence forces in village communities. By the beginning of 1962 the number of American military training personnel in Vietnam had more than tripled to over 3,000. Despite these efforts it was estimated that at least twenty per cent of the South Vietnamese population was now under North Vietnamese control, along with almost half of the Mekong Delta's thirteen provinces.

As North Vietnamese men and equipment continued to infiltrate the

Transporting goods on the Ho Chi Minh Trail from North to South Vietnam

South along the Ho Chi Minh Trail, Prime Minister Diem with US support rolled out the rural self-defence programme called the Strategic Hamlet Initiative, while in Operation Chopper, US helicopters ferried a thousand South Vietnamese troops to engage the Viet Cong near Saigon. Technically the airlift was a combat operation, but no one in the American military was saying so publicly. In February 1962, *New York Times'* journalist James Reston drew attention to what he claimed was now an open secret among other nations:

> *'The United States is now involved in an undeclared war in South Vietnam. This is well known to the Russians, the Chinese Communists, and everybody else concerned except the American people... Has the President made clear to the Congress and the nation the extent of the US commitment to the South Vietnam government and the dangers involved?'*
>
> (Robert Mann, *A Grand Delusion: America's Descent Into Vietnam*)

In January 1963, the Viet Cong scored a resounding victory against the South Vietnamese Army at Ap Pac, a hamlet just forty miles from Saigon. As news of the incident caused a considerable public relations setback for the American war lobby, the military responded with optimistic mission statements and progress reports. *'The situation in South Vietnam has been reoriented,'* claimed Army Chief of Staff General Earle Wheeler, *'in the space of a year and a half, from a circumstance of near desperation to a condition where victory is now a hopeful prospect.'*

Others such as Colonel Daniel B. Porter were less self-congratulatory, and had the decency to point out the human cost of the ideological struggle America had chosen to fight thousands of miles from its shores.

> *'In many operations against areas of hamlets which are considered to be hard-core VC [Viet Cong] strongholds, all possibility of surprise is lost by prolonged air strikes and artillery bombardments prior to the landing or movement of troops into the area. The innocent women, children and old people bear the brunt of such bombardments.'*
>
> (Andrew F. Krepinevich Jr., The Army and Vietnam)

In July 1963, a few weeks after a Buddhist monk had set himself alight in Saigon in protest at the persecution of his sect by the South Vietnamese government, President Kennedy told the world, *'We are not going to withdraw... for us to withdraw would mean a collapse not only of South Vietnam, but of Southeast Asia. So we are going to stay there.'* Five months later Kennedy was dead from an assassin's bullet. In the same month Prime Minister Diem also died. The war in Vietnam had only just begun.

The Communist government of North Vietnam was now being led by a former railway clerk named Le Duan. A veteran of the Japanese occupation and the first Indo-China War, under French colonial rule Le Duan had spent several years in prison for his political beliefs. He had subsequently been leader of the South Vietnam Central Office until 1954, when political divisions had obliged him to move across the border. Committed to reuniting his country, his 1956 manifesto 'The Road to the South' had advocated a non-violent revolution to bring the two sides together. Although the nominal leader in the North at this time was still Ho Chi Minh, Le Duan's natural abilities soon allowed him to take the important decisions over policy.

> *'Within the first few years of his role as general secretary, Le Duan became the most powerful figure in Hanoi, enlisting support from many allies. According to the biographer William Duiker, from the late 1950s Ho Chi Minh's role was largely ceremonial, with him increasingly delegating authority to his senior colleagues in the party and the government. Although Ho's international prestige and experience meant that he became Hanoi's chief diplomat, real power at home rested with Le Duan and his trusted deputies.'*
>
> (Quynh Le BBC Vietnamese service, 14 July 2006)

With South Vietnam still unstable, the non-violent revolution Le Duan had advocated seemed in doubt. Urging that the North, still in the process of implementing socialism should support the Communist movement in the South, in 1957 he travelled to Moscow to discuss his strategy.

By 1964, as peaceful Buddhist protests against the South Vietnamese government increased, the Viet Cong supported by Hanoi won further military victories. Kennedy's successor in the White House, Lyndon B. Johnson, was now being advised by the Chairman of his Joint Chiefs of

Staff to begin bombing North Vietnam. Johnson, mindful of forthcoming presidential elections, demurred. However, when US Defence Secretary Robert McNamara told him that the Viet Cong had taken over almost half of South Vietnam, and recommended a bombing campaign combined with funding for 50,000 more South Vietnamese Army recruits, Johnson gave his assent and took personal charge of the necessary proceedings. Fighting the Communism menace in any and every corner of the world was, it seemed, the overwhelming imperative of American foreign policy. Republican Senator Barry Goldwater was even advocating nuclear weapons to destroy North Vietnamese supply lines to the South.

Within the US government establishment there was at least one dissenting voice: '*There are no Chinese soldiers in South Vietnam,*' declared Senator Wayne Morse, '*there are no Russian soldiers in South Vietnam. The only foreign soldiers in South Vietnam are U.S. soldiers.*' Richard Nixon, formerly a Vice President, having visited South Vietnam was of the opinion that Johnson's strategy would not succeed. Later he urged the US military to '*win this crucial war and win it decisively.*' In May 1964, however, Johnson admitted to misgivings and suggested that the conflict was being perpetuated as a result of pressure from US Senate Republicans. In a phone call to his adviser he reportedly did not think that South Vietnam was '*worth fighting for and I don't think we can get out. Its just the biggest damn mess I ever saw.*'

In the summer of 1964, military engagements between US and North Vietnamese vessels in the Bay of Tonkin were judged as provocation towards Hanoi. Neighbouring China issued a statement: '*Aggression by the United States against the Democratic Republic of Vietnam (North Vietnam) means aggression against China. China will not stand idly by without lending a helping hand.*' The pledge was backed by the supply of fifty-one MIG fighter aircraft and arms for the Viet Cong. China's Mao Zedong was at the same time swift to assure Le Duan that his country's gesture was a precaution not an incitement to broader conflict: '*because no one wants to fight a war, there will be no war.*'

My Tho, Vietnam. A Viet Cong base camp being burnt to the ground in 1968

Independent observers were meanwhile making their own predictions for the outcome in Vietnam. In the opinion of Robert Thompson, leader of the British Advisory Mission in South Vietnam, 'Defeat by the Viet Cong, through subversion and increased guerrilla activity is inevitable, and this prospect will become gradually more apparent over the next few months.'

If the Americans failed to enter negotiations with North Vietnam said Thompson, 'they could be forced to insert combat troops in some strength.'

Thomson's prediction proved correct. From 1965 as American involvement intensified, anti-war demonstrators took to the streets in the US, while the military campaign on both sides deteriorated into a bloody tit for tat. Le Duan was determined to break the stalemate through increased use of the tactics Thompson had described – small scale hit and run, morale sapping attacks against the technologically superior US Army, but by January 1968 a major Viet Cong operation known as the Tet Offensive was in the final stages of planning. It has been pointed out that in North Vietnam there was also significant opposition to pursuing the war. Even President Ho Chi Minh and Defence Minister Vo Nguyen Giap spoke out against Le Duan's Tet Offensive, claiming the Communist forces were not strong enough to bring about a wholesale uprising.

Le Duan would brook no such dissent, and such was his power that Ho was exiled to Beijing and the Defence Minister to Hungary, and their deputies and supporters imprisoned. On the 30 January the Tet Offensive went ahead, with some 80,000 North Vietnamese troops launching attacks on over one hundred towns and cities across South Vietnam. Although the element of surprise had a significant impact on the South Vietnamese and US forces, counter-attacks were swiftly launched and many of the centres of population were taken back.

The war would rumble on for a further seven years, bringing the estimated total death toll to almost one and a half million. Of this figure over half a million were Vietnamese civilians from North and South. The reunified Socialist Republic of Vietnam now embarked on a war with neighbouring Kampuchea, and in deposing the Khmer Rouge would uncover a programme of systematic barbarity unknown since the Holocaust.

In 1980 I spent eighteen days in Vietnam, and in the course of visiting four provinces stood on the former borderline that had divided the war torn

Above and below: Part of Vagif Guseynov's tour of Vietnam in 1980

Just one of the ruined buildings

country for three decades. My colleagues and I were there as part of a large delegation to foster good relations between the socialist countries. In my home city of Baku we had a lot of Vietnamese students at the time learning construction and agriculture. There was an extensive programme of meetings for our stay, and our Vietnamese hosts took us around and introduced us to agricultural workers, students and people engaged in the huge amount of reconstruction that was going on. Seeing the bombed out buildings – the once thriving factories, schools and houses, whole communities reduced to piles of rubble was a stark reminder of the devastating effects of modern warfare on the human environment. Then there were the effects of Agent

Orange and napalm that still scarred the landscape and many of the people. Meeting some of the survivors, the victims of these horrific atrocities, was difficult to stomach.

Yet in the midst of all the destruction there was a positive spirit, the sense of a new beginning. Wherever we travelled by train or car, looking out across the rice fields and along the roadsides we saw people working. From dawn till dusk no one was sitting around idle or smoking, all were hoeing, digging, building, sweeping – busy and industrious, and however frail or poor seemed always ready with a cheerful smile.

A very different experience was to follow. Our Soviet delegation had all heard of Pol Pot and what had happened in nearby Cambodia and naturally the subject came up in conversation with our Vietnamese colleague. 'Would you like to see the place for yourself?' he asked me one evening. I thought sure, why not since we are here. I assumed it would be a long journey, and asked how we would get there. 'We can arrange that,' said my colleague, and with that proceeded to telephone the Vietnamese Minister of Defence. When the call was done he said, 'Okay, tomorrow a chopper will arrive and take you there.'

Sure enough the following day a helicopter touched down outside our accommodation. Already on board was the Minister of Defence, who ushered us in beside him. As the chopper soared over the rice fields we had a fantastic panoramic view of the landscape, while our hosts pointed out the sites of past military operations, as well as the opium growing region of Laos, part of the south east Asian Golden Triangle.

Finally we reached our destination in Cambodia. To this day I wish I had not made the journey. What I saw that day shocked me profoundly. The broken and burned out villages one could recognise as a result of so-called normal warfare, but the makeshift gallows used for the multiple hangings of innocent people was chilling in a quite different way. Then we came to the now legendary legacy of the Khmer Rouge: seeing mountains of skulls in a photograph is one thing, standing in front of them was for me quite another.

The legacy of the Khmer Rouge

Other human remains lay around – bones, skeletons – some of them still wearing torn and burnt clothes and what even looked like flesh.

In the midst of all this again we saw people building, planting crops, life going on. Either they had not had time to deal with the aftermath of the Khmer Rouge's horror, or they could not bear to go near it. Pol Pot's idea of year zero included killing people simply for wearing glasses on the assumption that they were intellectuals. Yet he too had supposedly been a thinker, a student of radio electronics in Paris. It was said though that he repeatedly failed his exams. During the war with Vietnam he vowed to destroy those in his own country deemed to have 'Khmer bodies with Vietnamese minds' and in the space of six months over 100,000 were murdered. Such exhibitionist demonstrations of power and cruelty showed the dark side of Asia, an atavistic cult of death harking back centuries.

Before leaving for home though, there were three things that would take my mind off the horrors of the Khmer Rouge for a while. The first occurred during a trek through the Vietnamese jungle, when I suddenly felt a pain in my leg. On examining me my Vietnamese colleagues informed me that a scorpion had stung me. The leg was blowing up like a balloon. With no hospitals within reach, without fuss or further ado our local Vietnamese guide cut open my flesh and set about sucking the poison from the wound. Already I could feel my temperature soaring as the sting took effect. The guide worked on me for a good twenty minutes. Taken to our waiting vehicle I was then ferried to a hospital in Saigon for further medication and aftercare. It took me several days to recover. Having come from minus thirty degrees in Moscow to a tropical climate, my body had already been struggling to adapt, and the trauma in the jungle had tipped it over the edge. A local person, having natural antibodies perhaps might have been back to normal quicker, but I still felt slightly knocked out for the next couple of weeks. Scorpion stings are often fatal if not quickly treated, and the speed with which the guide had got the poison out of my body had been critical to my survival and I owe him my life.

The second surprise was a pleasant one: the beauty of Vietnamese arts and crafts. Despite the war a number of galleries and their contents had survived intact, and I found that the people here were wonderfully talented artists. The paintings were amazing, likewise the embroidery work, which was still being regularly produced, and all so inexpensive for foreigners to buy. For a very poor country with so little in the way of natural resources, the artistic skill and output was breathtaking.

Surprise number three came a couple of days before we were due to leave, when my Vietnamese colleague told me we were going to call in at the main party building in Saigon to see Le Duan. I was thrilled, but in my head we were about to meet an old man. Instead we were greeted by a very alert, vibrant and well informed person. Le Duan was extremely interested to hear our impressions of the country, and eager for our thoughts on how it could best be rebuilt. This was a man who had taken on everyone and

Vagif Guseynov's surprise meeting with Le Duan in 1980

everything – the Japanese, the Americans, hunger and hardship – and he knew all about working hard, yet even at his advanced age he was more than willing to listen to advice.

He was also very well informed about the Vietnamese students studying in the Soviet Union, and knew which Soviet specialists were in his country at the moment and where, and was grateful for their presence and input. He said he was very glad to meet us, as he had received letters from students studying in the Soviet Union and from those working with our specialists in Vietnam, and had heard favourable reports. His colleagues were very happy with the outcomes, and he wanted to thank the Soviet Union for the support, help and attention given to his country's young people.

Le Duan was a legendary and heroic figure, and it was an unexpected and very inspiring experience to meet him in the flesh. This was a man who with his fellow countrymen and women had challenged the technological might of the American military machine and after years of struggle won. As Confucius said: 'in the fight between the sword and the spirit, the spirit will always win.' The Vietnamese people certainly had that spirit.

Le Duan on an official visit to Baku in 1982

5 May 1976, Escheverria speaks at a major UN Conference held in Vancouver, Canada, devoted primarily to the problems of rapid, unplanned urban growth

LUIS ECHEVERRIA

Of all the many parts of the world that I have visited, none has made so great an impression on me as Mexico. The sheer vibrancy of the people, their positive, life affirming spirit, even – or perhaps especially – those with little in the way of modern material wealth, was an inspiration to the soul. Of course such vivacity is helped by the abundance of bright sunshine in Mexico, the shimmering landscapes, the joyful Mariachi bands on every street corner, and sometimes the ready availability of tequila.

However, it would be misleading to attribute such preponderant optimism and warm heartedness to climate and alcohol. Mexico's history is a turbulent one, and its people have known what it is to struggle, to fight, to win and to lose. Difficult experiences build character, and from what I saw of the Mexican national character, the impulse is most often to see the glass half full, a belief that life is for living and that tomorrow – *manyana* – is not something to worry too much over.

That being said, Mexico has been built by the struggles of idealists and visionaries. Those visions and ideals have in some cases been political, in others artistic, and there are Mexicans that have committed their lives equally to both, as we shall see. Mexico emerged as an independent state in 1821 after finally breaking free from the Spanish Empire. Twenty-five years later the country was at war with America over Texas. A resounding defeat led to both Texas, and the then Mexican territory of California, being subsumed into the USA. The position of their shared border would remain a contentious issue between the two countries and not until 1909 would an American president, William Taft, set foot on Mexican soil. Taft was keen to preserve US investments in Mexico, while Mexico's President Porfirio Diaz hoped the visit would demonstrate America's backing for his upcoming re-election bid. With emotions over the disputed Chamizal strip

The vibrancy of Mexican art

section of the border running high, both sides deployed a large military presence to attend the presidential meeting.

Following the invention of the internal combustion engine, Mexico's rich oil reserves would become a major economic asset. America's Standard Oil Company had staked its claim early, however, using Mexican workers to extract the product while taking the lion's share of the profits. In 1938, when an industrial dispute could not be resolved via the courts, President Cardenas took over the wells and set up PEMEX – Petrolios Mexicanos – a nationalised oil company. It was a bold move on Cardenas' part, which might have provoked American retaliation but for Roosevelt's 'Good Neighbour' policy. The US had already been involved in one World War, and with events in Europe signalling the potential for another crisis, the benefits of cooperation in one's backyard were being recognised. Neighbourly feeling though had at the same time been somewhat compromised during the Great Depression, with the coercive repatriation of over half a million Mexicans from the US. With many of those sent out believed to have been American born, the programme has been compared to a form of ethnic cleansing.

World War Two brought greater solidarity to American-Mexican relations, though the pragmatic foundations for this improvement, chiefly the increased requirement for Mexico's workers and commodities, would last only as long as the conflict. The following decades would see a marked upswing in Mexico's industrial development, the so-called 'Economic Miracle' of the post war years. The income that had been earned during the conflict from export of materials and manufactured goods would be invested in agriculture, infrastructure and perhaps most importantly, education. The benefits of oil revenue added to the growing prosperity and urbanisation accelerated.

In 1968 Mexico was to host the Olympic games, an occasion one might imagine of huge national pride and excitement. The government was certainly pulling out all the stops, with President Gustavo Diaz Ordaz having pumped $150 million dollars into the event to be held in Mexico City. But who would benefit from this investment – the population as a whole or mainly big business? There was a degree of unrest in the country; unions demanding wage increases had been suppressed and large numbers of university students, in general step with their peers in Europe and America that year, were in rebellion against the status quo. In Mexico the National Strike Council, a delegation of representatives from colleges and schools across the country, was asking for the curbs on free assembly of more than three persons to be lifted, for those responsible for the violence against previous demonstrators to be identified, for political prisoners to be released and for the chief of police to be removed. The National Strike Council also strongly opposed the government's interference in the autonomous management of the universities.

In July, clashes took place between rival gangs at Mexico City's Vocational Schools, the violence adding to the general mood of restlessness and agitation among the youth population. Brigades of students handed out leaflets accusing the government of corruption, gave impromptu speeches and collected donations. The public was divided in its response, some voicing their support, others seeing young people intoxicated with the adrenalin of anarchy. One commentator described the atmosphere as inspiring:

> *'The year 1968 in Mexico City was a time of expansiveness and the breaking down of barriers: a time for forging alliances among students, workers, and the marginal urban poor and challenging the political regime. It was a time of great hope, seemingly on the verge of transformation... A revolution was happening – not Che's revolution – but a revolution from within the system, non-violent, driven by euphoria, conviction, and the excitement of experimentation on the ground.'*
>
> (*From Che to Marcos*, Jeffrey W. Rubin, *Dissent Magazine*, Summer 2002)

At the beginning of August 1968 some 50,000 students undertook a peaceful anti-government march from the National Autonomous University of Mexico led by the university Rector, Barrios Sierra. Despite the National Strike Council's assurances that it did not wish to disrupt the imminent start of the Olympics, when a silent protest was then proposed for the 13 September, President Ordaz decided to prevent it and sent the army onto the campus. Heavy-handed tactics were employed against students, and the Rector resigned his position in protest. Within weeks pitched battles had broken out between police and activists at two Polytechnics, leaving conflicting reports on the fatalities, put at three by the authorities, fifteen by French newspaper *L'Express*.

With the Olympic opening ceremony just days away, on 2 October thousands of people filled the Plaza de las Tres Culturas in the Tlatelolco area of Mexico City. Some were now expressing distinctly anti-Olympic sentiments. As military forces began to surround the Plaza and helicopters circled overhead, shots rang out. Who had fired them was uncertain. What ensued was a tragedy. As people ran for cover more gunfire followed, with a so-called 'Olympia Battalion' rounding up students, herding them into nearby buildings and beating them. By the following morning twenty-eight civilians including children were counted dead.

When I arrived in Mexico City in 1973, Luis Echeverria had been President for three years. He had been born in the city in 1922 and from 1947 taught political theory at the National Autonomous University, the institution into which Ordaz sent troops in 1968. Founded in 1910, the university became a secular replacement for the Royal and Pontifical University of Mexico, which, as the name suggests, held the Catholic Church and the monarchy as core values. Entry to the new seat of learning would become highly competitive, but with the Mexican revolution still in flux its intellectual independence remained under prolonged pressure from the conservative establishment. Carrying the motto *The Spirit Shall Speak For My Race*, Rector Jose Vasconselos' design of the map of Latin America encircled by an eagle and a condor was adopted as the university's coat of arms in 1921. As throughout much of Latin America, the uneasy relationship between religion and left wing ideology on the campus would not be easily resolved.

Echeverria began his political career in the Institutional Revolutionary Party and became Secretary of the Interior in the Ordaz administration in 1964. The first five years of his presidency he had devoted to major economic reforms and social welfare policies. Health and education services were improved, a large-scale home building programme was rolled out and electricity companies and mines were nationalised. Whilst these measures predictably made him unpopular with the business community, Echeverria stuck to what he believed was right for the Mexican people. On taking office he had also pledged to allow some of the 1968 student protesters that had been exiled to Chile to return home. In addition, a number of political prisoners being held in Mexico were released.

In 1971, however, trouble flared again between the universities and the authorities over the principles of academic autonomy and democratisation. On 10 June, Corpus Christi Festival day, the dispute culminated in the death of 120 students, allegedly at the hands of Los Halcones (the Hawks) a specialist undercover riot squad trained by the CIA at the behest of the Ortaz government following the 1968 protests. Echeverria vowed that the Corpus Christi day killers would be brought to justice, but as time went on there seemed less possibility that this could be achieved, which angered those on the left.

When I met Echeverria it seemed very strange, because although a Secretary of International Affairs of the All-Union Komsomol, I was by no means a big party official. An introduction to the President certainly wasn't on the planned agenda for my visit. However, it turned out my opposite number in Mexico's youth organisation was very close to Echeverria. I noticed soon after I arrived that he called him a few times, and my impression was that it was he who arranged our meeting. When it became known where I would be going, even our ambassador to Mexico was surprised, as there was a Soviet minister amongst our delegation and he had not been invited.

I was told I would only have twenty minutes with the President, but in fact I was with him for two hours. My Mexican colleague remarked to me afterwards that I had been behaving like 'a real Mexican.' He thought I had been masquerading, playing the part. But it wasn't difficult here to get into the Hispanic mindset, I felt very in tune. During the conversation Echeverria covered a range of topics. America was discussed in not very positive terms. In public the diplomatic relations between the two countries appeared cordial; the following year for example US President Gerald Ford was to visit Mexico and lay a wreath on the tomb of Padre Eusabio Kino, the 17th century Jesuit priest and explorer who had set up a mission and helped peasant farmers in what was then the Spanish Empire. Kino caused controversy among his fellow priests by speaking out against slavery in the silver mines.

Symbolic gestures between nations were important, but in terms of what the United States got up to behind the scenes it would be understandable for Echeverria to have reservations; the role of the CIA in training the

Los Halcones riot militia for example, for whose actions he was still held responsible in many quarters. Few could guess at the full extent of any secret service operation, and cover-ups were endemic. In 1975, a Rockefeller Commission report into CIA domestic activities and assassination plots would be significantly altered by the Ford administration prior to publication. The alteration would not be revealed until several years later.

Echeverria was very pleased that Brezhnev and the Soviet Union were supporting his country, and that Mexican students were being invited to study in the Soviet Union, especially at the oil and gas institutes in Baku – oil was of course a big industry for Mexico, and over one hundred nations were represented among the student population at the Baku academies. I explained that part of my job with the youth organisation when I was back home was to meet representatives of the different national student groups each month, see how they were getting on, if there was anything they needed and to sort out any problems they might have. The Mexican leader was also very interested in our Soviet cosmonauts and delighted that we had brought one with us in the delegation. Keen to have his country represented in space exploration, Echevarria said he had written to Brezhnev to ask if a Mexican national could be included in one of the Soviet missions. I replied that he should perhaps try a more personal approach, take Brezhnev a bottle of Tequila and sit down with him.

Being passionate about art, before flying to Mexico I had researched the country's treasure trove of galleries and famous painters. Among the most interesting was David Alfaro Siqueiros. As a young man Siqueiros had joined the armed struggle of the Constitutional Army against Victoriano Huerte, known as 'the Jackal', who in 1913 had usurped the elected President Madero, and who is a hate figure to many Mexicans to this day. When Huerte was toppled, Siqueiros stayed loyal to the Constitutional Army, now battling Zapata and Pancho Villa's rival bids for power. In 1919, he travelled to Europe, looking at cubism and Italian frescoes, and meeting fellow Mexican painter Diego Rivera. Returning home, it was Siqueiros,

David Alfaro Siqueiros

From the Dictatorship of Porfirio Diaz to the Revolution: The Revolutionaries (1957–65) by David Alfaro Siqueiros

Rivera and Jose Clemente who led the Mexican Muralism movement, creating inspirational works aimed at uniting the country socially and politically during the post-revolutionary years.

Siqueiros made it clear that for him politics and art were inseparable. His military experiences had shown him life in the raw – the struggles of ordinary Mexicans to survive amid grinding poverty and conflict. As an artist his work would now be informed by Marxism, but above all by the fusion, or collision, of classical painting with the manifestations of the modern age. Early mythological imagery is employed to serve 20th century agrarian and proletarian revolutionary themes, and it is the common people – men, women and children – who are the heroes of his pictures. Never afraid to speak his mind, Siqueiros had spent time in jail and was at one time ejected from the United States for political activity. In 1938 he joined the fight against Franco with the Spanish Republican Army, and two years later back in Mexico City, as a staunch supporter of the Soviet Union, he led an attempt to assassinate Leon Trotsky, a mission fulfilled by others with the infamous ice pick a few months later.

Never one to retire gracefully or compromise, for his criticisms of Mexican President Adolfo Mateus in 1960, Sequeiros was again imprisoned. While behind bars he continued to paint and sell his work and was released only after four years of campaigning by supporters in the art world.

I understood that Sequeiros lived somewhere within the outskirts of Mexico City, and during the conversation with Echeverria I mentioned that if there were one artist I should love to meet it would be him. Within moments of my having expressed the wish, arrangements were being made. Sequeiros's home and studio were located on the other side of town. This, however, was a city of several million people and what seemed like as many cars. Crawling through the dense traffic, encountering every half mile or so a donkey blocking the road, it took a good three hours to reach our destination. Sequeiros welcomed us warmly, coffee was served and we spent a good twenty minutes talking about art, Mexican history, and the Soviet Union, and took photographs together. It had been a privilege to meet David Sequeiros, a unique experience made possible by another person I had not expected to meet, President Echeverria.

The terrible night of the Tlatelolco Massacre had left a permanent scar upon Mexico's collective consciousness. People had been rightly aggrieved, and along with President Ordaz, who was his Interior Minister at the time, Luis Echeverria was identified by many as a prime culprit. He was suspected, on his own authority or directed by Ordaz, of ordering the troops to open fire. Others believed that some unknown person had either panicked or deliberately provoked the slaughter. During his presidential campaign Echeverria had called for a moment of silence for the victims of the massacre, a gesture that had angered Ordaz, who threatened to dismiss him from his ministerial post.

Luis Echevarria seemed a man of principle. In 1976, with his presidential term coming to an end, he had no desire to see the progressive social achievements of the previous six years undone:

> *'Aware of the gathering of conservative forces... Mr. Echevarria seems determined to prevent a reversal of his reformist policies.'*
>
> (Alan Riding, *New York Times*, 21 November 1976)

The issue of Tlatelolco would not go away and further investigations produced fresh evidence, pointing the finger of blame again towards the authorities:

> *'...the government version is that the students opened fire. Well, there's been pretty clear evidence now that there was a unit that was called the Brigada Olympica, or the Olympic Brigade, that was made up of special forces of the presidential guard, who opened fire from the buildings that surrounded the square, and that that was the thing that provoked the massacre.'*

Katie Doyle, All Things Considered, National Public Radio, 14 February 2002

A march to commemmorate the Tlatelolco Massacre, October 2014

In 2006 charges of genocide were brought against Echeverria, by then eighty-four years of age. It would be another three years before he learned the outcome of the case.

> '...*after a convoluted appeal process, the genocide charges against Echeverria were dismissed. The Mexican newspaper The News reported that "a tribunal of three circuit court judges ruled that there was not enough proof to link Echeverria to the violent suppression of hundreds of protesting students on 2 Oct. 1968".*'
>
> Nacha Cattan, *The News*, Mexico City, 28 March 2009

Hearing the news naturally reminded me of my 1973 trip to Mexico where, before I left, President Echeverria had presented me with the medal of Latin American liberator Jose de San Martin for work between nations. I had spent almost a month in Mexico and still recall it as an incredible experience. I found the people just amazing, and loved the Hispanic culture, the architecture and in particular the magnificent museums. Many of the buildings housing the collections are in themselves breathtaking works of art, and have been much improved in recent years. Entering the baroque splendour of the Museum of the City of Mexico, built in the 17th century as the Palace of the Counts of Santiago de Calimaya, one can now explore twenty-six rooms of beautiful exhibits telling the story of Mexico, from the time of the Aztecs and through the Spanish colonial period to the present day.

There was one more person I met in Mexico whom I must mention. One of my Soviet colleagues, a journalist who happened to be living in the country at the time was a friend of a woman called Consuela Velazquez. Those who don't know the name might well recall the song she wrote in 1940, *Besame Mucho* – 'Kiss Me a Lot' – is among the best selling records of all time, was at number one in America in 1944 and has been performed by a host of artists from the Beatles to Placido Domingo. Consuela is said to have written it after a heartbreak experience of her own, and the lyrics carry a poignant, bittersweet rapture, which anyone who has ever been in love cannot fail to be stirred by. The day Consuela and I met I drank a great deal of tequila, and on saying farewell presented her with some bottles of fine Russian vodka and a nest of matryoshka dolls. She in turn pressed more of her best tequila on me to take home. All I needed to complete my Mexican transformation was a Sombrero. Fortunately Echeverria had already given me one.

Consuela Velazquez

Left: Medal of Latin American liberator Jose de San Martin, given to Vagif Guseynov by Luis Echeverria

Below: Photograph taken during a visit to Mexico City, 1973

HÉLÈNE D'ENCAUSSE

Hélène Carrère d'Encausse, Permanent Secretary of the Academie Français, must be one of the top twenty intellectuals in the world. An expert not just on the USSR but also on Russia before and after the Soviet years, her fluency in the Russian language is amazing. In fact I believe she has some Russian ancestry. I first met Hélène in Munich then in Moscow in the late 1970s and we renewed our acquaintance in the 1990s as fellow members of the Council on Foreign and Defence Policy. She and I were preparing a book along with a number of other contributors within the Council. Whilst this was a friendly and convivial group, we naturally did not agree on everything – that was the whole point of meeting, to bring differing points of view to the international table. Our discussions in the '90s focused mainly on Russia's relations with Hélène's native France and its role within NATO.

More recently, with the Western military alliance drawing closer to the Russian border, Russia has intervened covertly and openly in Georgia. The French contingent within the Council on Foreign and Defence Policy tended to be very negative about this involvement in Georgia and would openly attack my colleague Karaganov and myself for what our government was doing. We told them the reason Russia was attempting to keep some kind of hold on Georgia was because of NATO. Ten years earlier there had been an agreement to maintain the status quo, and then NATO had moved its troops further towards the Russian border. The Kremlin had seen this action as a provocation and then were accused of revanchism. Admittedly having someone like Putin at the helm did not help.

Although an intellectual who strives always for objectivity, Hélène d'Encausse, like all of us, speaks from an inherited cultural and geographical perspective. The basis of her ideas could be called Atlanticist – a belief in the values of Europe, the US and Canada – the West. Having said that, Hélène has a tremendous liking for Russia and its culture, is immensely knowledgeable about Russian history and politics, and from the early 1960s has written a series of detailed books on the country and its most prominent figures. The title of her 1982 work *Confiscated Power: How Soviet Russia Really Works*, first published in French in 1980, carries an inbuilt suggestion of something wrong or dishonest at the heart of the Soviet system. Western reviewers gave the book a favourable response:

> *'This excellent study of Soviet government by a distinguished French scholar describes not only the apparat but the political culture in which it operates. Beginning in 1917, but dealing only summarily with the Lenin and Stalin eras, then more fully with the turbulent Khrushchev era, the author devotes most of her attention to the past two decades. Bureaucratic interests and conflicts have become institutionalised and are managed by the party elite in ways which have brought stability but also immobility, and a question remains whether petrified power will indefinitely contain the forces of a changing society.'*
>
> (John C. Campbell, *Foreign Affairs*, Spring 1983)

Written at around the same time was *Decline of an Empire: The Soviet Socialist Republics in Revolt*, in which, according to one reviewer, Hélène d'Encausse concluded that at the beginning of the 1980s '*...power in the USSR still lies with the Communist Party,*' (*Kirkus Review*) and that this assessment of the author's ran '*counter to recent conjectures that the seat of power might have moved to the army or the state bureaucracy. Lenin, Carrère d'Encausse notes, tried to institute two incompatible policies: a leading role for political and technical experts, resulting in unequal authority relations, and material egalitarianism, whereby the experts would receive modest wages.*' (Ibid)

The reviewer describes the author as painting a picture of a two tier society having emerged in Russia, with institutionalised corruption, the means by which people might gain a little more in terms of material benefit: '*plant managers used their positions to skin wealth off the top, party insiders were given sole access to stores selling foreign goods, etc. Stalin's purges disrupted but did not end this system; and, says Carrère d'Encausse, it was Khrushchev's attempt to undermine this arrangement – through the introduction of economic incentives and the decentralization of decision making--that led to his overthrow by a troika bent on preserving the status quo.*' (Ibid)

From the troika referred to, Brezhnev emerged the leader, and for the reviewer of Hélène's book at least, this only served to confirm the strong hand of the Communist Party. As for the development of Soviet military resources during the 1960s and 1970s, *Decline of an Empire* was read as attributing this growth to a degree of abnegation elsewhere: '*Whatever strides the Soviet military has made over the last twenty years are not a result of significant new power for the army, Carrère d'Encausse claims, nor do they represent victories for a "hawk" faction over a "dove" faction. Rather, the Soviet leadership, rejecting domestic reforms, has turned to foreign policy as a substitute; and in that realm they have succeeded.* (Ibid)

The *Kirkus Review* concluded that, '*The one value the Soviet leaders share is maintenance of the power system that benefits them. The one great stride the Soviet system has taken, since the tumultuous Stalin years, has been toward regularization of its governmental processes; today, the system is both internally weak and externally strong.*' How far this reflects Hélène d'Encausse's own view, or is an interpretation, would require very close reading of the original text. The verdict on *Decline of an Empire* was, '*For both novices and Kremlin watchers: a thorough, knowledgeable look at the Soviet scene.*' (Ibid)

In May 1985, Hélène presented a paper to the thirty-third Bilderberg Meeting, a three-day international forum on world affairs held in New York.

Nineteen European nations were represented, along with Canada and the USA. The 113 delegates were drawn from a cross section of organisations and professions – diplomats, lawyers, politicians, trade unionists, lecturers, journalists, financiers, business people and the military. According to Bilderberg's stated protocol, *'All participants spoke in a personal capacity, without committing in any way the organizations or governments to which they belonged.'*

In the opening address it was also pointed out that the meetings were taking place close to the fortieth anniversary of VE Day, out of which event, *'had grown the NATO Alliance, and Bilderberg, while not formally a part of the Alliance, had been born alongside it.'* Hélène d'Encausse's paper was one of two submitted to provide the background to the second topic of discussion on the agenda: *How Should the West Deal with the Soviet Bloc?*

Hélène opened her paper by referring to the long-running debate in the West about the future of the USSR and how this had divided opinion. The debate had centred, in her view, on the question of how to turn the Soviet Union *'towards more moderate attitudes at home and in international life.'* She then broke the debate down into two parts: economic and military/political relations. Within the former, there were as she saw it two conflicting attitudes: those of people like Samuel Piszr, who assumed that economic cooperation and technical assistance would enable the West to promote reformist Russians, thereby leading to a liberalisation of the Soviet Union. Another group held the opposing view that trading with the Soviets was only helping them to enlarge their military capacity, potentially imperilling the West, thereby scoring an own goal one might say.

The military/political aspect of relations was, Hélène claimed, split along similar lines: the so-called 'doves' in their attitude to the Soviets being opposed by those who saw any relaxation of the West's guard being exploited, as in the case of Angola and Afghanistan. It was observed that in the 1960s and 1970s there had been a perception in the West that the Soviet Union would in time drift away from rigid socialist ideology and turn out *'behaving like every modern power, especially in its international policy.'* In the current decade of the 1980s, Hélène saw the West returning to a more traditional attitude to the Soviet Union, implying that the regime's ideological basis remained essentially unchanged, and that central to that status quo came the impulse to expand its territory and its influence abroad.

Hélène claimed that observers in the West had attributed the Soviet expansionist drive to a domestic malaise within its borders. She said there was also the perception that the advanced ages of the Kremlin leaders signalled a moribund political establishment, unable or unwilling to hand on power to the up and coming generation. However, since the advent of Gorbachev, the first leader to be born after the 1917 Revolution, this charge of a problem of succession could no longer be justifiably levelled. At the same time Hélène was not predicting an easy ride for the incumbent: *'…we know from Soviet history that the leader in charge of supreme power needs several years to establish his authority over the whole system.'* With the Soviet Union also facing serious economic challenges, what were the prospects she asked, *'in such a gloomy situation, for some dramatic initiative due to Gorbachev's fresh authority?'*

Hélène identified two positive factors: that a large number of the Soviet elite was looking for a change in economic policy, and that Gorbachev was young enough to inspire the confidence that he would see such changes through. Whilst suggesting a reduction in central planning and target driven management in favour of small-scale private enterprise, encouragement of craft activity and innovation in agriculture, Hélène also mentioned the role of law, order, discipline and hard work, invoking Andropov in this context.

Hélène's paper then came to what she called the imperial issue, and pointed to the demographic shift between Russia and the peripheral parts of the Soviet Union: *'The USSR, with a population of 273.8 million as of January 1984, has its North, with developed Slavic, Baltic and other European populations constituting 77 per cent of the total population (1979 census)… its South, made up of people of Turkish Moslem origin, located primarily in Central*

Asia and the Caucasus... represents 22.7 of the population (1979 census) with an average natural increase in the 1970s... four times that of the north.'

A growing population in the republics would obviously be harder to manage and contain, especially when fused with a growth in nationalist sentiment. In flagging up these statistics Hélène was alerting her fellow delegates to a trend that, as we all know, would contribute to serious consequences for the Soviet Union. Whilst Hélène d'Encausse's 1985 paper delivered to the Bildersberg stopped short of predictions – who would have dared make any at such time of flux in international affairs – many of the points she made in relation to the Soviet Union proved prescient. By 1993, with the Berlin Wall down, Gorbachev gone and Yeltsin doing his best to hold things together, there was the opportunity to take a look in the rear view mirror and try to see the twists and turns that had led us to where we now were. For some commentators, the Soviet Union's demise had been a foregone conclusion, but for Hélène d'Encausse this was not necessarily so, and there were those who agreed with her, some of them having just discovered her talent for perspicacious analysis:

> *'Having never read anything by one of France's most eminent and prolific historians of the Soviet Union, I decided to take a look at Hélène Carrère d'Encausse's 1993 book,* The End of the Soviet Empire... *Carrère d'Encausse explores the role of nationalism in the Soviet Union's collapse but focuses on the Soviet regime's bad management of nationalism in great detail....Close examination reveals, perhaps, that the Soviet Union didn't just suffer from nationalism, it often promoted that nationalism, however unintentionally. That is to say, Stalin and his successors exported ethnic Russians to the peripheries in order to exert control on those areas, but created fearful ethnic tensions in the process... The irony is that Gorbachev began ...by insisting that although socialism had stumbled economically, and had perhaps unnecessarily stifled other forms of human initiative, it had at least solved the nationalism question. As Carrère d'Encausse reminds us,*

although Gorbachev avoided party cliches on a variety of different questions, he entered the age of reform relying almost exclusively on the old rhetoric of proletarian internationalism. The breakdown of the empire had roots in Baltic memories of independence, a partly Iranian-inspired Islamic revival, Caucasian geography, a Khazak population explosion, and Russian chauvinism. But Carrère d'Encausse's contribution to our understanding of these ethnic revolts is to show that this wasn't entirely inevitable. If Soviet leaders in Moscow had had experience in the smaller socialist republics, or Russians hadn't been exported elsewhere, or Gorbachev had thought to do something other than reenergize the drive toward Russification of the cadres, things might have worked out a little differently than they did.'

(*Soviet Roulette*, 30 January 2013)

Vagif Guseynov and Héléne during the International Conference of Council on Foreign and Defence Policy in Moscow, 2009

Hélène d'Encausse's open mind on the trajectory of Soviet history from the mid 1980s is characteristic of her intellectual approach in general. She brings a wealth of facts and statistics to any debate and uses them with intelligence and judgement. Her study of the founding father of the revolution has also been updated in the light of new evidence:

> *'Lenin… is a one-volume, concise study of Lenin and his role in the Russian Revolution. It concentrates on his years in power between 1917 and 1924. The book draws on recent historical work in Russia and the West, and makes use of new documents made available since the Gorbachev era and the end of the Soviet Union.'*

She is also not afraid to express unfashionable views. In 2005, during the civil unrest in France, she suggested that one reason why some young Parisians of African origin might have problems with accommodation was because of their family structure: *'Why can't their parents buy an apartment? It's clear why. Many of these Africans, I tell you, are polygamous. In an apartment, there are three or four wives and twenty-five children.'*

Inevitably the remarks were judged to be racist, and in the face of the backlash Hélène compared the political climate in her country with that of Soviet, and post-Soviet Russia.

> *'It's true that the Russian television follows Putin step by step. But French television is so politically correct it is a nightmare. We have laws Stalin could have thought up… People cannot express an opinion about ethnic groups, World War Two, and plenty of other things. You'll be quickly convicted of a crime.'*
>
> (*Worse Than The Riots Themselves*, Jared Taylor)

Hélène d'Encausse is the author of over twenty books, has contributed to many more, and written a mountain of articles, treatises and research papers. A woman of great style, she is admired by men and women as much for her intellectual rigour and breadth of learning as for her elegance, grace and charm. With huge authority in academic and political circles she is also warm, communicative and culturally aware. I was in touch with her quite regularly until about 2014, when I became quite busy with my family, my children and grandchildren. However, we still call each other on the phone at Christmas and other occasions to catch up. Only recently I saw an excellent programme presented by her on Russian television, offering a lucid and highly informed commentary on the current state of world politics.

In 2010, Russia's current leader spoke about the global impact of Hélène's work: '*During his meeting at the Kremlin with the renowned linguist and Russian historian, Mr Putin underlined that the research done by Hélène Carrère d'Encausse was important and interesting for the entire world, and not only for Russians and the French.*'

Hélène speaking at the Place de Nancy, Luxembourg, September 2013

General Secretary, Hélène d'Encausse arrives at the Elysée presidential palace to attend Emmanual Macron's formal inauguration ceremony as French President on 14 May 2017, in Paris

The publication *Russia Today* also spoke with Hélène in 2010, and when asked among other things if she thought that Russia now had imperial ambitions, she emphasised that Russians were quite capable of being both sentimental towards their past, and level headed about the present. *'I don't believe it. I would rather say there is some kind of nostalgia, but that's a completely different thing. What country can forget overnight that it used to be a powerful empire? Some Russians say that it's a shame it's forgotten about. But still Russian people and specifically those in power have common sense, and they understand too well that it's over and that Russia's future is not to be an empire, but rather to build up its reputation and influence via soft power, rather than by force.'*

As to the future of the country she had studied and written about for five decades, she made it clear she was not a crystal gazer but a historian: '*I don't make forecasts, as a rule…I look at the past and try to figure out what's happening in the present. I think Russia has come a long way over the past twenty years. It is having some difficulties, as countries do. It's not easy to introduce democracy or capitalism. It took Western Europe centuries to do that. Doing it within twenty years isn't so easy.*'

Yet although offering no predictions about the difficult journey Russia was embarked upon, there was a small note of reassurance: '*I think Russia is following the path it chose in 1991. There have been ups and downs but I don't see any discontinuity so I think we can be calm about Russia's future.*'

From a thinker of the calibre of Hélène Carriere d'Encausse, such words give grounds for optimism.

YURI GAGARIN

Time: 10.29 pm, 4 October 1957. Location: A top-secret government base in the remote steppes of the Kazakh Republic. A metal sphere measuring 56 centimetres in diameter – about the size of a beach ball, although at 83 kilos considerably heavier – is attached to a rocket and launched vertically into the air. The metal sphere is called *Sputnik*, a Russian word meaning travelling companion, and the journey it has embarked on will signal the dawn of an awe inspiring new era of exploration for humankind.

Climbing steadily, *Sputnik 1* left the Earth's atmosphere and commenced its first elliptical orbit of the planet. Moving at a phenomenal 18,000 miles an hour, at the furthest point of the ellipse the satellite was over 500 miles from Earth, at its nearest less than 150 miles, making it visible with binoculars after dark. Each orbit took an hour and a half, while from its four long antennae the satellite sent regular radio signals back to Earth. Around the world people watched and listened, radio hams excitedly picking up the bleeps from their sheds and living rooms, children begging to stay up late to catch a glimpse of the remarkable phenomenon. Four months later the joy ride was over. *Sputnik 1* had, as predicted, burned up in the atmosphere, its fragments forever lost in space.

Khrushchev was eager to build on the success of *Sputnik 1*'s voyage. It would prove to be just the beginning for space exploration, and what was now referred to as the space race between America and the USSR. The reaction in the United States was that Russia had stolen a march on them with the *Sputnik*, which had been ten times larger than a planned American version. Fears about the potential military applications of the new technology spurred the US authorities to press ahead with their own programme. Meanwhile Khrushchev was pushing to have a second satellite launched to coincide with the fortieth anniversary of the October

revolution, 7 November 1957. He was also calling for the event to be a 'space spectacular' – something that would surpass *Sputnik 1* and amaze the world. It was decided therefore that *Sputnik 2* would have a passenger. From the streets of Moscow was found three-year-old Laika, a stray female mongrel dog, thought to be of terrier and husky parentage. Laika's conveyance was fitted out with food, water, a life support system, cooling fan, as well as an electrocardiogram to record her heart rate.

Precisely how an animal's physiology would react outside of the Earth's atmosphere was largely a matter of speculation at this time, but there was agreement on one thing: Laika would not return. Prior to the launch, one of the scientists working on the project took her home to play with his children: 'Laika was quiet and charming, I wanted to do something nice for her: she had so little time left to live.' (Vladimir Isachenkov *Space Dog Monument Opens in Russia*, MSNBC, 11 April 2008.) Though Laika did not make it back to Earth, she would be immortalised in history as the first living creature in space. The Soviet Union had also leapt ahead again in the space race, America's first satellite *Explorer*, which carried no passenger, not being launched until two months after Laika's voyage in *Sputnik 2*.

The next big date in the Soviet Calendar being Lenin's birthday on 20 April 1958, a launch of *Sputnik 3* was planned for the day. Mechanical glitches, however, held the event back until the 27th. A more serious glitch

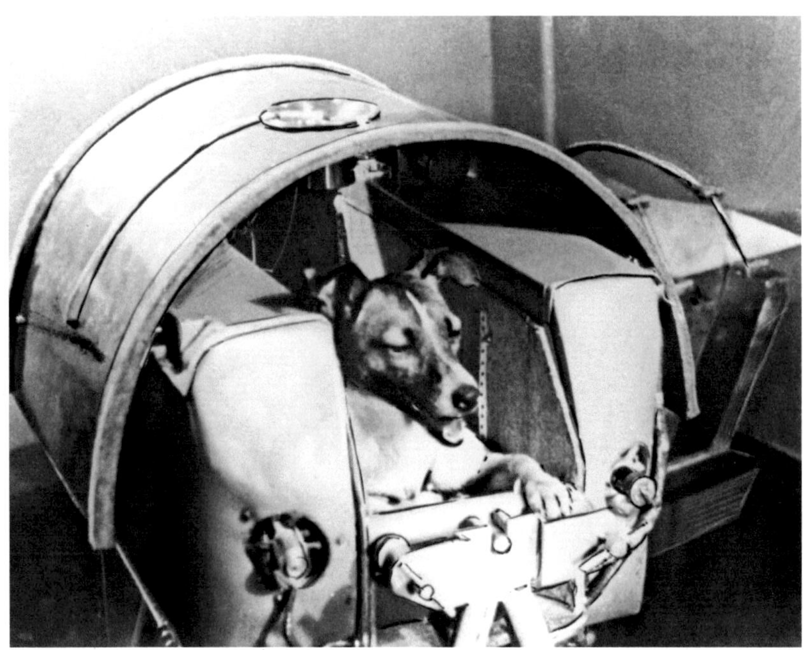

LAIKA was the first dog in space via Russia's 'Sputnik 2' in Ocober 1957

was in store as within two minutes of lift-off, as it reached a height of approximately 140 miles, the vehicle fell back to Earth. On examination it transpired that the satellite had at some point detached itself from the rocket carrying it. On 15 May a replacement was successfully re-launched, where it's onboard instruments measured and relayed atmospheric conditions in space for the next two years until burning out.

The burning issue now was the possibility of a human flight beyond the Earth's atmosphere. It was certainly the wish of the Soviet Union that such a mission should be attempted, and it was now not a matter of *if* but *when* it would happen. Who though would be brave enough to embark on such an incredible journey? The answer was thousands of ambitious young pilots. From the initial swathe of volunteers, twenty were enrolled into the Soviet Space Programme to undergo a series of examinations, gruelling endurance tests and training exercises. From the twenty, six finalists – the 'Sochi Six – would compete to pilot *Vostok 1*, the first ever manned voyage into space. Among them was a twenty-six-year-old carpenter's son called Yuri Gagarin.

The surname Gagarin was said to be derived *'from the Russian for wild duck, and was also that of an ancient princely family that held vast estates in the Smolensk area before the Bolshevik revolution.'* Gagarin, however, *'angrily denied any connection with that aristocratic lineage'* (*New York Times*). Born in the small village of Klushino in Smolensk Oblast, Yuri, whose mother was a milkmaid, had been seven years old when the Nazis invaded the Soviet Union. As the enemy forces moved towards Moscow, the village was occupied and the family home commandeered by a German officer. While Yuri, his mother, father and younger brother Boris lived in a mud hut his older brother and sister were sent to a Nazi labour camp in Poland. In 1945 the family was reunited, and a year later they moved to Ghatsk. By 1951 Gagarin had completed an apprenticeship in foundry work. It was after moving on to the Saratov Technical Institute that he also developed an interest in aeronautics. Joining a Soviet air cadet programme at a nearby club, he had his first taste of flying. After his army call-up in 1955 Gagarin was admitted to the First Chkalov Air Force Pilot's School, and in 1957 flew solo in a MiG 15.

In terms of physical fitness for the Soviet Space Programme, Gagarin scored highly; a keen sportsman since joining the Air Force he excelled at ice hockey, a game requiring quick reactions and agility. A natural feature favouring his candidacy was his stature: at 5ft 2in he could move with relative ease in the small interior of *Vostok 1*. Psychological fitness was equally important, both for dealing with practical tasks and problem solving, and in terms of attitude. A member of the medical staff judged Gagarin to have a 'high degree of intellectual development' and a 'fantastic memory,' with the capacity to handle 'celestial mechanics and mathematical formulae with ease.' Perseverance was also noted along with painstaking preparation for duties. Gagarin stood out from his colleagues said the doctor, by virtue of a 'sharp and far ranging sense of attention to his surroundings.' There was in addition modesty, an occasionally embarrassing 'racy humour', and an ability to understand life 'better than a lot of his friends'. As part of the selection process, the opinion of the prospective cosmonaut's peers was also sought, and in the original heat of twenty each candidate had been asked to say anonymously which of the others they would most like to see fly the mission. Out of his nineteen comrades, sixteen had picked Gagarin. Their superiors agreed with the choice.

With its cosmonaut selected, *Vostok 1* was prepared and a launch date scheduled. To ensure his own preparedness, Gagarin was given a medical. The doctor who examined him that day remembered her impression of the young man about to become world famous: '*Gagarin looked more pale than usual. He was unsociable and quiet, which was not like him at all. He would answer by nodding or a short 'yes' to all questions. Sometimes he would start humming some tunes. This was a different Gagarin. We geared him up, and hugged. And I said, 'Yuri, everything will be fine.' And he nodded back.*' (*Celebrating a Star: 50 Years Since Gagarin's Spaceflight. Russia Today*, April 2011.)

Cosmonaut Yuri Gagarin aboard 'Vostok 1' spacecraft

At the Baikonur Cosmodrome, its location in southern Kazakhstan still a closely guarded state secret, in the early morning of the 6 April 1961, Yuri Gagarin ascended the thirty-metre rocket to enter the tiny capsule attached above. While the last minute preparations and safety checks were run, Gagarin sang Soviet hymns. As the seconds till blast-off ticked away, who knew what lay ahead for him in the distant skies? At 09.37 am, on receiving the signal from launch control, Gagarin replied with the now legendary phrase *'Poyekhali'* – *'Let's go!'*

Released suddenly from gravity, he described the experience of weightlessness in a matter of fact way, like *'hanging in a horizontal position in straps… as if you are suspended,'* while what met his eyes from space moved him deeply: *'What beauty, I saw clouds and their light shadows on the distant dear Earth.'* On receiving his messages the people below were also in awe, as fellow cosmonaut Georgy Grechko recalled: *'The most emotional moment was when we heard he was walking and waving; his arms and legs were whole…*

we understood in one sigh that our five to six years of hard work had paid off and we had achieved something huge.' (*Daily Mail*)

Orbiting the Earth at over 17,000 miles per hour, after an hour and forty-eight minutes it was time for *Vostok 1* to return home. What was not revealed at the time was that as the craft began its descent, things did not go according to plan. Instead of separating from the equipment module as intended, the capsule remained connected and went into a rapid spin. *'It happened over Africa,'* said Gagarin. *'One moment I see Africa ... another the horizon, another the sky. I barely had time to shade myself from the sun, so the light did not blind my eyes.'* A back up system designed to take over took a further ten minutes before activating. Gagarin quite probably thinking he might never see his family again, began to sing the patriotic song *The Motherland hears, the Motherland knows/Where her son flies in the sky.* When the mechanism did right itself the capsule re-entered the Earth's atmosphere safely, and at 10.44 am the parachute deployed and the pilot ejected.

On landing Gagarin found himself in open countryside, where a Volgograd farmer and his daughter stared at him in utter disbelief.

> *'When they saw me in my space suit and the parachute dragging alongside me as I walked, they started to back away in fear. I told them, don't be afraid, I am a Soviet citizen like you, who has descended from space and I must find a telephone to call Moscow.'*
>
> (Jim Ensom, *Voice of Russia UK*, 9 March 2014)

Khrushchev was at his holiday home on the Black Sea when he received the news that Gagarin had landed safely back on Earth, and sent the cosmonaut a message of congratulation: *'The flight made by you opens up a new page in the history of mankind in its conquest of space.'* (BBC report, 12 April 1961) America's President John F. Kennedy likewise offered his congratulations to '*the people of the Soviet Union for their 'outstanding technical achievement'.*

For Gargarin the adulation and celebrity status had only just begun. The

ONLY JUST THE U.S.

see page two

Daily Worker

THE ONLY DAILY PAPER OWNED BY ITS READERS

CANDID ON POLARIS

see page three

(9185) 3d WEDNESDAY APRIL 12 1961

Soviet astronaut circles the earth three times

THE FIRST MAN IN SPACE

Back alive—but suffering from effects of his flight

From DENNIS OGDEN MOSCOW, Tuesday.

THE Soviet Union has launched the first man into space and brought him back to earth alive, according to well-informed sources here.

The astronaut, said to be the test-pilot son of a top-ranking Soviet aircraft designer, is understood to be suffering after-effects from his flight.

Top aviation medical specialists and leading space scientists are in constant attendance.

They are keeping him under close observation.

EAGER WAIT

A Soviet astronaut ready for his space flight with (left) an artist's impression of the Soviet space capsule. A. Pressurised cabin; B. Foam-padded seat to relieve pressure on take-off; C. Parachutes to slow speed of capsule on descent; D. Air supply; E. Television cameras, microphone for relaying back to earth; F. Porthole; G. Instrument panel.

EDITORIAL

Big Business butts in

Long neglect

Interference

Holy cow!

De Gaulle threat to Algerian talks

By the FOREIGN EDITOR

Partition threat

Release refused

Six million dead accuse Eichmann

EFFORTS by Adolf Eichmann's West German lawyer to prevent his trial going forward were passionately combated yesterday by the prosecution.

LONG WAIT

TWITCHING

GAS CHAMBERS

TELL TORIES TO QUIT TOMORROW—GOLLAN

TOMORROW in London and Middlesex, and in the counties polling in the next few days, the people have a chance to serve the Tories nationally with a notice to quit, Mr. John Gollan declared yesterday on behalf of the Communist Party.

Housing misery—Tory hypocrisy rapped

Daily Worker Reporter

COMMUNIST candidate in North Battersea in tomorrow's London County Council elections Mr. John Evans yesterday attacked the hypocrisy of the Tories in trying to make capital out of London's housing misery.

Stand for unity

40,000 FEET SAY JOBS!

Daily Worker Reporter

BELFAST, Tuesday.

Busmen, dockers

Menzies warns S Africa

Trevor Williams

TV's West news

WEATHER: Bright periods, perhaps some rain later. Lighting-up time: 8.20 p.m.

Adolf Eichmann, in the bullet-proof dock yesterday.

Motorman dies in rail crash

Daily Worker Reporter

TV electricians return to work

On the agenda

It's YOUR paper

IT HAS GREAT PLANS

Come and discuss the Daily Worker's future. Put your own ideas at the

Annual General Meeting of the People's Press Printing Society

LONDON

Monday, April 24, 7.30 p.m. Conway Hall, Red Lion Square, W.C.1

Speaker: George Matthews

The front page of the 'Daily Worker' showing cosmonaut Yuri Gagarin as the first man in space, 1961

voice of Yuri Levitan, who two decades earlier had covered all the important developments of the Great Patriotic War, announced the success of the *Vostok 1* mission to the Soviet people over the radio. Massive parades and gatherings were held in cities across the country, while around the world the press and TV featured stories about the space flight. The focus of all the attention was the man who had undertaken this astonishing feat and returned to tell the tale. After landing, Gagarin was brought to Moscow, where, surrounded by the Communist Party elite and amid huge crowds, he was kissed profusely by Khrushchev and awarded the title of Hero of the Soviet Union.

There followed an international tour that included Finland, Germany Italy, Egypt, Brazil, Japan, Canada and the UK. As he was driven in an open top car through cheering onlookers in Manchester it was raining heavily, but Gagarin refused to put the hood up or even use an umbrella, insisting that if his hosts could stand in the rain to see him he should at least do the same for them. There were rumours that being constantly in the limelight began to affect him, and while previously a moderate drinker he now felt

Yuri Gagarin observes the Air Parade at the Air Base near Cairo, Egypt in 1962

obliged to down several toasts at every social engagement, of which there were many.

Gagarin seemed to survive all the pressures unscathed and over the next couple of years took up a number of official appointments, including a deputyship to the Soviet Union, as a committee member of the Young Communist League, and by the end of 1963 a promotion to Colonel in the Soviet Air Force and as Deputy Training Director for cosmonauts at the Star City base. However, his desire to continue flying was now being discouraged by the authorities: the first man in space was too precious a national treasure for such dangerous endeavours. Gagarin's passion for the air was too strong though, and although banned from further space missions, by 1965 he was renewing his training as a fighter pilot.

It was the following year that Gagarin added another city to the many he had now visited since his momentous space flight. Yes, our legend, our hero was coming to Baku! I was a young man of twenty-four. On the big day the streets were crammed with people brimming over with excitement at this chance to see the great man, who was going to be passing through on his way to meet the Azerbaijani oilrig workers. As the open car approached, everyone began throwing flowers. I remember catching just a glimpse of him as he went by. He had a very kind, open face and that radiant smile that had adorned the covers of a million newspapers, almost Biblical in its sweetness and innocence. There were thousands of people along the road, all craning their necks waiting and watching for him to appear. The atmosphere was very emotional, very charged, like a religious experience. People all around were crying, and I remember as Gargarin went by a woman standing beside me exclaimed in an awestruck voice, '*He saw God, and came back!*'

Everywhere Gagarin went, children and adults alike were filled with wonder, for each generation felt in its own way a very special connection to him. For that woman beside me on the street, who must have been in her seventies and who clearly believed devoutly in God, he really had been to meet the Creator of the universe. For others he represented the most amazing human achievement in their lifetime. What he had done was such a huge event, and what it symbolised was for each person to interpret, but however spiritual one felt about it we all loved Yuri Gagarin. He was a wonderful, inspiring symbol not just for the Soviet Union but for the whole planet, this son of all humanity leaving the Earth and journeying thousands of miles into the wide blue yonder for the first time ever. It had been a phenomenal moment in history and he was a unique individual. Now I too had seen him in the flesh, and I would never forget that moment.

Watching Gagarin pass by that day, I little imagined that later I would have the privilege of meeting him. The occasion was a conference of youth organisations in Moscow at which Gagarin had come to deliver a speech. He was seeing lots of people and had an extremely busy schedule, but he was very relaxed and personable and spent about twenty minutes chatting to us, during which time we asked him all kinds of crazy questions – how do you become a cosmonaut, what do you need to know, what was it like up there, etc, etc. I think his scientific understanding must have been way ahead of everyone in the room, for he had recently been expanding his theoretical expertise and working towards a thesis on space plane aerodynamic configuration. Gagarin spoke about his experience, and discussed the future of space travel when cosmonauts would travel to Mars and beyond. He emphasised that this would not take place during his lifetime, but thought it could conceivably happen in ours, not that he was that much older than most of us. The man was absolutely charming with amazing oratorical skills, but to be honest if he had just stood there people's jaws would have dropped just to look at him, as they had done in Baku.

On the 27 March 1968, a few weeks after successfully completing his academic thesis, Gagarin took a flight in a MiG-15 UTI from Chkalovsky with instructor Vladimir Seryogin. The following day we were shocked to hear the following statement from the Soviet Union news agency Tass: *'It is officially announced here that Hero of the Soviet Union Yuri Gagarin, the world's first cosmonaut, has perished during an air crash.'*

USSR, 1976. Postcard with commemorative Airmail stamp. 'The 15th anniversary of the world's first manned space flight'

On 30 March thousands of mourners congregated in Red Square, many holding aloft photographs of Gagarin in his uniform with full honours. As the ashes of Gagarin and Seryogin were interred in the Kremlin wall people wept. Tributes flowed in from all parts of the globe. Perhaps the most apt in its simplicity and choice of last words was from the Soviet space journalist Vladimir Gubarev *'Yura (Gagarin) was a very quick learner. He assimilated everything new. His mind was stellar.'*

In the wake of the tragedy a number of conspiracy theories circulated, most of them postulating the idea that Gagarin had been killed because of some unspecified disloyalty to the state. Some claimed that he had deliberately crashed the plane to commit suicide, and there were even rumours of him crashing into a UFO. A KGB report pointed to incorrect meteorological data being given out by ground control. Further clues would take several more years to emerge, and it would be Gagarin's friend and fellow cosmonaut Aleksey Leonov who would provide them.

Yuri Gagarin had celebrated his thirty-fourth birthday a few days before his plane came down. For the Soviet people and for the whole world it was a time to remember and celebrate a very special person, whose radiant smile had lit up their lives and shown them that when thinking about what human beings can achieve, nothing should ever be taken for granted.

RAJIV AND SONIA GANDHI

1980

Following independence from British rule in 1947, India's first Prime Minister, Nehru, at first kept his country politically non-aligned. America in the meantime became the first country to open a dialogue with the newly created neighbouring state of Pakistan, and Dwight D. Eisenhower's announcement in 1954 to supply it with arms prompted a re-think on India's part. In 1955 Nehru and Khrushchev exchanged visits, and the warm relations established between their two countries have continued to this day. During this time India has been involved in a series of diplomatic and military conflicts with Pakistan, the first coinciding with partition, and in 1965 a seventeen-day clash resulting in thousands of casualties over Pakistan's territorial claims on Kashmir and Jammu brought the Soviet Union in to act as successful peace broker. A larger confrontation in 1971 saw some ten million East Pakistanis fleeing across the border into India, and the creation of the People's Republic of Bangladesh. The same year, India signed the Indo-Soviet Treaty of Friendship and Cooperation, article two of which pledged the two nations to:

> *'...contribute in every possible way to ensure enduring peace and security of their people...declare their determination to continue their efforts to preserve and to strengthen peace in Asia and throughout the world, to halt the arms race and to achieve general and complete disarmament, including both nuclear and conventional, under effective international control.'*

Following the loss of East Pakistan, Bhutto embarked in earnest on a nuclear weapons programme, and called on Pakistan's scientists to assist in the development of a bomb within the next three years in the interests

Rajiv, Indira and Sanjay Gandhi

of national survival. India had meanwhile been conducting its own nuclear programme from as early as 1944, instituted at the behest of Nehru. But Nehru had also publicly stated that such a capacity must only be used for defence as a last resort: '*We must develop this atomic energy quite apart from war – indeed I think we must develop it... for peaceful purposes.... Of course, if we are compelled as a nation to use it for other purposes, possibly no pious sentiments of any of us will stop the nation from using it that way.*' In 1974, on an army base in Rajasthan, under the operational codename 'Smiling Buddha', the Indian military carried out its first successful testing of a nuclear bomb.

Pakistan continued to receive American backing, although support

Jawaharlal Nehru and Rajiv Gandhi on horseback, 1940s

wavered during the 1970s, with Pakistan's request for America to impose sanctions against India after the 1974 nuclear test was turned down, Kissinger telling Pakistan that it would *'have to live with it.'* Two years later Kissinger warned Bhutto of consequences unless Pakistan cancelled or restricted its own nuclear weapons development, to which Bhutto replied, *'For my country's sake, for the sake of people of Pakistan, I did not succumb to that blackmailing and threats'.* Nixon was then ousted from the White House and replaced by Carter, who pledged a worldwide ban on nuclear weapons. When Bhutto persisted with his programme, there were predictions of a catastrophic war between Pakistan and India. In 1979, however, Bhutto was declared corrupt and hanged, and Pakistan's positive relations with America were restored. In December of the same year the Soviet Army moved into Afghanistan.

It was just a few months on from these last two major events that I

Rajiv and Sonia Gandhi shortly after their wedding

sat with Rajiv and Sonia Gandhi in their elegant home in Bombay. As a Secretary of International Affairs of the All-Union Komsomol Central Committee of the USSR Communist Party, my brief was to meet those working in a similar role throughout India, listening and talking to leaders and young people, and exchanging thoughts and ideas about the values, aspirations and challenges faced by the fledgling citizens of our respective countries. The trip would take twenty days, travelling east, west, north and south of the country and visiting several of the biggest cities including Delhi, Bombay and Chennai, in the process covering nine of India's twenty-two states.

Rajiv Gandhi's leadership of the Indian National Congress Party's youth movement in India at this time placed him at the very top of the list of those to meet on the trip. Born in 1944, Rajiv was the eldest son of Indira and Feroze Gandhi. No relation to Mahatma, Indira was the daughter of Nehru, and had served as India's first female Prime Minister from 1966 to 1977. In January 1980 she had swept back into power with the Congress Party a second time. In the same year, her son Sanjay, like his elder brother, Rajiv, a keen pilot, would be killed in a flying accident near New Delhi.

Sonia, two years younger than her husband, had been born in Italy, the daughter of a builder of modest means. Interestingly, her father Stefano Maino, had apparently been a self-declared supporter of Mussolini, and during World War Two had fought alongside the Wehrmacht on the Eastern Front against Russia. Sonia had been raised as a Catholic and in 1965, while studying English at a language school in Cambridge, England, she met Rajiv, an engineering undergraduate at Trinity College. Three years later the couple married, settled in New Delhi, and had two children. Rajiv, avoiding politics at that time, worked as a pilot for the state run Indian Airlines.

The differences in Sonia and Rajiv's cultural and religious upbringings seemed to have been no bar whatsoever to the success of their marriage. On the contrary, what impressed me most while in their presence was the sense that they were in total harmony with one another, almost like one person, an organic whole as it were. Both clearly highly educated, one could immediately tell that they were not just a devoted husband and wife who loved each other, but also the best of friends. I had been invited to meet them not at a government building, but in their home in a wealthy district of Bombay, now Mumbai. The house was beautiful, with lovely gardens and a swimming pool. At the same time it was not palatial, and there was nothing that struck one as ostentatious or over the top. I was also very surprised that the Gandhis' clothing was really quite plain and unadorned, and at first glance Rajiv could easily have passed for a clerk. Sonia I have to say was extremely beautiful, and the photographs I had seen of her hardly did her justice.

I gathered the impression that the Indian elite at this time, whatever their party, did not display their wealth or status; it was almost a religious point, a matter of social etiquette not to show one's material distance from the masses, who were extremely poor. Of course as a high-ranking family the Gandhis had Mercedes cars, drivers and servants, but neither of my hosts were wearing expensive watches or any kind of extravagant jewellery, it was all very modest. A late breakfast was served and alcohol offered, which I politely declined, telling them the famous old saying from the white officers of the Russian civil war, that anyone seen taking strong drink early in the day must be either a general or an aristocrat.

The choice of their home environment for the meeting was matched by the Gandhis' welcoming demeanour, and although our talk focused on the political rather than the familiar, their tone throughout was friendly, warm and accommodating. Both members of the Indian Congress Party, as well as accompanying Indira in her election campaign, both Rajiv and Sonia were now extremely active with the party's youth organisation, and interested to learn about the experiences and concerns of young people in my country. My translator spoke very good English, and amazing Hindi with a Bombay accent, so I was able to gain a clear understanding of their thoughts and ideas. We discussed current Soviet–Indian relations, and one could see that Rajiv had prepared very well for our meeting. In the past ten years trade between India and Russia had seen a tremendous increase, and I had only recently been in Moscow talking to the Indian student community to get an insight into how they felt about their studies and their impression of life in Russia. I had also met a large contingent of Indians at the naval academy in my hometown of Baku, and I remembered how I had struggled to learn all their long surnames by heart from a list the night before, and how the next day as the door had opened and they all trooped in one after another, it had seemed like the endless procession of names reeled off in the 'Court of King Caractacus' song.

There were, in fact, a huge number of Indians in Moscow and elsewhere in Russia, studying agriculture, engineering, medicine, biology, geology and other intensive scientific subjects. India would ask to send a quota of maybe fifty students for a particular course or discipline being taught in the Soviet Union. In my hometown of Baku, among the universities and twenty polytechnics, one of the main institutes was devoted to oil and chemistry, which had about forty Indian students. India needed specialists to develop the country's food production and technological capabilities, and the training they could obtain in Russia was obviously highly prized.

I was, however, aware of some cross-cultural issues among Russia's Indian community. In this regard I mentioned to Rajiv and Sonia that it might be useful to employ or brief a student representative, someone who could explain to the young Indians leaving home for the first time perhaps, the differences they were likely to encounter in Russia, the things that might come as a surprise. Apart from the practical issues, such as sensible preparations for living in a considerably colder climate and finding unfamiliar food, there were also social differences, perhaps the most important being that Russia did not recognise the caste distinctions that were still an integral feature of Indian society. Such a representative could, I suggested, also come over and visit those studying in Moscow, Baku and elsewhere, see how they were faring, and generally oversee and help them to settle in, counselling them to avoid hierarchical systems and attitudes to one another, thereby ensuring that all the students felt equal. Rajiv took this on board and I was pleased to learn later that such a scheme had been put in place.

In our discussions there was close agreement about the need to stem the proliferation of international arms, in accordance with article two of the Indo-Soviet Friendship and Cooperation Treatment signed ten years previously. Rajiv reiterated his grandfather Nehru's point that India did not want to fight, but while the arms race continued, along with the huge Cold War tensions playing out close to the country's northern borders and American support for Pakistan, there was great pressure to maintain spending on defence. The sums involved were vast, and with a dramatically increasing population, many of whom struggled to survive, money spent on arms seemed an obscene waste. This was a massive concern. Rajiv expressed India's gratitude for the support of Russia politically, and for the provision of Soviet arms in defence against Pakistan in the past.

Sonia, a great supporter of India, was an absolute equal in all these conversations, and I noted that they sat close together most of the time, not in separate parts of the room. Again, this seemed quite different to the typical diplomatic husband and wife scenario. They complemented one another perfectly, almost like Siamese twins on an intellectual level, and though they would be speaking separately and not interrupting one another, I would sometimes have the impression that it was just one voice I was hearing, not two. They had their own special aura.

As the grandson of Nehru, a top barrister and India's first Prime Minister, Rajiv was of the absolute elite and extremely clever, but there was no showing off or imperiousness; his diplomacy and manners were impeccable and he had a special charm, at ease with himself, with a sense of quiet, internal wisdom. When my colleagues and I itemised a list of places and people we would like to visit while in India, Rajiv was extremely helpful, pointing out which might be possible to include in our itinerary and offering advice and arrangements. I left feeling that the biggest political message of the meeting was that Rajiv and Sonia had chosen to receive me in private, in their home setting, and that this symbolised the close and friendly relationship they were keen to maintain with Russia. Rajiv's interest in Russian affairs had been genuine, and one could feel that fascination and curiosity pouring out of him with utter truth and eloquence, a very sincere human being.

With the death of his younger brother Sanjay, Rajiv was persuaded by his mother to enter politics fully in 1981. Three years later on the 31 October 1984, while walking in the gardens of her official residence in New Delhi, his mother Indira was shot dead by two of her bodyguards, in what was believed to be a reprisal for the storming of the Sikhs' Golden Temple at Amritsar. The assassination was followed by mass riots against Sikhs, killing almost three thousand. Rajiv said of the events, '*When a big tree falls, the earth shakes.*' Taking over immediately as Prime Minister at the age of forty, the youngest to hold the post, he served for the next five years, afterwards continuing as President of the Congress Party. On the 21 May

India's 7th Prime Minister, Rajiv Gandhi with Sonia, being greeted warmly by the crowds

Vagif Guseynov speaking during a visit to India in 1980

1991 while Rajiv was out campaigning in the elections, a woman bent down to touch his feet and detonated a bomb, killing him instantly.

I have met so many people during my lifetime but none have stayed in my memory in quite the same way as Rajiv and Sonia Gandhi. I loved them, they were amazing, and you could feel the love between them, like a fairy tale but at the same time so natural and unforced, which was also apparent in their attitude to other people. My feeling was that Sonia was highly intellectual and a complete equal to her husband. After Rajiv's death, she stayed away from politics until 1998, when she accepted the post of Congress Party President. Several times in recent years Sonia Gandhi has been cited as among the most powerful and influential women in the world.

President Ronald Reagan, Sonia Gandhi, First Lady Nancy Reagan and Prime Minister Rajiv Gandhi in the Yellow Oval Room during a state dinner, June 1985

CHE GUEVARA

The year is 1965 and I have just arrived in the heart of Africa, the Congo. This vast territory, rich in minerals, was formerly known as the Congo Free State, so named by King Leopold of Belgium who in 1888 at the Congress of Berlin claimed it for himself. For the indigenous people their country was anything but free, with millions dying as a result of forced labour in the colonisers' rubber plantations. Little changed apart from the name, when in 1908 Leopold's rule was removed and the Free State became the Belgian Congo. By 1960, however, with the mood against colonialism throughout Africa gathering pace, Congo was declared a republic under President Joseph Kasa-Vubu and Prime Minister Patrice Lumumba.

With the region still unstable, Lumumba asked the United Nations for peacekeeping assistance. When he made a similar request to the Soviet Union, however, Kasa-Vubu, disapproving of such a link sacked him within a few months of taking office. It has been stated that Kasa-Vubu's actions were steered by America. In the ensuing power vacuum, the head of the army, Joseph Desire Mobutu, staged a rapid military coup. Patrice Lumumba was shortly after executed, with American and Belgian military personnel thought to have assisted in his apprehension. Adding to the drama and intrigue, the following year a plane carrying United Nations Secretary-General Dag Hammarskjold crashed in unexplained circumstances over nearby Ndola, Zambia, killing all fifteen people on board. Hammarskjold had been en route to the Congo to attempt ceasefire negotiations in the civil war that followed Mobuto's coup. Examination of the plane's wreckage fuelled rumours that Hammarskjold had been assassinated, possibly by those with vested interests in Congo's mineral wealth.

Facing continued instability and sporadic conflict, the people of the newly liberated country remained in need of food, health-care, education

and other basic provisions. In the Soviet Union, Brezhnev and his comrades were glad to assist, and in addition to sending supplies and specialists to train the population, invited young Congolese to come and study at universities in Moscow and elsewhere. The students acquired valuable knowledge and skills, particularly in agriculture and medicine, and in Baku at the oil and gas colleges, to take back to their country. Alongside this practical support, fraternal relations began to be established between the people of Congo and the Soviet Union, with regular cultural and industrial trips and exchange programmes for young people, workers', women's and artists' groups.

As a leader of our Soviet youth organisation, Komsomol, I have been invited with a party of students to visit the Republic of Congo and meet some of its people, and we have brought with us an orchestra. As everyone is aware the political situation has remained fragile. The previous year, 1964,

The young Vagif Guseynov emulating Che Guevara

Cyrille Adoula was struggling to maintain overall leadership, but with no United Nations presence, the various factions here have continued their armed conflict. Since the closure of parliament by Adoula, a coalition under the title of the National Liberation Council assumed command. Rival militia remained active in the northeast under Gaston Soumaliot, while over other large parts of the country, a former associate of Lumumba, Christophe Gbenye, supported by the Soviet Union and China, had achieved extensive control and set up a government in Kisangani.

One month after a visit from US envoy, Averell Harriman, in March 1964, an American airlift was initiated. When Adoula's rule crumbled in July, his successor Moishe Tombe called on America, South Africa and Belgium to assist in restoring order. Backed up by white Rhodesian and South African mercenaries, Belgian officers and British paratroops – sent with Prime Minister Harold Wilson's approval – the Congolese Army set about removing Gbenye and his supporters. News of this international involvement prompted offers of military help for Gbenye from Egypt, Algeria and Cuba, and as we arrive in Congo in 1965, the foreign troops on both sides are still there.

Having earlier hosted a party of African students in Baku, we were familiar to some extent with the culture and particular challenges of the Congolese people at this time. Congo was a divided country and afflicted by internal strife, the Congolese, along with many people in the developing world were looking at Cuba as a success story; it's perceived high standards in medical and educational care and its egalitarian ethos under Castro a model to which they might aspire. Cubans were popular here and shortly after our arrival, along with an official from the Soviet Embassy in Congo, whom I assumed was KGB, I was given a fraternal introduction to a representative from Havana.

Our Soviet delegation likewise intended to show solidarity with the socialist cause, and our orchestra is to play in the city square. This turns out to be a huge affair with around 30,000 Congolese people flocking to

Che Guevara while participating in an guerrilla insurgency in the Congo in 1965

listen to the music and celebrate. When the concert was over, the Cuban representative came over to speak to me. He said the orchestra had been amazing and asked if it would be possible for them to come and play for a brigade of Cuban soldiers who were here building villages and supporting the local people. I replied something to the effect that I was sure we would all be honoured to oblige. Cubans were also very well liked and respected among Soviet people, so it was not at all difficult to persuade the musicians and our whole delegation to agree to this request. Just show us where the soldiers are billeted, I told him, and we will go and prepare.

A short while later the orchestra, their instruments and the rest of our delegation were loaded into trucks and we were heading out of the city. Entering the jungle, the temperature began to soar along with the humidity, and I found it difficult to breath. After travelling along unmarked tracks for a couple of miles or so we arrived at a clearing with a few huts and a cluster of tents and were greeted by an officer in uniform. The orchestra piled out and set up; the soldiers and villagers gathered around and the second concert began. I was seated beside the commander of the brigade, and during an interlude in the proceedings he turned and whispered in my ear that the brigade was honoured to have a very important person staying nearby at the moment. This person was travelling incognito, but would I like to meet him? Intrigued, I replied that I would, but who was he?

'*One of our Cuban leaders*,' replied the commander. '*He's here only for a few days, we love him very much and he really wants to meet you.'*

'A Cuban leader wants to meet me – well yes certainly.'

'Okay,' said the commander, *'I'll just have to send a message into the jungle.'*

The orchestra played a little more, until after about twenty minutes a small group of men in army fatigues appeared though the trees. The commander brought them over and introduced one of them to me. I knew immediately who it was, though for a few moments I was utterly speechless. When the commander had said 'a very important person' I had no idea how important, and that I was about to meet the one and only Che Guevara. Like a lot of young men and women at that time I had a T-shirt with his image emblazoned across the front, and now here he was standing in front of me shaking my hand. I was completely star-struck. It was like meeting a rock star, more than that, the Son of God.

The Soviet Embassy guy remained impassive. It seemed Che's presence in the Congo was no surprise to him. Staring at the living legend, all I could think to say to him in Spanish was *'What are you doing here?'* He smiled and told me about the work he and his comrades were doing with the Congolese people, building infrastructure, bringing in medical care, whatever they could do to help. Of course they were also fighting a war, supporting the local Simba forces against Mobutu's army. He then asked me, *'How is comrade Brezhnev?'* as if I was chatting to Brezhnev on a daily basis! But Guevara had visited Moscow only the year before and knew many of the Soviet leaders, especially the old guard, people like Suslov, the true revolutionaries.

The concert resumed and Guevara took a seat. Afterwards he and I began talking. We discussed the Soviet Union and he reminisced fondly about his visits there, and asked about my family and my work. Friendly, and with a ready smile, he could create a comfortable and pleasant atmosphere around him very quickly, yet there was no question of his earnestness. Talking about his vision for Africa and what needed to be done, he said that the Cubans would always help any nation that was prepared to fight imperialism and colonialism. *'Cuba,'* he emphasised, *'will never leave the patriots without support.'* He was also very interested to hear my thoughts as an outsider on Cuba, and how I perceived developments there. The conversation got around to Castro, and I gathered that although in public his relationship with the Cuban leader was harmonious, in private Fidel was jealous of Guevara's celebrity. One could understand it; he was a towering figure, a romantic legend, women were crazy about him, men hero-worshipped him. I could feel that magnetism. The aura around him was immense.

As Guevara continued to talk about politics, the future, the tasks that lay ahead, there was the sense that Cuba was already behind him. Although he had held government posts there, it was clear that he was not a career politician and would never be content to rest on laurels. Now he had moved on to the revolution here in Africa, then it would be the rest of Latin America. Wherever there was work to do and people to help, one felt certain he would be there. When the time came for him and his comrades to depart, I felt as if over the last couple of hours I had been talking to an old friend. I spoke to the Soviet official and obtained a bottle of Vodka and some albums of Soviet music. I presented these gifts to Guevara and he thanked me heartily. We wished each other well. The next minute he was gone, vanished back into the darkness of the jungle.

Guevara's inspiration and ideas were strongly rooted in theory – he was extremely well read – but equally in what he had seen of the real world early on in his life. Born into a middle class family in Argentina, in 1948 he had won a place at Buenos Aires University to read medicine. During the holidays, however, wanderlust and an innate curiosity took him on long journeys throughout Latin America. Riding a homemade motorcycle in 1950 he covered almost 3,000 miles of northern Argentina, visiting remote villages and small communities, talking to people, learning about the hardship and poverty of their lives. During what students nowadays call a 'gap year' he worked for free among lepers in Peru, and in Chile was angered by the inhumane conditions and exploitation which copper miners were forced to endure at the hands of large corporations. The United Fruit Company, an American monopolistic concern that operated throughout Latin America and accused by critics of paying indecently low wages while bribing government officials in return for favours, was a particular object of his ire. In 1953, just after Stalin's death, he swore on a picture of the Soviet leader that he would not rest until *el pulpo* (the octopus: a reference to the United Fruit Company's tentacles having an economic stranglehold on workers throughout numerous host countries) had been slain.

Guevara realised there was not just one octopus, and his journeys through Latin America had marked the turning point in his life. Accepting that one doctor could only do so much, and that the scourge of poverty and disease could only be cured by addressing the capitalist system grinding people ever downwards, he abandoned his medical studies and turned his energies towards political action. In 1953, the year of his pledge to defeat *el pulpo*, he moved to Guatemala, where a progressive government under President Jacabo Arbenz Guzman was making great strides in reclaiming large tracts of land from the United Fruit Company and other foreign owners and redistributing it among the local inhabitants. However, when the US government targeted Arbenz using aerial propaganda, bombing raids and local mercenaries, he was forced to flee to the Mexican Embassy, leaving the country in the hands of the pro-American Castillo Arbas.

Guevara, who had openly supported President Arbenz, likewise took flight for his life and spoke about the loss of the one beacon of hope in an exploited and beleaguered continent, and of who in his view was responsible:

> *'The last Latin American revolutionary democracy – that of Jacobo Arbenz – failed as a result of the cold premeditated aggression carried out by the United States. Its visible head was the Secretary of State John Foster Dulles, a man who, through a rare coincidence, was also a stockholder and attorney for the United Fruit Company'.* (Kellner, 1989)

El pulpo had proved itself a formidable adversary, with even more formidable allies, yet the experience in Guatemala only strengthened Guevara's revolutionary resolve. There followed a period in Mexico – working at a children's hospital, lecturing and taking photographs for a news journal – and it was here during the mid-1950s that he met brothers Raul and Fidel Castro, sworn enemies of the Batista regime in Cuba. Their cause said Guevara, was what he had been waiting for: long the playground of wealthy Americans while its people remained downtrodden and poor, Cuba was ripe for overthrow. Signing up as a medic with Castro's 26th July Movement, Guevara took part in arduous guerrilla warfare training alongside the other members of the group, practising the arts of reconnaissance, ambush and stealth fighting in readiness for the planned revolution.

On 25 November 1956, with just eighty-two men, the Castro brothers set sail from the coast of Mexico in a rusting cruiser and headed for Cuba. Engaged soon after landing by Batista's troops, fierce fighting ensued. Twenty-two of the invasion force survived and took to the Sierra Maestra mountains, linking up with local revolutionaries. As the weeks in hiding went by, Guevara impressed Castro with his ingenuity and commitment, not only employing his medical training to heal the sick, but teaching the hill people to read and write while baking bread for them and producing makeshift hand grenades.

But by now Guevara would become known not only for his care and compassion; promoted by Castro to second in command of the rebel army, he exerted steely discipline, pursuing and sometimes shooting those who deserted. When a local peasant confessed to selling information to the Cuban army, Guevara summarily executed the man. At the same time there seemed no lack of courage. One young comrade wounded in action owed his life to Guevara's bravery, which stunned even the enemy soldiers:

> *'Che ran out to me, defying the bullets, threw me over his shoulder, and got me out of there. The guards didn't dare fire at him ... later they told me*

he made a great impression on them when they saw him run out with his pistol stuck in his belt, ignoring the danger, they didn't dare shoot.'

(Samuel Landua, *Poster Boy of the Revolution. Washington Post,* 19 October 1997)

Having seen the effectiveness of propaganda in bringing down Arbenz in Guatemala, Guevara set up a pirate radio station to broadcast to the Cuban people. Meanwhile the Batista government strengthened its tactics and ignored the Geneva Convention by torturing and executing rebel prisoners. When they began shooting civilians at random, the US baulked and threatened to withhold arms sales.

Guevara's skills as a military tactician were by now astonishing, time and again hitting the enemy with lightning attacks then melting into the countryside. Towards the end of 1958 he began leading his men towards the capital Havana, moving by night and starving themselves to avoid observation. After a successful attack on the city of Santa Clara on the 31 December, three days later Havana was in the hands of the revolutionaries. Suffering from asthma, Guevara retired to a house in Tarara to write and to help in planning the new Cuban society. What then followed has been seen as a dark period for Guevara personally, during which, to purge the military he ordered the execution of up to one hundred men. In his defence, others have claimed that the individuals concerned were guilty of rape, murder, treason or desertion, crimes that would normally have been subject to the death penalty in a time of war.

'I have yet to find a single credible source pointing to a case where Che executed "an innocent".... I should add that my research spanned five years, and included anti-Castro Cubans among the Cuban-American exile community in Miami and elsewhere.'

(John Lee Anderson, *Che Guevara: A Revolutionary Life*)

Now declared a citizen of Cuba for his achievements in the revolution, in the summer of 1959 Guevara was sent to a series of countries in the Middle and Far East and to Greece and Yugoslavia. Ostensibly this was a diplomatic and trade mission, but some thought he was being got out of the way by Castro who felt uncomfortable with Guevara's hard line Marxist image. With American banks, oil companies and plantations being nationalised and the new government forging ties with the Soviet Union, Cuba could hardly expect to feel relaxed about its position in its own back yard, as witnessed in the blowing up of a freighter in Havana harbour and the subsequent Bay of Pigs invasion intended to remove Castro. To forestall further threats to the legitimacy of his government, Castro asked Khrushchev to equip Cuba with the ultimate deterrent. When an American U2 spy plane took back pictures of a ballistic missile facility in place less than one hundred miles from Florida, the terrifying reality of a nuclear confrontation for the first time seemed possible. After tense negotiations, the Soviet Union agreed to remove the missiles in return for a public guarantee from the US to leave Cuba in peace.

Guevara's reaction to the Bay of Pigs invasion is interesting. In a note sent to US President John F. Kennedy he wrote: '*Thanks for Playa Girón* (Bay of Pigs). *Before the invasion, the revolution was shaky. Now it's stronger than ever.*' (Ibid) The idea that a movement would be consolidated by virtue of being challenged makes sense. Some of what Guevara is reported to have said about the missile crisis, however, sounds more disturbing unless one views it as hyperbole to make a point: regarding the Soviet withdrawal of the missiles as a betrayal, Guevara allegedly told the *Daily Worker*, Britain's Communist newspaper, that had the Cubans been controlling them they would have fired them, adding later that the possibility of 'millions of atomic war victims' might have been a price worth paying to end imperialist aggression.

By the end of 1964 Guevara was a world statesman, speaking out at the United Nations in New York against South African Apartheid and continued exploitation in Latin America, meeting human rights leaders and appearing on television chat shows. The American visit was followed by a world tour taking in Ireland, France, the UAE, North Korea, China and

From left to right: Fidel and Raul Castro with Che Guevara in Havana, Cuba, 1961. (Photo by Osvaldo Salas)

several African countries including Congo, which brings us to the time of my meeting with him.

He had arrived in the country in April, an admirer of Patrice Lumumba, *'whose murder should be a lesson for all of us'* and determined to bring about the kind of society that Lumumba had fought for. It was not an easy proposition, even for the hero of the Cuban revolution. Stacked against him and the Simba guerrillas was Mobutu's Congolese Army supported by white mercenaries, Cuban opposition forces in exile and the covert operations of the CIA: from the Indian Ocean off Dar es Salaam, a US naval ship was monitoring his communications and relaying them via the American National Security Agency to his enemies on land.

Despite valiant efforts, after seven months Guevara and his comrades were on the back foot in Congo. Weakened by a bout of dysentery he urged his six surviving Cuban comrades to go home and leave him to die with his boots on. The comrades felt differently, however, as did Castro, and between them they persuaded Guevara to evacuate. A letter of farewell he had left with Castro to be opened in the event of his death had apparently been revealed in Cuba, signalling his intent to fight for world revolution till the end. In the event this is what happened. On 7 October 1965 while leading the National Liberation Army of Bolivia, Guevara was captured and two days later executed.

Che Guevara's legacy is immense, and the subject of endless discussion. As a military and political figure, his supporters and opponents alike have testified to his stature: '*There was no person more feared by the company (CIA) than Che Guevara because he had the capacity and charisma necessary to direct the struggle against the political repression of the traditional hierarchies in power in the countries of Latin America.*' These are the words of Philip Agee, a CIA operative between 1957 and 1968. Agee subsequently defected to Cuba. While there is disagreement over Guevara's methods and strict ideology, there can be little doubt about his commitment to bringing about a fair and just society. While some might disparage this as the quest for a Marxist utopia, it should be remembered that Guevara had seen the opposite of utopia – a world in which corrupt corporations and governments murdered, bribed and stole from the poor to maintain their power.

There is a postscript to this story. On one of my trips to Spain, my friend Boris Khananashvili introduced me to a famous Spanish surgeon,

Dr Nami. We struck up a friendship and began to meet regularly. Dr Nami and I enjoyed talking about history and current affairs, and our debates could be long and sometimes heated. In the course of one such discussion at which a number of other friends were gathered, Dr Nami said to me, *'During your work in the Komsomol youth movement in the Soviet Ministry of Foreign Affairs you visited many countries, saw and spoke with many well-known people. Tell me, who made the biggest impression on you? Who has remained in your memory as unique, unlike anybody else you have ever met?'*

The question rather threw me. I thought about the Cardinal of Krakow and future Pope Karol Wojtyla, about Brezhnev, various army commanders and World War Two heroes, Soviet Marshals K. Rokosovsky and S. Budenny, Vasilevsky and numerous others, all remarkable individuals. After mulling the question over for some time I replied, *'Ernesto Che Guevara.'* I could tell from my friends' reactions they were not surprised by my choice.

Several months later, when I had quite forgotten about our conversation I received a telephone call from Dr Nami. Could he pop over to my house and see me on a very important matter? Mystified, I replied that my family and I were always very happy to see him. He arrived within the hour with a large square box. My daughter Rena and my grandchildren Alessandro, Sofia and Massimo sat down on the rug as Dr Nami opened the box and took out a bust of Che Guevara.

The gift was completely unexpected and absolutely wonderful to behold. My grandchildren were all very interested in who this person was, and of course I explained to them, in a way they could each understand, that Che was someone who wanted to help and protect good people. The bust continues to stand in our house and whenever my grandchildren pass it they stroke Che's head. Massimo sometimes even kisses it. More recently my eldest grandchild, Alessandro, says he too wants to protect 'good people'.

MIKHAIL GORBACHEV

In the 18th century, sometimes called the Golden Age of the Russian Empire, Catherine the Great ordered the building of a line of ten fortresses stretching from Azov to Mozdok. One of the fortresses, situated several hundred miles south of Moscow was Stavropol, and in 1809 Catherine's successor Alexander I, in the interests of trade, encouraged a number of Armenians to come and live there. The Armenians stayed and established a community.

Two hundred years later, revolution followed by civil war came to Russia, and Stavropol was one of the places hotly fought over by the Bolshevik Red Army and the Capitalist White Army. Control of the city swung back and forth between the two sides, until in January 1920 the Red Army achieved a decisive victory.

Move forward to 2 March 1931, when in Privolnoye, a rural district in the north of Stavrapol Krai, Mikhail Gorbachev enters the world. Born to a peasant family, Mikhail is ten years old when almost half the people in his village, including two of his sisters and a paternal uncle, die in the Soviet famine. When the Great Patriotic War comes, the fascists attack and occupy the city of Stavrapol for six months; the Luftwaffe using the airport as a base to bomb Soviet oil supplies at Grozny. Mikhail's father leaves his work as a combine harvester driver to fight in the war. Mikhail takes up his father's job and works on collective farms. '*Impressing local officials as bright and disciplined, he was sent to study law at the prestigious Moscow State University.*' (Jim Gallager, *Chicago Tribune*, 1991

After further study in farming economics via a correspondence course from Stavropol Institute, Gorbachev begins his political journey in 1970 as First Party Secretary of Stavoropl's Regional Committee. By 1978 he has been summoned to Moscow again to take up the post of Central Committee

Secretary for Agriculture. The number two figure in the Politburo under Brezhnev at this time is Suslov, who has himself spent time in Stavropol earlier in his career. Having this link will be seen to have assisted Gorbachev's promotion and by 1980 he is a full member of the Politburo. The Stavropol connection extends to another powerful figure, Yuri Andropov, who was born in the region. Andropov will become known as a zealous opponent of corruption in the Soviet Union, and for him and Suslov, Gorbachev is seen as something of a protégé.

'Suslov and Andropov helped pave the way for Gorbachev after he was transferred to the capital at the age of 47 and began impressing colleagues

there. Gorbachev had the good luck to arrive in Moscow at a time when there were few men his age in either the Politburo or the party secretariat, which ran the country on a day-by-day basis. In the mid-1970s, Brezhnev, guarding his flank, began removing younger men from both organizations and replacing them with elderly allies. Against this background, Gorbachev`s meteoric rise within the Kremlin hierarchy was impressive.' (Ibid)

Following Brezhnev's death and Andropov's succession to the leadership in 1982, Gorbachev's importance likewise grows: *'As one of Andropov's chief deputies, Gorbachev helped plan far-reaching reforms in the country's economic and political systems, which had stultified and become alarmingly corrupt under Brezhnev.'* (Ibid)

In February 1984 Andropov dies and is replaced by Chernenko. Gorbachev retains a prominent position in the government and his well-publicised visit to Britain later that year raises his profile further on the international stage. Chernenko's death on the 11 March 1985 is Gorbachev's opportunity; within three hours he has been elected General Secretary of the Communist Party, becoming the first leader of the Soviet Union to have been born after the revolution. At fifty-four he is also the youngest since Stalin, and the only one never to have experienced service in the military. At the 27th Communist Party Conference the following February, the two words that will become almost synonymous with Gorbachev enter public discourse: *glasnost* meaning openness and *perestroika*: restructuring. Also flagged up are *demokratizatsiya*: democratization and *uskoreniye*: acceleration.

The acceleration refers to the economy, and for this Gorbachev stresses the need for increased technological advance in agriculture, commerce and industry. He appears to believe that modernisation should not involve a compromise of Soviet principles. Speaking to a meeting of East European Communist Party secretaries in 1985 he tells them, *'Many of you see the solution to your problems in resorting to market mechanisms in place of direct*

Mikhail Gorbachev taking questions from a crowd on the streets of Moscow.

planning. Some of you look at the market as a lifesaver for your economies. But, comrades, you should not think about lifesavers but about the ship, and the ship is socialism.' (*The Genesis of Gorbachev's World*, Bialer, Seweryn & Joan Afferica, *Foreign Affairs* no. 64)

How far his apparent commitment to socialism is compatible with allowing private ownership, under the new Law on Cooperatives of 1988, is debatable. It seems the idea is for some kind of mixed social and economic model inspired by the Prague Spring of 1968; when asked the difference between his policies and Dubcek's, 'socialism with a human face' Gorbachev replies: '*About nineteen years*'.

The socialism comes in the form of heavy taxes and rules governing employment in the new private sector, but these are not always observed in some of the Soviet republics. Later these restrictions are relaxed in the interests of continuing to encourage enterprise.

In 1989, Gorbachev holds the first open election in Russia since the revolution, and is voted Chairman of the Supreme Soviet. In an election the following year he becomes the country's first Executive President, and in emulation of the American system, chooses a Vice President: Gennady Yaneyev.

Yaneyev, whom I had worked with during my time as Secretary of the Youth Division of the All-Union Communist Party, had been running the All-Union Central Trades Unions Council and had a seat in the Politburo when Gorbachev selected him. I knew Yaneyev as a committed socialist, what outsiders called a 'hardliner', and one had to wonder how far he would support the changes underway in the Soviet Union. As for the international community's response to the supposedly brave new world of Gorbachev's, the West in general was approving. Margaret Thatcher expressed a liking for Gorbachev, a man with whom she could '*do business*'. Reagan and Gorbachev had already met in Geneva in 1985, the first face-to-face talks between Soviet and American leaders for eight years. Reagan's successor, George Bush, however, appeared less accommodating: '*Bush, it seems, unlike Reagan was not convinced that the Soviet Union was no longer an 'evil empire'*' (Bob Livingston, Personal Liberty Media Group). Slowly though, progress was made on the START programme for mutual arms reduction, and an agreement was reached in 1991.

Within the Soviet Union, however, the mood was now far from harmonious. With economic, ethnic and political tensions growing, Gennady, seeing the negative effects of *glasnost* and *perestroika*, became alarmed that the Soviet government was losing its grip and was in danger of sliding into chaos. He was not the only one to question the wisdom and competence of Gorbachev; KGB Chairman Vladimir Kryuchkov was now asking him to take heed of the signs, and take steps to avert disaster.

The final straw for Gorbachev's opponents was his worrying proposal to change the USSR into a federation. The so-called 'Gang of Eight' high-ranking officials who in August 1991 attempted to pull the Soviet Union back from the brink did not include Yeltsin, but Yaneyev, Defence Minister

Vice-President Bush and President Reagan, meet with Soviet General Secretary Gorbachev on Governor's Island, New York, 1988

Soviet leader Mikhail Gorbachev at No 10 Downing Street with Prime Minister Margaret Thatcher, 6 April 1989

Dmitry Yazov and KGB Chairman Vladimir Kryuchkov were among them. Their coup, which consisted of confining Gorbachev in his house in the Crimea while Yaneyev assumed leadership and demanded the imposition of a six-month state of emergency, lasted three days The trials of the conspirators took three years. One of them, Interior Minister Boris Pugo, had already killed his wife and shot himself dead to avoid arrest. Another supporter, Akhromeyev, who was not even under suspicion, hanged himself in the Kremlin. The remainder were eventually granted amnesty, though General Valentin Varennikov, who had been charged for assisting the Gang of Eight, said he would only accept this if Gorbachev were now prosecuted for plunging the Soviet Union into political disarray. The court, and a subsequent appeal rejected his plea.

Although Gorbachev was ostensibly restored to power, the coup attempt had damaged his reputation irreparably. In December he resigned the presidency and Boris Yelstin took the helm.

The fact that Gorbachev was the first leader born after the revolution did not, I think, have any particular bearing on his outlook. Yaneyev for example, born in 1937, became his sternest critic when it came to the destructive impact of *glasnost* and *perestroika*. Gorbachev was a very talented person obviously, capable of many things, one cannot deny that. For the first part of his life he did live as a Soviet person. So what changed him? There were a lot of conversations and discussions in the party about this; rumours that while he was abroad in the West on official duties he had been converted to capitalism. I think this is really all just speculation and gossip and there is no evidence for it. When people who hated Gorbachev could not find any direct explanation or any specific negative things to hang on him, they created myths, spreading vague rumours that somewhere down the line he had been 'turned' by the CIA. It was a way of smearing his character, saying that in effect he was a traitor to the Soviet Union.

My view of Gorbachev is that he was not a great manager and an average party official. His intellectual level and general outlook on the world was for the most part mediocre, and his use of the Russian language was unimpressive, certainly not beautiful; he had some kind of south Russian dialect and his speech was not flowing, there were no great oratorical skills there. These were little things of course. But the worst aspect of the man was that as a government leader he was also completely involved with himself, not to say in love with himself. Very self-centred, he thought himself the cleverest and the best. He would therefore undermine everyone and everything, and he also under-estimated everyone else.

On the other hand there were those that liked Gorbachev, but what is largely undisputed is that he came to power because of Andropov. The two men had roots in the same town of Stavropol, and Andropov picked him up and helped him up the party ladder. It was not nepotism exactly, but a kind of favouritism based on a shared past. This happens, the tendency to bring people from your place of birth, your hometown or your college, and those who know Russian, indeed world political history, will be familiar with the pattern. Basing one's political decisions on these incidental associations though is very bad because it clouds the judgement. However, in the case of Andropov and Gorbachev, a lot of people thought, and I agree with them on this, that it was not just a random choice on Andropov's part and that there was another and more particular reason for singling out Gorbachev. Otherwise why would a shrewd and committed Communist like Yuri Andropov promote such an apparent wild card as Gorbachev? Unless he was completely misled by Gorbachev and could not predict how he would turn out, I believe Andropov's support was unlikely to have stemmed from the Stavropol connection alone. Perhaps the details will emerge one day.

I met Gorbachev a number of times – and very tense encounters they were, especially during the war in the Caucasus between Azerbaijan and Armenia, simply because Gorbachev was supporting Armenia. I was Chairman of the Azerbaijan Committee for State Security (KGB) at the time, when Kryuchkov was head of the Soviet KGB. Kryuchkov had a very clear understanding of the kind of man Gorbachev was by this time, and knew exactly the kind of mayhem and disaster that was likely to occur as a result of his policies. After a year of Gorbachev coming to power small conflicts began to break out in the Russian republics. In some instances the small conflicts became all out wars. The Soviet Army was in a poor state having been deliberately undermined and degraded, and was lacking the morale and capability to deal effectively with these incidences of violent nationalism and ethnic strife.

The Politburo had been changed completely and the decisions being made by the new people in the government were very strange, going against the interests of Russia in a way. In terms of everyday life, in a country that had been used to producing and exporting millions of tons of grain and other food every year, people were now queuing outside shops; the bread, the meat, the sausages were gone, and this kind of situation had not occurred in Russia for many years. During the Great Patriotic War people could understand why there were severe shortages and they had ration cards and accepted that almost everyone was struggling against a common foe. Now, however, there was no credible or reasonable explanation for the lack of food other than corruption – the borders were open and people were selling goods abroad but nothing was coming back in; the money was going into the pockets of officials.

Gorbachev did invite representatives of the republics and the big cities to discuss all these issues. When the Azerbaijan–Armenia war was at its height I had a direct phone line to him, and though reluctant to do so I had no choice but to speak to him. During the Party Congress at Kremlin Palace, in the breaks between sessions, Gorbachev went inside the building, and from one of the dozens of telephone booths rang every three to four hours. The situation was extremely heated, as groups of militants from Armenia continued to force their way into Azerbaijani territory. They were bombing the railway tracks, systematically firing at the Azerbaijani villages, taking more hostages and stealing cattle. On one of the Congress days, a large group from Armenia had killed three Azerbaijanis and taken hostage two agricultural workers.

I was in Moscow and had gone to the Kremlin. When Gorbachev came out to the foyer I went over and introduced myself. He flashed a smile, '*I read your telegrams attentively and try to deal with them.*' I informed him about the latest hostage situation and said that thousands of people – men, women and children – were protesting on the railway tracks, demanding that the members of Congress be informed of the attack. I said it was proving almost impossible to control and that all attempts by local leaders to defuse the situation had failed. I asked Gorbachev as Chairman of the session to inform the delegates of Congress of these events as a matter of urgency. Rallies had taken place in Baku and other cities, condemning the attack and demanding that the members of the Azerbaijani delegation leave the Congress immediately. I told Gorbachev that his succinct address and condemnation of the attack should have the desired effect. The railway workers were also going on strike again. '*Your words will carry a lot of weight,*' I said. Gorbachev looked thoughtful and replied, '*We'll see.*'

The break over, Congress resumed. The chair gave the floor to Gorbachev, who gave a convincing account to the delegates of what I reported. A lot of shouting was then heard in the room, but the majority of the delegates supported Gorbachev.

Unfortunately this was a rare example of prompt and firm support from the Soviet leadership at the time. On most other occasions he would lend an apparently sympathetic ear and even agree to my requests and say yes, yes, great, action will be taken, but then nothing would happen. He would never say what he really thought and never give his real opinion. He was for the most part all talk. The Soviet Army, which was supposed to be neutral, was helping Armenia against Azerbaijan and the whole situation was very one-sided because of Gorbachev's bias. This again was due to a form of nepotism and the Stavrapol connection, where there was a massive

Armenian diaspora; it was a case of looking after old friends. Kryuchkov tried to discuss the conflict with Gorbachev from a neutral perspective, encouraging him to see Azerbaijan's position also, and confront him with what was actually happening in the region and other parts of the Soviet Union, but it was impossible. In fact it was already too late. Gorbachev had waved the flag and the train had left the station. Now it was steaming down the track towards anarchy and the country was being destroyed.

In the Great Patriotic War, how did the Soviet Union manage to win against fascism? If there is any single answer it surely has to be unity – of the nation, of the government, and a united faith in the leader. Now there was no such faith. Rather our leader was a figure of fun, new jokes or anecdotes about him circulating around the country daily. Some of the jokes were rather nasty, like the one about the man who has been queuing three hours for bread: '*I blame Gorbachev for this and I'm going to kill him!*' he exclaims angrily and storms off. A while later he returns. '*Did you kill Gorbachev?*' ask the other people waiting for bread. '*No,*' sighs the man, '*the queue was far longer.*'

Every time we turned on the TV Gorbachev seemed to be talking about what a great life everyone was going to have in Russia now, which of course was wonderful to hear, but again these were empty words; the function and duty of any government is not only to talk positively but also to take positive action. When people go to the shops and the shelves are empty – no meat, no sugar, no butter – and they cannot even obtain the basics they need to live on, no amount of fine words will compensate for the realities that are facing them. In such circumstances a leader could only remain credible for so long, and sure enough Gorbachev was destined to lose all his authority, and when that moment came it was like a line in the sand.

There were so many wars, especially in mid-Asia, that the whole place seemed to be on fire, nation against nation, and both the KGB and the military realised they should have done something sooner to halt the slide. In the August putsch, when they tried to get rid of Gorbachev, one has to say the British and American secret services did a very good job in helping him regain power, but that was it for the Soviet Union. The worst part was that the wars continued and Georgia was terribly traumatic, a dreadful human tragedy. It was exactly what had happened in Yugoslavia; when the central authority, the hand that has held everyone together and distributed power equally among regional and ethnic groups becomes drastically weakened, the traitors and nationalists rise to the surface. Where there are no longer laws, there are no longer rules of any kind, might becomes right and anarchy and bloodshed are the result.

This is the tragedy of Gorbachev. Maybe his intentions were good but things should have been done differently. Sadly he did not have the intellect; funnily enough for a so-called populist he did not know Russia very well at all, or the real mentality of the people. He should have analysed the situation better, thought things through more carefully. For the leader of such a massive country he did not have sufficient intelligence or knowledge. Stalin, who wrote fifty-three books on how to rule the country and what was needed, did not have a great education, but he had a profound natural ability and understanding. The sheer size and diversity of Russia has always made it a very difficult place to govern, and over the centuries only strong personalities and big leaders have succeeded. Peter the Great, Nicholas I, Alexander III who did so, were also all great reformers. Peter lived and studied in Europe for long periods, gathering new ideas; during his time as Tsar he worked in the docks helping to build ships, gaining a genuine understanding of what life was like for ordinary people.

Gorbachev had no comparable experience, not even by way of military service. His populism was all fake. The Soviet Union had to change undoubtedly and needed someone to lead that change, but Gorbachev, though talented and with perhaps a few good ideas, was a mediocre leader. He destroyed the Soviet Union's culture and arts, its military and other institutions, including the youth organisations and so many people hated him for that.

ERICH HONECKER

Now let us go back in time. I am in East Berlin. The year is 1973 and it is the turn of the German Democratic Republic to host the International Festival of Youth and Students. My East German colleague here is Egon Krenz. Egon is about four years my senior and is a member of the People's Chamber. Following his military service, like myself he became involved with youth work in his country, first with the Ernst Thallman Pioneer Organisation, and since 1971 as the leader of 'Free German Youth'. Together we are going over the programme for the upcoming festival, in which young people from around the world will gather in East Berlin to enjoy shows, talks, music, discussions and the arts. The slogan chosen for the festival is 'For Anti-Imperialist Solidarity, Peace and Friendship'.

Many of the events will take place in and around Alexanderplatz, which a few years ago was modernised and made a pedestrian area, allowing people to walk and mingle, and go shopping even. There are already lots of people who want to visit East Germany, for while the general standard of living in the West is higher, goods in general are much cheaper here, about thirty per cent less in most cases. The stories about West Germans crossing the border to take advantage of this disparity are true. I have seen for myself the cars coming over and people loading their boots up with food and beer.

In the office of the Central Committee on International Issues, Egon and I are chatting with the Committee Secretary about organisation and logistical details. I am the Secretary of International Affairs of the All-Union Komsomol Central Committee of the USSR Communist Party, and my role here is to make sure that everything from A to Z is organised and running smoothly. This is just a general conversation to keep him informed about the current state of affairs regarding the festival, ticking off what has been done in terms of things like travel arrangements, accommodation,

scheduling and announcements, and making sure there are no outstanding tasks.

Egon and I also inform the Secretary of a few problems that had arisen with the organisers of some of the youth groups coming from Yugoslavia and Romania, but that these have been dealt with now. In the midst of our discussions the telephone rings. The Secretary answers it, speaking in German, so I understand little of what is being said. When he replaces the receiver he turns to us and says, '*Honecker is going to pop in to see you shortly.*' The leader of the German Democratic Republic, the top man in the country, is coming to talk to a couple of youth administrators? I am very surprised. In the Soviet Union, if a party leader or senior official wants to see someone they summon the person to their office. The East German leader clearly does not stand on such ceremony, nor expect it of others, regardless of rank.

When Honecker arrives he greets us all warmly. He is very friendly and seems genuinely interested in the work that Egon and I are doing. He also asks my opinion on a number of issues, and wants to know if I am happy with the way things are being handled. It turns out he is acquainted with a number of other youth leaders in the Soviet Union and asks me who else will be attending the festival. He spends a lot of time discussing all the details with us, and when he asks if we are aware of any problems, the three of us assure him of the issues that have been resolved, that the working groups of our organisations are currently in Havana, and that everything is ready for the grand opening. Honecker then shares with us a few of his memories of past youth festivals and forums; as the founder and Secretary of Free German Youth from 1946 to 1955, his experience is unique and such projects are clearly close to his heart. After half an hour he wishes us good luck and says farewell.

My strongest impression from this meeting was that Honecker was a very democratic man. Here was a person whose political career began in an era of turbulence and dramatic polarisation. Born in 1912, on the other side of Germany, close to the French border in the coal rich area now called Saarland, his father a miner and political activist, Erich Honecker joined the Young Communist League of Germany at the age of fourteen. On leaving school he worked for a while on the land and then as a roofer before being selected to study at the International Lenin School in Moscow, and in 1930 became a fully-fledged member of the Communist Party of Germany. When the Nazis came to power in 1933, the young man was arrested briefly in Essen, took flight to the Netherlands and the following year came back

Erich Honecker, founder and secretary of the Free German Youth meets with some the members, with a poster of Stalin in the background, 1951.

to help those trying to stop Saarland being swallowed into the German state. When the attempt failed, Erich, along with several thousand fellow inhabitants, fled his homeland. Erich now devoted himself to the resistance cause, countering the Nazi regime with illegal pamphleteering for the Communist Party. Using the alias of 'Martin Tjaden', in August 1935 he smuggled a small printing press into Berlin. In December his luck ran out: arrested by the Gestapo he spent eighteen months in detention before being charged with a treasonable offence and given a ten-year prison sentence.

After Berlin was liberated by Soviet troops, Honecker met the prominent Communist Walter Ulbricht, the man who would become his mentor. When the Socialist Unity Party (SED) was formed, Erich Honecker would rise quickly to a position on the Central Committee. Meanwhile, at the Yalta Conference of 1945, Churchill, Stalin and Roosevelt had sat down together to discuss the future of Europe. These were all very clever men, astute politicians, well read, erudite and bringing a wealth of experience – failures as well as successes – to the table. The iconic photograph from Yalta – Churchill with his trademark cigar, Roosevelt looking cerebral yet tough, Stalin, veteran of the Russian Revolution and civil war, the man of steel – conveyed above all a sense of optimism. Stalin of course was a tyrant, no one can now dispute that, but in that moment, on the peaceful shores of the Black Sea, it seemed that a wonderful opportunity to leave the past behind and to make the world a better place than before had been given.

The unity that America, Britain and Russia had forged in overcoming fascism was remarkable, a precious achievement won with immense sacrifices by the people of all three nations. Full and proper acknowledgement could at that time have been given to Russia for the hundreds of thousands of lives lost in the struggle to defeat the Nazis. The blood that had been spilt on all sides should surely have been put to the common good, building on that wartime alliance to work as heroically together in a new era of peace for the benefit of all mankind.

Instead, what happened? Europe was effectively carved up, and the Soviet Union and Eastern European countries became one power bloc, the United States, Western Europe and Britain another, setting the stage not for a world of openness, freedom and humanitarian fraternity, but for one of rivalry, anxiety and fear – the ideological standoff that became known as the Cold War. Why did this come about? After four years of being on the same side, why did these three great nations split two ways? It is not entirely clear, and there is no one simple answer.

From my own historical analysis based on a range of authors and perspectives – English, French, American and Russian – I have tried to form a balanced and impartial view. Broad reading is essential, for as we know not all authors are objective. One thing that emerges is that Churchill

Erich Honecker speaking at the award ceremony for the best pioneer leaders in the House of Youth, 8 March 1952

had a great influence on Roosevelt, and of course the two men and their countries shared a common language and Anglo-Saxon roots. Churchill was anti-Stalin, though perhaps not so much anti-Russian as baffled by the country that he described as *'an enigma wrapped in an enigma,'* a cultural and historical Matryoshka doll. Whatever the misunderstandings and concerns, it is my belief that if the Yalta conference leaders had thought more carefully and striven to continue cooperation, together they would have educated the whole world, and the quality of life for everyone could have been much improved. Sadly, mutual suspicion, egoism, territorial ambition and vested interests gained the upper hand.

By 1949, any idea of an imminent re-unification of the German nation had receded. In the western zone the founding of the Federal Republic, known as West Germany, was followed swiftly by the Socialist Unity Party (SED) leading a coalition in the formation of the German Democratic Republic in the east. While West Germany aligned with NATO, the GDR created a new constitution, modelling the country's political system on that of the Soviet Union. As leader of the Free German Youth movement, Honecker organised the first 'Deutschlandtreffen der Jugend' in East Berlin in May 1950, and the following year the '3rd World Festival of Youth and Students'. The latter event was not without its difficulties, which Honecker had alluded to during our meeting. Coming in the midst of the Korean War and with Mao's Communist Party consolidating its rule in China, the international mood was tense and NATO countries were fearful about the spread of leftist ideology. The 1951 festival's motto, 'For Peace and Friendship – Against Nuclear Weapons' did little to allay such anxieties, and a number of students trying to cross into East Berlin to attend were shot at by West German police and American soldiers.

In 1955 Honecker passed the Free German Youth baton on, and at the request of Walter Ulbricht, spent two years studying at the School of the Soviet Communist Party in Moscow. Here he would have heard Khrushchev's public repudiation of Stalin, who had died in 1953. Nevertheless, in July 1956, when Ulbricht became East German leader, the country, now ostensibly autonomous of the Soviet Union, embarked on a second, Stalin-like five-year plan of industrialisation under the slogan of 'modernisation, mechanisation, and automation'. One obstacle to progress cited by the authorities was the number of people migrating from East Germany to the West, and the loss of skilled workers in particular was said to be causing a 'brain drain'. Stemming this outflow of the population, condemned as disloyalty to the country, was seen as a priority and resulted in what many people now most associate with Honecker, his staunch defence, physical and ideological, of the Berlin Wall. When the structure failed to stop the more determined migrants, it was Honecker as Party Security Secretary who would be held responsible for issuing the infamous standing order to fire on those trying to escape.

By the end of the 1960s Honecker had risen to number two in the East German government under Walter Ulbricht, but when differences of opinion between the two men emerged Honecker's former mentor had him removed. Brezhnev however stepped in, Honecker was retained, and in 1971, again with Soviet backing, became General Secretary (then known as First Secretary) of the Central Committee, the leader of East

Erich Honecker (left) head of the State Council of the German Democratic Republic and Leonid Brezhnev (second left)

Germany. Whilst Ulbricht had flirted with the idea of détente with the West, the ideological differences remained entrenched; if there were ever to be a unified Germany, it would be a Communist Germany seemed to be the message. Similarly, Honecker was not opposed to détente but rejected the notion of unification in favour of 'Abrengzung' (separation) combined with allegiance to the Soviet Union. Cognisant that East Germans much preferred to think of themselves as simply German, Honecker promoted a new, dual definition: 'citizenship GDR, nationality German'.

Erich Honecker may have been an old-school Communist, a person of ideas and inflexible in his beliefs perhaps, yet he was arguably not without imagination or enthusiasm, such as for youth work that belied his famously dull and wooden style of presentation. After meeting him, throughout the remainder of the 1970s and into the 1980s, I followed his career with great interest. At the end of the 1980s the economic and political situation within the Soviet Union under Mikhail Gorbachev began to deteriorate sharply. Right from the beginning, as soon as Gorbachev came to power and started promulgating the idea of Perestroika, things began to take a turn for the worse. Erich Honecker did not hide his views and was critical of Gorbachev, which would only reinforce his reputation as a 'hardliner'. Regarding the hated Berlin Wall, as late as January 1989, Honecker told a Western journalist: *'The Wall will still be standing in fifty and even in a hundred years – if the reasons for it have not been removed by then.'*

At the German Democratic Republic's 40th Anniversary celebrations in October that year, as the military parade passed by it must have been galling for him to hear members of the public chanting in front of Mikhail Gorbachev and the Warsaw Pact leaders, 'Gorby save us!' Demonstrations that same evening occurred in East Berlin and across the country, but when Honecker dispatched troops to a particularly large gathering in Leipzig, local party officials had them withdrawn. Two weeks later, hoping to fend off the growing calls for change, the Politburo forced Honecker's removal.

By this time I had met Honecker's daughter Sonja, and was on very good terms with her and the rest of the family. A very pleasant woman, Sonja had married a Chilean communist, and it was in the Chilean Embassy in Moscow in 1991 that Honecker, by then almost eighty years old and unwell, sought refuge; an arrest warrant had been issued against him for alleged human rights abuses concerning the East Germans who had been shot while attempting to cross the Berlin Wall. Declining an offer of assistance from North Korea, Honecker, accompanied by his wife Margot, hoped to be granted asylum in the Soviet Union, and at the same time applied to enter Chile as a number of Chilean refugees from Pinochet had been welcomed to East Germany during his leadership. The Chilean authorities, however, stated they could not admit him without a valid German passport, and while Margot was allowed to enter the country, in July 1992 Honecker was flown back to Berlin, apparently by force, to stand trial. In his statement to the court, Honecker admitted responsibility for maintaining the Berlin Wall and for the shootings, but said that on a human level he regretted every single death. He said he believed that the wall had prevented escalation of the Cold War into an armed confrontation between East and West that would have incurred far larger numbers of casualties, and cited West German leaders that had shared this view. After a period of legal debate and political argument, taking into account his poor state of health, Honecker, having been held for a total of 169 days, was freed and joined his family in Chile, residing there until his death on 29 May 1994.

In my view people understood Honecker very well, but when East Germany imploded they wanted a scapegoat. The GDR had continued to exist largely because the Russians had helped them, but when Gorbachev effectively came up with a plan to destroy the Soviet Union, that support disappeared. Honecker opposed Gorbachev's plans, which he regarded as a complete betrayal of socialist ideals and in my opinion he was right. Being a highly educated and very well read man, and more importantly having been imprisoned by the fascists in his youth, he knew the fragmentation, violent nationalism and chaos towards which Gorbachev's unrestrained approach would lead. Resolutely he told Gorbachev, '*We have done our Perestroika, we have nothing to restructure*'.

In terms of human rights abuses, apart from the shootings on the Berlin Wall, one of the great criticisms of East Germany is the role played by the secret police, the Stasi. It is hard to say exactly how much Honecker was involved in the day-to-day operations of the Stasi, but it is safe to say he would have been aware of the general set-up and how it was run. If the system were anything like that in the Soviet Union, and almost every other country in the world for that matter, the person at the top would know what the internal security services were doing; certainly the moment that something went wrong, that person would be fully in the picture as regards developments and who was involved.

Yet for Honecker, I think he would have believed in the necessity of the Stasi, that everything he did in fact was in pursuit of a socialist ideal. In the popular imagination there is a tendency to lump him together with Ceauşescu, yet the Ceauşescus were not hardliners, they had no line other than their own aggrandisement and the total neglect of ordinary people. It is also perhaps to Honecker's credit that in his hour of need he refused the offer of help from North Korea, a country that appeared to prioritise huge military spending to the detriment of humanitarian needs. If Honecker had been like Gorbachev, he would by the end of his career have owned a private plane, written his memoirs and auctioned them for several million dollars. But this was a man with very strong ideological beliefs, a man that never sold out, and never forgot his early experiences of fighting against the Nazis, a true revolutionary to the end. It was somewhat ironic that having risked his life and been imprisoned for trying to stop the fascists taking over his country, that his fellow countrymen, most of whom had never engaged in that struggle, should seek to condemn him. Did Germany really have such a short collective memory, and did those who hounded Honecker really know nothing of history? Their memories, collective or otherwise were good I think. I am more tempted to say they were just b*******.

My erstwhile youth worker colleague Egon Krenz, who succeeded as leader briefly until the fall of the Berlin Wall forced his own resignation, spoke highly of the moral qualities of Erich Honecker, and talked at length about his underground activities during the reign of Hitler, along with much more. In later years many consider his greatest achievements to include bringing the German Democratic Republic into full membership of the United Nations and harmonising the country's relations with the outside world.

We now have a phenomenon known as 'Ostalgie', a nostalgic view of a putatively simpler and happier way of life in the old East Germany. Precisely what Honecker would have said of this trend we can only speculate on, but it is reasonable to assume he would have approved the general sentiment. In 1993, in what is believed to have been his last public speech, he observed that, '*Socialism is the opposite of what we have now in Germany. For that I would like to say that our beautiful memories of the German Democratic Republic are testimony of a new and just society. And we want to always remain loyal to these things*'. Evidence enough it seems that Erich Honecker belongs resolutely to the early 20th century cohort of genuine revolutionaries and anti-fascists, people who from a very young age dedicated themselves to the struggle for a better life for the working classes and intelligentsia, and that until the day he died he remained faithful to that idea.

RUSTAM IBRAGIMBEKOV

Having graduated from Azerbaijan State University (Department of Journalism) in 1970, I had since been working as a correspondent for Azerbaijan TV and radio. A journalist in print as well as broadcast, my interests included arts and culture, the latest exhibitions, plays, novels and films. A Soviet movie had just been released about young people in the post Stalin era – the effects of Khrushchev's thaw, what life was like at that time, the social milieu. I was keen to write a review, particularly as the screenplay was the work of a Baku born filmmaker.

Rustam Ibragimbekov was already making his mark in the world of cinema. *White Sun of the Desert*, for which he had co-written the script with Valentin Yezhov, told the story of a Red Army soldier's adventures on the shores of the Caspian Sea during the long running Civil War. Comradeship, shootouts with bandits, valour, yearning for home, music and comedy spill gloriously out along the way, together with the hero's attempts to rescue a harem. This rich concoction, combining elements of the American Western with the Russian folktale tradition, was destined to become a classic.

Ibragimbekov being extremely busy, I arranged to go over and meet him on the promenade in Baku, about an hour-long journey. I would then need to hurry back to the studio to broadcast the last minute news items of the day, which always tended to be the hottest – 'hold the front page' as they say in the newspaper industry. With such a tight schedule everything had to be done briskly and efficiently that day, but at the same time I was concerned that my interview with this exciting filmmaker should go well and that we would get on. Any worries were soon dispelled. When people meet for the first time, it is often the case that they either click or they don't, and there is no in-between. Sometimes you get instant recognition, rather like planes on a radar screen, you can identify whether an aircraft entering your vicinity is

on your side or not – friend, neutral, or perhaps foe. It was exactly like this that day, and my radar told me immediately that here was a friend.

It was a friend I would come to value and admire, and whose career I would follow with great interest over the coming decades. Rustam had initially taken a degree at Azerbaijan's Oil and Chemistry Institute, but his father being a professor of art history, perhaps it was not entirely unexpected that he would find his true vocation in connection with pictures. Rustam's forte though would be in creating the words that accompanied pictures. This he attributes to another early influence at home, while acknowledging that his switch of career was not planned:

> *'It was purely accidental. By training, I'm an engineer. I had been involved with science for quite some time before I started writing. But in our family there is an incredible regard and respect for the written word. My older brother Magsud is known as a prose writer. I wrote my first story when I was 23 in 1962. My own work in professional writing began in 1966 when my first novel was published.*
>
> (*Azerbaijan International*, Summer 1995, Interview by Betty Blair)

The change of direction involved a move to Moscow to study at the world's oldest film school, the All Union State Institute of Cinematography, whose former teachers included the legendary Sergei Eisenstein, director of the 1925 Soviet epic *Battleship Potemkin*. Following his early success with *White Sun of the Desert*, Rustam wrote the screenplay for *Interrogation*, a crime thriller set in Riga involving embezzlement, murder and corruption in high places. *Urga*, a collaborative production with Nikita Mikhalkov, portrayed the marital problems of a couple in rural Mongolia, and their chance friendship with a drunken Russian truck driver. Released in America as *Close to Eden*, the film won the Golden Lion at the Venice Film Festival.

Rustam paired up with Mikhlkov again to write the 1994 release *Burnt by the Sun*. This picture would garner considerable praise from audiences and critics, along with that year's Cannes Festival Grand Prix and the American Academy Award – an Oscar – for Best Foreign Language Film. Set in the Soviet Union of the 1930s, the fictional central protagonist is Kotov, a senior Red Army commander who has retired to the beauty of the Russian countryside. When military manoeuvres threaten to destroy the local farmers' crops, he decides to intervene. An American reviewer described his fate in a nutshell: *'When army tanks begin to roll over his neighbours' wheat*

Filmmaker Rustam Ibragimbekov (left) talking with the Kyrgyz film director Bolot Shamshiyev

fields, Kotov uses his influence and status as a hero to turn the tanks back. But because it is 1936, the beginning of Stalin's great terror, Kotov has unwittingly made the kind of gesture for which he will pay. In… Burnt by the Sun *no one escapes Stalinism.* (Caryn James *New York Times*, 29 April 1995) James thought the film had rigour as well as charm: '*…exquisite, lyrical and tough-minded.*' (Ibid)

The drama of human beings struggling to connect meaningfully in the midst of forces beyond their control, also made a positive impression on critics: '*What* Burnt by the Sun *does best is elegantly intertwine the personal and political themes of love, trust and betrayal.'* (Kenneth Turan, *Los Angeles Times*, 21 April 1995)

Speaking after the Oscar ceremony, Rustam said that the win came as a complete surprise to him and to director Nikita Mikhalov. Neither of them had even thought to bring a camera to the event. Nikita and his eight-year-old daughter, Nadia, had also acted in the film, playing Kotov and his daughter. When the award was being presented, Nadia was asked what it meant to her, and she replied she hoped that at last she would be bought a bike. When in a later interview Rustam was asked a similar question, he laced his reply with characteristic humour:

> *'I don't know exactly what my "bike" will be, but this honour is extremely important. We've always grown up with the idea that the Oscar is something extraordinarily unique – something very honourable. As a professional cinematographer, I feel a deep respect for this prize. Somehow, it seems that among Europeans there's always a feeling that the Oscar is much more difficult to win than, say, the Cannes Festival. Perhaps, it's because Hollywood is geographically further away that this perception exists.'*
>
> (*Azerbaijan International*, Summer 1995, Interview by Betty Blair)

The comment on Hollywood suggests that whilst grateful for its recognition, Rustam also maintains a sense of proportion about the perception of status within the film industry. A similar candour comes over when he is evaluating his own abilities: *'I'm fully aware that there are others who can write much better than I do. To write – you need a lot of self-confidence because you quickly become very conscious that there are a lot of extremely talented people out there. My strength comes from realizing that I know things that nobody else does and that I can tell some things that others can't – despite how talented they may be.'* (Ibid)

Certainly, having known him for so many years I would say Rustam is

Scriptwriter Rustam Ibragimbekov (centre), with a group of actors of the Azerbaijani Akhundov State Academic Opera

most of all passionate about his craft, and concerned more than anything to create stories on screen or stage that will stimulate and entertain people. In the course of his career he has written more than forty scripts for film and television, together with numerous plays and works of prose. When starting out in his career, he was not actively involved in public affairs. In fact he has told me he hates politics. When a growing group of young intellectuals calling themselves the Popular Front, seeking democratic reform in Azerbaijan, approached him to be their leader, to lend his voice to their cause, they felt rightly that Rustam's achievements as a filmmaker and writer, his deserved reputation for decency and integrity would be invaluable. The fact that he was not a politician but a cultural figure outside of the ruling establishment, could lend even greater weight – his opinions could carry an independent moral authority.

Rustam remained a staunch advocate of fair play and anti-corruption in Azerbaijan. He would also continue to worry about the future of his country:

> *'I'm very much concerned about what is happening in Azerbaijan. The ultimate question is whether Azerbaijan can continue to exist as an independent state. There are tremendous influences at work, pulling from opposite ideologies and geo-political tensions. I'm absolutely convinced that there are outside forces that wish Azerbaijan's annihilation as an independent state. Fortunately, the standards of the international community are placing restraints on these tendencies; otherwise, we would have already been wiped out.'*

Rustam's distress at the way governments and those in power sometimes operate should not be confused with love of his country and its men and women, whatever their religion, race or hue. That love comes across in his 2014 novel *Solar Plexus*, described by the publishers of the UK edition as *'a compelling saga of family and friendship, love and betrayal, set against the backdrop of Azerbaijan's rapidly-changing capital, Baku, as the country struggles with the transition into a post-Soviet world...'* (*Glagoslav Publications*)

Beginning in the 1940s, the novel charts the lives of a group of friends from Baku that grow up together and have to navigate their way through the Great Patriotic War, followed by Stalin's purges and eventually the break up of the Soviet Union and its aftermath. Told from the characters' separate perspectives, *'Ibragimbekov evokes a world of passion and honour, of proud men and hot-headed women, of great tenderness and complex humanity, where "the truth is always just one of many truths." The novel is equally a paean to the multiculturalism of Baku, and a time when a person's worth was measured by their qualities, not whether they had been born an Azeri, Russian, Jew or Armenian.'* (Ibid)

Rustam Ibragimbeekov's contribution to cinema is a track record to be proud of. Outstanding among what might be called his more serious films

Rustam Ibragimbekov taking a break by the sea in 1982

is of course the Oscar winning *Burnt by the Sun,* with its evocation of the stunning Russian countryside, a land in which the hero Kotov's hero is Stalin. When Kotov defies the state he assumes his personal connection to the leader will guarantee his safety. The tragic irony of Kotov's faith in Stalin to look after him, brought home in the film's dramatic ending, is that it was a belief shared by countless Russians at the time.

However, whilst B*urnt by the Sun* illuminates past injustices, Rustam felt that people should not jump to conclusions about any simple ideological message regarding the Soviet era: '*These days, there is a rush to destroy everything that relates to the past. But we must be careful not to discard and purge everything... We shouldn't eliminate everything from our past or as you say, "Throw the baby out with the bath water!" We can't dump everything before acquiring new values to fill the void...In my opinion, we have to deal objectively with the previous system. Though it may have been monstrous, it contributed many positive dimensions to our lives. We don't say it directly in the film but it's there.*'

When *Burnt by the Sun* was adapted for the stage by Peter Flannery and performed at the National Theatre in London, it received critical acclaim: *'This one's a cracker... As an extended family of characters spanning four generations take breakfast and bicker on the veranda, we might be in the world of the Cherry Orchard ... But then comes news that Russian tanks are destroying the villagers' wheat field and we realise life has changed,'* (Charles Spencer, *Daily Telegraph*, 2009). The stage version also seemed to capture something of Rustam's nostalgia for pre-glasnost Russia, despite its darker elements: *'The show, complete with marching band, sinister secret policeman and young, uniformed Pioneers celebrating the splendours of Uncle Joe, creates a superb sense of place and time.'* (Ibid)

From Rustam Ibragimbekov's earliest cinematic work, a picture closer to the purely entertainment end of the artistic spectrum has survived the test of time and is finding a new generation of fans. *White Sun of the Desert*, the rip roaring, comic tale of heroism and adventure in the Civil War, has also provided some immortal lines; while Hollywood has given us *'Play it again Sam'*, *'I'll be back'* and *'Make my day'*, consider these philosophical gems from the script of Rustam Ibragimbekov and Valentin Yezhov, all of which have become everyday catchphrases in Russia and the former republics: *Mahmud, light the fire*, said when setting off spiritedly on a perilous undertaking; *Gyulchatai, show your sweet face*, a romantic invitation from a boy to a girl, and often used in the context of international relations: *The Orient is a delicate matter.*

From the date of its release in 1970, *White Sun of the Desert* was seen by over thirty million Russian citizens and was the most popular showing of that year, yet throughout the whole of the Soviet era no official accolades were ever awarded. In 1998, however, its creators collectively received the Russian Federation State Prize in Literature and Arts from Boris Yeltsin. The film is so mainstream to national culture that it is required viewing for all cosmonauts before launching into space. There has more recently been a computer game based on the plot and characters, and in Donetsk and Samara statues of the hero Sukhov have been erected. A restaurant in Moscow now bears the name *White Sun of the Desert*, and among the new wave of fans around the world, the film receives ecstatic reviews from bloggers, who regard it as highly deserving of its cult status and a 'true Russian classic.'

To be an integral part of giving such enjoyment to millions of people is amazing, and this from someone who by his own account was withdrawn as a child. What appeared to have brought him out of his shell were the performing arts:

> *'There's no doubt that childhood is the source of what I am doing today. If a person is not tied to his childhood, then he can never become a writer, producer or anything else…when I was thirteen I became involved with a drama circle, and we organized a play called "Hard Task". I had a role in that play, but it was so hard for me as I was extremely shy. Perhaps performing in that play somehow influenced my career.'*
>
> (December 1999, Mazahir Panahov and Aynur Hajiyeva *Azerbaijan International*)

Rustam Ibragimbekov has not only done great things in the world of cinema and literature, both during and since the era of the Soviet Union, but he has taken a stand against injustice and put himself on the line for others. He has also enriched the world simply by being who he is – throwing himself into every project, every party, every chance meeting and every friendship – of which he has many – with undiluted enthusiasm, humour and vivacity. He is a very funny guy and a terrific person to dine out with. Being a dedicated *bon viveur* has brought a tendency to put on weight, and every so often he will check himself into a health spa. But for Rustam this experience is simply a necessary means to an end, as his favourite saying puts it, *'The only reason I like to lose weight is so I can go out and enjoy putting it all back on again!'*

Whether at work or play, Rustam is like a human tank, driving forward all the time. Always eating, drinking and partying, one might wonder when he found the time to create his amazing screenplays, novels, stories, apart from all the input he gives to numerous arts organisations and unions. The answer he once told me was that he would sleep for only three hours a night. He has always been a people person, who loves to have his friends around, and our families have become very close. In fifty years of friendship, during so many dramatic changes in Azerbaijan and Russia, through thick and thin our friendship has never wavered. Rustam now splits his time between Moscow and his house in Venice Beach, Los Angeles, but thanks to the marvels of modern communications we speak to each other once or twice a week. Even though our lives do not coincide and we live thousands of miles apart, we also make an effort to meet up whenever we can. For my seventieth birthday I had a family celebration in Marbella. Rustam came all the way from Los Angeles to be there. He has not changed a bit – as happy, funny and witty as ever, and a true friend.

These following words of his, might be a good summary of his philosophy:

'A man can try to do his best, and yet circumstances may turn everything upside down. For whatever we manage to achieve, only a small portion depends on us; the rest is circumstance and fate. God gives us paths to walk upon, but we have to choose our own route. Many things depend on us, but a lot of other things are determined by God, fate, circumstances or something or somebody else. That's why you should never generalize or get disappointed. Despair is the most fatal tragedy of life. Whatever happens, life is life.' (Ibid)

Rustam Ibragimbekov poses for a picture with Vagif Guseynov and his extended family by the poolside in Marbella.

VALENTIN KATAEV

In the days of the Soviet Union you could call up the most popular and acclaimed artists and writers in the country and say, '*In a few weeks' time in our town we are getting together a group of talented thirteen- to fourteen-year -old children who are keen on books and the arts – would you care to come and speak with them?*' The answer would almost invariably be, '*Sure, I'll be there, delighted, just give me the time and place and tell me what I have to do.*' And sure enough, they would be as good as their word and come, and feel it a great pleasure and honour to do so.

Such people were genuinely thrilled to be asked and to be able to contribute in such a way to the culture of their country. There was still that sense of duty and vocation among artists, especially when it came to young people. Indeed, among most citizens of Russia in those days, there was the feeling that children really were our future, that inspiring them with a love of literature and art, teaching them to appreciate novels, poetry and stories, and to excel in their own artistic endeavours, was the ultimate good. We had artists who were generous in sharing their time and their talents with children.

Valentin Kataev was one such person. Born in Odessa in 1897, Kataev started writing stories as a schoolboy. His education was cut short by the war, when he volunteered to serve in the Russian artillery in 1915. When the revolution came he fought on the side of the Red Army. A career in journalism followed, firstly in Odessa, and by the early 1920s he was living and working in Moscow, writing for the magazine *Whistle*. Kataev's style was already leaning towards comedy and satire, and his stories were often to depict ordinary, powerless people carried along by big events and a changing world, sometimes prone to temptation, or simply trying to make sense of the circumstances in which they found themselves.

Kataev would also become the curator for other writers' work, discovering and nurturing new talent through his editorship-in-chief from 1955 to 1961 of the Russian literary magazine *Youth*. Being by this time a celebrated author himself, Kataev attracted a large readership to the magazine, as well as the most promising, yet so far unheard of younger writers, several of whom went on to achieve high renown themselves, including Bella Akhmadulina – acclaimed as *'one of the Soviet Union's literary treasures and a classic poet in the long line extending from Lermontov and Pushkin* (*New York Times*, 13 May 2011) and Yevgeny Yevtushenko, *'one of the greatest poets of the modern age…"Bratsk Station" offers the greatest insight into Soviet life of any work in modern Russian literature.'* (Tina Tupikina Glaessner, 1967) We should also mention author and screenwriter Boris Vasilyev, winner of the 1975 USSR State Prize, and whose 1969 novel *The Dawns Here Are Quiet*, a story of Russian women's heroism in the Great Patriotic War, sold almost two million copies.

All these authors contributed to *Youth* magazine, through which Kataev opened the door to a new wave of Russian writing. It has to be said that the political climate of the time was also very conducive to this flowering of literary and artistic endeavour. After Stalin, under Khrushchev's thaw from the mid-1950s the relaxation of censorship and the encouragement of a much greater degree of free expression, enabled writers in particular to be bolder in their work. Khrushchev made many mistakes throughout his leadership of the Soviet Union, but this opening up of cultural discourse and creativity should be recognised as one of the good things he did.

The visual media also benefited from such liberalisation, although Khrushchev was notably unappreciative of what some of the new kind of artists had to offer. The episode which best illustrates the leader's bewilderment and suspicion regarding the avant-garde, occurred in 1962 at a thirty-year anniversary exhibition for the Moscow branch of the Soviet Artists' Union. The story goes that Khrushchev had been reluctant to attend the event and would have much preferred to go and look at the latest tractors. But go he did, along with Brezhnev, Suslov and a few others. Walking around the exhibition his eye was caught by a collection of abstract paintings. He exclaimed that the pictures were degenerate and looked like they had been painted by a donkey's tail. Angered, he demanded to see the leading artist of the exhibition.

Modernist sculptor Ernst Neizvestney was summoned. He told Khrushchev that he could only comment on his own work, and then proceeded to give the Soviet leader a piece of his mind: '*You may be premier and chairman, but not here in front of my works. Here I am premier, and we shall discuss as equals.*' He also told Khrushchev that he had been 'duped' and that he '*was neither an artist nor a critic and was illiterate when it came to*

Valentin Kataev in 1929

aesthetics.' The implication was that Khrushchev had been set up by party hardliners who sought to bring back censorship of the arts. At the end of the heated exchange the two shook hands, though not without a warning from Khrushchev: '*You're an interesting man — I enjoy people like you — but inside you there are an angel and a devil. If the devil wins, we'll crush you. If the angel wins, we'll do all we can to help you.'* (Reported by William Grimes, *New York Times*, 17 August 2016)

While not crushed exactly, Neizvestney found that he was ostracised in official Soviet circles for the next few years. On Khrushchev's death he had a revenge of sorts. When asked by Khrushchev's family to create a monument to the deceased, '*The artist responded with a bronze head placed in a tower of white marble and black granite blocks, representing the progressive and reactionary impulses that competed for primacy in Khrushchev's soul.'* (Ibid)

I first met Kataev in Baku when I was working on the main radio station in Baku as a journalist in the mid-1960s and had the honour of interviewing him for a broadcast. The second time I met him was in 1975 during a month long cultural forum in Baku on the theme of *Books for Children and Youth*. About seventy authors working in the field had been invited and all had accepted. Kataev was going to be one of the star attractions. His work was legendary and enjoyed by thousands, if not millions of readers. He had also won the Stalin Prize, and was by now a huge figure. The prize money that came with the Stalin Prize was also a huge figure – 100,000 roubles. To average Russians like us this seemed like winning the pot of gold at the end of the rainbow.

My job as one of the founding members of the committee of the cultural forum was organising the Baku festival – the meetings, the logistics, transport arrangements, and who would be speaking where and when – the whole programme. Our literary guests would be visiting the city's twenty-four universities, along with other Baku colleges, several massive public halls and a large number of schools. At each of these venues the authors were to deliver talks about their lives, how they started, their inspirations, methods of working, discussing their latest projects and answering questions from their eager audiences. This all added up to them speaking to some two to three thousand people a day over the course of about ten days – a total of twenty to thirty thousand young people of Baku given the opportunity to see and hear these much-admired authors face to face.

At one point during a brief lull in the proceedings, Kataev came up to me. He said he was really sorry to bother me as he could see I was so busy, but he would like to ask me a favour. I replied it was no bother at all and asked how I could help. He told me he was in the middle of writing a book about Stalin, and knowing that as a young revolutionary the former Soviet leader had spent time in Baku, he was very interested to see the particular places in which he had lived and operated.

Stalin himself regarded his time in Baku as a significant phase in his political development: '*Two years of revolutionary activity among the workers in the oil industry steeled me as a practical fighter and as one of the practical leaders. Contact with advanced workers in Baku, with men like Vatsek and Saratovets, on the one hand, and the storm of acute conflicts between the workers and oil owners, on the other, first taught me what leading large masses of workers meant. It was in Baku that I thus received my second revolutionary baptism of fire.'* (*Pravda* no. 136, 16 June 1926)

Stalin's exploits however were not confined to pamphleteering and making speeches. *'Koba (one of Stalin's nicknames) was not afraid to take physical risks when it came to refuelling the party's coffers through expropriations and racketeering.'* (*Stalin's Baku Curve: A Detonating Mix of Crime and Revolution*, Fuad Akhundov)

Being a wanted man, Stalin was obliged to use a number of apartments or 'safe houses' in and around Baku to meet his local Bolshevik comrades and partisans, away from the eyes of the police. On two separate occasions though – in 1908 and 1910 – he had been captured and put behind bars for several months in the city's Bailov prison. Kataev was especially keen to go out there and see the prison for himself. When we arrived I introduced him to the director of the prison and explained the purpose of our visit. It was not the first such request – indeed the cell that Stalin had occupied here had in recent years become something of a visitor attraction. Kataev was shown in. He looked around, tapped on the thick walls, and remarked that surely it must be an impossible place from which to escape.

The Bailov was also where Stalin gave an early display of his phenomenal strength of body and mind, as recalled by a fellow inmate:

> *'In punishment of rioting by the prisoners, the authorities ordered that they be marched in single file between two lines of soldiers who proceeded to shower blows upon them with rifle butts. With head high, a book under his arm, Stalin walked the gantlet without a whimper, his face and head bleeding, his eyes flashing defiance. It was the kind of grit he demanded from others, the kind that helped save Russia from Nazi conquest and domination.'* (Reported in *New York Times*, 6 March 1953)

Kataev stayed in the prison cell for half an hour, sometimes walking around, sometimes sitting, sometimes peering through the narrow window, all the while in absolute silence, wrapt in thought and immersing himself totally in the atmosphere. This was Kataev the writer, the artist at work. It was the ultimate, most intimate form of research, like a method actor of the Stanislavski school – surrendering himself to the place in which his subject had lived and breathed, and in this way 'becoming' Stalin during those long days of incarceration before the revolution.

There was an actual connection between Kataev and Constantin Stanislavski, for it was the great theatrical pioneer had who suggested to him the dramatisation of Kataev's first novel *The Embezzlers*. Kataev duly wrote the script, which was performed at the Moscow Arts Theatre in 1928. The storyline, based on a number of true stories Kataev had read in Russian magazines, concerns a plot by three office workers to steal a large sum of money from the companies that employ them. Assigned to collect 12,000 roubles from the bank, the three rogues – accountant Fillip Stepanovich, cashier Vanechka and courier Nikita – make off with the cash. On a tour of the country they enjoy the high life until everything is spent. On their return home they are apprehended and flung in prison.

Such incidents were reportedly rife in Moscow at the time, and the Communist Party was engaged in a concerted effort to eradicate such corruption and outright theft. Kataev's fictionalised version was well received by critics, and he remembered it as the springboard of his career: 'The Embezzlers *endorsed me as part of a literary mainstream, marking the beginning of the whole new life for me. I received a phone call from the Stanislavski quarters and was asked to write a play...*'

Every morning during Kataev's stay in Baku I would ask my driver to take us along the sea front. We would stop and have a stroll along the promenade. Kataev loved this, it reminded him of his birthplace of Odessa. He could not live without the sea, he told me – we humans came out of the oceans and a

Michail Fainsilberg, Valentin Kataev, Mikhail Bulgakov, Yury Olesha and Iosif Utkin at the Funeral of Vladimir Mayakovsky, Russian Soviet poet, playwright, artist and actor.

natural affinity with the water remained in us. Kataev's love and fascination for that magical place where the land meets the sea is conveyed powerfully in his writing:

> *'...the entire sweep of the sea was like burning magnesium...here the steppe ended suddenly...This sand was amazingly white and fine...deep, soft, marked all over with the shapeless holes of yesterday's footprints, and looked like semolina of the very finest quality. The beach slanted almost imperceptibly towards the water. The last strip of sand lapped by broad tongues of snow-white foam, was damp, dark and smooth...this was the most wonderful beach in the world...'*
>
> (*A White Sail Gleams* by Valentin Kataev. Translated from the Russian by Leonard Stoklitsky. Progress Publishers Moscow)

Six months after his visit to Baku, Kataev called me on the phone and asked to meet up again. He wanted to make sure the details of the places I had taken him to were correct for his book on Stalin – that the names of streets, the description of the prison and the various houses and local people from the past were accurate. Afterwards he sent me the relevant pages of his manuscript and I was able to check everything off again for him. It was a task I relished. At school, history and literature had been my favourite subjects, both of which I excelled at. Within a short space of time I had memorised the whole of Pushkin's *Eugene Onegin*. When my teacher heard me recite this long work, cherished in the Russian canon, I was told it would take me to the top of the class for the rest of the year. This did not go down well with my fellow pupils.

The impressionistic side of Kataev's research that I had witnessed – visiting the locations depicted in his books and immersing himself in the sensual atmosphere in which the events he describes are set – was a technique he practiced in both fact and fiction. In the same way, his novelistic approach was to blend his own experiences with an imagined storyline, in what he referred to as his 'lyrical diary' style of writing. Frequently these personal experiences are also those of Russian history, its epic moments, its momentous turning points and heroic struggles. Kataev's fondest childhood memories were of the sea and the Crimean coast, a place of idyllic charm and beauty where the Romanovs would spend their holidays.

Odessa, Kataev's home city, was also a vital Russian port and naval station. In 1905, when Kataev was eight years old, sailors on the Potemkin, a battleship of the Imperial Russian Navy's Black Sea Fleet, weary of the harsh punishments, maggot ridden food and brutal conditions on board, sent one of their number, Valenchuk, to the ship's commander to protest. In a fit of temper the commander shot the man dead. A mutiny immediately broke out in which the commander and several other officers were killed. The crew hoisted the red flag and made for Odessa. When the *Potemkin* arrived, the dead sailor was brought ashore with a piece of paper attached

The Battleship 'Potemkin', 1925 Goskino film written and directed by Sergei Eisenstein

to his chest: '*This is the body of Valenchuk, killed by the commander for having told the truth. Retribution has been meted out to the commander.*'

As news of what had happened spread through the port, locals brought food for the sailors and placed flowers on Valenchuk's body. People began making speeches, singing revolutionary songs, and drinking vodka. Within a few hours the harbour area was ablaze and looters ran amok. A telegram arrived from Tsar Nicholas II ordering a military response. Troops were deployed and opened fire on the crowd, trapped within the confines of the harbour. By the end of the day some 2,000 citizens of Odessa lay dead.

In 1925 Eisenstein made his remarkable film about the events of that day. For the young Kataev, the drama had unfolded before his eyes: '*I clearly remember the Battleship Potemkin, a red flag on her mast, sailing along the*

This bronze sculpture is dedicated to Odessites Petya and Gavrik – literary heroes of Valentin Kataev's story 'Lone White Sail'

coast past Odessa. I witnessed the fighting on the barricades, I saw overturned horse-trams, twisted and torn street wires, revolvers, rifles, dead bodies.' (Ibid: Author's Introduction)

These momentous scenes were to be filed away in his imagination for one of his most compelling narratives, *A White Sails Gleams*. Described by many as a prose poem, the novel portrays the *Potemkin* episode from the perspective of two schoolboys in Odessa at the time. The result is a captivating tale of adventure for young people, and the book, later made into a film, remains a classic of Russian children's literature. There is also much eulogising of the sea, whose supreme spell for the author, '*...lies in the eternal mystery hidden in its expanses.*' (Ibid)

As well as creating a hugely entertaining story, Kataev stated that his aim in *A White Sail Gleams* was '*...to convey the invigorating spirit that had been infused into the life of Russia by her first revolution.*' (Ibid). At the time of that novel's setting, 1905, Stalin was still a young outlaw, in and out of prison. Three decades later he was the leader of Soviet Russia and embarked on the second of his five-year plans to industrialise the country on a scale comparable or in advance of America and Western Europe. The focus of the second plan was heavy industry, and in the iron rich region of Magnitogorsk on the southern tip of the Urals, a massive steel producing plant was under construction. Kataev's novel *Time Forward,* describes the workers' struggle to bring the project to completion ahead of time. Again, his writing is rooted in direct experience: '*I was struck by all I saw in Magnitogorsk, by the great enthusiasm of people building for themselves. This was a revolution too. It inspired my book.*' (Ibid)

Kataev had experienced two world wars, as a soldier in the first, in the second, the Great Patriotic War, as a news correspondent. In the 1940s conflict, he saw '*a great deal, but for some reason it was the youngsters that made the biggest impression on me – the homeless, destitute boys who marched grimly along the war-torn roads. I saw exhausted Russian soldiers pick up the unfortunate children. This was a manifestation of the great humanism of the Soviet man. Those soldiers were fighting against fascism, and therefore they too were beacons of the revolution.*' (Ibid)

In Kataev's literary portrayal of Soviet soldiers, their compassion is matched by their courage and sacrifice in battle:

> '*In my short story "The Flag" which is based on a wartime episode, the Nazis have surrounded a group of Soviet fighting men and called on them to give up. But instead of the white flag of surrender they ran up a crimson flag, which they improvised from pieces of cloth of different shades of red. Similarly, Soviet literature is made up of many works of different shades which, taken together, shine like a fiery-red banner of the revolution.*' (Ibid)

Valentin Kataev's greatness lies not only in his subject matter and his skilfully woven storylines but the way he uses the Russian language. His style is beautiful and enchanting. From meeting him I had seen proof that he was not only a writer with a wonderful imagination but one who paid meticulous attention to detail. Stalin, himself a writer of poetry knew that Kataev was a genius equal to Pasternak, and that he could not come within a mile of touching either of them.

His willingness to go out and engage with people by the thousands, particularly the youth of the country, stemmed from an overriding belief in the social value of art. It was a principle instilled in him early on in his career by another celebrated figure in Russian literature. Kataev had received an invitation to the International Pen Conference in Vienna. Flattered by the honour, he went around in great excitement telling everyone he met. On breaking the news to the renowned writer and actor Vladimir Mayakovsky however, he received a salutary reply:

> *'They invited me too, but I'm not bragging about this. Because they did not invite me, of course, as Mayakovsky, but as a representative of the Soviet literature. The same applies to you. Get it? Reflect, Kataich (as he called me when he was in a good mood), on what it means to be a writer in the Land of Soviets.'* (Ibid)

The advice was not lost on Kataev:

> *'Mayakovsky's words made a lasting impression on me. I realized that I owed my success as a creative writer to the Soviet people, who had backed me. I realized that being a Soviet writer meant marching in synch with the people, being always on the crest of a revolutionary wave.'* (Ibid)

Valentin Kataev working from home in 1962

KERIM KERIMOV

Kerim Kerimov

In 1865, the French author Jules Verne wrote a whimsical tale about three members of an American gun club attempting to build an enormous cannon that would fire them to the stars. From the *Earth to the Moon* ends as the friends hurtle into the sky. In the sequel, *Around the Moon*, we follow the heroes' adventures in space. Was the book intended as prophecy or to be merely an entertaining story? Nearly a century earlier the Montgolfier brothers had staged the first balloon flight with passengers – a duck, a rooster and a sheep. But by the time Verne's tale appeared aeroplanes were still unheard of, let alone a machine that could venture beyond the Earth's atmosphere. The idea that people might one day travel in space remained the stuff of fantasy.

Like so many scientific developments it was the field of warfare that would accelerate mastery of the skies. Napoleon had already used balloons for aerial reconnaissance, and by 1914 German Zeppelins were dropping bombs and heavier-than-air military planes were in service. World War One marked a new and frightening paradigm in armed conflict. For the first time in history, death and destruction could came raining down from the sky, inflicting large numbers of civilian as well as military casualties in a matter of minutes. What diabolical inventions would military planners and scientists come up with next?

Rockets had been around since the 13th century in China, but these had been fired with gunpowder: in World War One the use of liquid

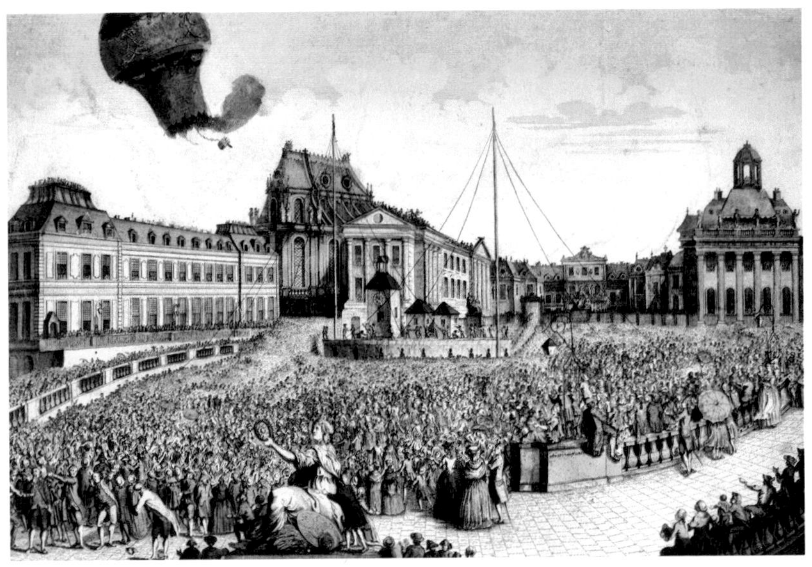

Montgolfier Brothers launch of the Aerostat Reveillon at Versailles, 19 September 1783

propellants lent them far greater efficiency. In terms of sending rockets on a vertical trajectory, in other words into space, it was a Russian, Konstantin Tsiolkovsky, a teacher of mathematics, who had written one of the earliest known studies of such a possibility. In *The Exploration of Cosmic Space by Means of Reaction Devices*, published in 1903, the author outlines the theory of rocket propulsion — a concept already thought of but which came to be known as the Tsiolkovsky Equation. Tsiolkovsky's writings led to the founding in Moscow in 1924 of the Society for Studies of Interplanetary Travel, of which he became a leading member. Tsiolkovsky had also theorised on the potential of liquid propulsion, and by the 1920s scientists in Germany had built an experimental liquid propelled rocket.

By the early 1930s, scientists and engineers at Leningrad's Gas Dynamics Laboratory were advancing the Soviet Union's progress in this new field of endeavour, developing prototype rocket engines. However, in 1938, when director Valentin Glushko was arrested along with Tupoloev, Korolev and other scientists during Stalin's purge, the programme stalled. With Hitler having already launched an attack on Spain in 1936, and the warning signs of further aggression flashing, it might seem surprising that Stalin did not recognise the military significance of such work. The wake up call was about to come:

> '*...research of outer space had been forbidden as it was considered a waste of time. In fact, Stalin had had chief scientists, Nikolai Tupolev and Sergei Korolev, arrested in 1938 and imprisoned for six years... Stalin changed his mind when he heard that the Germans had produced rockets (surface-to-surface missiles) that were used in bombing London. Churchill, himself, informed Stalin. That's when he began to realize the potential for such technology and released his scientists to rush to Germany to study these rockets. Germany had attacked England from a distance of 300 kilometers – an unprecedented feat in the history of military warfare up to that time.*'
>
> (Betty Blair. Interview in *Azerbaijan International*)

The speaker is Kerim Abbas Aliyevich Kerimov, around twenty-three years of age at the time of Hitler's attacks on London, and whose talents and energy were destined to make him the driving force behind the Soviet Union's astonishing achievements in space exploration. Born in Baku in 1917, Kerimov was the son of Abbas-Ali Kerimov, an engineer from the St. Petersburg Institute of Technology. When the Great Patriotic War began, Karim had just completed his studies at the Azerbaijan Industrial Institute. He then enrolled in the Dzerzhinsky Artillery Academy, which had been evacuated to Samarkand, and it was here that his aptitude for rocket technology developed. On completion of a thesis on mortar production, with the war still raging he worked with the Soviet invented Katyusha rocket launchers, mobile artillery systems mounted on various means of transport – from trucks and trains to river and ocean going vessels. Although comparatively slow to reload, the Katyushas were exponentially effective,

Soviet Katyusha Rocket Launcher in action near Breslau in February 1945

a battery of four rockets capable of sending over four tons of ordnance raining down on the enemy in under ten seconds, around the same volume as seventy field guns. For his contribution to the defence of his country Kerimov was awarded the Order of the Red Star.

In 1945, aware of the devastation wrought by Hitler's V2 rockets, the Soviet Union was keen to acquire the technology. Kerimov was dispatched to Germany, following on from Korolev, who unlike many comrades had escaped the death penalty during the purge. However, the brains behind the German rocket programme, Wernher Von Braun, along with several associates had surrendered to the Americans. Korolev and his comrades, determined not to leave empty handed, headed for Nordhausen to undertake an exhaustive examination of the V2 factory and study FAU II rocket construction.

Knowing that Von Braun and his colleagues would be working with the US military, the Soviet objective now was to produce a long-range ballistic missile and launch the first satellite. The Ministry of Defence sent Kerimov to Kapustin Yar, a remote spot between Astrakhan and Volgograd where a testing and launch site had been set up in 1946. Utilising components brought back from Germany, he and his team were able to put together ten rockets, seven of which were launched. Kerimov later spoke candidly about his impressions at that time, and how he had little notion of where, other than for military use, the technology might go:

> *'We didn't really understand the essence of what we were doing. We had no idea what would evolve. Our task was simply to create rockets. The further they could reach, the better. Our first efforts in 1950 were directly patterned after the German R-2 Rockets, the only exception was that ours had twice the range… 600 kilometres. Two years later, we produced rockets with the capability of 1500 kilometres… an inter-continental range of 10,000 kilometres was only a matter of time.'* (Ibid)

By the end of the 1950s, Kerimov having proved his worth he was put in charge of the Space Objects Control Department, responsible for monitoring rocket tests across a variety of high security locations throughout the country. According to latter day outside observers, Kerimov's role in space development did not come about through preference: *'As an artillery man, Kerimov's first priority was military missiles, and he moved from head of the Strategic Missile Forces to become the first commander of the new Central Directorate for Space Assets. Although he and Korolev apparently got on well together, this was regarded as a setback for Korolev, who was pushing for piloted space flight on behalf of the Soviet Air Force.'* (*Daily Telegraph*, 3 April 2003)

Exactly who regarded Kerimov's advancement as a setback for Korolev is unclear, but Kerimov would later express his admiration for Korolev. In October 1960 fate delivered Kerimov a cruel blow – a plane crash that killed his younger brother. Like all his comrades, Kerimov regularly worked a seven-day week, and was due to attend the launch of a new Soviet ICBM aircraft at Baikonur Cosmodrome. Given his sad news, however, he was granted time off to go to his brother's funeral. On the day of the launch at Baikonur, a malfunction on the aircraft caused it to explode on the ground. One hundred and twenty-six engineers and military personnel, including Nedelin, the Strategic Missile Forces commander, were left dead. *'Under normal circumstances, I would have been standing right beside Marshal Nedelin,'* recalled Kerimov. *'It was such a mysterious twist of fate that my brother's death, in essence, saved me from mine.'* (*Independent*, 6 April 2003)

Six months later on 12 April 1961, the whole of the Soviet Union was celebrating, as Gagarin became the first man in space. Kerimov credited Korolev for the success of this phenomenal endeavour: *'Actually, the idea of sending a human being into space originated with Korolev. At first it seemed like a fantasy, so unbelievable...Eventually, Korolyov gained the support of the government and we began building Vostok...'* (Betty Blair. Interview in *Azerbaijan International*)

Behind the scenes Kerimov himself had played a key role, and was on duty the morning that the young man about to become the most famous cosmonaut ever, prepared to leave the Earth. It was an occasion he would never forget: *'It was a beautiful day... near the Aral Sea. Gagarin, and his backup, Gherman Titov, had slept very comfortably the night before – in fact, much better than we had. We knew because, unknown to them, we had monitored their sleep via sensors under their beds. Lift off was at 9:07 a.m. and less than two hours later at 10:55 a.m., the spacecraft had already circled the earth and landed. It was an incredible moment in history.'* (Ibid) The Soviet Union rewarded Kerimov with a promotion to the rank of General.

Over the next four years the Soviet Space Programme streaked ahead, sending the first woman, Valentina Tereshkova into space in 1963 and Leonov on his momentous space walk in 1965. Meanwhile American Alan Shepherd quickly followed Leonov, and the teams at NASA remained committed to pushing the boundaries. But military implications aside, what was the reason for such intense competition between the world's two most

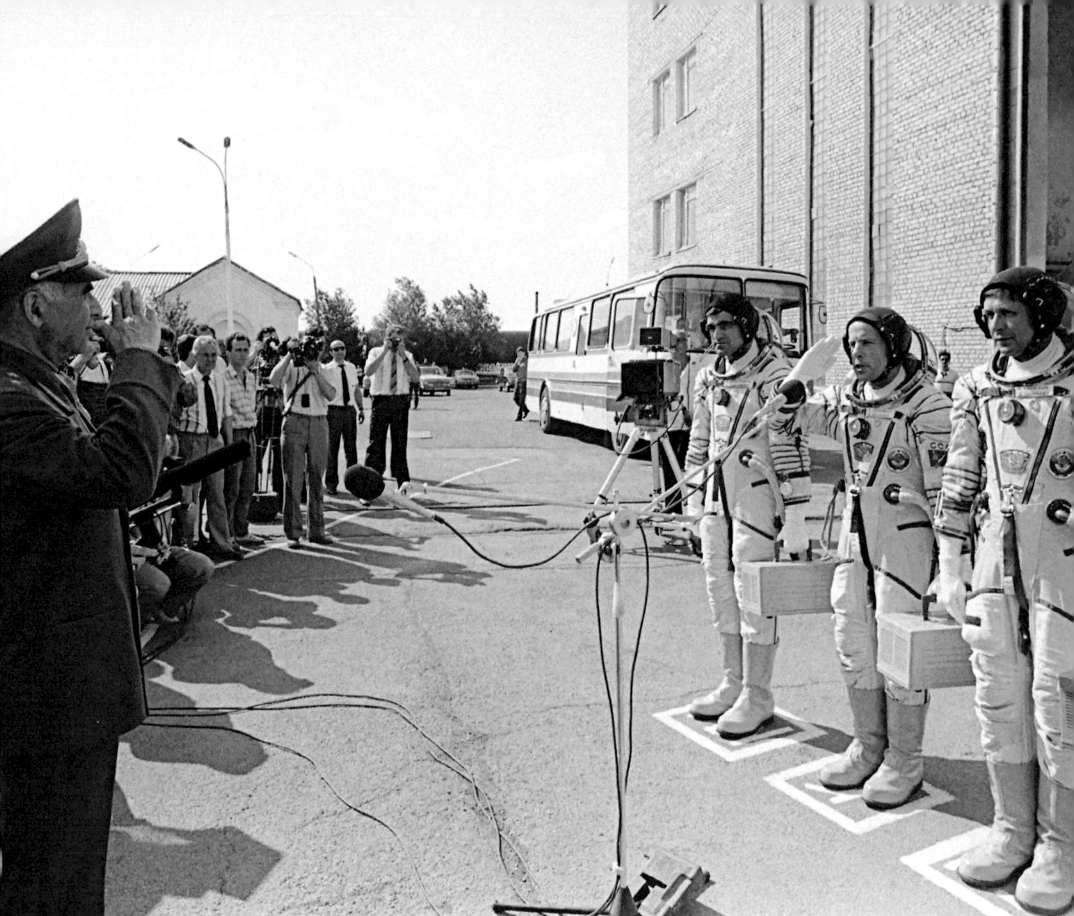

Anatoly Solovyev captain of the international space crew reporting to Kerim Kerimov head of the state commission for space

powerful nations? Kerimov, from his unique inside position, saw it this way: *'Space flights are not play toys; every single aspect of their journeys is highly calculated. Consequently, the space race became symbolic of the intellect of each nation; advanced technology signalled national superiority – at least, that's how it was perceived by both sides.'* (Ibid)

Even the most advanced of calculations, produced by the finest minds could not predict the unknown quantities in outer space, nor the dangers. Following the great triumphs – Gagarin, Tereshkina, Leonov – would come disaster and tragic loss of life. In January 1966 Kerimov mourned the death of his comrade Korolev, who having survived brutal treatment during his years in prison, had now succumbed at the age of fifty-nine from a botched surgical operation. To fill the vacuum Kerimov was put in charge of the newly formed body, the State Commission for Flight Testing of Soyuz Spacecraft. The Soyuz would be the successors to the Vokshod craft that had carried Gagarin, Tereshkina and Leonov. The debut flight of the new rocket series did not go well: in November 1966, cosmonaut Vladimir Komarov, returning in Soyuz I was killed when the main parachute on his capsule failed to open during its descent. Kerimov, who had rushed to the landing site by helicopter found the remains of the craft still smouldering. He would later confirm rumours that for a time he and his team had been held personally responsible, and that he had only kept his job because 'Brezhnev understood the nature of these projects.' (Ibid)

Kerimov later reflected that if his old boss Korolev had still been around the accident might not have happened, a view shared by many of his comrades. Korolev's passing would continue to affect him deeply: *'His death was a terrible loss. It made me feel incredibly lonely. I had relied on him immensely as he was the Number One man in the industry up until that time. On every space mission, there is always incredible anxiety and pressure that something could go wrong and the mission end in failure and tragedy. With his passing, the entire responsibility fell upon me.'* (Ibid)

Kerimov acknowledged his late comrade's role in developing the technology to join satellites together in space. In October 1967 those ideas would be brought to fruition when Kerimov and his team succeeded in docking together Kosmos 186 and Kosmos 188. Kerimov duly informed Brezhnev, who thanked him. The same day Kerimov received a call from the Deputy Chairman of the Cabinet of Ministers who told him he had been made a Lieutenant General. The event would also pave the way for a more cooperative era of space endeavour between nations, marked by the joining of Russia's Mir with the American space shuttle Atlantis in 1995.

The Soyuz programme continued apace. Soyuz 2 was unmanned, while Soyuz 3 in October 1968 became the first successful manned flight in the series, carrying forty-seven year old Georgy Beregovoy, a hero of the Great Patriotic War and the oldest person to travel in space, on a four-day voyage, making eighty-one orbits of the Moon. There can be little doubt that as Beregovoy came safely home, he had the most famous cosmonaut of all time in his thoughts: Gagarin's fatal plane crash had taken place only a few months earlier. Beregovoy's achievement might have provided some balm to the nation in the wake of Gagarin's death, though a few months later those toiling at the heart of the Soviet space programme might have felt more than a twinge of envy as American astronaut Neil Armstrong became the first human being to step onto the Moon.

For Kerimov the work went on, the Soyuz missions occupying most of his waking hours. The Kosmos 186 and 188 docking had convinced Kerimov and his comrades that long term manned satellites – space stations – could provide a platform for far more extensive research into interplanetary phenomena. Thus in 1971 began the Salyut space station programme in which Leonov would participate. For the design of the stations, Kerimov again paid credit to the late Korolev, who had originally had the idea for a separate compartment, enabling a spacecraft to operate independently for longer periods and which could be invaluable in an emergency. One of the greatest dangers for cosmonauts however was at the point where space ended – the moment of re-entry. In June 1971, Kerimov was given a sobering reminder of the fact: *'The orbital station (Soyuz 10 and Soyuz 11) had docked and the crew, Dobrovolsky, Volkov, and Patseyev, had managed to conduct research for 24 days. When the spaceships disconnected from each other, all seemed normal. We didn't worry much when we lost connection with the crew as these things sometimes happen and the craft was coming down without difficulty. The flight landed as expected. However, when we opened the hatch, we were shocked to find all three cosmonauts dead.'* (Ibid)

Kerimov remembered that fateful day as *'a tragedy that I can never forget that deeply influenced our work.'* (Ibid) Lessons were learned however; because of the cramped conditions in the capsule the cosmonauts had not been wearing the space suits that might have saved their lives. This would not be the case on future flights.

Over twenty-five years of service, Kerimov launched every cosmonaut who went into space during that time. *'I almost didn't have a personal life. I used to work Saturdays and Sundays. I couldn't fall ill. I didn't have the right to get sick.'* (Ibid)

To the Soviet people his voice became very familiar, for at the moment before blast-off it was he would issue the order: *'I authorise you to go.'* Yet all one ever saw on the TV coverage was his back; the man behind the voice remained completely anonymous, his name never revealed, his face never seen. Kerimov was a 'secret' general, his official job title bearing no mention of rockets or space flight; he was referred to only as the 'Chairman of the Commission', his government department the 'Ministry of General Machinery'. Only in 1987 after glasnost was Kerimov first mentioned

The Invisible Man from Baikonur – the legendary Azerbaijani Kerim Kerimov.

publicly by name in *Pravda*. Then suddenly everyone wanted to know who he was and what he had done.

It was during a 1st May celebration in Moscow's Red Square that I was given the privilege of meeting Kerimov. By tradition on these occasions the Secretary of the Central Committee of Komsomol would sit on the left hand side of the guest rostrum. It came as a complete surprise to me when the secretary that year, Semyon Kuzmich Tsvigun, came over, and taking me under the arm said, *'Let's go, I'll introduce you to your countryman.'* (Like me, Kerimov was born in Baku) Karim Abbas Aliyevich was standing with a group of Soviet Generals. Catching sight of Tsvigun waving to him he came down and joined us. When Semyon Kuzmich introduced me, Kerimov replied with a smile: *'I saw Vagif on the 17th Congress of Komsomol, and once we sat together at the Presidium, in the Column Hall, celebrating the 23 February.'*

I must say he had a good memory. For looking at him I realised it was true, we had sat together on the occasion to which he referred. But at that time I had no idea that this was the man who during his career had overseen the launch and flight of every Soviet cosmonaut. I remembered how for many years I would watch the TV coverage of the space missions, hearing the cosmonauts report to the 'Chairman of the State Commission' – the shadowy figure with his back turned always to the camera – that they were ready to fly. Then the Chairman's order: *'I authorise you to go…'*

I met Kerimov several times after that, and we often spoke on the telephone. To say that he was an interesting man would be an understatement. Highly educated, he was also friendly and extremely tactful with people, sensitive to their feelings. Occupying a unique position in the Soviet Space Programme was not only about making history, for Kerimov it carried enormous responsibility, making daily decisions that could mean the difference between life and death for the people around him. In his own life there had been sadness and loss – the early death of his younger brother, and his wife, whom he had known since their schooldays, had passed away aged only fifty, after which he had not remarried.

Commemorated on an Azerbaijani stamp in 2007

Kerimov remained Chairman of the State Commission until 1990. After retirement he lived on his farm, still rising at 6 am every morning and enjoying swimming and working with his hands on repairs and restoration. He would also lend his professional expertise occasionally, consulting on space projects such as the Mir Shuttle. Able at last to talk openly about his career, he set it all down for people to read in *Way to the Stars*, charting the story of the Soviet Space Programme – the exciting, nerve-wracking experimental work, the long, laborious hours of planning and modifications to the spacecraft, the many fascinating people and places he had known. There is a wealth of technical detail in the book, and while rightly proud of the space programme's achievements, Kerimov's account is also scrupulously honest about the failures and mistakes, emphasising that no launch was ever without hitches.

In the game of life, fate had dealt Karim Abbas Aliyevich Kerimov a unique hand, which he had played with integrity and honour. After decades of service to his country and making a major contribution to the advancement of science and technology, for which like many comrades he received no public recognition, his attitude was above all one of gratitude:

> *'I've had incredible experiences in my lifetime, most of which I wouldn't trade for anything in the world.'* (Ibid)

HENRY KISSINGER

It was 1975. Thirteen years since the Cuban missile crisis and the subsequent installation of the 'red telephone' line between Moscow and Washington. Talk was better than war, certainly the nuclear kind, and the notion of mutually assured destruction – MAD – was recognised on both sides of the Atlantic as just that, insanity. The policy of détente, bringing the world's two largest superpowers together to talk, improve their relations and promote greater safety had begun under Richard Nixon and Leonid Brezhnev. In November 1969 the first Strategic Arms Limitation Talks (SALT 1) had taken place in Helsinki, resulting in the 1972 Anti Ballistic Missile Treaty. It was a worthy achievement. Nixon and Brezhnev had managed to find common ground, and a productive dialogue on a par with that of Stalin and Roosevelt.

In 1973, Nixon, disgraced over the Watergate Hotel bugging scandal, had resigned and been replaced by Gerald Ford. Détente had continued however, and an important feature of the process was for members of the two governments to visit one another on a regular basis, getting together and talking face to face. If you have met and got on with someone in the flesh, it's much harder to think of them and their family as an enemy or an anonymous target. This was the theory. If there was agreement and understanding, the results were even better.

For the previous few years a major challenge to transatlantic diplomacy had been the Vietnam War, in which the Soviet Union had backed the North against the high-powered American forces in the South. By 1975, however, the war was effectively over, and in April, as 100,000 North Vietnamese soldiers surrounded Saigon, panic set in and US Embassy staff and large numbers of other foreign nationals were evacuated by helicopter. The end to this long, bloody and tragic conflict in South East Asia, combined with the progress on the de-escalation of nuclear weapons, gave grounds for increased optimism, the belief that harmonious relations between America and the Soviet Union might now develop further. A symbolic gesture in this direction took place on 17 July 1975, when Soviet Cosmonaut Alexei Leonov and American astronaut Tom Stafford shook hands in space. This event, watched around the world on television by millions of people, was the first such encounter in human history, and something I will talk about further in the chapter on Leonov.

Back down on Earth there was to be more handshaking. As Secretary of International Affairs of the All-Union Komsomol Central Committee of the USSR Communist Party, I was part of a Soviet delegation invited that year to the White House. After the traditional American brunch we were conducted to the State Department's Ministry of Foreign Affairs to meet a number of US officials. Chief among them was Henry Kissinger. As Secretary of State and National Security Advisor under Nixon and now Ford, it was Kissinger who had been the main organiser and engine behind these US-Soviet meetings.

Naturally I was thrilled at the chance to be introduced to Kissinger, but before we went in we were briefed that the meeting would be short and sweet and advised therefore not to get carried away in our expectations. Kissinger was open and charming, asked lots of questions and listened carefully to one's replies. To him I was a new person entering his arena, and I felt this fact alone stimulated his interest – what kind of individual was I, what motivated me, what were my views? On learning that I was from Azerbaijan he talked about the country's large Jewish community in the mountains of Quba, across the river from the city, and was very well informed about the history of the settlement.

When the discussion turned to Komsomol, Kissinger was particularly interested in the degree to which our organisation was connected to the Soviet Communist Party. I said that my colleagues and I were obliged to discuss our programmes and ideas with party officials, and that we had to obtain permission before holding events, issuing invitations and spending money. I stressed, however, that we formulated our own planning and were not directly controlled or run by the party. Neither, I added, were we financially dependent on it. Kissinger was curious. If we had no state support, where then, he wanted to know, did we get our money from? I explained how all Komsomol members paid monthly subscriptions linked to their incomes – students for example might pay the equivalent of a few cents a month, higher earning professionals a few dollars. Times those small amounts by the entire membership of around forty million, and there was ample revenue for Komsomol to be self-sufficient. The organisation also produced its own newspaper, the *Komsomol Pravda*, priced at the equivalent of about three pence with a daily print circulation throughout the Soviet Union of some eighteen million copies. In addition we had several magazines and periodicals, plus a book publishing house, *Young Guards*, all bringing in extra revenue which could be used to fund conferences, festivals and other activities.

Kissinger then asked me how much money Komsomol earned overall in a year. '*It's a secret,*' I said, '*but I'll tell you. It equates to roughly 300 million sterling per annum.*' '

And the government gives you nothing?'

'*If anything the situation is the reverse,*' I replied, '*our main problem is guarding our money from the government!*'

We had to show Komsomol's income and make the case for any change in expenditure, with everything itemised to the exact rouble. The government could sometimes refuse us things for no obvious reason, as in the case of one of our magazines, entitled *Youth*, for which demand was outstripping supply with more and more people wanting to take it. The press ministry was not allowed to print more than three million copies per issue. Sometimes, I told him, we had confrontations with the party over such matters.

Having been advised that the meeting with Kissinger would be brief, in the end I spent over an hour in his company. It was clear that he was extremely clever, so sharp that second by second as you talked to him you could almost see his mind working – taking in what one said, assimilating information, making mental notes of the salient points and asking the most pertinent questions. In my view, such skills are a mark of true distinction in a diplomat, and the qualities of a great person.

Although I was the leader of Komsomol at the time, I was a very minor player on the diplomatic stage, and especially so at these high level meetings. I was also junior to Kissinger in age, and obviously way, way below him in terms of rank. Yet this world-renowned statesman had taken time to discuss with me one to one the current state of international affairs, as if I was an equal. He never once interrupted me nor did he show condescension or disrespect. There was no bombast, presumption or lecturing, but instead the skilful encouragement of mutual understanding. Throughout our conversation he would politely enquire along the lines of, *'Do you mind if I add to this…?'* or *'May I offer a further thought on that…'* It wasn't a game either; this was his style, utterly dignified, an incredible human being I felt.

Where did such exceptional abilities come from? If they were natural gifts, they had been honed and developed by a remarkable aptitude for hard work and a very diverse range of life experiences. That life began in Furth, Bavaria, in 1923, when Heinz Alfred Kissinger was born into a Jewish family, his father Louis a schoolmaster. Heinz devoted much of his time to playing football for the youth side of one of the top clubs in Germany. As for so many in Europe however, especially Jews, his life was about to change. In 1938, shortly before the 'Kristallnacht' attacks on Jewish shops and homes, the Kissingers fled to London, then on to New York. The fifteen-year-old was enrolled in the George Washington High School and then went on to study accountancy. Meanwhile he worked part time in a factory.

The Japanese attack on Pearl Harbor in December 1941 had brought America into World War Two, and with the introduction of wholesale conscription, in 1943 Kissinger was among those called up for military service. It was while serving in the 84th Infantry Division that his German background, along with his intellect and a good deal of courage and tenacity, would prove to be a great asset in fighting the fascists. At the end of 1944, the Germans launched a major counter-offensive in the forests of the Ardennes in Belgium. This surprise attack, the Battle of the Bulge, would claim the lives of 19,000 US soldiers. As a member of the army intelligence staff, Kissinger put himself forward for reconnaissance operations, a dangerous position amidst the fierce fighting. When the Allies finally entered German soil, his doggedness and organisational skills would also come to the fore in leading a team to hunt down members of the Gestapo in Hanover. Awarded a Bronze Medal for this work, Kissinger was then assigned to the de-Nazification programme, during which time, according to record, he safeguarded German citizens against reprisals. (Walter Isaacson, *Kissinger A Biography*)

What path now lay ahead for this bright and capable young man? Politics it seemed was what now drew him, and in 1950 he achieved a first degree in political science from Harvard. Post-graduate studies followed, and a PhD thesis whose title signalled the direction in which Kissinger was headed: *Peace, Legitimacy, and the Equilibrium (A Study of the Statesmanship of* Castlereagh *and* Metternich).

After fulfilling a series of academic and consultancy roles throughout the 1950s, Kissinger entered the world of politics in 1960 as a supporter of Nelson Rockefeller, and with Nixon's ascendancy to the White House in 1968 came the appointment as National Security Advisor. A longstanding concern for US foreign policy was Communist China. Since 1950 and China's involvement in the Korean War, diplomatic relations between the two countries had been frozen. In the spring of 1971, an American table tennis team had made a much-publicised visit to Peking (Beijing) to play against their sporting counterparts. In this groundbreaking event Kissinger saw an opportunity. In July 1971 he made a covert trip, reportedly arranged via diplomatic contacts in Romania and Pakistan, to meet with Chinese premier Zhou-EnLai. A follow-up visit in October ushered in a

H. R. Haldeman, John Ehrlichman, Henry Kissinger, William P. Rogers with Richard M. Nixon and Charles de Gaulle in the foreground, 3 February 1969

historic meeting between Nixon and the Chinese leader Mao Zedong in 1972. Ending a twenty-two year diplomatic rift, the meeting was a major achievement on Kissinger's part, and would arguably have led to closer and faster ties with China if Watergate and Nixon's downfall had not come about.

On taking office Nixon had also become the inheritor of 'Johnson's War' – the now highly controversial engagement in Vietnam. Nixon had pledged to end the conflict and bring 'peace with honour', a phrase that must have sounded ominous to those recalling Chamberlain's confident return from Munich in 1938. Kissinger, however, had already been on the ground in Vietnam in 1965, visiting Saigon in a consultancy capacity at the behest of the US ambassador. From this experience he concluded that the war was unwinnable, and in 1967 he had begun mediation with the North Vietnamese. Subsequent negotiations led to the Paris Accords. Ceasefire agreements were signed, and in December 1973 the Nobel Peace Prize was

Henry Kissinger, Henry Ford and Mao Zedong

bestowed on Kissinger and his North Vietnamese counterpart Le Duc Tho.

The award to Kissinger provoked a hostile reaction with the resignation of two Nobel committee members and Le Duc Tho refusing to accept his prize on the grounds that a lasting peace was far from restored. Kissinger was also judged to be instrumental in, or at the very least a party to the bombing of Cambodia. He did, however, accept his Nobel Prize, though did not attend the ceremony and donated all of the prize money to families of American servicemen killed or missing in the conflict. In 1975, the year I met him, he had apparently had a change of heart and attempted to return the award.

The relationship between Nixon and Kissinger is known to have been complex, and has been the subject of much debate. To begin with there were cultural differences, Nixon coming from a Quaker background, and there is evidence of anti Semitic utterances on his part, both towards and about Kissinger. Some commentators allege that Kissinger used flattery on Nixon, while Nixon was *'simultaneously eager to exploit Kissinger's diplomatic skills and resentful of his emergence as someone who could overshadow the president. The dynamic was tense and never-ending.'* (Robert Dallek, *Vanity Fair*, 2 April 2007)

Tension among high-level politicians ostensibly on the same side is hardly uncommon of course. The same author quotes a phone call made by Kissinger as the Watergate crisis mounted: *'After returning from the Middle East in June of 1974, Kissinger spoke by phone with Jacob Javits and told the New York senator, "You know, what really worries me, Jack, [is that,] with the President facing impeachment, what's been holding things together is my moral authority abroad and to some extent at home. If that's lost we may be really in trouble."'* (Ibid) In another source he is quoted as saying, *'I was the glue that held it all together in 1973 – and I'm not being boastful...'* (Alistair Horne, *The Case For Henry Kissinger, The Independent*, 17 August 2009)

What sounds here like self-regard on Kissinger's part, may in fact be

Kissinger and fellow Nobel Prizewinner, Le Duc Tho

President Gerald Ford and Secretary of State Henry Kissinger, conversing in the grounds of the White House, Washington, DC in 1974

an accurate assessment of the situation. In 1973 he had been praised for his key role in ending the Yom Kippur. Israel National Security Councilor William B. Quant described his press statement, which led swiftly to a United Nations resolution, as 'a brilliant performance, one of his most impressive. Engineering the Nixon visit to China, the Paris Accords over Vietnam, and bringing resolutely hostile parties in the Middle East to some kind of agreement – these were the events that had built Dr. Henry Kissinger's reputation as an exceptional global peace-broker. In the fallout from Watergate and Nixon's demise, Kissinger's concern seemed to be that he could become similarly tainted in the public's perception, and that this would only add to the destabilizing effects the crisis was having on American diplomatic efforts: '*Every gambit of US foreign policy in 1973 was…overshadowed by the darkening clouds of the Watergate scandal.*' (Ibid)

In the event, despite criticism for the so-called 'Berlin Wall' of secrecy with which he and other members of the White House team had supposedly surrounded the President, Kissinger's career survived Watergate. Nixon may have had a hand in this, for it is believed that on his departure from office he urged his Republican successor Gerald Ford to retain his former colleague's services. Thus Kissinger served another three years at the centre of US politics, until the arrival of Democratic President Jimmy Carter in 1976.

Opinion was, and remains sharply divided about Kissinger. To liberal America it seems he has largely been regarded as a manipulative, Machiavellian figure. The planned endowment of a chair at Columbia University in 1977 was abandoned when student protests caused a media furore, while US domiciled British writer Christopher Hitchens called for him to be prosecuted. Hitchens' 2001 book *The Trials of Henry Kissinger,* implicates his subject in alleged war crimes in Vietnam, East Timor and Bangladesh, and suggested involvement in a plot to assassinate Cypriot President Archbishop Makarios in 1974. While some applauded the book, others questioned its premise and novelistic approach to historical events: *'Dr Kissinger is not a fictional character. In an account that purports to be factual, pretending to read a person's mind, then utilising it as a confession is so transparently malicious and misleading as to make one discount everything that*

Henry Kissinger in a heated debate with Nixon at the White House

follows it.' (George Jonas, *Daily Telegraph*, 4 May 2001)

Kissinger is frequently associated with the concept of 'realpolitik' – politics as the art of the possible, rather than an adherence to any ideology. But this identification may be too simplistic. In 1974, by which time 50,000 American servicemen had died in Vietnam, Kissinger had argued for significant military and financial aid to support the South Vietnamese. Congress turned down the request, and Kissinger maintained in his memoirs that, '*...the thrust of my appeal was to such unfashionable concepts as 'honor' and 'moral obligation,' not to realpolitik as our critics had it.'* (John Bew, *The Kissinger Effect on Realpolitik – War on the Rocks*, 29 December 2015)

From other remarks, however, it seems clear that Kissinger never discounted realpolitik, seeing it rather as an unavoidable fact of political life: '*The test of a statesman, argued Kissinger, in a phrase Ludwig von Rochau – the originator of Realpolitik – might have written, was "his ability to recognise the real relationship of forces and to make this knowledge serve his ends."'* (Ibid)

Biographer Alistair Horne found the jury appeared not so much out as in stubborn disagreement over Kissinger: '*...no Americans – and few Europeans – could be neutral about him. They either loved him or hated him. For everyone who would happily have seen him arraigned on war crimes charges there were others who applauded his contributions to the cause of world peace.'*

After four years of research, Horne concluded that, '*I think I have come out with the latter group. This is not to say that I consider his record irreproachable. It is just that, on balance, I cannot avoid the conclusion that he is a great man.'*

That greatness could be seen and felt in Henry Kissinger's personal charisma. He could also employ a ready wit on occasion: Alistair Horne quotes a waspish reply he sent during a spat with Washington's Soviet Ambassador Dobrynin, telling him to '*...hold his water or I will send him to Siberia – I know Brezhnev better than he does. Ask him if he's ever been kissed on the mouth by Brezhnev as I have...?'*

ALEXEI KOSYGIN

By his early thirties Alexei Kosygin was one of the youngest ministers in Stalin's government. With a growing reputation as a very good economist he was also seen as what today we might call a workaholic. Stalin, who by this time was over sixty, certainly liked and respected Kosygin a great deal and put him in charge of Russia's imports and exports. Whilst Stalin is portrayed as a monster, it has to be remembered that the individuals he brought into his government were all comparatively young, most of them all under forty. Given what else we know about him he might well have regarded young people as a particular threat, ambitious and eager to depose him. Instead, he promoted them and Kosygin was one of his favourites; precise, meticulous, analytical and industrious, very clear in his goals, how he expressed them and how he was going to achieve them.

What gave Joseph Stalin, the feared and by all accounts paranoid dictator, such faith in this extremely competent if rather unassuming young man? The answer can perhaps be found in one word: Leningrad. In 1904, the year Kosygin was born, it was St Petersburg, the magnificent city built by Peter the Great. Baptised at the St. Sampsonievsky Cathedral, Alexei grew up in a Tsarist Russia that was still to a large extent a society of serfs and landowners, its vast inequalities justified by the Orthodox Church as God's preordained pattern: '*The rich man in his castle the poor man at the gate, he made them high and lowly and ordered their estate,*' to borrow from the English hymn. There had been new ideas and anarchists and revolutionaries and bombs thrown, but the age-old feudal system remained the norm throughout much of the country. The 1905 Revolution brought limited reforms and a gesture towards democracy in the form of the State Duma, or parliament. There had also been the growth of a new middle class, to which Alexei's father as a skilled factory worker in effect belonged. Alexei's mother died when he was young, but his father was able to provide him and his siblings with a reasonable education in St. Petersburg.

In the civil war that followed the 1917 revolution the young Kosygin was conscripted into Trotsky's Labour Army and after entering the Communist Party in 1921, four years later graduated from the School of Commerce in St Petersburg, now named Petrograd. For the next three years he engaged in co-operative enterprise, mining for Siberian gold in partnership with a British company. Family affairs then brought him back to his home city, now renamed Leningrad. Here Kosygin studied textile engineering for the next five years. Fellow students recalled his amazing ability with figures and for making complex calculations in his head. It was a talent that would help both him and his fellow citizens in the monumental test of fate about to be unleashed upon them. Kosygin's managerial skills had already been recognised by his appointment to Leningrad's Chair of Industry, and at the age of thirty-four he became the city's youngest ever mayor. Stalin, hearing good reports, in January 1939 summoned him to Moscow to join the central government.

In November 1939, Stalin shook hands with Germany's foreign minister Jaochim von Ribbentrop to seal the non-aggression pact negotiated by Molotov. Within two years of the handshake Hitler had ordered an attack on Soviet territory in Eastern Poland, and German troops were marching towards Leningrad. Germany's allies the Finns were meanwhile drawing in from the north and the complete encirclement of the city was imminent. Russian troops and civilians fought a courageous defence and managed to hold off the enemy, but cut off from the outside world and with dwindling supplies how long could they last? As winter arrived starvation set in. Those with strength to find and kill rats ate them gladly, or peeled off wallpaper to lick the fish-oil glue. For some, cannibalism, a resort they thought they would never come to, was keeping them alive. In a poignant and stirring gesture of human solidarity a group of feeble and emaciated musicians assembled to play the premiere of Shostakovich's 7th Symphony. The music, relayed around the city by loudspeakers, may have provided spiritual succour but the enemy had not gone away, and it seemed that Leningrad and its inhabitants were ultimately doomed. According to folklore Hitler had already printed invitations to a victory party in the city's Astoria Hotel.

If that were true he had not reckoned on the strategic brilliance of one man: Alexei Kosygin. With all roads in and out of Leningrad sealed off by the enemy Kosygin decided on an alternative route: Lake Ladoga. Using the freezing weather to his advantage Kosygyn, working under heavy bombardment from land and air organised makeshift roads to take truckloads of food, fuel and ammunition across the thick ice covering the lake. On their return the trucks were filled with people. At the same time underwater pipes and cables were laid to carry electricity and fresh water to the beleaguered citizens. As well as preventing Leningrad from being overrun this 'Road of Life' would successfully evacuate over one and half million workers in key industries vital to the country's overall defence. Most of these people would probably have died otherwise, along with an estimated one million of their fellow inhabitants.

Including the men, women and children found clinging to life inside

Women flee Leningrad with the aid of Alexei Kosygin and his 'Road of Life'

the city at the end of the 900-day siege, Kosygin's master plan had saved around two million people from starvation or extermination. The survival of Leningrad was also the first failure of the enemy offensive and a great boost to Soviet morale. It proved the Nazis were not unstoppable and when they tried to take Moscow it was the Russian winter and her people's determination that would teach them that lesson a second time. For his outstanding achievement at Leningrad Kosygin was awarded the Red Star and made a Premier of the Russian Federation.

Photograph of the Soviet leader Alexei Kosygin and the Finnish president Urho Kekkonen giving autographs to two young Finns in 1966

More important was the enduring respect that Kosygin had earned, and it was a legacy I was well aware of when, during one of the big Politburo meetings towards the end of the 1970s I had my first brief conversation with him. The second occasion followed soon after. The Chairman of the Committee of Youth Organisations, Gennady Yanayev (later Vice-President under Gorbachev), myself and another colleague were in the planning stage for Soviet participation in the 11th World Festival of Youth and Students due to take place in Cuba. A key priority was financing the project, and for this we thought we might hold a Subbotnik – a Saturday workday – whereby workers throughout the country would donate whatever they earned on the agreed date towards the cost of transportation, accommodation and other necessities. We were hoping to encourage several thousand young people in Russia to attend the festival, as well as their peers in other countries.

As it was a big world we had divided up the responsibilities, with Yanayev liaising with the capitalist countries while my other colleague and myself looked after the Soviet Union and the other socialist states. We had agreed that to travel to Cuba by air would cost a huge amount in flights and be complex logistically. Instead we planned to go by sea, setting out from Odessa and picking up people from Europe on the way to the Straits of Gibraltar, thence steaming across the Atlantic to Cuba.

This was a difficult time for Kosygin. The historical consensus now is that from the 1960s Brezhnev and Kosygin had been engaged in a power struggle within the Kremlim, which by the mid 1970s Brezhnev had more or less won. While Kosygin remained an important figure, his health had not been good recently, and after suffering a heart attack in 1976 he had according to some observers become dispirited, and there were rumours of his imminent retirement. Knowing a little about Kosygin's situation I wondered what sort of reception he would give us. Knocking on the door of his office we were asked to come in. Kosygin got up immediately and came around from his desk to greet us. He asked would we like some tea or coffee. We thanked him and the beverages were brought in. Kosygin was quite amiable and asked if we liked jokes and anecdotes. When we nodded he asked if we had a good one. I told him the story of the priest who is visiting one of his neighbours. The neighbour offers him a choice tea or coffee, to which the priest replies, '*Yes vodka please.*' Kosygin laughed and said, '*If I give you vodka I'll get kicked out of the Party!*'

Vagif Guseynov with Alexei Kosygin

With the ice now broken he asked to hear about our request. We told him we were arranging for Soviet youth and people from other countries to attend the festival in Cuba and that we would like as many to go as a possible. We made it clear at the outset that we had not come to ask for money from the government but to appeal to Russian workers to hold a Subbotnik in order to raise funds. Kosygin nodded and asked a few more questions. He then picked up the telephone and asked to speak to Brezhnev. He explained our idea and said he thought it was a good one and asked Brezhnev what he thought. From the conversation it was clear that Brezhnev was all in favour, and told Kosygin jokingly that we were not to drink the proceeds. Kosygin put down the phone and signed a declaration there and then that $400,000 – the rouble wasn't worth very much – should be earmarked from a Subbuotnik to pay for a vessel and other expenses. He was very interested and said he would put us in touch with the Soviet shipping department to discuss booking a suitable vessel.

All three of us were very surprised that the two people at the top of the Russian government had given us a decision on a youth project on the spot. We had been expecting to wait possibly for days, be summoned to further meetings and provide all sorts of detailed information in advance. In the following days Kosygin continued to show great interest in the festival plans and was very democratic in discussing all the ideas and problems and going over the arrangements with us. Though obviously no longer a young man himself, he seemed fully engaged with the thoughts and concerns of young people, their hopes and expectations. At the festival I was in touch with Kosygin via telegrams to Moscow about the Ortega brothers, who were keen to visit the Soviet Union. Kosygin was extremely efficient and when he sent his permission along with specific dates the Ortegas were most impressed. They also thought I must be a very important person to be in direct contact with Kosygin, which also said a lot about his reputation outside of Russia.

Throughout the siege of Leningrad Kosygin's plans and the ways in which he implemented them had been immensely clever, and his commitment to the people and the needs of his country unquestionable. When it came to managing situations in peacetime he displayed the same calm and rational executive ability, and a precision and doggedness in seeing the job through. Reading the various accounts of Kosygin the descriptions that recur most often refer to his strengths as an administrator, his organisational skill and capacity for sheer hard work.

There seems also to have been a strong streak of individuality or knowing his own mind at least; one anonymous assessment, believed to be that of a colleague reads: '*He always had an opinion of his own, and defended it. He was a very alert man, and performed brilliantly during negotiations. He was able to cope quickly with the material that was totally new to him. I have never seen people of that calibre afterwards.*' (Amin Sakhal, *Modern Afghanistan: a History of Struggle and Survival*, 2006)

The rivalry between Kosygin and Brezhnev is well documented. There were differences over policy including the intervention in Czechoslovakia in 1968, which Kosygin at first opposed then supported, leaving Brezhnev as the sole dissenting voice in the Politburo. Kosygin also strove with some success to supplant Brezhnev as the Soviet Union's representative overseas. After the 1962 Cuban Missile Crisis, regarded as the downfall of Khrushchev, Kosygin had stepped into his shoes as Chairman of the Council of Ministers, becoming in effect Soviet Prime Minister and attempting to rebuild diplomatic relations with the United States. In 1965 he was in Hanoi meeting the North Vietnamese and promising them Soviet military aid, and then, following a seventeen-day war between India and Pakistan over the territories of Jammu and Kashmir, under the auspices of the United Nations, he invited Indian Prime Minister Lal Bahadur Shashtri and Pakistan's Ayub Khan to Tashkent in Uzbekistan for peace talks. In the resultant Tashkent Declaration of 1966 both sides agreed to withdraw their troops to pre-conflict positions and enter negotiations concerning economic and refugee issues. While Tashkent was seen a success by outsiders, Indians criticised the lack of a 'no-war' clause, while in Pakistan disappointment at the absence of a national victory led to considerable unrest.

The following February Kosygin paid an official visit to Britain and met with Prime Minister Harold Wilson, who was keen find an end to the war in Vietnam. The conflict was going badly for the US both militarily and politically, and continued Soviet support for the North meant that any diplomatic solution was largely in the hands of the two superpowers. In June 1967 however, an additional crisis broke out on the world stage in the shape of a direct confrontation between the Arabs and Israelis. With the memory of the Cuban Missile Crisis still fresh in everyone's minds, both the Kremlin and the White House held back:

'Both U.S. President Lyndon B. Johnson and Premier Alexei Kosygin of the USSR pledged not to intervene. But the Middle Eastern political temperature continued to rise in spite of the superpowers' restraint, and the Six-Day War began on June 5th.' (Sherada C. Rempe Rowan Magazine Summer 1997)

Alexei Kosygin USSR Council of Ministers Chairman (right) and Harold Wilson Great Britain's Prime Minister, 1967

On June 10th Kosygin, in typically succinct style wrote a 'hot-line' letter to the White House:

> *'Dear Mr. President: The events of the last days have forced me to express to you with all frankness our view. As the situation shows, the resolutions of the Security Council are invalid. Israel has completely ignored them. As you can understand, after the many attempts taken in this direction and the resolutions of the Security Council concerning the termination of aggression on the part of Israel in the Near East –these attempts have proved ineffective.*
>
> *A very crucial moment has now arrived which forces us, if military*

actions are not stopped in the next few hours, to adopt an independent decision. We are ready to do this. However, these actions may bring us into a clash, which will lead to a grave catastrophe. Obviously in the world there are powers to whom this would be advantageous.

We purpose that you demand from Israel that it unconditionally cease military action in the next few hours. On our part, we will do the same. We purpose to warn Israel that, if this is not fulfilled, necessary actions will be taken, including military.

Please give me your views.

A Kosygin'

The next day, after the loss of an estimated 20,000 Arabs and 1,000 Israelis, and a considerable expansion of the territory under Israel's control, a ceasefire was signed. The fear now was that the Israelis would either try to press home their advantage or that the Arabs would seek retaliation, in short that the conflict could re-ignite at any time. Would Russian military assistance now be sent to bolster the Arabs against any further possible incursion? The perception in America was not: '*The Soviets were still unwilling to engage their troops directly by backing the Arab states, but on June 19th, Kosygin came to New York to condemn Israel and the U.S. in a special session of the U.N. General Assembly.*' (Ibid)

It might seem obvious that Kosygin and President Johnson would now sit down and talk face to face about both the Arab-Israeli situation and Vietnam. Apparently though this was not so easy: '*Kosygin was under strict orders not to go to Washington, and Johnson felt it was not customary for a president to receive visitors in New York. A compromise, negotiated by then New Jersey Governor Richard J. Hughes, was to meet halfway between in Glassboro.*' (Ibid)

Others allege that Johnson was reluctant to go to New York for fear of encountering anti-Vietnam war protestors. The university campus of Glassboro in New Jersey would therefore provide the backdrop for an intense three-day summit with Kosygin:

Soviet Premier Aleksei Kosygin and President Lyndon Johnson during the Glassboro Summit Conference, 23 June 1967

> *'Suddenly, with only 16 hours notice, the official residence of Glassboro State President Thomas Robinson and his wife Margaret had to be converted from a quiet campus home into a secure and sophisticated location for an international press corps, secret service agents and the world's two most powerful leaders. Prayers and hopes from around the globe were focused on Hollybush during those meetings June 23rd and 25th.'* (Ibid)

Those hopes and prayers were answered in the sense that direct military confrontation between America and the Soviet Union remained off the agenda. The commitment to peace, striven for since the Cuban Missile Crisis, remained strong, and might now be built upon in the 'Spirit of Glassboro' – a reference to the amicable tone of the impromptu summit. Meanwhile the peace in the Near East would remain tense and sporadic, while the war in the Far East, pursued actively on the one side by the US, supported on the other by the Soviets, continued.

On the covers of 'Life' and 'Time'

On his visit to Britain Kosygin had been referred to in the media as the Prime Minister, while his meeting with Johnson had put him on the cover of *Life* magazine. To the world he was often perceived as Soviet leader, the number one man in Soviet affairs. Back home it seemed that Brezhnev held the balance if not most of the power. Some say that Kosygin consistently declined to socialise with Brezhnev, in particular that he would never deign to take a drink with him. For Brezhnev, who liked to live it up a little this reticence may well have felt like a snub. Kosygin's abilities, however, were such that Brezhnev was reportedly reluctant to lose him from the government. Furthermore, Kosygin remained popular with the public, fuelling rumours of jealousy on Brezhnev's part.

Much garlanded throughout his lifetime, receiving no less than six Orders of Lenin and numerous other official awards, in 1982, two years after his death, Kosygin was immortalised with a bust in the centre of Leningrad. If it had not been for his Road to Life that had rescued so many people, including vital workers, from the besieging Nazi and Finnish troops, the city would almost certainly have fallen, and with it conceivably the whole of Russia. His immortalisation in 2006 with the naming of Moscow's Kosygin Street seems the very least tribute owed by the Russian people.

VLADIMIR ALEKSANDROVICH KRYUCHKOV

It is easy and at the same time difficult to write about Vladimir Aleksandrovich Kryuchkov. Easy because I have known him a long time, ever since the 1970s, when I was First Secretary of the Central Committee of the Komsomol (All-Union Leninist Young Communist League) of Azerbaijan. Kryuchkov, who was eighteen years my senior, had begun his own career with Komsomol before going on to take a law degree. In 1967 he had joined the KGB under its new chief, Andropov, who was to nurture his career. Around the time I first met him he was Chief of the KGB's First Main Directorate, the department responsible for overseas surveillance – spying.

Between 1980 and 1983, when I was First Secretary of the Baku City Committee of the Communist Party of Azerbaijan, Kryuchkov came to visit the city. Then in 1989, on the instructions of the leadership of Azerbaijan I was moved from the position of Deputy Head of the Department for Organisation Work and Personnel, Central Committee of the Communist Party of Azerbaijan, to that of Chairman of the Azerbaijan Committee for State Security – the KGB – a post I would occupy until 1991. Meanwhile Gorbachev had come to power, and in 1988 had appointed Kryuchkov overall head of the KGB. Thus he and I were to meet again on a number of occasions to discuss issues of security, my own particular concern at that time being my country's war with Armenia over the disputed territories of Nagorno-Karabakh.

The broader picture for the Soviet Union was not looking good. Since assuming office in 1985, Gorbachev had pushed ahead with his much-

publicised plans for *glasnost* and *perestroika* – openness and restructuring. But while the new leader bandied these slogans airily, by 1990 corruption and illicit exports were causing widespread shortages of food and medicines. Inflation had reached 300 per cent on an annualised basis, with stocks of vital heating fuel running drastically low. Meanwhile the forces of nationalism and ethnic tensions, evident in the fighting over Nagorno-Karabakh, and in South Ossetia were spreading. Armenia, a Soviet republic, had already declared itself independent of the Soviet Union, as had Georgia and Estonia, Lithuania and Latvia, having also unilaterally broken away, were internally divided and politically unstable.

Lending legitimacy to nationalist causes, the Declaration of State

Sovereignty of the Russian Soviet Federation of Socialist Republics, signed on 12 June 1990 by Boris Yeltsin, Chairman of the Presidium of the Supreme Soviet of the Russian SFSR, included a formal recognition of the 'need to significantly expand the rights of the autonomous republics, regions, districts, territories of Russia.'

In an attempt to gain legitimacy, impose some kind of order on the chaos, or both, Gorbachev had arranged that on the 17 March 1991 a referendum – the first ever such event in the country's history – would be held throughout the Soviet Union. It asked the following question: *'Do you consider necessary the preservation of the Union of Soviet Socialist Republics as a renewed federation of equal sovereign republics in which the rights and freedom of an individual of any nationality will be fully guaranteed?'*

Almost 150 million citizens voted, amounting to a turnout of around eighty per cent. The governments of Latvia, Lithuania, Georgia, Moldova, Armenia and Estonia boycotted the referendum, however in the remaining nine republics the vote was over seventy per cent in favour of maintaining the Soviet Union.

The results appeared to give a clear message of grass roots support for the political status quo. The boycott by the six republics strongly suggested that those in charge of these states were seeking nationalist power in their own right, and did not want to risk hearing what their own people might prefer. To many of the nomenklatura throughout the Soviet Union – what one might define as the Soviet establishment, the traditional bureaucrats and officials – the situation the country and the republics had slid into since Gorbachev's succession seemed not so much restructuring as the abandonment of any kind of structure, a kind of anarchy in short. Kryuchkov, as we know, though originally supportive of Gorbachev, had for some time now been warning of imminent catastrophe.

He was not the only one. On 23 July 1991, A *Word to the People*, an article published in the conservative, anti-perestroika newspaper *Sovetskya Rosiya*, claimed that *'An enormous, unforeseen calamity has taken place...Motherland, our land, a great power, given to us to ward with the nature, glorious ancestors, it is perishing, breaking apart, falling into darkness and non-being. And this collapse takes place at our silence, toleration and accord.'*

The article, signed by a group of Soviet writers and politicians, was a moving appeal to the Russian people to save their cherished homeland from further and irreversible devastation, leaving a wreckage from which opportunists would divide the spoils: '*Let us unite, so as to stop the chain reaction of the disastrous collapse of the state, economy, human personality; in order to contribute to the strengthening of the Soviet power, to the transformation of it into a genuinely people's power, and not some manger for the hungry nouveau riche who are ready to sell off everything for the sake of their insatiable appetite.*'

Among the signatories to *A Word to the People* were Valentin Varennikov, Vasily Starodubstev and Alexander Tizyakov, who a few weeks later would be a part of the attempted coup.

The events of those three days in August 1991 were broadcast extensively at the time. The discussions since have focused on interpretation, and speculation about how things may perhaps have turned out differently, if say this or that course of action had been taken. With the benefit of hindsight, some believe that if the coup's leaders had also detained Yeltsin then their plans might have succeeded. Certainly if Yeltsin had been unable to seize the opportunity to climb aboard the tank outside the White House and deliver his speech on the morning of the 19th, urging the Soviet soldiers not to turn on their own people, things might well have progressed a lot further.

The capitulation of the plotters was not immediate however. In response to leaflets circulated quickly around the city, Moscow residents began to congregate around the White House, building makeshift barricades. In response to this resistance, at 4pm Yaneyev declared a state of emergency throughout Moscow. An hour later, in a statement to the press he announced that Gorbachev, who was being held under house arrest on the Black Sea, was 'resting' as he was 'very tired and needs some time to get his health back.'

For the next few hours the standoff continued and a night curfew was

Defenders of democracy on top of a tank deployed in Moscow, 19 August 1991

imposed. On the afternoon of the following day it was Kryuchkov, along with Pugo and Yazov that made the decision to enter the White House by force if necessary. At the same time they were hesitant. The crowd, largely unarmed, nevertheless seemed resolute, and sensing the mood the coup leaders were reluctant to inflict casualties. When later that day a skirmish with a military vehicle resulted in the death of three members of the public, however, it was agreed that Kryuchkov, Yazov and four others should go and speak with Gorbachev. When they arrived in the Crimea Gorbachev declined to see them. The coup was over, and within a few days all the conspirators had been apprehended, save for Pugo, who committed suicide with his wife. The KGB was quick to distance itself from Kryuchkov, declaring at a specially convened meeting that the other officials of the organisation had '*nothing to do with these anti-constitutional actions. They feel deeply upset by the fact that their honor was besmirched...*' (*After the Coup – New York Times*, 23 August 1991)

Considering a second 'if' in the story – if the storming of the White House had not been aborted – Kryuchkov stated at his trial that '*We did not want to spill blood to achieve our objectives.*' Had they gone ahead and done so, and gone on to form a new government, would its credibility have lasted or would it have been already dead in the water? Pending such speculations Kryuchkov and his co-conspirators were charged with high treason, a crime punishable by death. Having been in a similar position myself – not on a treason charge and through no fault of my own – I know how that feels. Kryuchkov, who had been head of the Soviet KGB, one of the most powerful men in the country, was now reduced to the status of a criminal, at the mercy of his fellow Russians:

> *'...in court Kryuchkov cut a forlorn figure. Bombast gave way to hesitancy under cross-examination, punctuated with frequent sips of water. He was nearly 70, and a lamp had to be brought into the courtroom so that he could read his notes, and he appeared to have difficulty hearing the prosecutors'*

Former Chairman of the Soviet KGB Vladimir Kryuchkov exits the courtroom after the GKChP trial

questions. Beset by procedural wrangles, the trial ended with the plotters being pardoned and freed.' (*Daily Telegraph*, 27th November 2007)

Though an active player in the events that had taken him to this juncture, Kryuchkov was, arguably, motivated by what he thought was right. As with other great Soviet figures we have looked at, he had lived through the Great Patriotic War, during which much of his home city of Stalingrad was pounded to rubble, throughout months of attack by the Nazis. Such events leave an impression. His parents were also staunch admirers of Stalin. Everyone is shaped to a greater or lesser extent by their background, by their experiences. As Andropov's protégé, he worked as an aide to the latter at the time of the Hungarian uprising, when the Budapest police officials were being strung up on lampposts within sight of the Soviet Embassy. Having been close to such shocking events, which among us would not be fearful of the hysteria and mob rule that can be fuelled by virulent nationalism?

In the many books published in Russia and other countries about the KGB, and in the memoirs of former intelligence officers, politicians and colleagues, almost all of the authors have paid tribute to Kryuchkov, praising his professionalism. While many might take issue with his actions most, nonetheless, give due credit to his qualities.

Such tributes might seem greatly at odds with Kryuchkov's standing in Russia in the years after 1991. He may have escaped execution, but the moral condemnation directed at him was severe. He remains notorious for his role in the State Committee on the State of Emergency – that group of eight high-ranking Soviet officials that orchestrated the attempted takeover. In the public domain he is described as the leader of this group, the driving force of the putsch. Many of Kryuchkov's colleagues in the Secret Services, young people and veterans, the party and the economic elite of the country berated him mercilessly for putting the state and the authorities under attack. As leader of the Soviet Union's KGB at the time, it seemed like the ultimate betrayal of his country. Indeed, the whole episode, regarded as

Vladimir Kryuchkov former chairman of the State Security Committee KGB (left) attends meeting in connection with Soviet Army Day

being instigated by Kryuchkov, was seen as the reason for the Soviet Union collapsing. He was not forgiven for that. After being released from prison at Matrosskaya Tishina, for a long time he stayed at home, forgotten by many of his former friends and colleagues, consigned almost to oblivion.

In the year 2000 I became Director of the Institute of Strategic Studies and Analysis. Two months after I had moved to Moscow to take up this position, I invited Kryuchkov to come and work in the organisation. Why did I do this? Because I felt he had a great deal to offer in terms of character, understanding and experience. Also I believe the 1991 coup attempt was widely misunderstood. It was precisely because Kryuchkov was so concerned about the chaos Gorbachev was sleepwalking into, and how the country was going to fragment and suffer as a result, that he did what he did.

With the collapse of the Soviet Union, the negative elements and forces that had been contained in the interests of public safety, harmony and wellbeing would be allowed an increasingly free rein. Concurrent with the development of new economic structures and methods, private ownership and entrepreneurship, the social and spiritual atmosphere throughout Russia began to worsen. Neither could Yeltinism offer any coherent substitute for a socialist system, no comparable moral ideology. On the contrary, the 'wild' 1990s have entered modern history as among the bloodiest and most terrible years that Russia has experienced – gang violence, high mortality, uncontrolled riots, bribery and prostitution, war in the Caucuses and more. Looking back now at this not so distant past, it is hard to believe that my friends, my colleagues and I were able to survive those horrendous and difficult days, that we managed to keep our families and our comrades safe, and to find strength to withstand such testing times.

Russia had become a place where individualism was given licence to run rampant – get what you can while you have the chance and don't worry about the country or other people. When Valentin Yumasheva and Tatyana Yeltsin – Boris Yeltsin's daughter and advisor – proposed Vladimir Putin as presidential successor, they thought least of all about Russia, but more about themselves. Remember, when it was suggested to Yeltsin to look more closely at Vladimir Putin, the response was: *'He did not betray Sobchak, he won't betray us either!'* The cause of Sobchak's sudden death has never been fully ascertained. A week, as someone once said, is a long time in politics and a lot can change in that time. For the much-reviled Kryuchkov, however, public forgiveness took considerably longer. After Putin became president he began to invite Kryuchkov to state functions. For his part, Kryuchkov praised Putin, warned of Western plots against Russia, and the dangers of in-fighting in his profession:

> *'By the end Kryuchkov had become something of an elder statesman of the intelligence community, warning that feuding within its ranks could lead to "big trouble", of which Russia's adversaries would be the beneficiary. The*

admonition came in an open letter to the newspaper Zavtra ("Tomorrow") less than a month before he died, after agents from the Federal Security Service, the KGB's successor, arrested officers from the anti-drugs service, allegedly for corruption and abuse of office. The quarrel, he said, would only weaken national unity. "Trust out experience," wrote Kryuchkov. He had seen his country disintegrate once, and had no intention of witnessing a repeat.'

(*Independent*, 26 November 2007)

In planning, and then withholding the storming of the White House in August 1991, Kryuchkov and his comrades changed the course of history in some way, but exactly how and by what degree it is hard to judge. These are the difficulties in writing about Kryuchkov. His critics on either side might accuse him of cold feet that day, but perhaps we should view his standing down more fairly, as genuine moral restraint. Perhaps the image of a ruthless

Vladimir Kryuchkov chairman of the USSR State Security Committee speaking at a session of the USSR Supreme Soviet

party official was undeserved. His demeanour certainly seemed to suggest a kinder sort of man:

> *'Kryuchkov's reputation as a hardline ideologue was at odds with his self-effacing personal manner. The KGB's spymaster was an avuncular, balding figure, inclined to chubbiness, with thick spectacles and a wry grin. Latterly he shed his army rank of general in favour of an anonymous civilian suit and preferred to be known as plain "Mr".'*
>
> (*Daily Telegraph*, 27 November 2007)

Another well-known saying is that a prophet is never honoured in his own time, or his own country. Kryuchkov's prophesy in 1991 was one of doom if the Soviet Union abandoned its ideals, and he acted to try to avert that fate. As we have seen, he was certainly not honoured for his prophesy, quite the reverse. Here again however, as the years go by one can discern a change in attitude, not only in the higher echelons of government, but among the people:

> *'Kryuchkov...benefited from the passing of time, from the disillusionment of many citizens with Yeltsin's Russia, and from nostalgia for the Soviet Union. When the most reliable Russian survey organisation, the Levada Centre, last year conducted a poll on the 15th anniversary of the attempted coup, only 12 per cent of Russian citizens said they would now support resistance to Kryuchkov's committee for the state of emergency, 13 per cent would support their attempt to take power, while the vast majority either refused to take sides or were "don't knows".'*
>
> (Archie Brown, *Guardian*, 30 November 2007)

Looking at these findings, on the question on whether Kryuchkov and his comrades were doing the right thing in August 1991 the jury seems at the very least undecided. As with so many of history's turning points, a lot of

KGB Chairman Vladimir Kryuchkov visiting Vagif Guseynov's family

people will reach the conclusions that suit them. In my view, Kryuchkov only wanted what was best for all Soviet people. For that he should be thanked. Here is his kind letter to our family, which we will always treasure:

To Khabiba, and Vagif Aliofsat!
With greatest respect I am Wishing you health, success on every life avenue and all of your beginnings, wishing you piece in your heart and happiness to you and your family, especially RENA.

I would like to highlight yet again that you inspire me and my family and give me support during our endless discussions and conversations and sometimes disagreements about life and life problems, which unfortunately do not diminish in sizes .

31 August 2004

V. Kryuchkov

ALEXEI LEONOV

In honour of Yuri Gagarin, the day of his momentous space flight was declared a national holiday throughout the Soviet Union. Each year on 12th April it became the tradition for people to gather together in Red Square and lay flowers on the Kremlin wall, where in 1968 Gagarin had been laid to rest. On this moving occasion there has always been a large contingent of the younger generation present. From Stalin's time citizens were encouraged to take an interest in aviation. Local Komsomol organisations in towns and cities across the Soviet Union, providing a network of advice and moral support for young people would often suggest that they join their nearest aeronautical club or air cadet unit. Some would then go on to a career in the Soviet Air Force, making a valuable contribution to this crucial arm of defence for their country. This was the path Gagarin had taken, and the era of the cosmonauts was born.

Gagarin being a national icon and a unique role model, he and the leader of Komsomol at the time, Sergei Pavlov, had agreed that it would be a wonderful idea to set up formal ties between the youth organisation and the cosmonaut community. Young people from all over the Soviet Union could attend talks and demonstrations on space travel, socialise and share their enthusiasm for the subject, and most inspiring of all meet their cosmonaut heroes. From 1963 there was a Soviet heroine and role model for women too: Valentina Tereshkova, who that year had spent three days in space while orbiting the Earth forty-eight times. Two years later another amazing first was achieved, and again it was a Soviet cosmonaut that had made it into the history books: on 18th March 1965, Alexei Arkhipovich Leonov became the first person to walk in space.

It was thanks to Yuri Gagarin and Sergei Pavlov establishing the close relationship between Komsomol and the cosmonauts, that I had the

opportunity to meet Leonov at one of the joint conferences. I found him to be a warm, sociable, humorous and highly intelligent man. Although obviously used to intense discipline of mind and body, he was by no means averse to a drink or two, and loved to socialise. I had of course read about his exploits, but the more one learned about precisely what had happened to him up there in space, the more one realised that it took a very special kind of person to survive such an experience and come back smiling.

Leonov, born in Siberia in 1934, was three years old when during Stalin's purge his father was imprisoned without trial and the family's name tarnished among the local community. At school Alexei displayed a prodigious talent for art, but instead chose aviation as a career. After qualifying as a fighter pilot he became one of the twenty Soviet Space Programme cosmonauts including Gagarin that were short-listed for *Vostok 1*.

At the time there were few if any reliable predictions about the effects space travel might have on the human body. Laika the dog had never returned. Cosmonaut training focused on extreme conditions: '*You needed to be physically fit,*' recalled Leonov. '*Every day I ran a minimum of 5km and swam 700m.*' To familiarise them with conditions in space, candidates were placed in darkened cabinets where they were unable to see or hear and spun around to produce the sensations caused by G-forces in space, several men fainting in the process. The high level of oxygen used in the locked cabinet made it highly combustible however, and when trainee Valentin Bondarenko spilled some cotton wool laced with alcohol he suffered fatal burns, prompting the scientists to henceforth use normal air.

Following Gargarin's successful manned flight, the Soviet Space Programme's chief coordinator Sergei Korolev was ready to take things to the next level. At the OKB-1 space design centre in Moscow, a group of cosmonauts was summoned to take a look at the programme's latest creation. It looked very much like the craft Gagarin had flown in, apart from one thing: a protruding tube that measured about 3 metres. Korolev explained that the plan was for a cosmonaut, breathing through the tube, to exit the capsule. '*A sailor must be able to swim in the sea. Likewise, a cosmonaut must be able to swim in outer space.*' *Singling out Leonov he commanded, 'You, little eagle, put on that suit.*' Leonov was given two hours to rehearse the manoeuvre and then to deliver his observations to Korolev. '*My heart started thumping,'* Leonov remembered, *'How would I do the report?'* When it was over Leonov presented his feedback and waited outside the room. Gagarin came to give him the news: *'I think they have selected you. You will be in charge of the space walk.'*

Preparations for the mission got underway. Leonov would not be going alone, and at his request the capsule was to be commanded by his friend Pavel Belyayev. Ten years senior to Leonev, Belyayev had fought bravely as a fighter pilot against the Japanese. Whilst Leonov was officially the navigator, in case of eventualities he and Belyayev practiced each other's roles exhaustively, including the space walk. As part of the training they looped the loop in an aircraft, which replicated the experience of weightlessness for a quarter of a minute on each circuit. With an American attempt at a space walk known to be imminent there was pressure to launch as soon as practically possible, and the date was set for the 18 March 1965. On the day, Yuri Gagarin was there to see his two comrades off. After Leonov and

Meeting of the leaders of Komsomol Youth Organisation of Azerbaijan with Leonov in Baku, 1977

Belyayev had been through their medical inspections, Gagarin gave them each a sip of champagne and resealed the bottle to save for their return. By 7am they were heading into the sky.

Once the spacecraft had completed an orbit of the Earth it was time for Leonov to begin the manoeuvre he had rehearsed so many times on terra firma, a journey of just a few metres, yet now so very different. The first move was into an airlock attached to the capsule, where he closed the hatch behind him. Belyayev then had to operate a mechanism to adjust the pressure in the airlock till it matched the zero pressure outside in space. Failure to do so properly could result in decompression sickness, what deep-sea divers coming up too quickly have traditionally referred to as the 'bends'. When Belyayev gave him the signal, Leonov opened the hatch and stepped out. A crucial unknown factor was whether the spacesuit would withstand conditions outside the capsule. So far there were no noticeable ill effects.

Back on Earth people would be able to see something of what Leonov experienced, as a film camera had been attached to the outside of the capsule. His own impressions were of the overwhelming magnitude and emptiness of his surroundings, and of his insignificance within it: '*You just can't comprehend it. Only out there can you feel the greatness – the huge size of all that surrounds us.... My feeling was that I was a grain of sand...it was so quiet I could even hear my heart beat. I was surrounded by stars and was floating without much control. I will never forget the moment. I also felt an incredible sense of responsibility.*'

To begin with Leonov stayed close to the craft. Connected by a cord designed to prevent him drifting further than five metres, it was now time for him to attempt actually walking in space. As he pushed himself off from the spacecraft, his body began to spin but the cord did its job and steadied him. After ten minutes he was instructed to return inside. '*I did not know that I was about to experience the most difficult moments of my life.*' For it was then that Leonov noticed that something untoward was occurring: '*My suit was becoming deformed, my hands had slipped out of the gloves, my feet came out of the boots. The suit felt loose around my body. I had to do something. I couldn't pull myself back using the cord. And what's more with this misshapen suit it would be impossible to fit through the airlock.'* To complete the nightmare, the spacecraft was in the process of hurtling towards the Earth's shadow, meaning that within five minutes he would be in total darkness.

Leonov had no option but to try to deflate the suit by opening a valve to release half of the oxygen. It was a balancing act: losing too much would suffocate him, too little and he would remain out in space to die. As the oxygen slowly left the suit he felt the bends kicking in: *'I began to get pins and needles in my legs and hands. I was entering the danger zone, I knew this could be fatal.'* Making it back into the airlock compartment head first, was a huge physical feat by itself: now he had to turn around in the small space in order to secure the hatch, and the copious amount of sweat in his helmet was making it almost impossible to see what he was doing.

With the space walk completed the airlock compartment had now to be jettisoned, which promptly sent the spacecraft spinning. More worryingly the oxygen reading was going up, and with it the danger of combustion as experienced by Valentin Bondarenko during training. *'Fortunately the engines produced no sparks,'* said Leonov. *'A spark would have caused an explosion and we would have been vaporized.'* With a concerted effort Leonov and Belyayev managed to reduce the oxygen levels in the craft, and a few hours later made ready for the return journey. But then another crisis occurred: the automatic mechanism designed to fire rockets and take them back into the Earth's atmosphere had malfunctioned. The emergency procedure for this eventuality was to set off the rockets manually, an unprecedented action. The timing for the rockets was crucial: if they burned for too short a distance there was a strong possibility the craft could ricochet back into space, while too long would increase the angle and speed of descent and burn the craft up on re-entry. As they made their decision on when to push the button, both men now sat on the brink of a homecoming or oblivion.

It turned out be the former, but where was anyone's guess. The Soviet

Union being so immense gave hope that they would fall to Earth somewhere within its borders. '*We landed and opened the hatch,*' said Leonov. '*The air was cold, it rushed in. We set up our radio channel and began to broadcast... Only after seven hours did a monitoring station in West Germany report that they had heard the coded signal which I had sent.*' Even now there was danger. For the wolves and bears that roamed the Siberian forest during mating season, two unarmed men were easy prey. There seemed no immediate prospect of rescue. After several hours a civilian helicopter appeared but was unable to land. Other aircraft flew overhead dropping out clothing, one a bottle of cognac that broke on landing. After his exertions to re-enter the airlock Leonov's space suit contained litres of sweat. They knew that the temperature could easily plummet to minus 20°C during the night, and as darkness fell, concerned about frostbite both cosmonauts wrung out their spacesuits to get them as dry as possible.

Next morning Leonov woke to hear movement in the distance: '*They landed 9km away and came on skis. They made a little hut for us and brought us a big cauldron which we filled with water and put over a fire. Then we washed in it.*' The party had also brought skis for the cosmonauts, and advised them that the following day they should make their way to a clearing where a pickup was being arranged for them. From the clearing a helicopter took them to the city of Perm. '*When we flew out of there,*' said Leonov, '*the rescuers said they saw wolf tracks around the spacecraft. Wolves are very smart, they came to look at what had come down from the sky into their territory.*' The next stop was Baikonur, and there to meet them were Korolev and Gagarin.

In the debriefing Leonov was asked why he had not informed his superiors before releasing oxygen from his spacesuit. '*What would you have done if I'd told you?*' he replied. '*You would have created a commission. The commission would have selected a chairman, and the chairman would talk to me. I knew I only had 30 minutes left and I didn't want ground control to panic.*' Korolev, the man who had selected the 'little eagle' for the unprecedented mission replied simply: '*Alexei is right.*'

These five men compose the two prime crews of the joint US–USSR Apollo-Soyuz Test Project docking in Earth orbit mission. Thomas P. Stafford (standing on left), Alexei Leonov (standing right), Donald K. Slayton (seated left), Vance D. Brand (centre), Valeriy N. Kubasov (seated right)

In the eyes of the world Leonov and Bayayelv were heroes, but not until years later would the public be told the real extent of the danger they had faced, and about the life or death battle they had fought throughout the mission The courage and cool thinking of both cosmonauts under such intense pressure only makes their achievement even more admirable. According to Sergey S. Pozdnyakov, the general director of Zvezda, the firm that manufactures spacesuits for the cosmonauts, human reactions to such conditions are impossible to foresee with any accuracy: '*The main doubt was the psychological condition of the person who was in outer space. In the ship, you have walls, you have communications with Earth, you are protected. But to go into outer space… the stress is, in my opinion, so high, that to predict how a person will behave in this situation is impossible.'*

It must have come as a great shock to Leonov when, three years after his space walk, his friend and comrade Yuri Gagarin met his end in a routine test flight. As with Leonov's own story, it was only much later that a more detailed version of events could be revealed. Leonov himself was in a good position to do so, not only because he was a highly experienced pilot himself but he had also been near the site of the crash when it occurred: *'He had overseen parachute jump training at Chkavlovsky airfield, northeast of Moscow – from where Gagarin had set out. At this point in his career, Gagarin was Deputy Training Director of the Cosmonaut Training Centre and was starting out as a fighter pilot again (as he had been in 1960).'* (*Daily Mail*)

The report from an official enquiry at the time suggested that Gagarin's plane might have been struck by a bird or swerved to avoid a weather balloon. It was also mentioned he might have been flying at an inappropriate altitude due to out of date weather information from ground control. In June 2013, following the declassification of the report, Leonov was able to reveal what he believed really happened: *'The [original] conclusion is believable to a civilian, not to a professional – but in fact, everything went down differently. Leonev went on to say that an SU-15 fighter jet on an unauthorised flight came into close proximity to Gagarin's plane. This sent it into a spin that led to the crash. I know this because I was there; I heard the sound and talked to witnesses. While afterburning, the aircraft reduced its echelon [plane formation] at a distance of 10–15 metres in the clouds, passing close to Gagarin, turning his plane and thus sending it into a tailspin – a deep spiral, to be precise – at a speed of 750 kilometres per hour.'* Leonov also saw that his name had been added to the original enquiry without his knowledge.

None of this would turn back the clock and bring Gargarin back, but Leonov had clearly felt a comrade's duty to tell the world what he knew and thereby honour his friend. It was a matter of personal responsibility. And as regards his own achievements, perhaps Leonov's most pertinent comment on how it felt walking out into space for the first time was the reference to responsibility. With millions of roubles being spent to get a cosmonaut into space and more importantly everyone's expectations upon you, the option to call in sick or change your mind about the mission does not exist. It is a job of which only a handful are capable. Thinking about Leonov's harrowing time up there outside the capsule, I could well appreciate why he liked to take a drink, unwind and enjoy life. His fellow cosmonaut Georgy Grechko expressed it succinctly: '*If there are some people who think that what we did was primitive, not very interesting, not worthwhile – let them fly into space, go for a space walk and experience the air leaking from your suit, or a safety hatch refusing to shut. Then they will understand that our pride and happiness is deserved.*'

After such experiences just the everyday pleasures of being among family and friends, dining out and enjoying a joke or two must seem like the most exquisite pleasure. In short, a cosmonaut of Leonov's stature knows how to count his blessings. As well as sharing his knowledge and expertise tirelessly at conferences and exhibitions over the years, he has developed his boyhood talent for drawing and painting to become one of the finest space artists in the world.

My family and I are proud to count ourselves among Leonov's friends. As well as being a workaholic he is very highly educated, well rounded and extremely sociable and has a good sense of humour. Even as I write this he travels, an octogenarian, all over the world giving speeches. In May of 2015 he was a guest of honour at London's Science Museum, delivering a lecture hosted by the British Interplanetary Society for an exhibition entitled Cosmonauts: Birth of the Space Age. When I heard about it I just had to go along and say hello. He didn't expect me to be there – he had just had breakfast with journalists and was flying home that day. He was completely surprised. For me it was a marvellous treat just to see him and talk for a while. Thank you Alexei.

DANIEL ORTEGA

In the chapter on Fidel and Raul Castro and my meeting with them at the 1978 Festival of Youth and Students in Cuba, I mention at the end of that story another pair of brothers, Daniel and Humberto Ortega. Two guys in their early thirties, just a little younger than myself, the Ortegas liked to go out drinking, have a good time and enjoy themselves. But these were no ordinary Latino sybarites. Castro had introduced them to me at their request. They wanted to get a message to the Kremlin to see if they could pay a visit to Moscow and to send some of their young fellow countrymen to the Soviet Union to study. During the festival I had been dealing with hundreds of applications for overseas student places in Moscow, Baku and other Soviet cities. This one though was rather different.

Six months earlier in the Ortegas' home city of Managua, Pedro Joaquin Chamorro, editor of the left wing newspaper *La Prensa*, and outspoken critic of the Nicaraguan dictator General Somoza, had been shot dead at close range. While the unknown killers remained at large, Somoza had laid the blame on a Cuban-American businessman with a grudge against the victim's paper. Chamorro's family pointed the finger at Somoza. Thousands of Nicaraguans agreed with them. Workers staged a national strike and in the streets of Managua cars were burned and Somoza's properties stoned. Somoza's response was to impose martial law, and *La Prensa*'s offices were repeatedly shot at and firebombed. This is the year that Daniel and Humberto's brother Camilo will be killed while fighting for freedom in Masaya, Monimbo. Because of these disturbing events in their homeland the Ortega brothers were not in Cuba just to drink rum. Nicaragua was at war with its government and so were they. How had the country descended into such darkness?

Nicaragua's story was a familiar one throughout Latin America, having

close parallels to the Cuban experience, and with colonialism playing a large part. The Spanish language was just one legacy of Columbus' first visit in 1502. The lure of gold brought warring conquistadors, Christianity and new diseases. Large numbers of the indigenous population were forced into slave labour, and over the years as the Spanish invaders took local women as wives or concubines, a new racial group emerged, the 'mestizo'. In 1821, Nicaragua was for a decade subsumed within Mexico's empire before joining an alliance of neighbouring states until finally emerging as an independent state in 1838. With internal conflict between the progressively minded citizens of Leon and the more reactionary elements in Granada, it was agreed that Managua should be the capital of the new republic.

Enter now the USA in the person of William Walker. A buccaneering young doctor-cum military adventurer who, when civil war broke out between Leon and Granada in 1856, managed to get himself elected as President of Nicaragua. The incumbent lasted only a year and in 1860 the Hondurans executed him. Half a century later the American government launched a full-scale occupation of Nicaragua, ejecting President Jose Santos Zelaya and installing a compliant replacement. In 1914 a treaty was signed granting the United States the exclusive option to build an Atlantic-Pacific canal across Nicaragua, effectively preventing competition with the US-controlled Panama Canal, which was about to open.

With Nicaragua's social and political landscape sharply divided, in 1927 Augusto Cesar Sandino led an armed uprising against the conservative status and the American occupation of his country. US troops drawn into the conflict began training local men into a loyal militia, which would subsequently become the country's feared National Guard. The reputation would not be unfounded. After a period of uneasy peace between Sandino and the ruling government, on the 21 February 1934, the rebel leader accepted a cordial invitation from a government intermediary to have dinner with the President and sign a formal treaty. On his way home afterwards Sandino was intercepted by members of the National Guard and shot while in his rural commune several hundred people, including women and children were executed.

The intermediary that lured Sandino to his death is believed to have been National Guard leader Anastasio Somoza Garcia, who two years later took the presidency. He would rule for the next ten years, and it was the Somoza family that would continue to hold the power in Nicaragua, either by title or in an eminence grise capacity for over four more decades. Meanwhile Augusto Cesar Sandino had not been forgotten. A message he had sent to Mexico City while on the run from American troops, found an answering echo in the hearts of the people he had championed: '*I will not abandon my resistance until the… pirate invaders… assassins of weak peoples… are expelled from my country.... I will make them realise that their crimes will cost them dear… There will be bloody combat…. Nicaragua shall not be the patrimony of Imperialists.'*

The Ortega brothers were not yet born when Sandino was killed, but growing up they would soon learn his name. Their working class parents held the ruling Somoza dynasty in contempt, not least because the boys' mother Lidia had been jailed by the National Guard on an accusation that her personal correspondence contained coded political messages. In his mid teens Daniel was also arrested, an experience that propelled him into Nicaragua's recently formed underground resistance movement, the National Liberation Front, which by 1963 had added the name 'Sandinista' in honour of the group's inspiration, Sandino. Aged twenty-two Daniel found himself in trouble again, having assisted in the armed hold-up of an American bank. As a known Sandanista, conditions in Managua's El Modelo prison were tough; beaten and tortured, he must have wondered if he would ever see the outside world again.

Fellow Nicaraguans were not having it easy either. At the end of 1972 just two days before Christmas, Managua was hit by a massive earthquake killing 10,000 people. If Daniel Ortega had not been in prison just outside the city he might have been one of them. In the wake of the disaster, money flooded in from around the world to help the injured and bereaved and the thousands who had lost their homes. It was alleged the National Guard embezzled the bulk of the donations, while President Somoza awarded the reconstruction work to firms run by family and cronies, swelling his personal coffers in the process.

For the Sandinista National Liberation Front, Somoza's profiteering so grossly from the tragic plight of their compatriots was like a red rag to a bull, but the time and place to strike had to be chosen carefully. In December 1974 they learned that the American ambassador would be a guest of the Nicaraguan Minister of Agriculture at his home in Los Robles on the outskirts of Managua. The ambassador's visit meant that several elite government figures would also be in attendance, along with members of the Somoza family. Waiting until the US ambassador had left, just before 11pm a group of fifteen young armed rebels led by Eduardo Contreras and Germán Pomares burst into the house. When the host opened fire on them they retaliated killing him on the spot. The group held the remaining members of government hostage and in a radio broadcast, which was also published in the *La Prensa* newspaper, demanded a ransom of two million US dollars.

The ransom was agreed to, along with later demands for a number of Sandinista prisoners being held by the government to be freed. Among the prisoners was Daniel Ortega, who had now served seven years. On his release Daniel and several others were banished to Cuba, forbidden to return. This would turn out to be a mistake on the regime's part. Fidel and Raul Castro had fought against a brutal military dictatorship twenty-five years ago, and won. They were more than willing to teach the Ortega brothers all they knew.

In Nicaragua, while Somoza bore down on dissent through ever more torture, indiscriminate killing and gagging of the press, the Sandinista movement kept to its strategy of building a Guerra Popular Prolongada – a prolonged popular war – robbing banks to fund campaigns (as Stalin had done) and gathering followers from the universities as well as among the rural poor. By the mid-1970s, however, some Sandinista members were expressing doubts about the viability of continuing to pursue a strictly communist agenda. These members argued that there were other elements within Nicaragua that were equally opposed to the Somoza regime. Whilst those elements might be far from ideologically pure in Marxist terms – some were even clearly on the right – if Somoza were to be toppled, did it not make sense to seek an alliance with them? Thus was formed the Terceristas, or Third Way, and among the leaders were Daniel and Humberto Ortega.

This brings the Ortegas' story back up to 1978, the year that I met them in Cuba. Following the murder of *La Prensa*'s editor, the Terceristas had carried out a number of attacks throughout Nicaragua, prompting further brutal reprisals from the National Guard. In previous years Somoza had always been assured of American support for his actions, since Democrat Jimmy Carter had been in the White House. Hearing reports of the human rights abuses by the Nicaraguan state, Carter, while maintaining the flow of humanitarian aid, refused to supply further arms to the regime. Meanwhile the Terceristas stepped up their game in August 1978 by carrying out a dramatic hostage taking operation on the government. The twenty-three guerrillas seized almost a thousand people, including every member of the Congress and a nephew and cousin of Somoza. The ransom was set at half a million dollars, with the release of political prisoners, guaranteed safe passage to Panama for the guerrillas and for a message calling for the uprising to be read over the media to the Nicaraguan people. Somoza assented on every point.

A fuse had been lit. Within days, people throughout the country were arming themselves with makeshift weapons and joining the Terceristas units to storm National Guard posts. In the end Somoza's forces proved too strong and thousands of civilians were killed. Nevertheless, the September rebellion would mark a turning point for Nicaragua. In the White House, Carter had by now decided that Somozo must go. He was not prepared to see a socialist administration take over, and in negotiations with the various opposition groups it was agreed that the Sandinista National Liberation Front should be excluded. The Nicaraguan people disagreed; fearing a continuation of the regime under a different name, they demanded that there be no *Somocismo sin Somoza* – no Somozaism without Somoza. Their voices were heeded, and the splintered Sandinista movement re-converged, with Daniel and Humberto Ortega among the nine members of a new National Directorate committed to the removal of Somoza.

All out guerrilla warfare now ensued, with Sandinista forces mobilising the civilian population to gain the support that was vital if they were to defeat the National Guard. A national strike was instigated, and in Costa

Rica, Daniel Ortega joined Chamorros' widow and three others to form a provisional government in exile. By the beginning of July 1979, the Sandinistas were in control of most of the country, and on the 19th they took the capital Managua. Somoza, who had resigned two days earlier, had already taken a plane to Miami.

East-Germany, propaganda, Nicaraguan soldiers holding rifles aloft celebrating the victory of the Sandinistas

The number of people who had died in the struggle to overthrow the dictator was estimated at 40,000. Of those that survived, over half a million were homeless. Somoza had also run Nicaragua into huge debt, over one and a half billion dollars' worth. To tackle the immense challenges facing the country and begin the process of forming a new government, a five member Council of National Reconstruction was set up and again Daniel Ortega was included. The Sandinista movement retained strong popular support within the new administration, and set out among its priorities land reform, housing provision, improved public services, a literacy campaign throughout the country, the outlawing of the death penalty and torture, and equal rights across the board, including for women. Humberto Ortega was also to assume leadership of a new people's army.

The literacy campaign's rationale was not simply to give people the pleasure of reading, but to equip them to participate fully in an open, democratic and progressive society. Thousands who were already educated became teachers, and within a few months over half a million people had learned basic reading skills. UNESCO was so impressed with the success of the campaign that it presented Nicaragua with the Nadezhda Krupskaya Award. Krupskaya, the Soviet Union's Deputy Minister of Education from 1929–1939, had championed the improvement and greater accessibility of libraries. The Sandinistas' emphasis on the importance of literacy was also in the tradition of Che Guevarra, who throughout his travels and campaigns took time to teach people to read and write.

Aware that not everyone in Nicaragua approved of the new order, and that counter-revolutionary elements lurked within its midst, the government established a network of Committees for the Defence of the Revolution. These local groups were part social workers part police force, looking after those in need, maintaining law and order, monitoring and where necessary dealing with any reactionary elements. While Jimmy Carter had opted to maintain diplomatic relations with Nicaragua, it was stipulated that economic aid was on the proviso that the Sandinista-led government would not incite or support unrest in other countries. Relations with the US deteriorated quickly after January 1980, however, with the arrival in the White House of Ronald Reagan, who saw the left-wing Sandinista government as a serious political and economic threat to American interests. When information about an arms shipment to El Salvador was discovered, it was the perfect opportunity to cancel a sixty billion dollar aid package to Nicaragua that had been approved by Carter. The CIA, at Reagan's behest, now began covertly encouraging 'Contra' groups operating in Nicaragua.

Not a unified organisation as such, the Contras were mostly ex-National Guard members and supporters of Somoza, or former Sandinista supporters who for one reason or another felt let down in the new Nicaragua. With CIA support the Contras now became an active force, bent on destroying the improvements achieved by the government and striking fear into local communities. Allegations of rape, murder and torture perpetrated by Contras were widespread, and the evidence of burned out schools and medical centres was incontrovertible. Meanwhile, the Reagan administration piled economic pressure on the country via a trade embargo, and even planted mines in the port of Corinto.

Another of our characters from the pages of this book now makes an entrance. Pope John Paul's visit to Nicaragua took place in March 1983. With Catholics comprising more than half the country's population, news of the upcoming event had stirred great interest. In their continuing struggle against the Contras, the Sandinistas were hoping for some words of moral support from the Pontiff. In previous years the Nicaraguan Catholic establishment, reviling the Marxist ideology of the Sandinistas had remained loyal to the Somoza regime, but after seeing the increasing atrocities and the bombing of churches, the allegiance of many in the church had shifted towards the revolution. However, sharp divisions still existed, specifically between the conservative Catholic hierarchy and the grassroots church community throughout Nicaragua.

It was the thousands of people in this community, living in daily fear of the Contras, who as the Pope stepped down onto the tarmac at Managua airport, held their breath. They were to be disappointed. Throughout the whole of his stay in Nicaragua there were no references to the internal strife tearing the country apart. In the square in which he spoke, the previous day a funeral had been held for seventeen Sandinistas killed by Contras, yet the Pope made no mention of it, not even to offer condolence to the bereaved.

Katherine Hoyt, National Co-Coordinator of the Nicaragua Network Education Fund, who was there at the time, recalled her experience: '*With all the misinformation being published right now about Pope John Paul II's*

Pope John Paul II listens attentively as Daniel Ortega, coordinator of the ruling junta of Nicaragua, gives a speech about American policy in Central America on the Pope's one-day visit in April 1983

previous visit to Nicaragua in March of 1983, I decided that I would make available a letter I wrote to my parents a few days after that visit. By the time of this letter, I had been living in Nicaragua for fifteen years, most of that time in Matagalpa. As a Catholic, I felt that the opportunity to attend a Mass celebrated by the Pope was a very momentous one. It was momentous, but not in the way I expected. Now, thirteen years later, following the lead of the Sandinistas, I had not wanted to rake up bad old memories. But since others are doing so and twisting the facts as I remember them, I felt moved to answer.

March 16, 1983
Dear Folks,

Daniel Ortega's impromptu speech at the airport as the Pope left was enough to make one cry. He almost begged the Pope to make one solid proposal for peace in Nicaragua, to say one word, to give that one crumb that he was not willing to give. We heard only part of it as we were walking back to Toyita's house, dirty exhausted and I, of course very distressed by the whole visit and certain we were headed for schism. One of the last slogans somebody had cried out as the Mass was ending was one of anguished defiance: "Because of Christ and His Gospels, we are revolutionaries." That seemed to just about sum things up.

What was the reason for the Pope's absence of comment on the desperate situation in Nicaragua? Perhaps he was wary that anything he said would be misinterpreted and inflame the situation further. Yet it was already dire, and as Ms. Hoyt also pointed out, the silence was claimed by the Contras as signifying the Catholic Church's disapproval of Marxism, as represented by the Sandinisa movement: '...it was a boost for the counter-revolutionaries and we are seeing an increase in the number of battles right now.'

If the many Catholics who supported the Sandinistas had been expecting to be given a sense of direction or some signal of support from their spiritual leader, they must have been left feeling let down or at least confused. Was belief in God incompatible with a just revolution? Could the Catholic Church not see the role of Christianity pointed out by the worshipper at Mass: '*Because of Christ and His Gospels, we are revolutionaries*' – did it even understand their desperate plight?

As the civil war continued, in 1984 the democratic process was enacted in a general election. Daniel Ortega's impassioned speech during the Pope's departure the previous year would have won many hearts. Now he was winning votes, 67 per cent of those cast to be precise. Reagan denounced the

Daniel Ortega's visit to USSR in 1985

result a sham. International observers monitoring the event gave a different verdict, an Irish government delegation declaring that: '*The electoral process was carried out with total integrity. The seven parties participating in the elections represented a broad spectrum of political ideologies,*' while New York's Human Rights Commission deemed it '*free, fair and hotly contested.*'

The US Congress had by now blocked further funding for the Contras. In the year of Daniel Ortega's election it came to light that members of the Reagan administration had got around the ban through secret arms sales to Iran, the money being then diverted to the Contras. The Court of International Justice found in Nicaragua's favour, and that the US was obliged to make reparation, '*for all injury caused to Nicaragua by certain breaches of obligations under customary international law and treaty-law committed by the United States of America.*'

1988 brought another meeting between Pope John Paul and Daniel

Ortega. This time Ortega flew to Rome, and according to observers the reception was 'markedly cool' (Robert Suro *New York Times*, 30 January 1988) with Vatican officials stating that the Pope *'sternly advised the Sandinista leader that respect for human rights and democracy was necessary to achieve peace in Central America'* (Ibid). A number of priests had been expelled from Nicaragua, presumably over ideological differences, which the Pope was said to be unhappy about. John Paul did, however, reiterate his support for a Nicaraguan peace plan agreed earlier in the year by the presidents of five Central American countries.

When the peace did finally come in 1990 it coincided with an electoral defeat for Daniel Ortega. His successor was former ally Victoria Chamorro, the widow of Pedro Chamorro the murdered *La Prensa* editor. With 55 per cent of the vote, Chamorro's margin was not huge, but Ortega said the result had come as a complete shock to him, and he pledged to continue 'ruling from below' and adhere to the principles of the Sandinistas. Threats by the Contras to continue fighting if the Sandinistas were re-elected might have played a large part in the result; the Nicaraguans had suffered more than a decade of civil war and no one could blame them for seeking a compromise. Ortega would not return as president until 2007. By now the Sandinista movement had split, with a 'Renovation' arm campaigning for a return to what its members saw as the original path. Ortega had changed too, controversially altering his position on abortion rights, which he now opposed other than in circumstances threatening the life of the mother, a shift indicative of a return to the values of the Catholic Church of his upbringing.

On 19 July 1979, just one year after I met him, Daniel Ortega was sat astride an armoured car riding victoriously into the Nicaraguan capital Managua. As I write this he is still President of Nicaragua. Like Fidel and Raul Castro, Daniel and his brother Humberto risked their lives for a better life for the people of the their country, while their brother Camilo lost his life early on in the struggle. Yet the flame of freedom ignited by them all burns on.

Havana, 28 January 2014. Cuban President Raul Castro (left) shakes hands with his Nicaraguan counterpart, Daniel Ortega, during the opening of the Second Summit of the Community of Latin American and Caribbean States

POPE JOHN PAUL II

During the late 1970s and early 1980s, in the course of my work as Secretary of the All-Union Komsomol Central Committee of the USSR Communist Party for International Affairs, I had frequent opportunities to visit the Polish People's Republic. Of the 120 youth organisations around the world with which we were in contact, our relations with our colleagues in the Polish student body and the organisation of Polish youth were especially warm.

This was also a time when new ideas were starting to flower, not only in Poland but also throughout the so-called Eastern bloc; people seemed to be seeking a way out of the commonwealth of socialist countries and looking to embark on an independent voyage. The direction of this voyage was clear and understandable; the concepts of democracy and choice, and the perception of a greater material plenitude enjoyed by those in the capitalist West, previously regarded with suspicion, were gaining wider credibility. The world was certainly full of possibilities, and the call of freedom was a seductive one. But like the siren of ancient mythology, might the call not also signal danger, luring the adventurous voyagers towards the rocks? This was the fear among the more cautious and conservative elements within Russia and the other socialist countries.

In 1978 we had planned a conference in Poland with the student and youth organisations. In several parts of Eastern Europe strikes and demonstrations were currently taking place demanding the resignation of the national leaders. In Poland the economic 'boom' under Edward Gierek had been short-lived, and with overseas debt rising, the government's increase in the price of food while wages remained static had caused unrest, culminating in violent protests at a number of factories in the summer of 1976. The authorities had clamped down and the people responded by forming the Committee for Defence of the Workers, or Komitet Obrony Robotników (KOR) in Polish, later renamed the Committee for Social Self-defence (KSS-KOR). Following these events the activity of the Catholic Church in Poland was to intensify sharply, which we will come on to shortly. Meanwhile, thinking the mood in Poland might be too volatile, it was felt we should cancel the youth conference. However, after some discussion it was decided we would go ahead.

Thankfully the conference was a success, and with two extra days in hand my Polish colleague and host, S. Yakubovsky, made a suggestion: '*If you remember, Vagif, I promised to show you the city where I was born and which I love very much. So if you do not mind, I suggest we visit Krakow, the university there, and meet the leaders of student organisations. You will not regret it and you will realise that Krakow is one of the most beautiful cities in Europe.*' I was pleased to accept. I already knew that Krakow, once the capital and still regarded as the intellectual heart of Poland, was the most patriotic place in the country; that at least was what everyone who came from Krakow said!

It took us a few hours' drive to reach our destination and after parking the car we made our way to the centre. Poland's second largest city after Warsaw, Krakow has a rich and dramatic history, and in the early 1100s was both the seat of government and a thriving trading hub. After almost complete obliteration by the Mongols in 1241 the entire city was rebuilt close to its original location. When the Mongols invaded again in 1259, fortifications were erected, which twenty-eight years later succeeded in seeing off a third raid. 1364 saw the foundation of the University of Krakow, also known as the Jagiellonian, one of the oldest universities in the world and the *alma mater* of Nicolaus Copernicus, the Enlightenment mathematician and astronomer whose work *On the Evolution of the Celestial Spheres* published in 1543 turned the revered concept of the physical and symbolic centrality of the earth on its head, causing a degree of consternation among the religious establishment.

However, it was six decades before the Catholic Church decided to ban the work, possibly because Copernicus like most scholars had written in Latin, making it inaccessible to the masses. Also, Copernicus died shortly after the book's publication, and could easily be dismissed as a sinner, with his calculations refuted by bogus theories to which he could not reply. The Jagiellonian University's motto is *Plus ratio quam vis* – let reason prevail over force. Some five centuries after Copernicus, another Pole destined to make a lasting impression on the world entered the halls of the Jagiellonian, his name Karol Wojtyla, whom we will of course come to in a moment.

Despite the obfuscating power of the church, the 16th century culminated in what became known as a golden age in Poland's history, attracting artists and thinkers to Krakow, the creation of fine renaissance buildings and artwork, the establishment of a printing press, and in the Jewish quarter the city's first synagogues. Caught between rival empires, Poland then endured a period of partitions and takeovers by absent rulers, an invasion by Sweden and in Krakow an outbreak of bubonic plague that killed 20,000 inhabitants. After the Napoleonic Wars the city emerged with a degree of political independence, once more drawing artists and intellectuals, and was even referred to as a 'Polish Athens'. From 1918, when Poland broke free from Austrian rule and formed the Second Polish Republic, Krakow flourished as a centre of culture and learning. At the same time the city's Jewish community consolidated, its various branches practising freely, including a growing Zionist youth movement. August 1939 brought fear and devastation; after the Nazi's blitzkrieg, or lightning raid from air and land had effectively immobilised the Polish Air Force and defeated its army, Krakow's inhabitants were forcibly removed and the streets renamed in German. Jews herded into the ghetto were later killed there or sent to Auschwitz. A young boy called Roman Polanski survived the horrors of the Krakow ghetto, and years later made a film called *The Pianist*, telling the similar experiences in Warsaw of the celebrated musician Vladyslaw Szpilman. Krakow would also be depicted in the cinema in the story of German industrialist Oskar Schindler, a Nazi party member who saved over a thousand Jews by employing them in his enamels factory.

1945 gave birth to the Polish People's Republic, and the country became a part of the USSR. Stalin's priority to industrialise saw the construction of the huge Lenin Steelworks on the outskirts of Krakow, and an expansion of the working class population. Meanwhile the Jagiellonian and other Polish universities were restricted in terms of their teaching and publications. In 1955, Poland signed the Warsaw Pact along with Albania, Bulgaria, Czechoslovakia, the German Democratic Republic, Hungary, Romania and the Soviet Union. The latter was the only nuclear power in the alliance, while Poland stood second in military strength with over 300,000 troops.

In 1978, Krakow was every bit as beautiful as my host had described, and being his home city that he loved, he was a natural fount of knowledge. The place could not fail to make a great impression on any visitor, for as Yakubovsky so passionately explained to me, it has a character like no other. Of course we had to go and see the Jagiellonian University, the ancient square and all the surrounding sights, art galleries, museums and ancient monuments. Remarkably given the ravages of war, much of the architecture of the old town remains untouched, including along the traditional coronation route of the Polish kings; through the 13th century Florian Gate that fortified the city against the Turks, and up to Wawel Castle with its wonderful view of the Vistula. Contrasting with this picturesque, fairy tale scenery is the Socialist Realist uniformity of the apartment blocks and avenues built in other parts of Krakow during Stalin's time.

We had been wandering around the city for several hours when we came upon a Catholic cathedral, where the beautiful sound of the organ and choral singing could be heard from within. Yakubovsky suggested we stop for a while and have a look at the architecture. He told me that the Nazis had intended to blow the building up whilst retreating under the onslaught of the Soviet Army, yet somehow it had survived. This was a blessing, for it was indeed a magnificent building. Yakubovsky then said that if we went inside he could introduce me to a very interesting person if I wished. I asked him who, and he told me it was the Archbishop of Krakow, Karol Wojtyla. I knew immediately whom he meant, for I had read a great deal about the man; his literary works, his knowledge of eight languages and his views on theology. I also knew that Wojtyla held anti-Soviet opinions. Nevertheless, I felt very keen to meet him.

The atmosphere inside the cathedral was magical. The service had begun and the pews were full of worshippers listening very attentively as the Archbishop spoke. What also struck me, and which I remarked on to Yakubovsky, was the large number of young people in the congregation. The singing resumed, the sweet harmony of the children's voices absolutely enchanting. At the end of the service we went over to say hello to the Archbishop. Still in his robes, he was a short, slightly stooping man in his late fifties. Yakubovsky introduced me as his colleague and friend. I was about to tell the Archbishop a little bit about myself when, speaking in fluent Russian, he said to me, '*So you are from Baku.*' I nodded, realising now that Yakobovsky had planned this meeting, and that the Archbishop was prepared.

Telling me that he had visited Baku in the late 1930s, the Archbishop said, '*Once upon a time there were many Polish people living there, and at the beginning of the 20th century they built a beautiful cathedral, tell me, is it still there today?*' I assured him that the place of worship he referred to was very much intact, and that it had been renovated only a few years ago. Over a century ago there were many Polish people living in the Caucasus but in Baku and elsewhere this community was now somewhat diminished sadly. '*However in my school class of about thirty children,*' I went on, '*there was a Polish boy and a beautiful Polish girl. I remember being very smitten with the girl.*' I said we found the Poles different from the Russians, who were chauvinistic, adding jokingly, '*I'm not Russian I'm Soviet.*' The Archbishop laughed and said, '*Yes, I know.*' He then graciously pointed out that the Poles had Stalin to thank for their independence as a sovereign state in 1918.

The Archbishop asked the purpose of my visit, and I explained about the conference involving about 500 people with artists and authors in attendance, and the festivals we organised at other times. He replied that he would be very interested in coming to one of the events. *'In my discussions with young people,'* he said, *'I always talk about the Russian authors, Pushkin, Tolstoy and Chekov.'* He said he loved poetry, and began reciting some pieces in Russian. I was amazed; it was so beautiful. Russian poetry, he continued, was *'full of humour and love, not violent but tolerant.'* The man was so educated, so intellectually aware of everything. Yakobovsky then went on to relate how he had accompanied the Archbishop and a group of students on a skiing trip, and it was clear that the two men knew each other very well. After we had said our goodbyes and left the cathedral Yakobovsky said, *'Well, what did you think?'* Rather lost for words I replied simply, *'What can I say?'*

If one cannot readily picture an archbishop hurtling down the ski slopes, then the idea can be even more surprising when it comes to a pope. The archbishop I had the pleasure to meet that day in Krakow was about to be elevated to that title. The event, however, was unexpected for all concerned. Only in the August of that year, Wojtyla voted with the papal conclave to choose a new pope. John Paul I died just thirty-three days after his election. The conclave was then split between the supporters of two candidates: the Archbishop of Genoa Giuseppe Siri and a close friend of the recently deceased pope, Giovanni Benelli, Archbishop of Florence, a conservative and a liberal respectively. With strong opposition from both sides, the Archbishop of Milan, Giovanni Colombo, was put forward as a compromise candidate. Colombo announced that he would not accept the offer of the papacy. A third Archbishop, of Vienna, then stepped in with an unusual suggestion: Karol Wojtyla; unusual because for the last four and a half centuries the pope had always been an Italian.

Wojtyla was born on 18 May 1920 in Wadowice, Poland. His father was an NCO in the Polish Army, and his mother, a teacher, died during childbirth when Karol was eight years old. Karol was an athletic boy and would often play football matches with a Catholic team against Jewish boys,

Archbishop's Palace or Palac Biskupi courtyard with a statue of Saint John Paul II, in Krakow, Poland

noticing in the latter their strong sense of Polish patriotism. The death of his older brother from scarlet fever affected him deeply. Moving to Krakow with his father in 1938, Karol enrolled in the university, studying languages and linguistic theory. A year later the arrival of the Nazis brought the closure of the university, and along with all other able-bodied males Karol was ordered by the occupiers to do manual work. When in 1941 the death of his father from a heart attack left the twenty-one-year-old Karol entirely alone, he made his way to the Archbishop's Palace in Krakow and asked about becoming a priest.

The seminary was being run secretly, and those in attendance had to be constantly on the lookout for the Nazis. In 1944 Karol was run over and injured by a military truck. Some German officers looked after him and got him to hospital. Recovering from serious concussion, it is said the experience confirmed his religious vocation. Six months later, to prevent an uprising, the Gestapo were hunting down all the able-bodied young men in Krakow. As over 8,000 were rounded up, Karol hid in the basement of his uncle's house, then escaped to the Archbishop's Palace until the Nazis had left the city. At some point Karol had helped a young Jewish girl called Edith Zierer who had fled from a concentration camp, carrying her to a railway station and looking after her on the train. Zierer maintains that in doing so Karol saved her life. Others have testified that he helped a number of other Polish Jews to escape from the Nazis.

Karol Wojtyla was ordained as a priest in November 1946, and was sent to Rome to study for a doctorate in philosophy. He returned to his homeland in 1948, as priest at the village of Niegowic, and shortly after to St Florian's back in Krakow. In 1953, Wojtyla defended his thesis at the Faculty of Theology at the Jagiellonian University, where he also taught ethics, along with giving lectures at Krakow Theological Seminary. It was around this time that his interest in skiing developed, as well as camping, hiking, cycling and kayaking, taking along groups of students, like my colleague Yakubovsky later, combining philosophical and religious discussions with charitable work for the blind and disadvantaged. Since it was not permitted in Poland at this time for priests to accompany students on holidays, Karol encouraged his companions to refer to him as 'Wujek' – the Polish for 'Uncle'.

In July 1958, Pope Pius XII appointed Wojtyla as an auxiliary Archbishop of Krakow *in absentia* – Karol was apparently on one of his kayaking holidays at the time and only on his return did the Polish primate invite him to Warsaw to give him the news. Between 1962 and 1964 Wojtyla took part in all four councils of the Second Vatican Council, and played an important role in the drafting of the Declaration on Religious Freedom. In January 1964 he was appointed as Archbishop Metropolitan of Krakow.

In the spring of 1976, Wojtyla surprised the church establishment by reading his sermons before the other cardinals in Italian, rather than Latin. Similar breaks with tradition would occur throughout his papacy, beginning with his inauguration, when instead of allowing the prelate of Poland Cardinal Wyszinski to kiss the papal ring, he stood up and embraced him. From the balcony in St Peter's Square in Rome he told the crowd that, '*I am speaking to you in your – no our – Italian language... if I make a mistake, please correct me.*' At fifty-eight he was the youngest pope since 1846, and it was in honour of his predecessor that he adopted the title of Pope John Paul II.

When I heard he had been elected pope I wrote him a telegram of congratulation. Shortly afterwards I received a phone call from the Polish embassy: could they come and see me? A member of staff arrived with a message back from the pope, which read:

> '*Dear Vagif, I remember our meeting very well, and our discussion about poetry, many thanks for your good wishes, I also remember we talked about the friendship between Russian and Polish young people. In my religious work I try always to remember the importance of young people in the world, and how we must bring them together.*'

In 1979, Pope John Paul II travelled to Ireland, Mexico and the Dominican Republic, and in the same year became the first pope to visit the White House. It was the beginning of a tour of the world that over the term of his papacy would take him to 129 countries, in many of them attracting huge crowds. In 2001, the year of 9/11, he prayed in a Syrian mosque and called for harmony between Christians, Muslims and Jews.

In certain aspects of theology John Paul II was deeply conservative, continuing to assert that abortion, contraception, homosexuality and even marriage of divorcees were sinful acts. At the same time he spoke out strongly against capital punishment. It was in 1979, however, returning to his native Poland for the first time as pope, he would have a profound and lasting effect on the country, and on the socialist commonwealth as a whole. The Polish people were galvanised by his presence, and according to Angelo

M. Codevilla, in Political Warfare: A Set of Means for Achieving Political Ends, '*...they came to him by the millions. They listened. He told them to be good, not to compromise themselves, to stick by one another, to be fearless, and that God is the only source of goodness, the only standard of conduct. "Be not afraid," he said. Millions shouted in response "We want God! We want God! We want God!"... the Pope simply led the Polish people to desert their rulers by affirming solidarity with one another.*'

The end of socialism in Poland did not come immediately, but as everyone now knows, the word 'solidarity' played a huge part in setting the train in motion, which we talk more of when we come to Lech Wałęsa. The direction of the train if you like, has also become apparent to historians: '*I would argue the historical case in three steps: without the Polish Pope, no Solidarity revolution in Poland in 1980; without Solidarity, no dramatic change in Soviet policy towards eastern Europe under Gorbachev; without that change, no velvet revolutions in 1989.* ' (Timothy Garton Ash)

Yet the same individual is also credited with ending fascist regimes: '*He was in Chile and Pinochet was out. He was in Haiti and Duvalier was out. He was in the Philippines and Marcos was out.*' (Jonathan Kwitny, *Man of the Century: The Life and Times of Pope John Paul II*)

Pope John Paul II was a very clever and able man. Aware of the huge following he had, he used it to instigate a momentous change in the political landscape of Eastern Europe and Russia. By paving the way for Gorbachev, in my view he did a lot of harm to the Soviet Union. But he will remain in history as an outstanding public figure, a significant and active politician in the modern sense of the word. For the first time ever, the head of the Catholic Church not only participated in world affairs, but was also prepared to discuss the role of the church and what he saw as the right direction for the future of humankind.

In what now seems the dim and distant past of the 1970s and 1980s, this unassuming character intrigued us with his unconventional way of life,

John Paul II on his journey through the Benelux countries, taken during his visit in Banneux in may 1985, seated in the popemobile

his erudition, his willingness to cross boundaries and reach out to people of other faiths. In doing so he survived two assassination attempts. His appointment coincided with a difficult time for religion as a whole, the growth of technology and its accompanying secularism in the West coming at the same time as a rising fundamentalism elsewhere. As far back as the 17th century Thomas Hobbes described the papacy as nothing but the ghost of a fallen empire. Three hundred and fifty years later, Karol Wojtyla proved that it was anything but.

YEVGENY MAKSIMOVICH PRIMAKOV

Primakov was a man with a remarkable biography. Just reeling off all the titles and positions that he held sounds impressive in itself: Minister of Foreign Affairs, Head of Central Intelligence Service, Director of Foreign Intelligence Service, Chairman of Soviet Union of the USSR Supreme Soviet, Doctor of Economics, Professor, Extraordinary Plenipotentiary Ambassador – the list goes on.

Yevgeny Primakov was born on 29 October 1929 in Kiev, spent his childhood and youth in Tbilisi, Georgia, and studied at nearby Marneuli. It is said that he never knew his father, who was believed to have perished in one of the gulags. At that time Marneuli's inhabitants were mainly Azerbaijanis, numbering around 500,000, and today the townsfolk are still predominantly Azerbaijani. This demographic make-up was the result of the administrative and political policies of the Tsarist government, which after the conquest of Baku, Erevan and Karabakh khanates, actively evicted Azerbaijanis from their native lands. Armenian ethnic groups were also re-settled there from a number of countries in the Middle East.

On leaving secondary school, Primakov attended the Moscow Institute of Oriental Studies, went on to post-graduate study, and between 1956 and 1962 worked as a correspondent, deputy chief editor, and then chief editor in broadcasting on Arab affairs. In 1959, he defended his thesis on Export of capital to some Arab countries – a means to ensure monopolistically high profits – and became a Candidate of Economic Sciences. In 1969 he met Saddam Hussein and Tariq Aziz during a stay in Baghdad, and often visited the North of Iraq where Kurdish insurgents were active, and met their leader M. Barzani. In 1969, he defended his thesis on Social and Economic

Development of Egypt and became a Doctor of Economic Sciences.

My first meeting with Yevgeny Primakov was at a conference at his *alma mater* at the Moscow Institute of Oriental Studies during the late 1970s. The delegates were giving speeches, exchanging opinions and ideas, having discussions. I was there as Secretary of the All-Union Lenin Komsomol Central Committee for International Affairs. With the formalities of the conference over Primakov and I got talking, and when I mentioned that I was from Baku, he told me he had attended the naval school there during his teenage years, but had been forced to leave in 1946 due to ill health. We also had a shared background in radio journalism, as he had been a Middle East correspondent for *Pravda*. Fluent in Arabic, and extremely well informed about the rich history and culture of that part of the world, it was the complex, often volatile world of Arab affairs that was Primakov's speciality.

After the conference, we bumped into each other a few times briefly over the next few years, but it was after Mikhail Gorbachev came to power that our paths were destined to cross far more frequently. Gorbachev, rightly recognising Yevgeny's intellect and diplomatic ability, was keen to adopt him as a key advisor during the 1980s glasnost and perestroika reforms. In 1990 he travelled to Kuwait to try to persuade Saddam Hussein to withdraw from the country and forestall a US-led coalition invasion. At the same time he was warning Gorbachev of the growing discontent among senior figures about how his policies were destabilising the Soviet Union, and that there might be a bid to remove him.

When the coup did come about in August 1991, Yevgeny supported Gorbachev and called the action illegal. Afterwards he appointed him First Deputy Chairman of the KGB and put him in charge of foreign intelligence. Yevgeny also remained Gorbachev's right-hand man as leader of the parliament, and as by now I was chief of the Azerbaijan KGB, we now began to hold regular meetings over the conflict with Armenia. For those who are unfamiliar with this period of history in the Caucasus, the inter-ethnic hostilities had begun in the late 1980s over long-standing and disputed claims to the territory of Nagorno-Karabach in south-western Azerbaijan. Gorbachev presented himself as neutral, but it soon became clear to me that his past association with Armenians was guiding his hand, and with it the actions of the Soviet military. In contrast to Gorbachev's empty words, it offered some relief to be able to sit down and talk such serious issues through with Primakov, a man of integrity who did his utmost to cast an impartial eye on the situation in Azerbaijan and to formulate a judicious and humanitarian approach as the dramatic events unfolded day by day.

At the beginning of 1990 the conflict would hit my hometown of Baku, when, following allegations of violence against Armenians and signs that an attempt to overthrow the Azerbaijani government was imminent, Gorbachev ordered a state of emergency and 26,000 Soviet special forces were deployed to the city. In his book *On My Country and World* Gorbachev claims that the soldiers had been fired upon by Azerbaijani National Front militia, a claim disputed at the time by an organisation called 'Shield Union' (reported in *Moscow News*, 12 August 1990).

Between 19th and 20th of what would become known as 'Black January' 133 Azerbaijanis and 137 Armenians were killed, though unofficial accounts put the figure higher. The crisis would also have a significant impact on my own life, with political intrigue leading to accusations of criminal behaviour, and my being flung in prison facing imminent execution. The only remote, if dubious consolation, was that the cell in which I was placed had once been occupied by Stalin at the time of the civil war. Those that would like to know more about this particular drama, and its outcome, can read the whole story in my autobiography, *More Than One Life*.

Towards the end of 1992 the sporadic clashes in Nagorno-Karabach were escalating into full-scale warfare, and within a few months Armenian troops were making incursions beyond the region. My meetings with Yevgeny continued, and we discussed issues of safety and security in the region, working very closely together for three to four years in total. With the criminal charges against me being finally dropped in 1993, I moved to Moscow to resume my writing career and find consultancy work in the new scheme of things in Russia. In 1996, Primakov, in his capacity as director of external security offered me a post in his department. I declined, which was probably a mistake, but after heading the Azerbaijan KGB, and my experience at the wrong end of it, I really felt I wanted nothing more to do with law enforcement.

Primakov's responsibilities and reputation meanwhile grew. Perhaps remembering the show of support for Gorbachev during the 1991 coup, when Yeltsin was also facing political discord as well the fallout from an economic crisis, he too was eager to have Yevgeny Primakov by his side:

> *'Primakov's name was unexpectedly proposed by Yabloko leader Grigory Yavlinsky at a roundtable with the president last week. At first the veteran foreign minister, who has no economic experience or expertise, said he was not interested in the post. Presumably, Yeltsin has now persuaded him to stand by – arguing that only his candidacy can rescue Russia from the*

political turmoil that has brought the country to the brink of disintegration.'
(Jamestown Foundation, 10 September 1998)

In 1996, Primakov was appointed Minister of Foreign Affairs, from which position it seems he viewed the changing world situation with a degree of realism, whilst also coming up with alternative formulations, in particular advocating '*…a new strategic triangle between Russia, China and India, a concept that later led to the establishment of the Brics group – Brazil, Russia, India, China and South Africa.*' (*Guardian*, 28 June 2015)

In 1999 the heated issue of whether military force should be used against Serbian forces engaged in ethnic cleansing of Albanians in Kosova was a huge moral dilemma, made more difficult for the Kremlin by the fact that the Serbian leader Slobodan Milosovich was Russia's strategic ally. Primakov was opposed to intervention, as demonstrated when, during a flight to the US on a separate issue, he was informed by a phone call from Al Gore that NATO aircraft had begun bombing Serbian positions. Yevgeny ordered his own plane to return to Moscow in protest. Later he would recall these events for *Pravda.ru*:

> *'I made the decision myself. After that, Yeltsin called me and I told him that I took such a decision. He approved of it. If I had not done this, I would have done very wrong thing. Al Gore told me directly: the decision to bomb has been made. I replied that he was making a huge historical mistake… He asked me to sign a memorandum of understanding that the visit is postponed. I refused. He offered to land somewhere in the United States, I again refused. If under those circumstances I would have landed and began my official visit, I would have been a traitor. There was no heroism there.'*

Despite this episode, which became known as 'Primakov's Loop', he did make it to America later. One of his key US counterparts, Madeleine Albright,

President of Russia Dmitry Medvedev and Chairman of Trade-Industrial Chamber of Russia Evgeny Primakov during Russia-Argentina talks at the Kremlin

has some telling memories of several meetings with him in different parts of the world. During their first encounter he told her, *'Given my previous job, you do realise I know everything about you.'* Albright later remarked, *'He was, without a doubt, referring to his time as the head of Russia's foreign intelligence service, the successor to the KGB.'* (Madeleine Albright, *Remembering Yevgeny Primakov:Foreign Policy.com*)

At that first meeting Albright also told him that she knew he was fiercely defensive of Russia's interests, adding that she felt similarly about America, and that if they both accepted this fact, they would get along well together. That they did not agree on the bombing of Yugoslavia was but one point of contention; the areas of conflict and concern around the world affecting both the US and Russia were manifold, and working out compromises was never going to be easy, even for the most talented of diplomats.

As Prime Minister, Primakov brought a mix of people into his cabinet, reformers alongside communists, and while criticising the oligarchs, channelled money into businesses where wages had stagnated or been withheld and encouraged more hiring. The Russian economy, helped by a rebound in the oil price that boosted overseas revenue, began to recover. Primakov's stand against NATO over Yugoslavia, together with his campaign against alleged corruption of the oligarchs, in particular Boris Berezovsky, was broadening his appeal among Russians throughout the country. This achievement was now to work against him as in 1999, Yeltsin, fearing that his popularity would make him a contender for the presidency, sacked him. Berezovsky's TV channel meanwhile launched a smear campaign, claiming that Primakov was a communist stooge and too old to lead the country effectively.

Seeing the signs, Primakov stood down from the 2002 presidential elections and in came Vladimir Putin. The following year Putin appointed Primakov as Chairman of the Russian Chamber of Commerce and Industry, an office he would hold for the next ten years. Though now possessing relatively little in the way of hard power, he remained a respected and influential figure in Russian public life, as well as on the world stage. Early in 2003 in the crisis over alleged weapons of mass destruction in Iraq, Putin dispatched him to entreat Saddam Hussein to reassure the US and Britain and thereby prevent an invasion. If anyone could achieve this, Primakov was probably the man, but given that the WMD were later proven to have been either a delusion or a fabrication on the part of the West, and that Bush and Blair were bent on war, it is clear that this was one peace mission that was doomed to failure. The same had been true of his attempt to broker a deal before the first Gulf War in 1991. However the two episodes were in the eyes of some observers, '*...rare failures for a man who managed to maintain a reputation for integrity, realism and consistency during some of Russia's most turbulent and ideologically divisive years.*' (Jonathan Steele, *The Guardian*, 28 June 2015)

As the second decade of the 21st century got underway the issues affecting international security seemed ever greater, and the problems more intractable. Former diplomatic colleagues Madeleine Albright and Yevgeny

Academician Evgeny Primakov, the president of the Mercury Club, attends a meeting of the Mercury Club at Moscow's World Trade Centre, 13 January 2015

Primakov had by now taken a back seat on their respective sides of the Atlantic, but they had both stayed very much in touch with global affairs. In 2014, the Russian Federation's occupation of Crimea had prompted sanctions by the United States as well as the EU. Primakov for one seemed not to relish the prospect of a return to the Cold War: in 2015 Madeleine Albright spoke to him on the phone: '*He was ill, but alert. "I am so worried because Russian-American relations are as bad as I have seen in a long time," he said. I agreed.*' (Madeleine Albright, *Remembering Yevgeny Primakov:Foreign Policy.com*)

Fortunately, like most diplomats these two heavyweights had some happy memories, of times when the politics were put aside and there was room for fun, like the annual ambassadorial gatherings at which all the delegates were required to perform a 'turn'. Madeleine Albright recalled a particular highlight with Primakov:

'I convinced him to join forces with me for a duet. In between difficult discussions on the Balkans and Iraq, we came up with our version of West Side Story. We called it the "East-West Story." We wrote the lyrics together and rehearsed with a lot of vodka. When it came time to perform, I entered the stage and sung out: "The most beautiful sound I ever heard – Yevgeny, Yevgeny, Yevgeny." He returned in his thick Russian accent, "Madeleine Albright – I just met a girl named Madeleine Albright." We were a hit.' (Ibid)

After Yevgeny Primakov died on 26 June 2016 there were many glowing tributes to the man and his achievements, in particular to his independence of mind, commented on by Irina Khakamada, *'He was extremely visionary about the world, generally... Both in parliament and in the government, he always asked very sharp questions and did not belong to any camp. The answers to these questions determined the country's future.'* (*Radio Free Europe*, 26 June 2015)

Along with the undoubtedly rigorous qualities of Primakov's intellect, I like to remember also the other side of the man – the real Yevgeny in fact: warm, witty and amusing, someone who knew the true meaning of friendship. Over many years I would meet him at conferences or for a drink, but on one memorable occasion, I was dining out with some friends and there was a birthday party going on in another part of the restaurant. Part way through the evening the conversation at our table stopped suddenly and my friends that were seated opposite were staring behind me. The next second I felt a pair of hands covering my eyes, and when I turned around it was Yevgeny. He was Prime Minister Primakov at the time, his face well known from TV and newspapers, hence the staring of my friends as he had crept up to surprise me.

Very well educated, extremely clever and highly intellectual, he knew his subject and many others inside out. An amazing character who, when he became your friend, was a friend forever. He had known me when I was a

KGB chief and when I was not; it made no difference to him. He attended my anniversary party, came to my home on numerous occasions, and our talk was always warm and informal, personal relationships for him had nothing to do with position.

Ironically perhaps for such a keen student of Arab history and affairs, Primakov was Jewish. Whether it was despite or because of this that he had such a huge reputation in Middle Eastern affairs is debatable, but his influence in the area was undeniable; he could speak to King Faisal whenever the need arose simply by picking up the phone, and there was a similarly close understanding with almost all the other Arab leaders.

A large part of it was that he had this great aura, and was such a very charming man. You could see that charm in any setting, formal or informal. I remember it particularly at one of his birthday celebrations and at an award ceremony held for him. At the birthday party, again, although he was Prime Minister at the time, out of forty government ministers there were only a couple in attendance, the rest of the guests being old friends, people he had known for years. With Yevgeny the accent was always on the personal. I will never forget how when I moved to Moscow and was still having a lot of problems after the trouble in Baku, he took the time to find my phone number and give me a call. He had nothing to gain from that, and didn't need to do it. Thank you Yevgeny. A friend for all seasons, not just summer.

PRINCE MICHAEL OF KENT

The Tsar was God. Each morning, schoolchildren recited prayers reverently facing Nicolas II's portrait, those infinitely tragic eyes looking down on his young subjects. So begins *Cousins Divided,* Ann Morrow's gripping account of the relationship between Russia's last Tsar Nicholas II and his British cousin King George V. Morrow paints an enchantingly romantic picture of the Tsar, a sublime figure who *'rode a white horse like a hero in a Pushkin fairy tale.'* Possessing a vast kingdom, hundreds of palaces, thousands of servants and immense wealth, Nicholas seemed to ordinary Russians as Morrow puts it *'indestructible'.*

By 1917 the Romanov fairy tale had reached a dramatic climax. As news of the Bolshevik uprising reached Britain the government offered political asylum to the Tsar and his family. Fearing the spread of revolutionary fervour at home the offer was withdrawn, and with the Red Army gathering strength, plans drawn up by the British secret service to smuggle the Romanovs out of Russia were aborted. Following his abdication in February 1917, Tsar Nicholas, his wife and children and a number of close servants who had chosen to remain with the family were placed under guard and later taken to the former Governor General's house in Tobolsk in Western Siberia. The civil war was underway, and when forces of the royalist White Army were reported to be approaching the Romanovs and their servants were placed in the hands of the Ural Soviet at Ekaterinburg. On 17 July 1918, the Soviet ordered Bolsheviks under the command of Yakov Yorovsky to execute the prisoners.

Nicholas' brother had been shot a few weeks previously and his sister-in-law Elizabeth, cousin Sergei and nephews Ivan, Constantine, Vladimir and

Igor battered and hurled into a sixty-foot mineshaft. Legend has it that as they lay dying they sang Russian Orthodox hymns, unnerving the soldiers into throwing grenades in after them. Meanwhile three more of Nicholas' cousins and his Uncle Paul remained imprisoned in Petrograd. A few months later, after a petition submitted by Maxim Gorky for their release was rejected, all four were also executed. Over the following months further relatives of the former Tsar were subjected to the same summary justice. The revolution seemed determined to erase all trace of the Romanovs from the new Russia.

This was a large family and amid the instability of the civil war and the divided loyalties within Russia's vast borders, obliterating an entire bloodline was not so simple. It is believed that by 1920, out of fifty-three members of the extended Romanov family at the time of the revolution, thirty-five remained alive. Most of these had managed to flee the country either by land or sea. Nicholas' mother Maria Feodorovna, his sister Xenia and brother-in-law Alexander were among a handful of survivors picked up by a British Royal Navy warship off the coast of Crimea on the orders of King George V. Settled as an émigré in Paris, Maria refused to believe newspaper reports of the death of her *'unfortunate Nicky'.*

When the White Russian army arrived in Ekaterinburg they were unable to locate any remains of Nicholas or his immediate family and servants. Rumours circulated that the heads of the deceased had been presented to Lenin as proof of their extinction. Of those killed in Petrograd the body of one cousin was buried by his adjutant, while those in the mineshaft were retrieved and taken eastwards by the White Russians who were by then retreating. Over time, an absence of *corpus delicti* allowed the Soviet state to distance itself from the brutal murders. In the 1940s the written account by Yurovsky, who had dispatched the family and servants at Ekaterinburg, was withdrawn from the Moscow Museum of the Revolution along with other books celebrating the 'revolutionary justice' meted out. By the latter part of the Brezhnev era the Romanovs' names barely appeared in school history books or public discourse.

In 1979, Ministry of Internal Affairs filmmaker, Geli Ryabov, and geologist Aleksander Avdonin began digging in the area around Ekaterinburg, reportedly with the backing of Interior Minister Nikolai Shchelokov, a figure close to Brezhnev. Three skulls believed to the Romanovs were found and taken to Moscow, but when, fearing state censure, the Russian

The three skulls found at Ekaterinburg, believed to belong to the Romanavs

Orthodox Church declined Ryabov's request to give them a religious burial he returned them to Ekaterinburg and placed a simple cross on the soil.

Ten years later, following the advent of Gorbachev and perestroika, information about the execution of the Tsar and his family was made public by playwright Edvard Radzinsky. The Russian public was astounded and in July 1991 President Yeltsin ordered the site near Ekaterinburg to be further excavated. Nine bodies were exhumed. But what proof was there they were Romanovs? An intensive scientific investigation commenced, drawing on the expertise of an international team of historians, archivists, forensic specialists and geneticists. Meanwhile at Ekaterinburg the local Soviet had given the site of the Ipatiev House where Tsar Nicholas, his family and their servants had spent their final seventy-eight days – and which in 1977 had been demolished by order of the Soviet government – to the Russian Orthodox Church to build a memorial chapel.

After seven years of research it was confirmed that the remains found near Ekaterinburg were those of Tsar Nicholas, his wife and children and their attendants. Vital to obtaining the proof had been the DNA testing

of known descendents of the Romanovs. The most prominent figure to provide such evidence was the grandson of King George V and first cousin of the Tsar: Prince Michael of Kent. An accomplished Russian speaker, Prince Michael had long held a strong emotional attachment to the country, which he first visited in 1992 following the dissolution of the Soviet Union.

Born in Buckinghamshire, England in 1942, when the Prince was less than two months old his father the Duke of Kent, fourth son of George V and Queen Mary, was killed in a plane crash in Scotland. After leaving Eton the Prince enrolled at Sandhurst Military Academy and was commissioned as an officer in the 11th Hussars, his service including peacekeeping duties in the disputed territory of Cyprus in the early 1970s. Although not a recipient of the Privy Purse, on leaving the army in 1981 Prince Michael went on to perform regular ceremonial duties on behalf of the British royal family and to represent the Queen on state occasions.

Having played a key role in the identification of the Romanovs, when their remains were officially re-interred in 1998, the Prince travelled to St.

Petersburg to attend the ceremony. He was by no means the only member of the family tree to turn up to the auspicious event:

> *'Among the fifty or so Romanovs who arrived from all over the world to bury their dead relatives was one who happens to be my American neighbor, Alexei Andreivich, the great-grandson of Xenia and Sandro, who had escaped Crimea aboard a British warship. From Alexei, I've learned how all those Romanov uncles, nieces and nephews scattered by the revolution suddenly recognized one another in the hallways of the Astoria hotel in St. Petersburg. That day, in a televised address from the Peter and Paul Cathedral, President Yeltsin called the nation to atone for its "collective guilt." Alexei told me what it meant to him and his relatives to see the last flag-draped coffin lowered into the family crypt there. "Whatever lack of familial sense existed," he said, "coalesced into a bond that couldn't be broken."'*
>
> (*Anastasia Edel The Remains of the Romanovs, New York Times,* 10 July 2017)

The interment, eighty years to the day from the executions at Ekaterinburg, was one of the major highlights of a huge resurgence of interest in the imperial family. Books, magazines and TV programmes about the Romanovs proliferated and everywhere one went people seemed to be discussing them – telling the stories of those who escaped in 1917 and speculating on where their offspring – nephews, nieces, second and third cousins and grandchildren might now be living. A particular talking point among the Russian elite was whether one might in some way be related to this fabulous dynasty suddenly restored to glory in the public imagination.

At the time I was working in Moscow as a lobbyist and vice-president for Systema, a company dealing in IT, telecommunications, construction and infrastructure. Systema's leader thought that since everyone was so fascinated by the Romanovs it would be in the company's interest to hold a social event focusing on the theme. Moscow's mayor, Yury Luzhkov, who oversaw a lot of the modernisation and construction projects in the city, was a great supporter of Systema, and had ambitions to run for the Russian presidency. If we could attract a topical VIP to our party it would be great publicity for both Luzhkov and Systema. The obvious choice was the grandson of the Tsar's cousin, Prince Michael of Kent. Through his contacts, Systema's boss issued an invitation, which the Prince kindly accepted.

The Systema function took place in a large mansion outside Moscow, and as predicted Moscow's journalists were thrilled to see Prince Michael and his wife Princess Marie Christine there as guests of honour. Systema also had its own TV channel, enabling us to broadcast the event direct. The Prince and Princess were reserved and dignified in their demeanour but certainly looked every inch royalty, and everyone commented on the Prince's remarkable similarity to portraits of Tsar Nicholas: *'Prince Michael has a beard like the Tsar did…There is an extraordinary physical resemblance. If you were casting a film and wanted a character to play the Tsar, he seems almost a double.'* (*Spunik News/Voice of Russia* 2012)

It was clear from the Prince and Princess' expressions that they were

The Prince and Princess on a visit to Moscow in 1998

enjoying the visit as much as their hosts. Luzhkov lavished gifts on them including a good deal of silverware. The royal couple stayed for a week in Moscow, where at the prestigious Plekhanov Economics Academy the Prince was awarded an Honorary Doctorate, before travelling on to St Petersburg. Meeting a variety of politicians and business leaders, the Prince and Princess were on an extensive, tightly programmed itinerary but nonetheless took time to go among the public, who were equally thrilled to see them.

The following year Prince Michael was back in Moscow, travelling not in the back of a chauffeur driven car but at the wheel of a vintage Bentley. Leading fifteen other Bentleys from the Brooklands Motor Museum in the UK, the Prince drove from the site of Tsar Nicholas' first resting place at Ekaterinburg all the way to St. Petersburg to mark the Tercentenary of the city. Completing the 1,700-mile trip in ten days, the rally raised £120,000 for the Russian Children's Fire and Burns Trust, the St. Gregory's Foundation and other charities. As patron of the Russo-British Chamber of Commerce, and through his philanthropic and humanitarian work, Prince Michael has since made regular visits to Russia. The Friends of Russian Children, the St. Petersburg based Nochlezhka Charity Foundation, which provides shelter and food for homeless people, and the Russian National Orchestra and St Gregory's Foundation have all benefited hugely from his patronage and involvement and earned him the deepest respect throughout Russia.

In 2002, Prince Michael was awarded the International Man of the Year Award by the Plekhanov Economics Academy, and the following year gave him the 'Glory of Russia.' He was also made an Honorary Professor of the Sinerghia Economics and Finance Institute. In May 2005, he took part in the White Knights Ride, setting off from Russia's eastern seaboard at Vladivostok and finishing at Khabarovsk. The rally raised vital funds for The Prince Michael of Kent Foundation, set up to benefit health, education, culture and heritage in Russia, and is administered by CAF. Money was also donated to the London's Royal Marsden Hospital, in great need of a new rapid diagnostic scanner, and Britain's Charities Aid Foundation Russia (CAF). In recognition of the Prince's invaluable contribution to Anglo-Russo relations, in November 2009 President Medvedev presented him with one of the highest honours in Russia: the Order of Friendship. In 2012, came an honorary doctorate from the St Petersburg University of Humanities and Social Sciences.

What though of the Prince's royal Russian ancestors? Although the feverish curiosity in everything to do with the Romanovs had subsided somewhat since the late 1990s, stories and rumours about the family continued to pop up. At Ekaterinburg two sets of remains had never been found, those of the Tsar and Tsarina's only son, thirteen-year-old Alexei, and one of two Grand Duchesses also believed to have been held captive with the family during 1918. Over the years a number of individuals had claimed to be these missing Romanovs, but with the advent of DNA testing putting paid to imposture it was now generally accepted that young Alexei and the Duchesses had also perished at Ekaterinburg.

A growing focus of interest was the Romanovs' symbolic place in history and their significance as part of the identity of the new Russia. As early as 1981 the Russian Orthodox Church Abroad had canonized Tsar Nicholas II, his family and the servants who had died with them. The church within Russia, however, had been divided over what official theological attitude should be adopted towards the Romanovs. Critics argued that the family should not be elevated to martyrdom, as they had not died for their religious beliefs; others felt that it was the Tsar's weakness as a ruler that had allowed the rise of the Bolsheviks. By the year 2000 the debate was resolved by canonizing them not as martyrs but 'passion bearers', having died with Christ like resignation, if not explicitly as defenders of their faith.

For their most devout followers though, martyrs are how the Romanovs are still regarded, with the location of their final days on earth now a pilgrimage site: '*The scene was both moving and slightly surreal. On an overcast day in mid-May, a group of Russian tourists – families, fashionably dressed students, ruddy-cheeked, middle-aged men – milled around the Holy Royal Passion-Bearers Monastery, a collection of log churches set among birch trees on the outskirts of Yekaterinburg. The mood was sombre. A few people made the Sign of the Cross; others bowed reverently, whispering the words "how awful" as they took in the sights.'*

But what of so-called mainstream Russia's feelings about Nicholas II? A poll of 16,000 Russians conducted by the Levada Centre in Moscow in 2013, the 400th anniversary of the Romanov dynasty, found that 48 per cent had a good opinion of the last tsar. In the same survey Boris Yeltsin was the preferred choice for 22 per cent of those questioned and Mikhail Gorbachev for 21 per cent. Top of the poll as most popular 20th century leader, by a small margin over Tsar Nicholas, was Leonid Brezhnev.

Over the passage of time positive sentiment towards the Romanovs has persisted. Whilst this might be mostly nostalgia for a colourful and romantic past, there have also been calls for a return to the values of the imperial family, even for their physical reinstatement at the heart of the nation.

In 2015 it was reported in *Izvestia* that Vladimir Petrov, a lawmaker from the St. Petersburg area, had written letters to Grand Duchess Maria Vladimirovna Romanova in Spain and Prince Dmitry Romanovich Romanov in Denmark, petitioning them to help re-establish Russia's stability and prestige: '*At the present time, a difficult process is under way in restoring Russia's might and of returning its international influence… I am certain that during such an important historical moment, members of the Romanov imperial house cannot remain aside from the processes that are going on in Russia.*' Petrov proposed that a Tsarist palace in Petersburg or Crimea be set aside as an official Romanov residence, and that he intended to draw up a bill granting 'special status' to the family's descendents.

The *Moscow Times*, quoting from *Izvestia*, subsequently carried a statement from a spokesman of the Romanovs that Grand Duchess Romanova was willing to move to Russia without claim to property or political authority, but asked that the status of the said imperial house as a part of Russia's 'historical heritage' be recognised in law. Petrov told the Duchess and Prince Dmitry that, '*Throughout the history of its reign, the Imperial dynasty of the Romanovs was one of the pillars of Russia's sovereignty,*' and that their return to the motherland would '*revive the spiritual power of Russian people.*'

Others begged to differ. Sergey Markov, head of the Institute of Political Studies, thought that the return of the Romanovs would have little impact on modern day Russia. In his view, most Russians regarded them, '*either as victims because they were shot by the Bolsheviks, or as traitors who behaved irresponsibly during the critical years of the monarchy. Many believe that it was Nicholas II's abdication that provoked civil war.*' (Reported by Rebecca Perring, *Daily Express,* 24 June 2015). It was also pointed out that the descendants of the Romanovs were not a unified family but a house divided, with Grand Duchess Maria Vladimirovna Romanova and Prince Dmitry Romanovich Romanov both claiming to be its head. Irrespective therefore of the Grand Duchess's claims of political neutrality, it was felt in some quarters that a return of the Romanovs in any official capacity could generate unnecessary conflicts within Russia.

Sergey Markov also commented that, '*Most of the countries pay no respect to Imperial Houses, except for Great Britain and the Netherlands.*' Having observed British royalty I have to say there seems a very positive side to many of the traditions, not least the expressions of wonder and delight on young faces when they see the guardsmen parading in their finery in Whitehall or the glittering spectacle of 'Trooping the Colour' outside Buckingham Palace. It is not only children who are enchanted by these fairy tale scenes, whose picturesque, magical quality are a world apart from the grey protocol of ordinary government.

Pending the return of the Romanovs, Russia has no resident royal family, yet tourists and Russians alike take great pleasure in appreciating the country's imperial heritage, thronging in their thousands each year to look over the royal palaces and experience the grandeur of a bygone age. It was just such a link to the past that so captivated people when Prince Michael of Kent visited us in 1998, yet more so: here was a living connection, someone who not only looked like Tsar Nicholas but shared his royal blood.

Prince Michael continues to win hearts and minds in Russia, while his charity foundation finances ever more projects in health, education, culture and historical preservation. When I met him he made a deep impression on me; this was a man of immense self-command, profound intelligence and attentiveness, able to lead a discussion on a wide range of political, economic, historical and cultural topics. Such personal attributes coupled with a royal pedigree and the Prince's fluent Russian can open doors and break down barriers between East and West that would defeat lesser mortals.

One other thing that puts the Prince in a class of his own, according to fashion gurus, is his appearance:

> *'Unlike his clean-shaven royal relatives, Prince Michael dons a voluptuous beard that could make him a style icon all on its own. These regal whiskers have been compared to that of Tzar Nicholas II, the last of the ruling Romanov dynasty of Russia whom the Prince shares an uncanny resemblance to… The cool thing is the contradiction this beard presents as it has an old world charm that makes it so modern and just plain bad-ass…quite current and edgy by royal standards.'*
>
> (*Get The Royal Look*, Anthony Bryant, *The Gentleman's Ledger*, June 2015)

GIORGIO NAPOLITANO

On the 24 October 1922, in the city of Naples, 60,000 people gathered to hear a speech by a thirty-nine-year-old army veteran named Benito Mussolini. Ejected from the Socialist Party for urging Italy's entry into World War One, Mussolini's message was unambiguous: *'We want to rule Italy!'* One week later he and his followers had marched into Rome where King Victor Emmanuel III, fearing civil war yet confident that Mussolini could be contained, appointed him Prime Minister with full legal authory to run the country.

While the new administration promised workers an eight-hour day, the rich were wooed with a cut in inheritance taxes, and to gain the backing of the Catholic Church religious education was made compulsory in primary schools. By no means all Italians supported 'Il Duce' however; his parliamentary manipulations, the blatant use of intimidation by his 'blackshirts' – *'a good beating did not hurt anyone'* declared Mussolini – and tacit admission to the murder of leading Socialist deputy Giacommetti for daring to stand in his way, fed a groundswell of opposition from MPs and the press. An appeal was made to King Victor to dismiss Mussolini, but since this request came largely from republicans the monarch demurred. Meanwhile the abstention of a growing number of protesting MPs played into Mussolini's hands. On 3 January 1925 he made a speech: *'I declare… in front of the Italian people… that I alone assume the political, moral and historic responsibility for everything that has happened. Italy wants peace and quiet, work and calm. I will give these things with love if possible and with force if necessary.'*

The accent was decidedly on force. Over the next three years all opposition parties and newspapers were outlawed, a secret police organisation was set up and the death penalty reinstated for *'serious political offences'.* Local mayors

were replaced by new magistrates appointed by the central government in Rome. In addition Mussolini amended the constitution to create a 'diarchy' – a twin political leadership of the prime minister and the monarch. A strong king might have curbed the extension and abuse of power on the

Mussolini with two of his children

part of his PM; Victor Emmanuel's pusilanimity left Mussolini unbridled in his quest for absolute authority and in 1939 the Italian parliament was simply abolished.

Lawyer Giovanni Napolitano, a citizen of Naples, a poet and a man of liberal political persuasion, would have witnessed with some dismay the crowds cheering Mussolini in 1922. Three years later as the fascist leader, now Prime Minister, gave his second landmark speech, Giovanni and his wife Bobbio Carolina were looking forward to the birth of their child. Giorgio Napolitano was born on 29 June 1925 in the village of Gallo in Comiziano, a province of Naples. At the age of thirteen he was enrolled in the Classical Lyceum Umberto, later moving with his family to Padova and the Titus Livius Lyceum.

It was at school that Napolitano first became interested in dramatic art, the techniques of which would no doubt come in useful in his later vocation.

At the University of Naples he studied for a law degree, wrote theatre reviews for the college magazine and acted in plays produced by undergraduates belonging to the young fascist group the Gioventù Universitaria Fascista. This early close acquaintance with the right wing only served to confirm his belief in liberal values, finding the group to be *'in fact a true breeding ground of anti-fascist intellectual energies, disguised and to a certain extent tolerated.'*

Napolitano also performed at the local Teatro Mercandate in a comedy by Salvatore di Giacomo, and cherished a dream of making acting his career.

Drama of a darker kind was about to cast all such considerations to one side, however. Mussolini had first met Hitler in 1934. The Führer admired the Italian leader and had emulated his 1922 March on Rome with his own 'beer hall putsch' attempt to seize power in Germany the following year. Mussolini dismissed Hitler's claims for Aryan superiority, dreaming instead of Italian hegemony and a return to the glory days of the Roman Empire. To this end in 1935 he invaded Abysinnia, a move condemned by the League of Nations. Hitler, who had taken Germany out of the League in 1933, lent his support to Mussolini. The two countries moved to a closer alliance and in May 1939 Hitler and Mussolini signed the Pact of Friendship, a ten-year agreement to provide mutual military and economic support. Thus was born the Rome-Berlin Axis.

When World War Two began Mussolini waited until 1940 and the fall of France before taking Italy into the conflict. He expected a swift victory alongside the Nazis, reportedly remarking to his Chief of Staff: *'I only need a few thousand dead so that I can sit at the peace conference as a man who has fought.'* While Italian troops were dispatched to southern France, Mussolini also sent forces across the Mediterranean to North Africa, eager to seize control of French and British colonial territories for his future empire. The North African campaign was not a success, and in 1942 the Axis powers there surrendered. Mussolini responded by purging his government of those suspected of sympathising with King Victor Emmanuel, who had voiced increasing criticism of Italy's involvement in the war.

Meanwhile the tide of the conflict continued to turn inexorably against Mussolini. By July 1943 the Allies had taken Sicily and in August launched a bombing raid of unprecedented magnitude on Naples. On 25 August a vote of no confidence was issued against Mussolini and the following day he was taken under armed guard to an undisclosed location in the mountains at Abruzzo. On the 3 September at the Armistice of Cassibile in Sicily, Victor Emmanuel made peace with the Allies. Just two months later in a daring raid by Nazi paratroopers Mussolini was sprung from captivity and taken to Berlin. In less than a fortnight, under pressure from Hitler he was back in Italy setting up a republic in Salo and pledging to retake the rest of the country: '*I am not here to renounce even a square meter of state territory. We will go back to war for this…Where the Italian flag flew, the Italian flag will return. And where it has not been lowered, now that I am here, no one will have it lowered. I have said these things to the Führer.*'

In Naples, the teenage Giorgio Napolitano had joined his local partisan resistance movement, taking part in guerrilla campaigns against Italian and German fascist forces in southern Italy. It was an experience that would stay with him, and he would later pay tribute to the sacrifice made by many of his fellow citizens who joined the struggle: '*The values and merits of the Resistance, from the Partisan movement and the soldiers who sided with the fight for liberation to the Italian armed forces, are indelible and beyond any rhetoric of mythicization or any biased denigration. The Resistance, the commitment to reconquer Italy's liberty and independence, was a great civil engine of ideals, but above all it was a people in arms, a courageous mobilization of young and very young citizens who rebelled against foreign power.*'

American archives also bear witness to the vital importance of courageous young Italians like Napolitano in defeating the fascists: '*The contribution of Italian anti-Fascist partisans to the campaign in Italy in World War II has long been neglected. These patriots kept as many as seven German divisions out of the line. They also obtained the surrender of two full German divisions, which led directly to the collapse of the German forces in and around Genoa, Turin, and Milan.'* (Peter Tomkins, CIA Library, 2007. Tomkins served in the Office of Strategic Studies [The OSS] spending five months in Italy behind the German lines.)

By the end of September 1943 Allied forces had landed in southern Italy and were approaching Naples. The beauty of the Mediterranean landscape seemed to them untouched by the war Among the British contingent was journalist Alan Moorehead: *'As we drove over the Sorrento peninsula and caught sight of the city for the first time it appeared that nothing had changed.... The island of Capri serenely floating beyond the mouth of the bay. The crenellated city spilled along the shore, and that same mesmerizing blueness in the water. Sunshine and orange groves...'* Soon, a more disconcerting picture began to unfold, *'Driving through Castellamare and Pompeii the crowd thickened steadily along the road. On the outskirts of Naples itself it was one tumultuous mob of screaming, hysterical people, and this continued all the way into the centre of the city. They had been cruelly bombed. There had been spasmodic street fighting for a week. And now they stood on the pavement and leaned out of their balcony windows screaming at the Allied soldiers and the passing trucks. They screamed in relief and in pure hysteria. In tens of thousands the dirty ragged children kept crying for biscuits and sweets.'*

Meanwhile, along with fighting the fascists in the streets and hills of his homeland, the young Napolitano had become a political activist and in 1942 took the initiative in forming a Neapolitan communist group. Under Mussolini the Communist Party of Italy had been outlawed and many of its leaders rounded up, but one notable figure, Palmiro Togliatti, had evaded arrest and travelled to Moscow to attend a meeting of the Comintern. By 1944 it was Napolitano who would be laying the ground for Togliatti's return to Naples.

The city's inhabitants had endured years of danger and hardship, but the arrival of the Allies did not mean that their ordeal would be instantly over. Overall the mood was one of celebration and the British and American troops were welcomed, yet most citizens were no better off in material terms.

In fact things had worsened since the Allied bombing had broken the supply lines to the Axis front in Libya, resulting in a severe food shortage in Naples. Throughout the war, prostitution had been rife, for many women the only way to feed themselves and their families, a situation that would continue to the end of 1943 and beyond. Even previously well off Neapolitans were forced to beg for a few lira or some tinned goods in exchange for 'favours' or for their trinkets and household ornaments. '*The streets of Naples are full of people hawking personal possessions of all kinds: pieces of jewellery, old books, pictures, clothing, etc. Many of them are members of the middle class, and the approach is made in a shamefaced and surreptitious way. One and all, they are in a state of desperate need.*' (Norman Lewis, *Naples, '44*)

Some war weary citizens trying to scrape a living now looked back on the Nazi occupation as a case of '*better the devil you know*'. One man appeared in court charged with stealing a quantity of telephone cable left behind by the Germans. The Allies claimed that any such abandoned supplies were rightfully theirs. When the judge asked the accused if he had anything to say before being sentenced he replied, '*Under the Germans we were fed once per day, under the Allies we are being fed once per week. Either way, you are getting screwed.*' (*Life in WW2 Naples*)

By the spring of 1945 Mussolini's days were numbered. With the Allies advancing through northern Italy, he and his mistress fled in the direction of the Swiss border, planning from there to fly to sanctuary in Franco's Spain, but on 27 April they were apprehended by partisans. A few days later they were executed along with several other fascist members of the Salo Republic.

For Giorgio Napolitano and his fellow Italians the task now was to rebuild shattered towns and lives. The latter stages of the war had also brought some unexpected changes. To the ethnically homogenous community of Naples, the sudden appearance of African-American and Indian servicemen on their streets was a complete novelty. Written just over nine months after the arrival of the Allied troops, *Io nun capisco 'e vvote che succede* (I don't understand what's going on) a popular song by E. A. Mario and Eduardo Nicolardi, tells of the surprise at the birth of a black baby to a Neapolitan mother. The influx of new cultural phenomena, according to Neapolitan playwright Eduardo De Filippo, hurled his city abruptly towards modernity: '*The new century, this twentieth century did not reach Naples until the arrival of the Allies; here in Naples, it seems to me, World War Two made a hundred years pass overnight.*'

Through the wider availablity of television, ordinary Italians would become further familiarised with the world beyond the blue waters of the Mediterranean. In international relations the focus would be on the tense military and ideological divide that had emerged between the United States and the Soviet Union – the Cold War. Freed from fascism with the help of the Americans, it seemed Italy was now obliged to choose allegience to one of these two opposing political systems. Giorgio Napolitano had made his choice, becoming an official member of the Italian Communist Party in 1945. In the first post war election in June 1946, the Christian Democrat party won 35 per cent of the national vote. However, with the Socialists and the Communists winning 20 per cent and 18 per cent respectively, the two parties agreed to combine, forming the Popular Democratic Front.

When the next election came around in 1948, the United States, fearful of further left wing gains in Europe following the ascendancy of the communists in Czechoslovakia in February of that year, embarked on a feverish campaign to influence the vote. '*They aimed to ensure that the Italian elections did not produce any unwanted surprises and to prevent the Italian Communists from mounting a Czech-type coup…America decided that its actions should fall short only of provoking civil war in Italy as a pretext for re-occupying it!*' (Effie G.H. Pedaliu, *The British Way to Socialism: British Intervention in the Italian Election of 1948 and its Aftermath*). Ten million letters were purportedly written by American citizens to the people of Italy warning them of the communist threat, while Britain joined the propaganda war against the Popular Democratic Front: The British decision to intervene with such ferocity in the Italian election of 1948 was based on strategic and ideological considerations. Bevin's view was that Britain should give all the support it could to anti-Communist elements in Europe in order to resist the spread of Communism westwards. He saw Italy as the *'weakest link in the chain of anti-communist states', which had to be strengthened to resist Communist advances.'* (Ibid)

Historian Gianni Corbi described the 1948 election as *'the most passionate, the most important, the longest, the dirtiest, and the most uncertain electoral campaign in Italian history.'* (Robert A. Ventresca, *From Fascism to Democracy*). CIA operative F. Mark Wyatt was involved at the time: *'We had bags of money that we delivered to selected politicians, to defray their political expenses, their campaign expenses, for posters, for pamphlets.'* According to Wyatt, the Soviet Union gave similar financial assistance to the Popular Democratic Front, some of it allegedly siphoned off by corrupt officials. *'As the elections approached, the amounts grew, and the estimates [are] that $8 million to $10 million a month actually went into the coffers of communism. Not necessarily completely to the party: Mr. Di Vittorio and labor was powerful, and certainly a lot went to him.'* (Ibid) The election result was a 31 per cent share of the vote for the Popular Democratic Front and 48 per cent for the Christian Democrats. A left wing government would not be elected in Italy for another forty-eight years.

Giorgio Napolitano meanwhile had returned to his laws studies, and while completing his degree became a member of the Secretariat of the Italian Economic Centre for Southern Italy, over two years making a valuable contribution to the post-war regeneration of the area. In 1953, he was elected to parliament and rose steadily through the ranks of the party to sit on the National Committee for economic issues. When the Soviet Union intervened to quell Imre Nagy's liberal revolution in Hungary in 1956, Napolitano was faced with the choice of supporting the country's bid for greater democracy or following the Italian Communist Party line that Nagy's cohorts were counter-revolutionaries and 'despicable agent-provocateurs'. With some qualifications he chose the latter position, explaining in his

Italian President Giorgio Napolitano and his wife Clio receive German President Christian Wulff and his wife Bettina at the Quirinal Palace in Rome, 13 February 2012

later autobiography that his decision was based upon concern about the influence of imperialist forces, and that he viewed the Italian Communist Party's position as '*inseparable from the fates of the socialist forces guided by the USSR.*' In the context of the time the Hungarian issue was not clear-cut and the party was split from that point. Napolitano would admit to having had qualms over his decision.

In the 1960s Napolitano served for three years as mayor of his native city of Naples and pursued greater cooperation between the Communist and Socialist parties. By the 1970s he had been given responsibility for the Communist Party's international relations, the role in which, as Secretary of Komsomol's international affairs I first met him at a youth conference. I found him very open minded, although we had some differences of opinion. He thought the Soviets were departing from Lenin's ideals and that Brezhnev's bureaucracy had left people behind. I knew that this was a man who was very much on the left. He was to mellow, however. The mid-1970s saw the emergence of what was termed Euro-communism, with Napolitano, by now a known moderate or 'meliorist' within the Italian Communist Party, regarded as a key representative of the trend. In an interview with Eric Hobsbawn in 1977, later included in a book called *The Italian Road to Socialism*, he explained what he saw as the way forward: *'The only path that is realistically open to a socialist transformation in Italy and Western Europe – under peacetime conditions – lies through a struggle within the democratic process.'* (Alan Woods, 24 October 2012, *In Defence of Marxism*)

What few people knew at the time was that Napolitano was having talks with the American Ambassador Richard Gardner with a view to establishing relations between the US administration and a moderated, Euro-Communism style Italian Communist Party. An important outcome of the meetings was a US visa for Napolitano, allowing him in the 1980s to speak and lecture at Harvard and other institutions across the United States.

Fast forward twenty or so years from my first meeting with Napolitano. I am in a Moscow hotel where Boris Yeltsin has provided me with a room for one month. Foreign delegates and other guests and associates of the government are also staying here. In the breakfast room a few tables away I see a figure I think I recognise but cannot quite place. I speak to the manager and ask him discreetly who is the man sat over there please? That is Mr Giorgio Napolitano the Italian politician, says the manager. Uncertain if Napolitano will remember me, I write a note and have it sent to his room. Later that day he sends a message back and we meet up and have a long chat, catching up on the last two decades. Napolitano is now President of the Italian Chamber of Deputies. Since we last saw each other momentous events have occurred in the Soviet Union.

In a discussion chaired by ITN Diplomatic Editor Jon Snow, with BBC

Foreign Correspondent Charles Wheeler, Editor of *Soviet Weekly*, Victor Orlik and British Labour MP Dennis Healy, Napolitano has already expressed the view that in responding to Gorbachev's leadership, the West should above all emphasise the importance of international stability. '*On this question of reciprocation, of the Western response First, I understand why we sometimes use the term 'to help Gorbachev'. But it's not completely correct. Of course, we want to give a positive answer to the opportunities Gorbachev is creating, not only for the West, but for peace and cooperation. But the basis must be mutual advantage, in disarmament, in resolving regional conflicts, in all fields. There is no other possible policy, neither for Gorbachev nor for the West.*'

It was Napolitano's vast experience in war and peacetime, combined with scrupulous honesty and a shrewd and judicious approach to public affairs – his sheer wisdom in short – that surely played a huge part in the decision to appoint him in 2006 as President of Italy. '*The eighty-year-old, who has served as senator-for-life, is known for his understatement, gentle manners and moral rigor.*' (*New York Times*, 10 May 2006). His reappointment seven years later 2013, stepping into the breach by popular demand in the wake of an electoral deadlock – '*I cannot shun my responsibility towards the nation*' – brought forth further plaudits: '*Italian President Giorgio Napolitano, re-elected on Saturday for an unprecedented second term in office, is known as a measured, mild and immaculately-mannered politician. His discretion and diplomacy, and his preference for working behind the scenes have earned him the respect of those in Italy and beyond.*' (BBC News, 2013)

Shakespeare famously tells us that '*Some are born great, some achieve greatness and some have greatness thrust upon them.*' In Giorgio Napolitano's case it is all three that are most decidedly true.

משרד ראש הממשלה
ישראל

BENJAMIN NETANYAHU

There is category of people one meets in life that is quite distinct. The individuals within this group are all unique in their own personalities and the way they apply themselves in their particular fields of endeavour, yet they all have one thing in common: they know exactly what they want – not just today and tomorrow and next week, but in ten, twenty, thirty years time. They have a grand design. Their aim is unerring and they go all out to follow it. Such a person is Benjamin Netanyahu.

When Theodor Herzl was working as a journalist in Paris in the 1890s, anti-Semitic attitudes were commonplace throughout much of Europe. In France the notorious Dreyfus Affair served to intensify negative feelings towards the Jewish community. For centuries the image of the wandering Jew, stateless, shunned, hounded and forever in exile had persisted. For those caught up in the pogroms, persecution had been a reality. Herzl, dreaming of a land where Jews could feel secure, a place they could truly call home, in 1896 set out this vision in his pamphlet *Der Judenstat* – The Jewish State: '*I believe that a wondrous generation of Jews will spring into existence… The Jews who wish for a State will have it. We shall live at last as free men on our own soil… The world will be freed by our liberty, enriched by our wealth, magnified by our greatness. And whatever we attempt there to accomplish for our own welfare, will react powerfully and beneficially for the good of humanity.*'

In 1948, Herzl's dream was realised on the eastern shores of the Mediterranean with the creation of the state of Israel, its first Prime Minister David Ben-Gurion. Forty-eight years and numerous major and minor battles later it was the turn of Tel-Aviv born Benjamin 'Bibi' Netanyahu to lead this small, controversial, immensely vibrant nation. It was 1996 and Israel's population had grown considerably. In 1990 alone around 200,000 immigrants had arrived from the Soviet Union, coinciding with the two countries entering into a trading partnership after a hiatus of over two decades. 1990 was the year that the United States House of Representatives adopted a resolution recognising Jerusalem as Israel's capital city, a move unlikely to please her Palestinian neighbours. Yet Israel was not just home to Jews; thousands of Christians and Arabs also lived, worshipped and worked in Jerusalem. Nasser may have once been rumoured to want to drive the Jews into the sea (it is disputed whether he or anyone else ever said this) but Egypt and Israel had in 1977 made a lasting peace, likewise with Jordan in 1994.

The continuing source of tension was the land inhabited by the Palestinians to the east of Israel's border, and the heated question of where that border should lie. More extreme Arab opinion was thought still to question the whole validity of the Israeli state. In 1993, Israeli Prime Minister Yitshack Rabin and Palestinian leader Yasser Arafat had met in Oslo to seek a treaty, or at least some way forward. A major breakthrough during these discussions came in the form of a letter written by Arafat acknowledging Israel's right to exist. The results of the Oslo Accords included Israeli recognition of a Palestinian Authority in future negotiations, a degree of Palestinian control over sections of the West Bank and the Gaza Strip and agreements on borders and Israeli settlements.

The terms that Rabin had agreed to with the Palestinians in Oslo did not find favour with all Israelis. Two years later in the centre of Tel Aviv one of them, an extreme nationalist, shot him dead. Shimon Peres of the Labour Party stepped into the breach. The following March Palestinian suicide bombings in Jerusalem killed thirty-two Israelis. The agreements reached at Oslo were again in doubt, and feeling the need for a mandate from the country Peres called an election. Netanyahu, by now leader of the rival Likud Party, ran with the slogan: '*Making a Safe Peace*'. He also brought in outside help in the form of US Republican campaign manager Arthur Finkelstein. The hard-hitting American style of winning votes paid off, and Benjamin Netanyahu became the youngest ever Israeli Prime Minister, and the first to have been born after the country's creation.

With Israeli citizens apprehensive about terror attacks on their streets and the Palestinian leadership apparently unable to prevent them, the peace process appeared to be in tatters. The memory of Rabin's assassination was also still fresh in everyone's minds. Was the situation the new Prime Minister had inherited a golden opportunity or a poisoned chalice? Netanyahu was not someone afraid of a challenge. His early teachers describe him as punctual and disciplined, active and brave, and in high school in America he had joined the debating club. Neither was he unacquainted with physical danger. Like most young Israelis he had undertaken military service, but Netanyahu's time had been served with the elite Sayerat Matkal unit. Wounded several times, his missions included the War of Attrition in the late 1960s and rescuing hostages from the hijacked Sabena Flight 571 in 1972.

For his university education Netanyahu chose architecture, though interrupted his studies at the Massachusetts Institute of Technology to return to Israel and fight with the Sayerat Matkal in the Yom Kippur war. Postgraduate degrees followed, but in 1976 while working for his doctorate,

The hijacking of Sabena Flight 571

his brother Yonatan, commanding the Sayerat Matkal in a mission to free hostages from a plane at Entebbe Airport in Uganda was killed. The loss had a profound effect on Netanyahu, and in a visit to Entebbe several decades later he would recall Yonatan as, *'a great writer, a great thinker, but he was also a man of action; he was a commander in battle unsurpassed, unmatched; he had the capacities of thought and action, rumination and purpose... He had a great soul.'* (*New York Times*, 4 July 2016)

Although three hostages also died at Entebbe, the daring mission was hailed a success, Israeli morale was given a huge lift and the incidence of hijackings in general subsided. The reality of terrorism had been brought home to Netanyahu in a very personal way, and the experience would harden his attitudes. His first response was to found an anti-terrorism institute in Yonatan's name, a project that brought him into the public spotlight and to the attention of the Israeli ambassador in Washington, Moshe Arens, who appointed Netanyahu as his deputy. The job was a major turning point in his life: *'Overnight, Mr Netanyahu's public life was launched. An articulate English speaker with a distinctive American accent, he became a familiar face on US television and an effective advocate of the Israeli cause.'* (*Benjamin Netanyahu: Commando Turned PM*, BBC, 18 March 2015). The next step for Netanyahu came in 1984 with a promotion to Israel's representative at the United Nations, and in 1988 he returned to his country and began his climb to the top of the Likud Party.

While his drive and tenacity made an impression on those around him, few realised his potential to succeed. As T. A. Karasova, the author of *A Political History of Israel*, translating the words of one of the Avoda (Labour) Party leaders, Haim Ramon in describing Benjamin Netanyahu writes, *'I have never met a man who had so much ambition and will to become the head of state. Right from the very beginning, he shocked his fellow party members with his stubbornness. He kept repeating that one day he will lead the party, however, nobody took him seriously including the Likuda leaders Ehud Olmert, Dan Meridor, and Roni Milo, the most popular figures in the leadership of Herut who did not doubt their victory and took no notice of Netanyahu's claims. It is likely that this trio, nicknamed the "Likuda Princes", was so sure of their success that they had forgotten one "golden rule" – you must fight for victory from the beginning until the end, only then the victory will be yours.'*

Although Netanyahu's competitors are remembered as calm and self-assured at this time, Likud was nonetheless suffering from a lack of morale, and there were those that saw in the newcomer the potential to revitalise the party. Let me quote the veteran of political battles Yitzhak Shamir, who after the defeat of Likud in 1992, explained his choice: *'I saw that the fighting spirit in the party was extremely weakened, comrades did not believe that it was possible to win over Avoda, Bibi however was of a different view. He was the only one who believed that he could win. I think that he inherited his strength of mind and the character from his parents. And, I said to myself: we need to work on this guy and see how he will withstand the tests of time during his journey.'*

The elections for the leader of Likud were scheduled for March 1993, and Netanyahu was up against the following people who had expressed their interest in running for the post: David Levy, Benny Begin, Mote Kanav, Meir Sheetrit. The ballot was cast and the results were as follows: Netanyahu received 52 per cent of party members' votes, Levy 26 per cent, Begin 16 per cent and Kanav 6.5 per cent.

Elected as the Likud Party's leader Netanyahu was on track to be Israeli Prime Minister, and it was shortly before this that I met him in Moscow. The Assembly of the Council on Foreign and Defence Policies (SVOP) was holding one of its regular conferences, and Netanyahu had been invited as our guest speaker. He spoke eloquently and participated actively, answering numerous questions with enthusiasm and insight. When the formal proceedings of the day were over a few of us gathered that evening at Sergey Karaganov's home, among them Netanyahu. My wife and daughter were also present, and over an excellent dinner enlivened by vodka we launched into further stimulating conversation, discussing in great detail the international situation and the hot topics of the day.

We sat up until 3am talking – covering everything from US foreign policy to Russia and the Middle East, obviously with a lot of debate about the protracted Israeli-Palestinian conflict. I particularly admired Netanyahu's ability to explain his position on a number of pressing political issues in a clear and coherent way. That is not to say he had no flexibility of vision, indeed he was quite willing to look at things from more than one perspective before making up his mind. He was also good at thinking ahead in his analyses, taking the long view and considering not just the current situation but about how things might pan out in two years' time or a decade or more.

I shall certainly not forget his contribution to a conversation with myself, the gist of which ran thus: '*Complex and hard years await the USSR, but I am not sure that your political elite and leadership realise that and take the necessary measures. It feels like the fundamental threat against your country is not taken seriously at all. Your society is gradually disintegrating from within and it feels like the society is losing those values that were cemented by the very people and the government. The elite has changed, and in my opinion, you are gradually losing the youth.*'

Hearing these views on the Soviet Union, a number of us disagreed and tried to convince him otherwise. I must admit that I was one of them. Netanyahu listened patiently to our thoughts, sometimes shaking his head. At the end of the discussion he said that he really wanted to believe what we were saying but felt obliged to stand by his observations. Time and events have shown that he was right. Even by the mid 1990s, we who lived and worked in the Soviet Union could not see with any proper clarity where things were heading. Possibly it was still too early for us to tell, perhaps we lacked objectivity – the perspective of a shrewd outsider like Netanyahu – or maybe it was wishful thinking on our part. Maybe it was all three.

There was another subject Netanyahu and I discussed that would have a far more heart-warming outcome. Discovering that I was from Baku he told me he believed he had a female relative born in Azerbaijan with whom he

Netahyahu being greeted at Andrews Air Force Base, Maryland, USA, 18 July 1996

had lost contact. He would dearly love to know if she was still living there and to get in touch. Could I possibly help? Baku's large Jewish community has for centuries lived peacefully among the wider population, and there are numerous synagogues and Jewish cinemas. Unlike in other parts of Russia, Azerbaijan's Jews have not been subject to oppression or social exclusion. Baku has always been a very tolerant, open and diverse place. From around 200 BCE traders and explorers of many nationalities passed through on the Silk Road between Europe and China. Some of these travellers, including Jews, stayed and settled in Baku.

I had previously looked through the statistics and discovered there were in all 112 nationalities represented and that around half of them had intermarried. After making a few enquiries I found Netanyahu's relative was alive in Baku, though rather impoverished and in need of looking after. I passed the information on to Netanyahu, who sent me a letter of thanks and said how pleased he was, and that he would straightaway be providing financial assistance and medical treatment for the lady.

Netanyahu's first term as Prime Minister lasted three years. During that time he met with Yasser Arafat, and despite his strong reservations about the terms of the Oslo Accords, made significant territorial concessions to the Palestinians. After spending some time away from politics, when Likud was returned to power in 2001 under Ariel Sharon, Netanyahu served in his government as Foreign and then Finance Minister. When Israel withdrew from the Gaza strip in 2005 he stepped down in protest. A year later though he was back, and has now been elected Israeli Prime Minister four times, equalling David Ben-Gurion, and at the time of writing is on track to beat Ben-Gurion's record as Israel's longest serving Prime Minister.

Strong leaders can never get along with everyone. The famous special relationship Israel holds with the United States came under particular strain during the Obama administration:

> *'From the start, the two did not see eye to eye. Idealistic and perhaps overconfident, Mr. Obama arrived in the White House certain that he could be the president who would finally resolve the decades-old dispute between Israelis and Palestinians. But Mr. Netanyahu saw a naïf who failed to grasp the existential threat to Israel and who demanded more of his friends than his enemies. The relationship was marked by one conflict after another, a reflection of not just personal differences but deeply held and diverging policy objectives of the men and their countries.'*
>
> (Peter Baker, *New York Times*, 23 December 2016)

> *'It is also often the case that those with a reputation for strength respect one another. A politician renowned for her purposeful character won plaudits from Netanyahu. Margaret Thatcher was he said, '...not only an economic leader but a world leader, helping, along with President Reagan, to end the Cold War bloodlessly...(and) inspired many around the world with conviction, determination and courage.'*
>
> (*Israel National News*, 17 April 2013)

As Prime Minister of a country like Israel, Netanyahu can never afford to drop his guard. Surrounded by potential and actual enemies, he remains crucially aware of the need for active diplomacy. In a visit to Moscow in September 2015 he expressed his concern over the implications for Israel of the conflict in Syria. *'As you know, in recent years and even more so in recent months, Iran and Syria have been arming the radical terrorist organisation Hezbollah with advanced weapons, which are aimed at us. Meanwhile, Iran, as the benefactor of the Syrian army, is trying to build a second terror front against us from the Golan. Our policy is to thwart the flow of these weapons...I thought it was very important to come here, both in order to make clear our positions, and also to ensure there will not be any misunderstandings between our forces.'* (*Guardian*, 21 September 2015)

President Putin sought to reassure the Israeli leader and said Russia was *'mindful of the many former Soviet citizens'* in Israel, adding that every Russian

Secretary of State Madeleine Albright (centre), Israeli Prime Minister Benjamin Netanyahu (left) and Palestinian Leader Yasser Arafat (right) in Houghton House at the Wye River Conference Centre, 16 October 1998

action in Middle East *'has always been very responsible. We are aware of the artillery against Israel and we condemn it.'* (Ibid) Maintaining the security of his country whilst attempting to keep both America and Russia on side can be no easy task for Netanyahu. *'Since the start of the Ukraine crisis, Israel has kept a low profile, attempting to maintain cordial contacts with Moscow, even as the US has criticised Putin's policies – a balancing act analysts believe will become ever harder to pull off.'* (Ibid)

As far as America is concerned, Netanyahu's relations look to be more positive at least with Donald Trump than they had been with Obama. After a meeting in the White House the two leaders:

> *'...discussed their continued cooperation across a range of issues and stressed their goals of countering Iran's malign influence in the region and resolving the Syria crisis in a manner consistent with American and Israeli security interests. The statement said the two also discussed their continuing efforts to achieve an enduring Israeli-Palestinian peace agreement, the optimism in the region about peace, and expanding economic opportunities to improve conditions for peace.'*
>
> (*Los Angeles Times*, 22 September 2017)

A handsome man possessing great charisma, Netanyahu has been married three times. One imagines it would be hard work keeping up with him. It was my impression that he was extremely well organised, very focused on going after what he wanted to achieve. People talk about a force of nature, and that is what he is. As soon as he enters a room you can feel his energy. I remember how he would get talking to people very easily, and that he had a very friendly, pally disposition. But straight away you could feel that he was leading you, and was quickly in charge of the conversation, taking it the way he wanted it to go. It was quite incredible, even if you thought you had the upper hand there was always a reason for his comments and questions. I would never wish to change places with the people working with him, as I believe he is very demanding of his colleagues and strong minded, difficult some might say. But in a culture like Israel you need someone of that calibre to take the reins. Just totting up the number of years he has been at the centre not just of Israeli politics but also of world affairs, Benjamin Netanyahu is clearly a man of exceptional qualities, a huge figure.

In September 2017 in a speech given to the United Nations, Netanyahu celebrated his country's achievements in modern industry: '*…cutting-edge technology in agriculture, in water, in cyber security, in medicine, in autonomous vehicles — you name it, we've got it.*' He also reminded his audience of the work Israel had done in fighting terrorism: '*In recent years, Israel has provided intelligence that has prevented dozens of major terrorist attacks around the world. We have saved countless lives. You may not know this, but your governments do, and they are working closely together with Israel to keep your countries safe and your citizens safe.*'

For a man who has always had the courage of his convictions, it is when Benjamin Netanyahu uses humour to make a point that he is perhaps at his most serious. Referring in the UN speech to his recent round of diplomatic visits he said, '*After seventy years, the world is embracing Israel, and Israel is embracing the world. One year. Six continents. Now, it's true. I haven't yet visited Antarctica, but one day I want to go there too because I've heard that penguins are also enthusiastic supporters of Israel. You laugh, but penguins have no difficulty recognising that some things are black and white, are right and wrong.*'

CONDOLEEZZA RICE

'My parents have convinced me that you might not have the money to buy a hamburger, but this does not mean that you cannot become the President of the United States of America.'

These are the words of Dr Condoleezza Rice. It was Sergey Karaganov, my friend and colleague at the Council on Foreign and Defence Policies who first introduced me to Dr Rice. Sergey is a person of high intellect, widely educated and energetic who put a lot of time and effort into running the council, bringing together Russian, European and US political scientists and journalists to share their knowledge and experience, learn from one another, and see what contributions between them they could offer to the public and the governments of the world in the pursuit of greater peace and security. Annual meetings were scheduled to discuss current problems and issues of the time, focusing in particular on the constantly evolving relationship between Russia, the countries of Western Europe and the US. Sergey has continued to work hard at keeping this stimulating and, I hope, valuable forum going.

Despite the heated tone of some of our debates, which could go beyond a polite exchange of views, I cannot remember in decades of meetings anyone ever taking offence. Believing passionately in what they were saying and eager to convey their ideas, people often expressed their views trenchantly but no one had a personal agenda. For a start most of the delegates were fully or semi-retired, they had taken a back seat so to speak and had nothing to prove. An atmosphere of comradeship and professionalism thus flourished, which was to the benefit of the debate. Between them people seemed committed above all to thrashing out the truth of whatever subject was under discussion, bringing their, often diverse, perspectives to bear on some of the thorniest and most controversial issues of the day.

Without a doubt Sergey Karaganov played a big part in keeping the proceedings of our meetings orderly and temperate, his gentlemanly diplomacy able to calm even the fieriest of debating opponents. Condoleezza Rice first took part in one of these conferences in Moscow in the 1990s. An attractive and confident person with an incisive, independent mind, Dr Rice could clearly have won the attention of any audience, while her academic standing and proximity to the upper echelons of the American government naturally stirred great interest. As a Fellow of the Council on Foreign Relations, from 1986 she had worked as special assistant to the Director of the Joint Chiefs of Staff, and been closely involved in nuclear strategic planning. 1986 was the year I had visited North Korea, which a few months earlier had signed the Non-Proliferation Treaty. A decade later they would be discovered to have broken the terms of this agreement.

Dr Rice's speeches concerning Russia and US-Russian relations, despite their straightforwardness sometimes, were at the same time apolitical and thought provoking. A number of the American delegates remarked in candid conversations that a wonderful career awaited her, and mentioned that she was close to the Bush family. I remember one evening about fifteen of us, Russians and Americans, were invited back to supper at Sergey Karaganov's home. Ever the welcoming host, Sergey created the most convivial atmosphere, the lively party savouring one another's shining wit and repartee along with the sumptuous cuisine.

Dr Rice, clearly remembering my role in Moscow as part of Mayor Yury Luzhkov's team, delicately led the discussion around to Russia's forthcoming presidential elections, the chances of the candidates, and so on. Recalling the details of our conversation, in which Sergey got involved from time to time, I can only applaud Dr Rice's subtlety and her sharp observations and assessment of the political situation in Russia.

As we continued talking I could sense Dr Rice slowly coming to the question, which I surmised for her was one of the most important ones: would Yury Luzhkov win the elections? With Yeltsin not riding high in the popularity stakes, the Russian people were certainly looking for a change, someone in whom they could place their trust. Luzhkov had the chance to be that person. His supporters, including myself, had discussed with Luzhkov the necessary protocol to put himself forward as a presidential candidate. He had preferred to ally himself with the business community, what came to be known as the oligarchs. When he took this course a number of people had been left disillusioned. When Dr Rice asked me whether Yuri Luzhkov might be president now, I had to tell her the answer was likely to be no.

That Condoleeza Rice had a sharp analytical mind was in no doubt. One imagines such talent would have been noticed early on and nurtured by her mother Angelina, a high school science teacher. Angelina also taught music and oratory, both important skills in a politician, blending the principles of harmony and modulation with clear and concise speech. Condoleeza's name comes from the Italian musical term *con dolcezza* – with sweetness – and such was her aptitude at the keyboard that an early ambition was to become a concert pianist.

With her father, John, being a church minister and pupil counsellor there was no shortage of moral guidance in the family. In the circumstances in which she grew up there were certainly difficult ethical issues for any caring parent to explain and for the young Condolezza to navigate, her hometown of Birmingham Alabama in the Deep South being still a racially segregated community by law. When her father applied to become a member of his local Democrat Party he was apparently turned down, yet the Republicans welcomed him. The loaded dice could also act as a powerful incentive, as John Rice's daughter, destined to become the African American Secretary of State, would later remark, '*You were told in segregated Birmingham that if you ran twice as hard, you might get half as far. And there were also people willing to run four times as hard so they could stay abreast. And once in a while, somebody was willing to run eight times as hard so they could get ahead.*' (*Guardian*, 16 January 2005)

Two incidents in particular from Condoleeza's childhood would stay with her. Just as most Americans of a certain age can recall the moment they heard Kennedy had been assassinated, so too they remember the Cuban Missile Crisis the year before. Condoleezza was almost eight years old in October 1962, and the incident remained for her, '*One of my most vivid childhood memories…in which the US and the Soviet Union engaged in a tense standoff over the placement of Soviet missiles in Cuba. We were glued to the set every evening during those 13 days. It was a very scary time. In school, we went through duck-and-cover drills. But the crisis in Cuba was no drill. I could tell that my father was worried, and I realized that this was something my parents couldn't save me from. It was the first time that I remember feeling truly vulnerable. The whole episode had a surprisingly strong impact on me.'* (Condoleezza Rice, *My Extraordinary Family*)

Aerial view showing missile launch site 2 on Cuba, November 1962

The second incident took place on 15 September 1963 and was much closer to home: a white supremacist attack on her primary school. *'That bomb took the lives of four young girls, including my friend and playmate, Denise McNair. The crime was calculated to suck the hope out of young lives, bury their aspirations. But those fears were not propelled forward, those terrorists failed.'* (Stan Corey, *Condoleezza, Condoleezza,* Australian Radio Broadcasting)

During the violent years of the Civil Rights movement, the possession of weapons was paramount to the safety of many African Americans in the South, a fact that strongly influenced Condoleezza Rice's later support for the second amendment to the American Constitution: the right to bear arms: '*We have to be very careful when we start abridging rights that our Founding Fathers thought very important. And on this one, I think that they understood that there might be circumstances that people like my father experienced in Birmingham, Ala., when, in fact, the police weren't going to protect you.*' (Quoted in *The Black Commentator* by George E. Curry from Dr Rice's interview on *The Larry King Show*)

When Condoleeza was thirteen the family moved to the state of Colorado, where John Rice became an assistant dean at the University of Denver, where Condoleeza, after attending a Catholic girls high school won a place to study Music. After moving on to a specialist music college, wondering if her abilities were sufficient for a career on the concert circuit, she enrolled for a course in International Politics. It was here, under the tutelage of Joseph Korbel, that Condoleeza Rice was to take the first steps towards her career as a stateswoman. Korbel, born in Austria-Hungary (subsequently Czechoslovakia, now the Czech Republic) in 1909, had lost both his Jewish parents in the Holocaust. Escaping to London with his wife and their infant daughter, Korbel worked with the Czech government in exile before returning home at the end of the war. He then served as the Czech Ambassador to Yugoslavia until the Communist Party took power in 1948, his views on democracy prompting him to seek political asylum in America.

Awarded a Rockefeller Foundation grant, Korbel joined the academic faculty at Denver, setting up the Graduate School of International Studies. By the time Condoleeza Rice became his pupil, Korbel's published works included studies of Tito, Czechoslovakia, Poland and the disputed territory of Kashmir, and was embarking on *Détente in Europe – Real or Imaginary*, examining the concept and practice of rapprochement between the Soviet Union and the US and Western Europe, and the extent to which it could progress. With the Cold War still very much on, this must have been a topic of great interest and concern to a bright young mind, especially one with such clear memories of the fear instilled by the Cuban Missile Crisis.

By her own account Condoleezza was greatly inspired by her tutor's knowledge and personal insight into the field of East-West relations. She also discovered that she had *'an inexplicable love for things Russian, that an adopted culture can teach you a great deal about yourself. Condi's passion for Russia seemed to have come out of nowhere, and for the next eighteen months Russia's history permeated her every waking moment. She quickly learned the language and began inundating herself with Russian media, even reading Pravda, the Soviet newspaper, on a daily basis. Shortly thereafter she began studying the Moscow press and military journals. She even named her car Boris after the country's leader, Boris Yeltsin.'* (L. Montgomery, *The Faith of Condoleezza Rice*, 2007)

Academically Condoleezza flourished, joining the prestigious Phi Beta Kappa society at age nineteen and going on to attain a University of Notre Dame Masters degree in Political Science. She took her first job in 1977, an internship with the Bureau of Educational and Cultural Affairs, a State Department office in the government of Jimmy Carter. In 1979 she travelled to Moscow, taking a summer course in Russian at the State University, and did further intern work with the Rand Corporation, the military research organisation funded by the American government and private endowment. Three years later she was awarded her Ph.D. in Political Science from her tutor Joseph Korbel's Graduate School of International Studies, her thesis the politics and military policy of Czechoslovakia. An interest in the international arms situation, and how to best manage it now led Dr Rice to a Fellowship at Stanford on its Arms Control and Disarmament Programme.

In terms of her own political alignment, Condoleezza was a supporter of the Democratic Party, the one her father would have joined in 1950s Alabama had he been allowed. In 1981, however, due to a course of action taken by Democrat President Jimmy, she changed her mind. Two years previously Soviet forces had occupied Afghanistan, which as Dr Rice pointed out, caused some dismay among the US citizens:

> *'...everyone was worried about growing tensions with the Soviet Union. I'd previously registered as a Democrat and voted for President Jimmy Carter in my first presidential election in 1976; I had this narrative in my head about reconciliation of the North and South and how he was going to be the first Southern president. Now I watched him say that he had learned more about the Soviet Union from this Afghanistan invasion than he had ever known. "Whom did you think you were dealing with?" I asked the television set. When Carter decided that the best response to the invasion was to boycott the Olympics, he lost me. I voted for Ronald Reagan in 1980.'*
>
> (*Condoleezza Rice My Extraordinary Family*)

As a born again Republican as well as a self-proclaimed Russophile, what though would Dr Rice have made of Reagan's description of the Soviet Union as 'the evil empire'? Perhaps she would have made a distinction between the Communist Party and the people of Russia and Eastern Europe. Speaking about one of the most iconic markers of the demise of the Eastern bloc, she quite bluntly attributed the event to simple incompetence. In 1989 the East German government relaxed travel bans, allowing its citizens to go in and out of the country more easily. It was hoped that this would encourage people not to leave permanently, as had been happening. It appeared, however, that the border troops had been given little guidance on managing this new policy, and as hundreds flocked towards the wall the officer in charge allowed them to go through. '*The unthinkable happened,*' *remarked Rice,* '*the Berlin Wall fell. The most momentous event in 40 years of international history occurred thanks to a gigantic bureaucratic screw-up in the GDR.*' (Ibid)

As had been whispered in my ear that night in Moscow, a wonderful career lay ahead of Condoleezza Rice, and the Bush family were to play a huge part in it. She in turn would make a major contribution to their foreign policy. They say talent will out, but how did this move into the inner circle of government begin? It was National Security Advisor Brent Scowcroft, who in 1989, having heard Dr Rice speak at a Stanford arms control meeting some four years earlier, appointed her to his team in the H. W. Bush administration as specialist in Soviet Affairs. The post was no sinecure or token gesture: *'Lacking a deep background in foreign policy, Bush counted on a team of foreign policy heavyweights with diverse expertise to help formulate policy based on his guiding principles, such as freedom, a strong military, and free trade.'* (What Happened, Scott McClellan, 2008)

Now thirty-five years of age and already with eight years at Stanford's Political Science department under her belt, Condoleezza Rice was stepping onto the world stage, doing politics one might say, for real. How would she fare? However smart or well informed an individual, diplomacy at any level calls for tenacity, adaptability and strong people skills. Personal chemistry, particularly with one's immediate colleagues is often crucial. The

Condoleezza Rice answers questions on the Middle East crisis with President George W. Bush, 7 August 2006

new Soviet specialist had all these qualities: *'Bush developed a strong personal bond with Rice and came to trust her judgment, instincts, and insights.'* (Ibid) Bush introduced her to Mikhail Gorbachev during her first year in the job, reportedly remarking, *'This is Condoleezza Rice. She tells me everything I know about the Soviet Union.'* (Ibid)

In 1991 Dr Rice took up private consultancy and returned to Stanford, where in addition to her academic work she proved herself a more than capable financial administrator, within two years turning the university's $20 million deficit into a surplus of $14.5 million. In January 1993, George Bush Senior was ousted from the White House by Bill Clinton. A Democrat with a youthful, modern image, the saxophone playing new leader needed skilled and experienced advisors, not least in the field of East-West relations. Dr Rice's track record with the Bush administration, despite the Republican label, made her a clear choice: *'Shortly after Clinton was elected, Strobe Talbott, his friend and closest adviser on Russia policy, had suggested that Condoleezza Rice be appointed the ambassador to Moscow, as a specialist on the Soviet Union.'* (*Rise of the Vulcans*, James Mann, 2004)

It was not until Clinton's tenure was coming to an end that Dr Rice began her return to America's main political area. The Republican opposition had already been regrouping, holding regular strategy meetings at which they analysed the weaknesses of the Clinton administration and planned their comeback. Among the foreign policy members at the meetings were Donald Rumsfeld, Dick Cheney and Paul Wolfowitz, who were joined later by Dr Condoleezza Rice. She more than pulled her weight, and put her personal stamp on the forum: *'Rice headed the group, referred to as the Vulcans…based on the imposing statue of Vulcan, the Roman god of fire and metalworking, that is a landmark in Rice's hometown of Birmingham, Alabama.'* (*What Happened?* Scott McClellan, 2008)

When George Bush Junior was elected president at the end of 2000, Rice was named as National Security Advisor. Over the next five years she would deal with a series of major emergencies, the 9/11 attacks on the World

Trade Centre probably the most serious by far. For Dr Rice, the incident would demonstrate that in times of crisis, the buck is often seen to stop before it reaches the presidential desk. Nine days before the attacks, CIA Director George Tenet had a meeting with National Security Advisor Rice at the White House to discuss a possibly imminent threat to the United States from Al Qaeda. Rice allegedly told Tenet to refer the matter to Donald Rumsfeld and the US Attorney General. Tenet later claimed this had been '*a tremendous lost opportunity to prevent or disrupt the September 11 attacks. Rice could have gotten through to Bush on the threat, but she just didn't get it in time, Tenet thought. He felt that he had done his job and had been very direct about the threat, but that Rice had not moved quickly. He felt she was not organized and did not push people, as he tried to do at the CIA.*' (*Washington Post*, 1 October 2006)

Condoleezza Rice meets Putin in the presidential residence near Moscow

The other enormously contentious issue in those early years of the 21st century was the Iraq War. When Bush appointed Condoleezza Rice Secretary of State in 2005, those who disapproved of the choice were said to feel betrayed by the bloody shambles of the Iraq campaign and the administration's seeming inability to successfully combat the war on terror. Some of the negative sentiment towards Dr Rice was unwarrantedly personal in tone, even racist, and an alleged slip of the tongue in referring to President Bush as 'my husband' during a public engagement, was pounced on unkindly by critics and gossip merchants. The detractors might have had a field day but there were plenty who spoke out in support of this immensely able and principled woman, calling not for a ban on criticism, but for it to be appropriate:

> *'Dr Rice... is admonished in many circles for her vision of American diplomacy and her handling of issues ranging from Iraq to the Palestinian elections to the rise of China, but such criticism is fair... As a conservative black woman, however, Dr Rice has had to endure an extra layer of deeply malicious and highly personal attacks... Dr Rice is eminently qualified to be secretary of state. She made it to the top because of her discipline, intelligence and political savvy...The Bush Administration's foreign policy is highly controversial and the subject of constant approbations and denunciations. The secretary of state, particularly one as powerful as Dr Rice, plays a key role in defining its day-to-day development. In assessing her successes and failures, let us – to modify the famous phase on Dr Martin Luther King – judge Condoleezza Rice not by the color of her skin but by the conduct of her statecraft.'*
>
> (Eric T. Miller, New Visions Commentary National Leadership Network of Conservative African Americans)

Condoleezza Rice has not (so far) become president. But she is the first female African American to have served as United States Secretary of

State. In 2009, as she returned to academic life, Barack Obama became the first African American President. In a country that many assert to be still racially divided, Dr Rice is clearly a positive role model, qualifying her support for affirmative action to achieve diversity in education with the view that race-neutral enrolment should be the goal of any institution. She has also opposed the removal of Confederate statues from the slavery era in southern states: *'If you forget your history, you're likely to repeat it…When you start wiping out your history, sanitizing your history to make you feel better, it's a bad thing.'* (*The Dothan Eagle*, May 2017)

A Republican for most of her adult life, Condoleezza Rice's belief in America as the land of opportunity regardless of race, creed or background seemed not in doubt in her 2012 Republican National Convention speech:

> *'When the world looks to America, they look to us because we are the most successful economic and political experiment in human history. That is the true basis of American exceptionalism. You see, the essence of America, what really unites us, is not nationality or ethnicity or religion. It is an idea. And what an idea it is. That you can come from humble circumstances and you can do great things, that it does not matter where you came from, it matters where you are going.*
>
> *Ours has been a belief in opportunity. And it has been a constant struggle, long and hard, up and down, to try to extend the benefits of the American dream to all. But that American ideal is indeed in danger today. There is no country, no, not even a rising China that can do more harm to us than we can do to ourselves if we do not do the hard work before us here at home. People have come here from all over because they have believed our creed of opportunity and limitless horizons.'*

As regards the East, when Condoleezza Rice asked me on that lively evening in Moscow several years ago which person I thought might replace Yeltsin, it seems she had a pretty good grasp of the situation in post-Gorbachev

Russia at that time. As to where she thinks the country is heading now, her more recent thoughts suggest it's still a matter of wait and see:

> *'Gorbachev is a complex man, but his biggest mistake was that he was a true believer in the Soviet Union. He was really convinced that if you got rid of Stalinism and you got rid of coercion, then it would emerge as the modern communist state... in the early 1990s... many Russians saw the privatization of the Boris Yeltsin years as deprivation and humiliation and chaos. It is a troubled country and it has not found a sustainable post-imperial identity.'*
>
> (*Der Spiegel*, 2010)

Condoleezza Rice and Daiane, 2003 world champion gymnast, met in Brazil in April 2005

Moscow International Book Fair
1987
arquitectura
popular
española

ANATOLY NAUMOVICH RYBAKOV

When Lenin returned to Russia from Switzerland in April 1917 and stepped off the train at the Finland railway station in Petrograd (later Leningrad, now St. Petersburg), the speech he made to the waiting crowd began with congratulations:

> *'Dear comrades, soldiers, sailors and workers, I am happy to greet in your persons the victorious Russian revolution, and greet you as the vanguard of the worldwide proletarian army... Any day now the whole of European capitalism may crash...'*

However, with the revolutionary movement in Russia still sharply divided, Lenin was also quick to warn that there must be no compromise with the side that for the moment appeared to be in control: *'I don't know yet whether you agree with the Provisional government. But I know very well that when they give you sweet speeches and make many promises they are deceiving you an the whole Russian people...comrades, you must fight for the revolution, fight to the end.'*

Lenin's speech signalled the beginning a few months later of the Russian Civil War, in which for the next four years his Bolshevik followers would be pitted against the White Army, a collection of factions united by broadly nationalist and authoritarian sentiments. Many of the White Army's supporters were anti-Semitic in their views and behaviour, although the largest common denominator was their antipathy to Bolshevism. In a country as large and diverse as Russia, however, it was not unusual for individuals to switch their allegiance according to expediency or whim.

For the Russian people these were unpredictable times, when even in the remotest areas of the country, violence and bloodshed could descend without warning.

Born in the Ukraine in 1911, and growing up amidst this political and military turmoil, Anatoly Rybakov was to turn the dramatic backdrop to his childhood into a gripping story for young people. The central protagonist of *The Dirk* is a boy named Misha, whose hero is Polevoy, a veteran of the Russian Navy who lives with the family and whom they call 'the Commissar'. One day, Misha notices Polevoy hiding something beneath an old dog kennel in the yard near his home. Intrigued, Misha decides to investigate, and looking under the kennel, he pulls out an exotic ceremonial looking knife: *'He turned the blade in his hand and noticed a hardly perceptible engraving of a wolf on one side. On the second side was a scorpion, on the third a lily. Wolf, scorpion, and lily. What could they signify?'* Misha's grandmother appears and he quickly tucks the weapon out of sight and takes it to his room, putting it under his bed till he can return it later.

That night Polevov's heroic persona is woven deeper into Misha's imagination as the sailor *'...spoke of voyages to distant lands, of mutinies on the high seas, of cruisers and submarines, of Ivan Poddubny and other famous wrestlers in black red, and green masks, of strong men lifting three horses together with the carts, each cart containing ten persons. Misha gaped in wonder....'* Polevoy also spoke of the *Empress Maria* on which he had served during the world war. The *Empress Maria* was a real ship of the Imperial Russian Navy, which had engaged the Ottoman fleet in 1915. The following year the vessel had sunk while anchored off Sevastopol. Spinning his tale, Polevov hints darkly that his ship was sabotaged: *'A black business that was...s he was not struck by a mine or a torpedo, but blew up on her own...the survivors, less than half the crew, were all either badly burned or injured.... Many people tried to get to the bottom of it... and then came the Revolution. You have to ask the tsarist admirals for an explanation.'*

Lying awake in bed that night and remembering the dirk secreted under his bed, Misha longs to join Polevov in some daring adventure: '*What a splendid thing it would be if Polevoy gave him the dirk. He would not be unarmed as now. And the times were alarming, with the Civil War going on. Bandits were running loose in the Ukrainian villages, and even the towns were not safe. Detachments of the local self-defence corps patrolled the streets at night, armed with old rifles with rusty bolts and no bullets.*'

Such a scenario was not pure invention. As throughout Russia, instability had continued in Ukraine after the revolution, with Bolsheviks, Anarchists, Nationalists and German and Austro-Hungarian forces among the factions fighting for ideological and territorial control. Rybakov's protagonist is just a boy, but one who longs for the day he is old enough to do his bit: '*…when he would be tall and strong… carry a rifle, hand-grenades, machine-gun belts, and wear a revolver on a creaky leather waist-belt. He would ride a raven-black horse, slender-legged, sharp-eyed, with a powerful croup, short neck, and a sleek coat… then he and Polevoy would go to the front and fight shoulder-to-shoulder; he would save Polevoy's life heroically and die, leaving his friend to grieve for him all his life; and he would never again meet a boy like Misha… And Misha went to sleep.*'

Misha's boyish dream is about to become reality. A few days later White Guards infiltrate the town, enter the family home and seize Polevoy. Hidden behind a coat stand, Misha hears them demand the whereabouts of the dirk. Polevov tells them nothing. Misha scurries upstairs, grabs the dirk, and as Polevov is being dragged away presses the weapon into his hero's hand. Polevov lunges at his captors and breaks free. However, before he can see whether Polevov has managed to escape, '*Misha is struck down by a terrible blow with the butt of a revolver and he sagged like a sack into the corner.*'

With this cliffhanging close to his chapter, a classic technique of great story telling, Rybakov has his readers hooked: what fate now lies in store for Misha and Polevov – and what is the secret of the mysterious engraved dirk that the White Guards are so desperate to obtain? Who would not want to read on!

Rybakov wrote *The Dirk* in 1948, by which time he had experienced considerable drama in his own life. At the beginning of Stalin's so-called Great Purge, in 1934 he had been arrested by the NKVD, the People's Commissariat for Internal Affairs, otherwise known as the secret police. On a spurious charge of subversion, Rybakov was sent to Siberia for three years. He was comparatively fortunate; Soviet records indicate that in 1937 and 1938 some 1,000 people a day were being executed for similar alleged crimes against the state, while some historians have estimated the killings at more than double that amount.

Among the victims were numerous writers and artists, and possibly what saved Rybakov was that he was not yet known as an author. On being released from Siberia he obtained a job as a transport mechanic, and when the Great Patriotic War began joined the military, becoming a tank commander. After publication of *The Dirk*, in 1950 he drew on his working experience to write *Drivers*, and in the years that followed devoted his energies to what would become his most celebrated work, *Children of the Arbat*. The central character of the novel is Komsomol member Sasha, an idealistic and mildly iconoclastic young man, whose attitudes change when, like Rybakov, he is arrested by the secret police. Shaken by his experience at the hands of the authorities, Sasha is now more circumspect, cautious and apprehensive for himself and his friends and family, and worried about the future of Soviet society.

The atmospheric setting of *Children of the Arbat* is the climate of fear and suspicion in the Soviet Union of the 1930s, in which the assassination of Sergey Kirov had signalled the start of the Great Purge. Kirov, who in the early 1920s was a senior figure in the Azerbaijan Communist Party and later party chief in Leningrad, had been a staunch follower of Stalin. His loyalty to the Soviet leader had not wavered through the years of compulsory collectivisation and the loss of millions of lives from famine. On 1 December 1934, in the corridor of his office at the Smolny Institute in Leningrad (St Petersburg), the forty-eight-year-old Kirov was shot in

Actors of the Brest drama theatre in the staging of Anatoly Rybakov's novel 'Deti Arbata' (Children of Arbat)

the back. Stalin had the killer and alleged accomplices executed. Despite no incontrovertible evidence ever being produced, some maintain that it was Stalin, fearful of a threat to his leadership, who had ordered Kirov to be killed.

A related theory is that Kirov's death gave Stalin a more credible pretext for his purge, letting loose the NKVD to root out and eliminate anyone suspected of disloyalty, or in many cases individuals whom they simply did not like the look of, or who were in the wrong place at the wrong time. *Children of the Arbat* tells the story of a group of people attempting to navigate this time of paranoia and state persecution, and conjures the feelings of anxiety and moral ambivalence that pervaded Soviet life.

The portrayal of Stalin is particularly striking, and although Rybakov had completed the work some time after the leader's death, it was not destined to see the light of day for several more years. '*The book had been intended as a reinforcement of the de-stalinisation process, begun by Khrushchev in 1956, but it had been an early victim of the move towards the policy pursued by Brezhnev, which was to leave things unsaid, rather than grasp uncomfortable nettles.*' (Harry Shukman, *Independent*, 4 January 1999)

Tentative permission to publish was then withdrawn repeatedly during the Brezhnev era, and although Rybakov could have found an overseas publisher he refused to do so on principle, feeling it would be a disloyalty to his fellow Soviet citizens. A number of copies were, however, printed and distributed in Russia through underground networks known as the Samizdat publishing, running the risk of severe punishment for those involved. (Vladimir Bukovsky, dissident and activist against the political abuse of psychiatry in the Soviet Union, coined his own definition of Samizdat publishing: '*I write it myself, edit it myself, censor it myself, publish it myself, distribute it myself, and spend jail time for it myself.*')

When the Gorbachev era and glasnost and perestroika arrived, *Children of the Arbat* hit the bookshelves, reaching a massive readership and creating a huge impact. The book was like a literary bomb exploding in the collective

Soviet writer Anatoly Rybakov holder of the USSR and RSFSR State Prizes visits Sixth Moscow International Book Exhibition

mindset. Rybakov had opened the door on history, showing the Russian people a past that the older generations already knew of, but which no one had been allowed to talk about. No one could deny that the past had been an immensely difficult time – the civil war, the executions of thousands of Russians without good reason or trial, the forced collectivisation, famines and deaths of five to six million people, the Nazi onslaught. But now the post revolutionary story was told in all its tragic detail – the lies, secrecy, conspiracies, mass murders, brutality, cover-ups, moral compromises and moral bankruptcies that had taken place alongside the sacrifices and heroism of a huge number of individual Russians.

Rybakov followed up with two more books reprising aspects of his own experience: *Fear,* in which a well-meaning young man publishes a joke in a student newspaper and receives three years in exile, and *Dust and Ashes,* charting the journey of a Soviet tank commander in the Great Patriotic War from Siberia to Stalingrad and ultimately to Berlin. The impression left on the Russian public and critics throughout the world by these three works, was to be a lasting one:

> *'In the Arbat trilogy Rybakov reveals his particular genius: an ability to combine a powerful sense of drama with a high degree of political and historical understanding. The work is neither a history with a thin veneer of fiction nor a story in which great historical events serve as mere background. It is not simply the product of a conscientious researcher, but a genuine work of art, a profound and moving tragedy… The lives of Sasha and his former companions are moulded by the terrible experiences of the 1930s: the Kirov assassination, the mass arrests, the frame-up, torture and murder of Old Bolshevik leaders and socialist opponents of the ruling bureaucracy.'*
>
> (World Socialist Website, 5 January 1999)

Following on the heels of the Great Purge and collectivisation came the Nazi invasion and occupation of large parts of Russia. Inflicting a further huge death toll and immense suffering, the war years had forged another deeply moving collective memory. A lot harder to confront were some of the events that had taken place in Ukraine during the 1940s. Rybakov chose to do just that in his 1978 novel *Heavy Sand,* the saga of three generations of a Jewish family living in a small town near Chernigov, the author's birthplace. When the Nazis arrive, the local Jewish population is rounded up and forced to work under the worst inhumane conditions. Eventually the captives rise up against their oppressors, and although most are killed, a few hundred escape to the forest. When the escapees attempt to join the Russian partisans, however, they are not always welcomed. Some are even murdered.

The theme of anti-Semitism that Ribakov addresses in *Heavy Sands* had long been taboo in Russia: '*It was not to be mentioned that Jews were singled out for extermination by the Nazis, or that the Nazis had much local help in the process.*' (Walter Z. Laquer, *Commentary Magazine*, 1 June 1979). Rybakov also took issue with the received wisdom that Ukraine's Jewish population suffered as a result of their own cowardice and inertia: '*He points out that most of those in the ghettos were either elderly people or very young or ill, since all men of military age were serving in the army. And he also notes the fact that hundreds of thousands of young and strong Soviet prisoners of war were also killed in the camps and did not resist – for what could they have done?*' (Ibid)

Rybakov recalled Ukrainian Jews being sent to their doom by the people who in peacetime had lived alongside them: '*Of the "good neighbors," Rybakov says, not a few betrayed the Jews, either because they coveted their houses and property or because they were simply scoundrels. The local police were equal in sadism to the SS.*' (Ibid)

Anatoly Naumovich Rybakov came to Baku in 1975, to the same Books for Children and Youth festival attended by Kataev. As the member of the festival committee for the event, I was working alongside an official of the Azerbaijani Writers Union and a representative of the Soviet Union Writers Organisation who had come down from Moscow. Each of our visiting authors was also assigned a young Komsomol member with a particular interest in literature to be their assistant during the festival. Like Kataev, Rybakov was eager for me to take him on the Stalin tour of Baku, visiting the houses and streets the leader had frequented as a revolutionary young firebrand in the early 1900s, including of course the Bailov prison, to sit in the cell and travel back in time in his imagination. I also took Rybakov to our local archives, and at that time we even had two people still living in Baku who had known Stalin during his stay in the city.

These visits formed just a fraction, but a meaningful one I imagine, of the research that Rybakov wove over the years into his writing. He has been criticised by some historians as misrepresentative, a charge that the author dismisses. The point is that he never claimed to write history textbooks, but rather interpretations of history – fictionalised accounts in his novels, and personal retellings of the recent past in his biographical work – describing Russia since the revolution and the people striving and suffering within in it as he saw them. Rybakov had a simple answer to his critics: if they thought the events in his books should be presented differently, then they should go ahead and write their own versions.

The other vital thing to remember is that Rybakov's aim was to do more than compile an exhaustive list of people, places and events; as a novelist his achievement was to take all those elements and bring them to life for his readers. This skill is seen at its height in his best known work, *Children of the Arbat*: '*The author has a deep insight into his characters, particularly the way in which the social experiences through which they pass shape their intellectual, political and moral development. This infuses the characters--and Rybakov's writings as a whole--with realness and life.... The chronicle of Sasha's disillusionment and alienation, of the accommodation of a number of his former acquaintances to the official regime, and the relative isolation of those who behave courageously and decently, including his mother and an intellectual neighbor, convincingly accounts for his transformation. At the same time it reveals important truths about the period in which Sasha matures.*' (World Socialist Website, 5 January 1999)

Comparing Kataev with Rybakov, Kataev's work has far greater lyricism and beauty. In his work Kataev is less interested in politics than in people – how they live, how they strive to maintain their integrity, how they love one another. I would say that Kataev is an absolute genius, and as a person he was very charming. Rybakov on the other hand, in the opinion of some, was opportunistic in using politics as the subject matter of his books and to further his reputation. Yet the political dramas he recreates are very compelling and played out by convincing actors, imagined and real.

A still from the film 'Vasily Surikov', 1959, directed by Anatoly Rybakov. It was a screened biography of the renowned 19th century Russian

How though can any novelist treat a figure of such magnitude as Stalin, for decades the most feared and loved man in Russia? Rybakov's approach was to reject the notion of a one-dimensional character:

> *'...one of Rybakov's most memorable portraits is that of the dictator himself: Comrade Stalin. The son of a cobbler, with a pock-marked face and a pronounced Georgian accent, Stalin is depicted by Rybakov as an astute manipulator of language. As a youth he was an aspiring poet and a candidate for the priesthood. Stalin's shrewd grasp of linguistic nuances undermines the literary aspirations of the novel's central protagonist: a*

young man steeped in the Russian classics, who can recite pages of Pushkin by heart.'

(Robert Shannon, *Peckham Independent*, 20 February 1993)

Rybakov was a master of his craft, a gifted storyteller. For a long time it was difficult for so many ordinary Russians, people just trying to survive, to escape the momentous events taking place in their county. The perennial, often tragic dilemma when a community or a nation is divided is the issue of whose side, if anyone's, the individual should be on. During Russia's post-revolution civil war, was it morally legitimate to sit on the fence? Given the dangers to life and property and the strife that was raging, the question was often redundant. Through his novels, Rybakov explores the bitter divisions that such predicaments inevitably created within towns and villages, families and friends, sometimes within each human heart. In *The Dirk*, Misha's Uncle Senya counsels against factionalism, instructing his nephew that the young especially should observe neutrality:

'The Reds are fighting the Whites and you're still too small to meddle in politics. Your business is to keep out of it.'

In the ensuing exchange, Rybakov endows his young hero with a defiant revolutionary zeal:

'Why should I keep out?' Misha said, touched to the quick. 'I'm for the Reds, you know.'

'I'm not agitating either for the Reds or for the Whites. But I consider it my duty, as a relative, to warn you against participating in politics.'

'Then according to you we should let the bourgeoisie rule? No! ...Uncle Senya...I don't agree with you.'

'No one's asking you whether you agree or not,' Uncle Senya said irritably, 'you listen to what your elders tell you!'

'That's exactly what I'm doing. Polevoy's my elder. My Father was…

And Lenin. All of them are against the bourgeoisie. And I'm against them too!'

Rybakov set young Misha's rousing speech several years before the Great Purge, the terror and the famines. Whilst *The Dirk* is on one level an exciting adventure story for young people, perhaps the author, consciously or otherwise displays here a hint of irony, a wry nod to the reader of what being 'against the bourgeoisie' was to lead to. Misha's idealism is presented for the most part as admirable, and the dark side of the Stalinist future is something he cannot predict. It is not until a later, adult novel that Misha's creator takes the reader forward in time, and suggests where his own sympathies really lie:

'In one passage in Dust and Ashes, Rybakov introduces the moving "testament" of Leon Trotsky by having Stalin read a copy of it. In this instant Stalin, the embodiment of police cynicism and reaction, is juxtaposed against Trotsky, whose message is imbued with optimism and faith in human solidarity. "Life is beautiful. Let future generations cleanse it of all evil, oppression and violence and enjoy it to the full." Stalin reads these lines in silent fury. Rybakov's message is unmistakable: in the end, Trotsky's vision will triumph over Stalin's brutality.'

(World Socialist Website, 5 January 1999)

TAHIR SALAHOV

Among the many celebrated Russian artists born during the last century, Tahir Salahov stands out as truly one of the finest in that gallery of fame. I had the honour of meeting Tahir for the first time in 1973. I was a young journalist on the radio in Azerbaijan reporting on culture and the arts. By then in his mid-forties, Tahir was already a leading figure in the art world both in Russia and abroad, and was about to become First Secretary of the Artists Union of the USSR. For the people of Baku there lay a special pride in Tahir Salahov, as it was the city of his birth, and where his journey to become a great painter had begun.

Around the time of that first meeting I was appointed Secretary of the Azerbaijan Komsomol, and it was in this capacity that I was soon to have the pleasure of working more frequently with Tahir. As well as encouraging student engineers and scientists, Komsomol was interested in new artists in all media – writers, poets, sculptors and painters. The first and most important requirement for any artist is to have the time and opportunity to sharpen their skills, to experiment, develop a style and produce a body of work. But without a wider audience to see and appreciate that work, who apart from the artist's family and friends is going to benefit? Our objective with Komsomol was to seek out promising artists, provide them with a platform and promote their work – finding gallery space, arranging exhibitions, reviews and public discussion. There were also a number of prizes and awards offered, all aimed at bringing gifted individuals into the public arena.

To fulfil this remit in the field of painting, Tahir and I travelled together to galleries and art schools, looking at the work on display and talking to young painters. Tahir lent his time and support generously, his discerning eye invaluable in spotting new talent, while his outstanding reputation was an inspiration to the young and a seal of approval to the whole project. In this way he was to play a key role in nurturing Russia's future artistic talent.

When the Union of Artists of Azerbaijan and the Central Committee of the Komsomol of Azerbaijan were jointly preparing an exhibition of young artists one year, as per usual an organising committee was approved, which included prominent Azerbaijani artists. Chairing the committee was Tahir, with myself as a deputy representing Komsomol. I was to learn a lot from this experience, not least about Tahir: from the very first meeting of the committee, it was clear that having him at the helm meant the exhibition was going to be a great success. I already knew him to be articulate and well organised, and now, seeing his attention to detail and perfectionism, combined with an ability to delegate and achieve results in a timely and efficient manner only increased my respect for him. When in 1978 I moved to Moscow as Secretary for International Affairs with Komsomol, I continued to liase with Tahir in his additional role of representing Soviet art and artists abroad. Spending more time together socially as well as professionally and getting to know one another's families, our friendship deepened.

Where had this man of such exceptional gifts come from? Always so industrious, positive and engaged, Tahir was rarely heard dwelling on his past. One day as we were talking, however, he began to reminisce about his childhood. He and his four siblings had lived with their parents in two rooms of a house in Baku, previously the home of an Iranian merchant. Following the revolution, the property had been divided up to take several families. Despite the cramped conditions, Tahir's sister Zarifa has some fond memories of those early childhood years:

> *'Once when Tahir and I were lying in bed, sick with scarlet fever, dad came home at night, bringing two yellow melons for my brother and me. After we got better, Father took us to the candy shop that was on the first floor of the building where the Literature Museum [Metropol Hotel at the time]*

> *is now located. He told us that we could order whatever we want. And as we had been on a restricted diet for a long time, I remember we ordered almost everything – as if we had never eaten sweets in our lives before. I always remember this when I think of Father. I know he loved us children very much.'*
>
> (*Azerbaijan International*, Winter 2005)

Tahir's first awareness of visual art came from a painting on the wall of the family home, left behind by the former occupants. Of unknown provenance, it depicted a lovely long-haired woman with her hands tied behind her back. The image stirred Tahir's curiosity, and a desire to create his own pictures. In the evenings when their father returned home tired from work, to keep his boys occupied while he took a nap, he would ask them to paint a picture of the Red Army hero Chapayev. Afterwards Papa would award a rouble for the best effort. Tahir was to find further inspiration at Baku's Belinsky Library, where one of the old librarians who taught children to read would also show them how to paint pictures and put them up on the wall. Thus Tahir had his first taste of an exhibition, and learned to appreciate the benefits of being nurtured as an artist.

Like many Azerbaijanis, Tahir's father Temur worked in the country's burgeoning oil industry. He was also political, having taken part in the 1906 strike in the rich Balakhani fields. In 1919 he joined the Communist Party and by 1935 had risen to a local government position in Lachin. Here he had met Mir Jafar Baghirov, First Secretary of the Azerbaijan Communist Party and a close associate of Stalin. Baghirov was frequently a guest in the Salahov home, and the two families both having summerhouses near the sea, the children would have tea and play together. At some point in 1936, Temur Salahov was accused of involvement in a plot against the government. Though strenuously denying the charge he was sacked by Baghirov, who also confiscated his Communist Party membership card. So angered and upset was Temur at being thrown out of work and unable to convince Baghirov of his loyalty, that in a heated moment he threatened that unless his card was returned he would kill him.

At 10 o'clock on the evening of the 29 September 1937, the life of eight-year-old Tahir and his family was about to change forever: '*I had just started school that year because I had been ill with scarlet fever the previous year. I remember lying in bed beside Father. He was reading the newspaper. Somebody knocked at the door. Father was wearing his white nightshirt, pants and slippers. So he got up and let those people in.*' (Ibid)

The late night visitors were two officers of the NKVD, the secret police, together with two of the Salakhovs' neighbours. Temur was asked to go with them, and while he got dressed they waited outside. When his wife asked if he had done anything, he replied that he had always been honest with the government and with her. It was an unforgettable moment for Tahir: '*Mom started to cry. Father kissed me. He asked mom where the money was and she replied: "Why are you asking? You know where the money is." And then he took some rubles and left. I looked out of the window and watched them leave – my father between those two NKVD agents. And that's the way it ended. For months, I used to look out of the window wondering when my father would be coming home again.*' (Ibid)

Tahir's father was sentenced to ten years imprisonment. No one in the family was allowed to attend the trial and Temur was forbidden to write letters. As the months passed Tahir's mother Sona would send parcels of clothes for her husband, and in one of them she included six handkerchiefs. In the summer of 1938 he returned three of the handkerchiefs, having written the names of his wife and children on them.

With Temur Salahov branded an enemy of the people, his family were shunned by most of their neighbours and relatives, who feared they too might be targeted. As Tahir recalled: '*People used to stay away from us – avoid us. Nobody would play with us at school or in the neighbourhood; nobody would befriend us. And so we started developing friendships with other kids whose fathers also had been arrested. There were two or three other children in my class whose fathers were gone: Toghrul Narimanbeyov's father had been arrested and Victor Galyavkin's father was at war. They both became artists and we all grew up together as friends.'* (Ibid)

Sona's brother Haji, the director of the Baku Botanical Garden gave what support he could, including paying 500 roubles in an attempt to get a letter to Stalin or someone in authority that might help his brother-in-law. Meanwhile, under constant fear that she might be exiled, to feed and clothe her family, Sona took a daytime job as a cloakroom attendant and spent her evenings being a seamstress. Later, being unable to comply with a local official's request to obtain food illicitly for him, she was transferred to a munitions factory, where she sustained an injury from the heavy labour and lost her job.

In 1947, Tahir's sister Zarifa wrote to Stalin that her father's ten-year sentence had now almost been served, and asking if he would be released. When the NKVD responded by asking her when her father had been arrested, the family began to hope that he might soon come home. As the months continued to pass with no further news, however, such hopes were hard to sustain.

Meanwhile Tahir's artistic talent had begun to emerge. On leaving school in 1944 he had begun studying at the Azim Azimzade Art College, while at night earning a little money from the show people in Kirov Park, painting advertisements directly onto the roads. With a wartime curfew in force, he had to obtain a pass to carry out the work. In 1950 he applied to study at the Leningrad Art Academy. As soon as his father's background became known to the academy, however, despite high marks in his school examinations, he was refused entry. A sympathetic member of staff instead found him a place on a one-year course at the Technical School of Industrial Art, but there was a further setback when a lack of adequate clothing saw him hospitalised from the intense cold of the Leningrad winter.

Returning to Baku, Tahir now set his sights on Moscow and wrote to the Surikov Art Institute, this time stating on the application form that his father had been killed in an accident in the oil fields. It seems that the story was accepted, for soon after he was offered a place. Until he was qualified, other kinds of subterfuge would be necessary in order to earn a living: during holidays, not yet a member of the artists union and therefore excluded from taking commissions, Tahir would produce work for fellow artists in return for a share of the proceeds.

In 1955, Tahir's sister Zarifa, by this time a member of the Soviet women's basketball team, was returning home from a match when she heard that the head of the Azerbaijan KGB was on the same train. A conversation she had with him that day led to the discovery that her father had been executed in 1938, on the day he sent his family the handkerchiefs with their names on. In 1956, eighteen years after his death, Temur Salahov was declared 'not guilty'. The Soviet Union granted Sona a widow's pension of 150 roubles a year, along with free supply of gas and electricity and medical treatment. Not knowing if her husband was dead or alive for almost two decades, she had slaved to keep her children from destitution. An agave Americana, commonly known as a century plant, which she had one day brought from the Crimea and planted in the garden of the family's summerhouse, many years later bloomed for the first time. For Tahir, the magnificent agave, which had grown to some seven metres in height, became a symbol of his mother's resilience, and his painting of her seated beside the plant that she had so lovingly nurtured became world famous.

Tahir Salahov graduated from the Surikov Institute in 1957. Stalin was gone and Khrushchev's thaw was underway. The artist's work was to provide a distinct contrast with the idealised imagery of Socialist Realism and usher in the 'Severe Style' that presented Soviet life in a more realistic light – focusing often on the sadness, struggle and isolation of ordinary people. The subjects of his graduation painting *The Shift Is Over* are the oil workers of his native Caucasus: *'I had lived for some time in Sabunchi on the Absheron peninsula, and pools of oil and the smell of kerosene were very familiar!'* (Ian Peart and Saadat, *Visions of Azerbaijan*, March 2012)

Critics noted similarities, and telling differences, to an earlier work

Vagif Guseynov and Salahov at the official XXV Soviet Party reunion at the Kremlin Palace in Moscow, 1976

by Aleksandr Deineka, *The Defence of Petrograd*: '*Exhibited in 1928 in celebration of a decade of the Red Army, Deineka's painting still reflects with a certain realism the pride in the initial struggle against the odds to establish a revolution.*' (Ibid)

Later, as power became increasingly centralised under Stalin, the uncompromising heroism of Socialist Realism was made the artistic status quo. From the mid-1950s, freed up by Khrushchev the wheel was ready to turn again, and Salahov and his contemporaries began to breath real life back into Russian painting. In *The Shift Is Over*, his oil workers '*are walking in similar ragged file, but in the opposite direction to Deineka's refugees, and their demeanour is not one of defeat... they are by no means in parade formation – this is no show, there is a real struggle going on, in this case with the elements, and it is being conducted by distinct individuals rather than a military machine.*

'Roofs in Old Baku' by Tahir Salahov

It is little wonder that their spirit and the energy in the painting, whether of the waves, the birds, the people, even the sky, brought acclaim from reviewers long subject to the monolithic mythology of Socialist Realism' (Ibid)

In its quest for truthfulness, the work of the *Severe Stylists* is often viewed as pessimistic. Some critics disagree with this assessment, and urge that whatever the subject of the painting, we should look more closely at

Salahov's work in particular: '*...for those with eyes to see, there was always a heartbeat in the images – even in an industrial landscape.*' (Ibid)

It is certainly true that in almost any work of art there is more than one way of seeing. In 1958, Salahov exhibited *Morning Train*, an industrialised landscape largely devoid of identifiable human presence or natural features. But it has been claimed that there are two ways to read this painting: '*Do you see featureless slabs of concrete and environmental pollution, or are you more impressed by the clean, open road to progress (with the promise of trees in the distance)?*' (Ibid)

Tahir would also make his mark in portraiture, notably with celebrated Russian composers Mstislav Rostropovich and Dmitri Shostakovich. Born like Tahir in Baku, Rostropovich was presenting some musical master classes in the city one year, and the two men met. Tahir began sketching a likeness of the composer and asked if he might complete a full portrait. Rostropovich told him to report to his accommodation at 7.15 am the next

Vagif Guseynov and Salahov at the official XXV Soviet Party reunion at the Kremlin Palace in Moscow, 1976

day. When Tahir arrived, however, the security staff would not let him into the building until 7.30 am. Rostropovich was allegedly disgruntled and unimpressed by Tahir's explanation for being late, but later wrote a note of thanks for the portrait.

Doubtless the most meaningful portrait for Tahir on a personal level was one that he painted in 2005. Based on seventy-year-old prison photos retrieved from the KGB's files, it was a picture of his father.

When Tahir was appointed First Secretary of the Artists Union of the USSR back in 1973, one of the governing members was asked why they had chosen him, as it was unusual for such a role to be offered to someone born in the republics rather than within Russia. The reply was that as well as being a great artist Tahir Salahov was a natural diplomat. It is true that throughout his career he has managed to find a common language with everyone, to share a joke and create harmony in an organisation which by the mid 1970s comprised over 14,000 members throughout the USSR – not just painters but sculptors, authors, composers, musicians, choreographers, all talented people, many with thin skins and neurotic tendencies. Tahir knew how to stroke egos when required, how to help people to relax and feel comfortable.

Valuing others earned Tahir their respect. I can honestly say I have never heard anyone say anything negative about him, and in all the years I have known him I cannot recall him ever losing his temper, let alone scream or shout or throw the kind of primadonna tantrums to which artists are thought to be prone. Whenever anyone has had a quarrel or created some kind of difficultly, Tahir is always cool and composed, an iceberg in that respect. Why does he possess such equanimity? Perhaps because so much of his emotional energy goes into his art, who knows? Tahir has also used his diplomatic skills to forge relationships in the arts at an international level, in 1989 arranging an exhibition by the American Robert Rauschenberg, the first of its kind in the Soviet Union.

After periods of not seeing one another for a while, when Tahir and I have met up again it seems like no time has passed at all, and we are talking as if we had parted only the day before. I shall never forget how when I moved to Moscow he arranged a surprise welcome party for me, and knowing my keen interest in painting had invited a bevy of other renowned artists to join us, a very kind gesture. Tahir is sociable and has always enjoyed a drink, but never to excess, just two or three shots of vodka is enough for him. A little alcohol has only a good effect on him, and again, I have never seen him annoyed or upset, a man of great poise and calm, always quietly in control. Yet at the same time he is warm, open minded and approachable, and enjoys nothing more than a good party. Whenever I had a delegation coming to Moscow, I would take them to meet Tahir at his large house and studio in the city. Even if it was a last minute request he was unfailingly welcoming, and my guests would always consider it a great honour to be introduced to him.

Tahir's work has become increasingly sought after. At a large sale in London in 2014 his portrait of Shostakovich fetched some £400,000; even though Shostakovich was a major figure, the performance of whose symphony during the Siege of Leningrad immortalised him in the eyes of Russians, this was a very large sum for a work by a living artist. Several of Tahir's paintings reside in the largest museums of Russia, Azerbaijan, Ukraine and elsewhere, as well as in private collections around the world. He has also contributed to the restoration of the Cathedral of Christ the Saviour in Moscow, at 103 metres the world's tallest Orthodox Christian church. From 1984 to 1992 he headed the Department of Painting and Composition at the Surikov Art Institute in Moscow, and has trained a plethora of famous artists.

The last words, with which I would wholeheartedly concur, go to the two people who talked to him on behalf of Visions of Azerbaijan in 2012: *'Tahir Salahov is undoubtedly one of the great painters of the modern era, but he is much more… we left our interviews with him enthused by his creativity, optimism and love for life. It takes someone special to live the experiences he has and still to give with a smile. Tahir Salahov is a very special man.'*

THE PRESIDENT
OF GEORGIA

EDUARD SHEVARDNADZE

'The town twinning movement started very soon after 1945, with the passionate support of mayors and citizens who vowed that Europe should never again be torn apart by war.'
(twinning.org)

The tradition of town twinning is found not only in Western Europe. In the Soviet Union it was a concept we grew up with, and fostering such cultural and political links within Russia was as important as doing so with other countries around the world. This was especially true of the republics; geographically distant from Moscow and with their own cultural identity, it helped enormously to have a structural basis for bridging the divide and developing friendships across these regions.

My own home city of Baku was twinned with Naples and with Tbilisi, the capital of the Soviet republic of Georgia. Azerbaijan and Georgia as a whole also had a very friendly relationship, and it was through this connection that I first met Shevardnadze. It was 1974, I was thirty-three years old and had been First Secretary of the Lenin Komsomol of Azerbaijan Central Committee for less than a year. Shevardnadze was by this time in his mid-forties.

It is established that Shevardnadze's father Ambrose, who was a teacher, despite being arrested at one point during the Stalinist purges of the 1930s, was a staunch communist. It was said he was saved when one of the arresting officers turned out to be a former pupil. Ambrose's cousin, the distinguished painter Dimitri Shevardnadze was not so fortunate: for his defiant campaign to save an ancient church in Tbilisi from demolition he was executed in 1937. Maybe this was one reason that Ambrose's wife did not share her husband's loyalty to the government, and why she even tried to prevent him, and in turn her son Eduard, from pursuing a political career.

The maternal disapproval may for Shevardnadze have acted as a spur. After joining the Georgian Communist Party at the age of twenty, he began his career as an instructor in the Ordzhonikidze District Committee of the Komsomol in Tbilisi, then in the Georgia Central Committee. He graduated from the Kutaisi Pedagogical Institute specialising in History, and in 1957 was elected as the Second Secretary of the Central Committee of Komsomol in Georgia. It was at the XII Congress of the Komsomol in 1958 that he met the man destined to have a significant impact on his life, and that of the Soviet Union: Mikhail Gorbachev.

In 1961, Shevardnardze became First Minister of the Georgian Republic's Komsomol, but it was here that he also experienced his first setback when his outspokenness caused him to fall foul of a local official and lose his position. Remaining active in politics however, his tenacious campaign against corruption among local government officials met with approval in Moscow, and in 1972 he was made First Secretary of the Georgian Communist Party.

An integral feature of the twin town relationship between Baku and Tbilisi were the various exchange visits and conferences undertaken throughout the year, with Georgian delegations making regular visits to Baku and vice versa. In 1974, I was with one such Komsomol delegation in Tbilisi, where I was required to give a couple of speeches as part of the programme. It was during the breaks in proceedings, where we would mingle or go for a walk around the conference buildings that I got talking to Shevardnadze. I found him to be a clever, highly educated person, very precise and someone who knew exactly what he wanted, would set his targets and as events would prove, frequently attain them. I met Shevardnadze again the following year in Tbilisi, and my impression of him as a man of keen intellect with clearly defined ambitions was strengthened. Getting to know him a little better, one could perceive other qualities, traits that later on in his career would earn him the soubriquet of the 'Silver Fox'. In other words, as well as having a firm grasp of politics he was flexible, communicative and sociable, open to new ideas and always trying to expand upon his knowledge and intellectual horizons.

These more imaginative talents – lateral thinking one might say – would be brought to bear on the problem of corruption. When Shevardnadze had taken over as First Secretary of Georgia in 1972, he inherited what was believed to be the most corrupt region in the Soviet Union. The problem was endemic and had become accepted as a way of life by many. To give just one example over 30 per cent of exports were being conducted illegally, with border officials and others lining their pockets in the process. Shevardnadze first placed a complete ban on all exports. Then, dressing up in peasant clothing one day, he drove incognito towards the border with a car loaded with tomatoes. When the police asked for cash to let him through, the subsequent investigation resulted in almost the entire border force being sacked.

First Secretary Shevardnadze's success in Georgia could be measured in economic terms. In 1974 when I first met him, he had, after just two years helped to achieve an almost 10 per cent increase in the republic's industrial output, while output in agriculture rose by a remarkable 18 per cent. In 1973 Shevardnadze had brought in reforms in the Georgian district of Abasha, allowing farming management to be handled at local level and offering a share of the crops if five-year agricultural plans were achieved ahead of target. With the crackdown on corruption such schemes could perhaps provide socially responsible rewards for hard work. When the Abasha experiment was judged successful, the methodology was extended throughout Georgia.

Whilst Shevardnadze favoured greater democratic and local engagement such as the Abasha agriculture project, he spoke out against nationalism, announcing at the republic's 25th Communist Party Congress that for Georgians *'the sun rises not in the east but in the north – in Russia.'* This clear commitment to the Soviet ideal of unity was tested in 1978 by Moscow's attempt to amend the constitution, removing Georgian from its position as the officially recognised sole language of the republic. Neighbouring Armenia and my own country of Azerbaijan had incidentally enjoyed a similar status in terms of their national languages, and the proposed amendment, giving equal status to Russian, would apply to them also.

In Georgia, however, a strong nationalist movement had arisen during the 1970s, and this element took particular exception to what they perceived as a threat to their language and culture. In April 1978, some 20,000 students and other protestors took to the streets of Tbilisi, 5,000 evading Soviet police and gathering outside the government building. As First Secretary, Shevardnadze was on the scene in person and spoke to the crowd, calling for calm and saying he wanted no one to be harmed, as in 1956 some students had been shot during a demonstration.

The mood remained truculent, and as people began to boo him, Shevardnadze contacted the Kremlin to request that in the interests of peace the constitutional amendment regarding the status of the Georgian language known as Article 75 be dropped. With no definitive reply forthcoming and armed Soviet troops facing the thousands of resolute protesters, the following few hours in Tblisi were tense. Shevardnadze stood between the two sides, expressing his sympathy with the Georgian people's demands and continuing his plea for everyone to remain calm. When the Kremlin answer finally came back it surprised many; the government agreed to abandon Article 75 and Georgian would remain the sole official language of the republic.

Today in Georgia, 14 April is unofficially celebrated as the 'Day of the Georgian Language.' As a result of the events of 1978 the Soviet government extended a similar agreement to Armenia and Azerbaijan, so I owe something perhaps to those students and to Shevardnadze for saving my national language. There were, however, other unintended consequences. The Abkhaz people of Georgia, emboldened by the success of the Tbilisi protests took the opportunity to demand that their region become a separate Soviet republic. Whilst the Kremlin refused to grant this change, a substantial amount of money was made available to improve the region's

USSR President Mikhail Gorbachev and USSR Foreign Minister Eduard Shevardnadze

infrastructure and fund cultural projects. If anything these concessions bolstered the Abkhaz's sense of being a separate group, and other Georgians living within the region complained of being marginalized. The problems brought by this trend towards ethnic and regional atomisation were destined to land in Shevardnadze's lap again a few years later.

I should mention now the relationship between Shevardnadze and Gorbachev, which certainly for the first part of their respective careers was a close and positive one. Like so many connections their friendship was regional in origin. Gorbachev's birthplace of Stavropol had very strong relations with the Republic of Georgia. When Gorbachev, three years older, had first met Shevardnadze while the latter was still leading Georgia's Komsomol, the two men had obviously established a rapport.

Gorbachev as we know would be the architect of glasnost and perestroika, and in the eyes of many the man who destroyed the Soviet Union. For

Shevardnadze, doubts about the system he grew up under perhaps first arose when he was in his late twenties. It was 1956, the year of the first Georgian demonstrations, when ironically the protests had been against the de-Stalinization promulgated by Khrushchev. 9 March was the third anniversary of Stalin's death, and Georgia being his birthplace the issue was a particularly sensitive one for local pro-Stalinists. When the demonstrations got out of hand Soviet troops opened fire killing twenty-two people, the incident that Shevardnadze would remind the Tbilsi protestors of twenty-two years later.

In the early 1970s, as First Party Secretary in Stavropol, Gorbachev had been giving greater local control in farming and offering incentives. Whether this provided the inspiration or cue for the agricultural reforms begun by his friend in the Abash region in Georgia is uncertain, but suffice it to say a common theme can be seen here. Gorbachev was always keeping an eye on Shevardnadze and perhaps to an extent guiding him. Then when Gorbachev became the effective leader of the Soviet Union in 1985, as soon as the opportunity arose he appointed Shevardnadze as Minister of Foreign Affairs.

Soon I would have reason to be particularly grateful to Shevardnadze, for in 1986 he offered me a job in his ministry. I say particularly grateful, because he was also on harmonious terms with the Aliev family, the ruling elite of Azerbaijan with whom, since exposing the corruption scandal, I was still highly unpopular. After being sacked from my post as First Secretary of the Baku City Committee of the Communist Party of Azerbaijan and then being kept out of the way for two years as President of the Azerbaijan National Olympic Committee, I was now out of a job again. Shevardnadze of course knew all about my problems with Aliev, but despite this he didn't have a problem with bringing me on board in his department, effectively going against Aliev. It was a big step to take, but he knew how unjust the situation was and saw through it. It was a balancing act in a way – the same way he had supported the Georgian language and local democracy while at the same time opposing nationalistic factions that sought separation from the Soviet Union. In this sense he was a pragmatist, as any successful politician has to be to a greater or lesser extent. Azerbaijan, and therefore Aliev, was Georgia's neighbour and you can choose to get on with your neighbours or not. Even though Shevardnadze was now in Moscow and a big player in the central government of the Soviet Union, Georgia was his home and as things were to turn out he would be back there again before very long.

Meanwhile, I now had the good fortune to work very closely with Shevardnadze for the next few years, my official title being First Deputy Director of a department in the Ministry of Foreign Affairs of the USSR working with the Directorate of Diplomatic Corps Servicing. The job entailed a great deal of day-to-day problem solving. We were liaising with all the diplomatic missions accredited to work in the Soviet Union, in other words the embassies and general consulates of 114 countries. Some embassies, not necessarily through any fault of their own demanded more attention than others, and the problems that arose were either with people or things, often both at once. The things tended to be buildings – providing, staffing and maintaining them – and transportation, which had to be arranged to collect and take personnel to and from every part of the Soviet Union, the vehicles fuelled, serviced and frequently repaired. Arranging building work to be carried out at an embassy could be particularly fraught, and minimising the noise and inconvenience to a tolerable level was not – in the opinion of the embassy staff concerned at least – always possible.

Then there were meetings, delegations, conferences and social activities, all of which had to be planned and supervised – all part of what was required to make an embassy work, times 114. It was very important to keep everything running smoothly at all times and to keep the foreign ambassadorial staff happy, as for every embassy based in the Soviet Union we had a similar representation in their home country, the Russian diplomatic staff there all expecting to be well looked after. Complaints about road accidents, trouble at night with the police or places of entertainment and diplomatic incidents were all part and parcel of my department's work, and as a matter of course I had to meet all the US, UK and other ambassadors, many of whom were charming and obliging, others less so. The state of international affairs at any given time could also naturally affect the mood, and during this period the war in Afghanistan was always likely to make for a tense conversation. Those at the British Embassy, mostly Oxbridge educated diplomats seemed to epitomise the word – intellectually inclined, courteous and correct, they stuck strictly to protocol and the rules of good behaviour.

In terms of the foreigners' perceptions of our government officials, Shevardnadze was seen by some as '*...an unlikely choice to be foreign minister of the world's largest country.*' (*Guardian*, 7 July 2014) It was believed he may have been reluctant to take the job and that it was Gorbachev who had persuaded him: '*The new Soviet leader wanted big changes—and the "Silver Fox", his friend since the 1950s, to make them.*' (Ibid)

Many in the West now remember Shevardnadze chiefly for his role in the post-Gorbachev era, as the first President of his native Georgia from 1995 to 2003. Yet his earlier achievements should not be forgotten. He became known in the Soviet Union as one of the creators of the campaign to fight corruption and the shadow economy, during which time he removed no less than twenty ministers, three secretaries of city committees and ten representatives of district committees, replacing them with colleagues from the Committee of State Security (KGB), the Ministry of Internal Affairs (MVD), and several young specialists. As a result of his clean-up campaign in Georgia several thousand people were arrested, among them almost half the membership of the republic's Communist Party. According to certain information, around 40,000 leaders of the higher, middle and other ranks were dismissed from their posts. In 1981 Shevardnadze was awarded an honorary title of Hero of Socialist Labour.

Unfortunately, during his time away from Georgia the virus of corruption re-emerged, and on his return as President, Shevardnadze found himself in a tenure that was fraught with challenges, divisions and physical danger. An

Monument of 'Courage' at the Fortress of Brest

attempt had already been made on his life in 1992, and in August 1995 a car bomb intended for him was detonated outside the Tbilisi parliament building. Then in 1998, a group of armed men attacked his motorcade killing two of his bodyguards. One might wonder why, by then in his seventies, he did not choose to leave politics and enjoy a peaceful retirement. One answer might be found in events that took place on the Black Sea port of Brest in June 1941. The Red Army were defending the Fortress of Brest against a superior force of the Wermacht. While civilians including children tended the wounded, the Russian soldiers, suffering heavy casualties held out for nine days. The achievement at the Siege of Brest became a symbol of Soviet endurance. Among those killed was Shevardnadze's brother. Tenacity it seemed ran in the family.

Shevardnadze displayed physical courage not only in the political arena.

At a football match in Tbilisi attended by some 80,000 fans, amid rumours the referee was corrupt, the crowd suddenly burst onto the pitch and a mass brawl erupted. As leader of the Georgian Communist Party, Shevardnadze ran out and tried to get between the warring sides to calm the situation. With every third person probably drunk it was two hours of mayhem and violence. This action, with no thought for his own safety, showed the character of the person.

Looking objectively at history, both Gorbachev and Shevardnadze were among the group of Soviet Union leaders that coincided with its end. To say that they destroyed the Soviet Union is just one opinion, though one I am often inclined to adopt in the case of Gorbachev. With Shevardnadze, although as Minister for Foreign Affairs he occupied one of the top positions in the government at the time, I have not come across specific evidence that he was instrumental in any deliberate act of destruction.

A lot of his decisions on foreign policy I thought were very brave, and making them could not have been easy in the particular climate in which he was operating. *'Deeds matched the words. He ended the Soviet Union's proxy wars in Africa, Latin America and Asia, hurrying the Red Army home from its futile and bloody mission in Afghanistan. At arms-control talks with America knotty negotiating problems unravelled overnight. The danger of nuclear war abated.'* (*The Economist*, 12 July 2014)

None of these things might have been achieved but for the fact that Shevardnadze was very determined. At the same time he had no problems expressing how he felt about people. He also read a great deal, and was never content to rest on his laurels or assume that he had the final or only answer to any problem.

As time goes on, comparisons with Gorbachev are inevitable, and according to some commentators, increasing hindsight will provide a clearer picture:

> *'...only historians will be able to tell which of them was the greater innovator in the drive for "new thinking". Towards the end, Shevardnadze*

had probably become the more visionary of the two. After his arrival at the foreign ministry, Shevardnadze surprised even himself when he quickly developed a grasp of foreign and security issues. He also brought in a new breed of Soviet diplomats, which eased the way when negotiating with foreign leaders…he won many friends. A man of small build, with a whiff of white hair and an easy smile, he may have lacked the Gorbachovian charisma, but he more than made up for it with charm, warmth, humour and acute intellect.'

(*Guardian*, 7 July 2014)

Without a doubt Eduard Shevardnadze was a gifted, intelligent and brave man who possessed many other positive qualities. He was one of the few great party and state leaders of the USSR who was able to find the strength and will to return to the highest level of leadership in his country. Those who know the history and psychology of Caucasus and Transcaucasia will agree with me that to succeed in this role was an almost impossible task. Yet when the Soviet Union imploded, amid the ensuing chaos of the 1990s it was Shevardnadze who ensured Georgia's rightful place in the new world community.

ANGELA STENT

The year 1947 saw a significant change for Britain. India, the jewel in the imperial crown, gained its independence, marking the start of a process of decolonisation which two decades later would see the British Empire that had once ruled three-quarters of the globe vanish. 1947 was also the year in which the English academic Angela Stent was born. Her father Ronald was a businessman who lectured part time in history with the London extension college. Angela would also see dramatic developments, as technology raced ahead, belief systems vied for dominance and new empires expanded. Growing up in this rapidly changing, often alarming world – she was a teenager at the time of the Cuban Missile Crisis – Angela, a gifted student, would turn her analytical mind to the conundrum of the two new post war superpowers – America and the Soviet Union: each claiming ideological superiority, both increasingly heavily armed, and perpetually it seemed prone to mutual misunderstanding and suspicion.

Angela's first degree at Cambridge was a BA in Economics and Modern History, followed by a Master of Science with distinction from the London School of Economics and Political Science. Later she completed an MA and PhD at Harvard.

My first meeting with her was during my first visit to the States. It was 1975 and I was one of the deputies of the young parliamentarians, a large youth delegation invited to tour around the US meeting young American parliamentarians. The trip took us not only to the big cities, New York, Chicago and Los Angeles but also to lots of small towns, the kinds of places you don't see so much in the movies, but where the majority of Americans live. We met students, teachers, university lecturers, business people, factory workers and farmers, a whole cross section of the community. There was a great book called *One Store America* written in the 1930s, which was all

about these small towns – the real America – I read it three or four times.

The trip I was making that year was part of a broad programme of exchange visits to improve cultural and political reciprocation between the West and the Soviet Union. After *Sputnik 1* in 1957 and then Gagarin's space flight in 1961, the outside world had realised that Russia was not the nation of peasants that many had assumed, but a country that had achieved huge progress in science and technology; the whole idea of unassailable Western superiority had crumbled. Thus had begun the arms race. But since the late 1960s, with the cost of attempting to maintain military parity ballooning for both sides, a rapprochement seemed not only desirable but also essential; the Darwinian fight between the two political species for survival of the fittest was becoming a no-win situation and could end only in mutual destruction, economically if not physically.

Faced with this doomsday scenario, the alternative had to be pursued energetically. 1968 saw the signing of the Nuclear Non-Proliferation Treaty, and in 1972 the first Strategic Arms Limitation Talks (SALT) resulted in the Anti-Ballistic Missile Treaty. 1975 was the year of the Helsinki Final Act, the culmination of two years of negotiations in Europe by the Conference on Security and Cooperation. Signed by thirty-five countries, the Helsinki Final Act recognised Estonia, Latvia and Lithuania as part of the Soviet Union, and allowed for the monitoring of human rights across Europe and Russia.

A closer, more cooperative relationship between East and West was already taking place at all levels and in multiple spheres – technology, industry, culture, sport, agriculture, art, music. The variety and plenitude of Western culture had a lot to offer for Russian people (enticements that would lead to problems in the years ahead) and likewise when Americans and Europeans listened to Rachmaninov and Tchaikovsky and saw the magic of the Bolshoi, they thought that these Russians really have something beautiful, something of deep value. Of course Soviet society was not democratic in the way democracy was always portrayed in America, yet the US also exercised control over its citizens through its hierarchical lobbies, the power of the media and most of all through money.

During our trip, in the midst of our spirit of goodwill between nations, mutual suspicion or curiosity at least, could occasionally creep in like an elephant in the room. But by pointing out the elephant it could be sent away with good humour. A good example was when we were in a bus in LA with some American colleagues, and they turned to us with a conspiratorial smile and whispered, '*Hey, are you guys really KGB?*' I replied, '*Tell me honestly hand on heart – who believes in God here, who thinks they are really honest? Okay here we have two KGB in our party – now you tell me, are three of you CIA – or is it four?*'

With everyone we spoke to in America, you could see they worked hard to achieve what they had, and I felt they wanted us to recognise that. We struck up very good relationships with those we met. People were interested

Vagif Guseynov with Angela Stent and Richard Weizekker at the International Conference on Foreign and Defence Policy in 1999

to hear from us what everyday life was really like in the Soviet Union. I enjoyed seeing America at first hand, seeing how people lived and listening to their stories. While politicians always had an agenda, what I would call the real people – those who made up the fabric of the nation as it were – were very positive about the Soviet Union. The further south we went the friendlier the reception – Southern hospitality we discovered was not just a myth. The cities were trickier, everyone was busy, honking their horns in traffic jams, bustling and in a hurry, tired from going to and from work in cars and buses and on the subway – that was the reality for them, a different, much faster rhythm of life, all cities tend to be the same in this respect.

The tour programme was not rigid – we would ask to visit a town or college, and we would be taken there – people weren't expecting us, but they would welcome us warmly and talk freely. In Cambridge Massachusetts we were invited to see Harvard, America's oldest university, the *alma mater* of eight US presidents and 130 Nobel Laureates and housing the largest academic library in the world. Women were now beginning to make up a higher proportion of the student intake, but not without a struggle: '*The fiercest opposition to women's inclusion at Harvard occurred during the 1970s… when students and the National Organization for Women fought for a one-to-one ratio in the admission of men and women instead of the four-to-one ratio that then prevailed.*' (Pat Harrison, *Radcliffe Magazine*, Harvard)

Arriving at the university my colleagues and I were introduced to the staff, among them Angela Stent, who was at that time a teaching fellow. '*I began my life as a Sovietologist at Harvard in the heyday of the 1970s, when interest in the U.S.S.R. was high, the United States and the Soviet Union were caught in the embrace of mutually assured destruction, and support for graduate students studying Soviet politics was abundant. The discipline had been established in the late 1940s as Washington came to realize how dangerously little it knew about its new Cold War adversary. The government funded area studies for the Soviet Union — and for other regions, from East Asia to Latin America — because it recognized the importance of training people who could bring together an understanding of the region and its languages, history, culture, economy and politics.*' (*Washington Post*, 14 March 2014)

1975 was also the year of Angela's wedding to Harvard research fellow Daniel Yergin, whose father was a publicity manager for Warner Brothers Studios, and his mother an artist and teacher. After a tour of the campus and a very stimulating meeting with the professors we invited them back to our hotel to continue the conversation over some Russian vodka. It was at the hotel that Angela noticed some books I had brought with me to read while on the trip – works on Russian history and politics – and asked if she might borrow one or two when I had finished them. I said sure. She had already visited Moscow, and with the Watergate bugging scandal that had recently toppled Nixon still resonant, her interest in Russia was equalled by a desire to communicate her perspective on American political life to those on the other side of the ideological divide: *'In 1974, I spent several months in the dusty main reading room of Moscow's Lenin Library, studying the troubled Soviet-German relationship. It was a thrill to glimpse the closed world of the Soviet Union, yet I soon found myself spending lots of time explaining the United States to incredulous Soviet students at Moscow State University. Yes, I said, Americans were outraged that President Richard Nixon's White House was listening to people's phone conversations. And no,* The Washington Post *was not in the hands of a capitalist-Zionist cabal out to destroy detente by fabricating Watergate. On the day Nixon resigned, I left Moscow, having failed to convince my fellow students about how America really works.'* (Ibid)

After I had returned home Angela and I began to correspond, exchanging books and ideas and meeting up whenever our paths happened to cross in Europe, America, Moscow or St Petersburg. By the early 1980s, now at Georgetown University, she was a published academic. Meanwhile the mood music between the Soviet Union and America, so upbeat in 1975, had begun to sound much less harmonious, due some said to unrealistic expectations of détente, while the Soviet occupation of Afghanistan in 1979 had raised hackles in the West. With the second round of SALT talks at a stalemate, rivalry and suspicion were once more at the top of the agenda, not helped by Reagan referring to the Soviet Union as the 'evil empire'.

Following the accession of Gorbachev in 1985, America's Soviet specialists were as agog with speculation as the rest of the world: *'Debates about whether Gorbachev was "for real" and how far his reforms would go consumed my colleagues and the U.S. foreign policy establishment.'* (Ibid) Six years later, in the wake of the attempt by Kryuchkov and his colleagues to restore order to the Soviet Union, Gorbachev was gone. The question of his precise role in the country's collapse remained open: *'People will long debate whether Gorbachev was the sorcerer's apprentice. Did he improvise when reality came crashing in on him and he was confronted by tidal forces he had unleashed but ultimately could not control? Or was the collapse of communism the result of a calculated strategy?'* (Angela Stent, *The Weekly Standard*, 26 October 1996)

As ever, further hindsight would assist in an evaluation. Angela's book *Russia and Germany Reborn: Unification, the Soviet Collapse and the New Europe*, first published in 1999, pulled a number of strands together. The work sets out to demonstrate that the relationship of both East and West Germany with the Soviet Union was a pivotal aspect of the Cold War. The author then provides a blow-by-blow account of how the Soviet Union responded to the 1989 East German revolution and the negotiations that followed, concluding with a study of Russian-German relations over the subsequent years, and their significance for the rest of Europe. This was the first book to look at the turbulent period from the perspective of both the Russians and Germans, and for a book written by a Western observer, albeit one with a deep knowledge of Eastern affairs, I found Angela's analysis to be very objective. There are interviews with a number of key players, Gorbachev among them, and the source material included recently de-classified documents.

The critics were full of admiration, '*Excellent.... Understanding the historic transformation of the German-Russian relationship is reason enough to read Ms. Stent's intelligent and perceptive book...Yet the more compelling reason to read it is for its history,*' wrote Frederick Kempe in the *Wall Street Journal*, while Jeffrey Herf of *The New Republic* judged it a '*thoughtful reflection on why this thoroughly unimagined outcome came about. The prose and tale are highly readable.*'

One person for whom Angela Stent has had a perennial fascination is the late American academic and policy maker George F. Kennan. In 1947 Kennan had asserted that the Soviet Union was an expansionist power, and that where its influence was deemed to threaten US strategic interests it should be contained: '*The main element of any United States policy toward the Soviet Union must be a long-term, patient but firm and vigilant containment of Russian expansive tendencies ... Soviet pressure against the free institutions of the Western world is something that can be contained by the adroit and vigilant application of counterforce at a series of constantly shifting geographical and political points, corresponding to the shifts and manoeuvres of Soviet policy, but which cannot be charmed or talked out of existence.'* (*Foreign Affairs*, July 1947)

Kennan's theory underpinned the Truman doctrine issued that year, in which US President Harry S. Truman announced to Congress that '*it must be the policy of the United States to support free people who are resisting attempted subjugation by armed minorities or by outside pressures.*' The 'outside pressures' in reality meant the Soviet Union, its sympathisers, supporters or recipients of its financial or military aid. However, within a year Kennan, the supposed instigator of the Truman Doctrine, now became its critic, appearing to have retracted this opinion. He claimed that he had never contradicted himself, but rather that his original words had been misinterpreted. In a 1996 American television interview he repeated that he did not consider the Soviets a military threat and that they could not be compared to Hitler. '*I should have explained that I didn't suspect them of any desire to launch an attack on us. This was right after the war, and it was absurd to suppose that they were going to turn around and attack the United States. I didn't think I needed to explain that, but I obviously should have done it.*' (*Online News Hour*, PBS)

In February 2007, at a symposium at the Kennan Institute in the Woodrow Wilson International Centre for Scholars in Washington, Angela Stent gave a paper on *George F. Kennan the Policymaker*. She told the delegates that it had given her great pleasure in preparing the paper to reread Kennan's memoirs and other works and described him as a gifted writer. She then recalled meeting Kennan at a conference twenty years previously, which had resulted in a book called *Containment: Concept and Policy*. She spoke about how some of the more conservative delegates at that conference had attacked Kennan personally, and she acknowledged that he was and remained a controversial figure.

Angela admitted that in her brief to talk about Kennan as a policymaker she had found it hard to separate this from his role as a historian of Russia, as it had so much informed his views on policy. She then recalled her time working as a State Department Policy Planning staff member from 1999

Angela Stent, Director of the Georgetown University Centre for Eurasian and Russian Studies, and British historian Dominic Lieven ahead of a plenary session titled 'The World of the Future: Moving Through Conflict to Cooperation', Sochi, Russia, 19 October 2017

to 2001, and reflected on how the working culture had changed since then: *'I remember how I always liked to look at the picture of the first head of Policy Planning, George Kennan, sitting there with his staff. I think there were only five of them…in the beginning. You look at these photos and the staff is depicted as thoughtful gentlemen discussing issues with the composure of people who have leisure. Maybe it is an illusion, but that is what it looked like. And then I think about the harried denizens of the current Policy Planning Staff, and I think it must have been much better in the late 1940s.'*

Angela then turned to the theory of containment, and looked at the origin of the concept. She talked about how Kennan had been selected for training as a Russia expert and sent to Riga to learn the language. At this time the Baltic States were newly independent. *'He describes Riga in those days as a lively cosmopolitan city, a cultural mélange of Latvian, German, Russian, Yiddish, and other different influences that made it such a lively city. His teachers in this Paris on the Baltic were highly cultivated Russian émigrés. They were well-educated intellectuals from the pre-revolutionary era, but their lives had been destroyed by the Russian revolution.'*

Angela read from this that Kennan's experience in Riga, where the Soviets believed that everyone in the US legation must be a spy, had imbued him with a negative view of Bolsehvism, and that Bolsheviks would always be suspicious of the outside world. She quoted from Kennan's memoirs: *'Never did I consider the Soviet Union a fit ally or associate, actual or potential, for this country.'* Angela then qualified this, saying Kennan was extremely complex, and in her view an idealist as well as a realist, who grew very fond of the Russian people and their culture, while remaining highly circumspect about the Soviet state machine. She described his subsequent arrival at the US Embassy in Moscow in the 1930s: *'He lived in the Hotel National, which was not the luxurious hotel that it is today.'* She talked of her shock on reading about the lax security in the Embassy at that time: *'No codes, no safes, no couriers, no security officers and regular telegraphs were used for communication with Washington.'* In Moscow Kennan observed again that under Stalin's regime almost all foreigners were assumed to be spies.

By the time World War Two began Kennan had been posted to Berlin, and it was believed, said Angela, that his experiences in Nazi Germany *'had a profound effect on his understanding of the USSR and its imperial policies in the post war world...he did see a similarity between the two systems.'* It was back in Moscow in 1946 that Kennan wrote what is known as the Long Telegram, outlining the views that would form the basis of his subsequent, initially anonymous article, and what is believed to have been the inspiration for the Truman Doctrine. His specific recommendation, according to Angela, was that his government should not *'assume a commonality of aims with the Soviets that did not exist, not to act chummy with them, and not to make requests of them unless we would take measures of them if they did not fulfil the request. In other words, he wanted U.S. policymakers to be consistent and to respond in kind if the Soviets did not respond to what they were supposed to do.'*

This sounds like reasonable diplomacy, nothing more nothing less. Angela re-emphasised that in Kennan's view he had been advocating political not military containment, and that he had not intended to imply that this containment should be applied globally, but only to Western Europe. *'Hence his criticism of the Truman Doctrine, which he felt was indiscriminately all-encompassing in its scope.'*

One cannot help but think that if Kennan's recommendations had not been misconstrued there may have been no Truman Doctrine – and no Bay of Pigs, no Cuban Missile Crisis and no Vietnam War. The list could go on. Angela Stent was right to recognise his pivotal role in post-1945 history, and rounding off her 2007 paper she quoted him again: *'In a phrase that I am afraid to say resonates very much in today's debates, Kennan said: "This whole tendency to see ourselves as the center of political enlightenment and as teachers to a great part of the rest of the world strikes me as unthought-through, vainglorious, and undesirable." He concluded that, "the best thing the United States could do is not to preach but to influence countries by the force of our example."'*

Angela and I have kept in touch ever since that first meeting at Harvard in 1975, and I am always grateful for her insights and observations as the world continues to surprise us. Let's be honest, which of us would have bet on Donald Trump reaching the White House? That particular event changed opinions everywhere; writing in the online magazine *Politico,*

Angela commented on a recent survey which found that a *'majority of Europeans now believe that Russia at least is a more predictable power and has a more stable leadership than the United States does.'*

MIKHAIL SUSLOV

In 1978 I received an unexpected phone call. '*Comrade Suslov would like to see you,*' said the voice on the other end. The Suslov? '*Of course,*' the voice assured me. To say I was incredulous would be an understatement. The legendary Suslov, Stalin's protégé and the man regarded under Brezhnev as the Communist Party's chief ideologue really wanted to see me in his office? My immediate thought was that a friend was playing a prank on me. Taking out the phone book I found the number for Suslov's office and rang it. The person who replied was the one I had just spoken to. '*Vagif? Yes, I'm Suslov's secretary, I rang you a moment ago – well are you coming?*' '*Oh, yes,*' I replied. One did not refuse a summons from a man like Suslov.

Mikhail Andreyevich Suslov was born on 21 November 1902 in Ulyanovsk Oblast. Situated north of Moscow, the region is divided by the upper reaches of the longest river in Europe, the legendary Volga. Flowing east and south and fed by some 200 tributaries, the Volga winds down central Russia for almost 3,700 km, through several of the country's largest cities to its outlet in the Caspian Sea, on the opposite shore from my own home city of Baku. The Volga has always had great symbolic significance in literature and folklore and is regarded as Russia's national river. In the winter months much of the Volga is frozen over, yet when navigable it provides crucial access for shipping to and from the Caspian. In the Great Patriotic War, Hitler had been intent on seizing control of the river both to cut off Russian supply routes and to strike eastwards across the Caspian to plunder the oil fields of Azerbaijan. On a bend in the Volga at the industrial city of Stalingrad, from August 1942 to February 1943, in what is considered one of the largest engagements in the history of warfare, the German 6th Army was destroyed and the Führer's ambitions sorely curtailed.

Twenty-five years prior to the Battle of Stalingrad, at the other end of the Volga in Ulyanovsk, then known as Simbirsk, the Bolsheviks took control of the city a few weeks after the October 1917 revolution, only to lose it the following year to a unit of White Russian Tsarist troops. By September 1918, however, Simbirsk was back in Communist hands and became the Revolutionary Military Council's eastern front HQ, the local munitions factory vital to the Red Army's victory. Simbirsk was also the birthplace of Vladimir Ulyanov Lenin, and on his death in 1924 the city was renamed Ulyanovsk in his honour.

Mikhail Suslov, aged twenty-two by the time of Lenin's death, would have grown up in close proximity to the legendary revolutionary and the earth shattering events he had inspired. For the young Suslov there seemed no hesitation in pursuing the socialist way; at sixteen he joined his local branch of Komsomol and later the Bolshevik All Union Communist Party. After studying at the Plekhanov Institute of National Economy, Suslov then undertook research and taught at Moscow State University.

Politics seemed to beckon, and by 1931 Suslov had joined the Party Control Commission and the People's Commissariat of the Workers and Peasants Inspectorate. Russia was still unstable politically and the time of Stalin's purges was about to begin; Suslov would play his part along with other party members in seeking to eradicate ideological deviationists. The so-called 'show trials' have received much condemnation and no one would now defend the arbitrary and totalitarian way in which people were treated. Yet leading up to the civil war in Spain in 1936, and more particularly the following year when Hitler ordered the attack on Guernica, Stalin may have known it was only a matter of time before the fascist regime turned on Russia and felt that it was vital to ensure loyalty to Communism throughout the country. He had already sent Suslov to pursue this aim in the Urals, Ukraine and the Caucasus, and there are allegations that here Suslov staged his own show trials accusing local party members of revisionism or disloyalty. Whatever the evidence it seemed that Stalin was impressed with

Suslov, who in 1937 was made Party Secretary in Rostov and in 1939 First Secretary in Stavropol.

At the outbreak of the Great Patriotic War Stalin ordered ethnic minorities to be sent to Siberia and Suslov was tasked with making the arrangements. It was in Lithuania, however, that the name of Suslov would leave bitter and lasting memories. In 1944, when the Nazis left Lithuania, there were concerns that the country's Communists were slow with their land reform and showing '*insufficient determination in uncovering Lithuanian-German bourgeois nationalists.*' (Re-quoted from The Soviet Machiavelli @ ianchadwick.com) the government set up a bureau for Lithuanian affairs and put Suslov in charge of reinforcing Soviet rule in the country. For the inhabitants, the intervention was to be a lasting reminder of an earlier unwelcome visitor:

> '*Mikhail Murav'ev, the suppressor of Lithuania's Insurrection of 1863, hung, killed, jailed or deported to Siberia around ten thousand Lithuanians. For his merits, the Tsar conferred upon him the title of 'Graf.' The Lithuanian nation 'baptized' him The Hangman. The number of Suslov's victims in Lithuania is ten-fold. The new Russian Tsar bestowed on him the title of Hero of Socialist Labor, the Order of Lenin, and several other orders. For a long time now the Lithuanian nation has considered him The Second Hangman.*' (Ibid)

These accusations were made in anti-Soviet samizdat literature in the 1970s, and deciding how far Suslov can be held personally responsible and condemned for events in Lithuania at a time of great instability, would require detailed investigation and debate. As far as Suslov was concerned the mission was to stamp out fascism and prevent its re-emergence at all costs.

His ideological commitment to socialism showed no sign of deserting him in the new post-war world order. Faced with the emergence of two intellectually and economically opposed power blocs, his outlook, perhaps understandably was both Manichean and suspicious:

> *'Having taken the path of military-political conspiracy against peace and the security of the peoples, the ruling circles of the U.S. and Britain drive at full speed preparing a new war and are declaring with increasingly cynical shamelessness and insolence, their claims for world domination, the "American leadership of the world," reviving the insane plans of German fascism and forgetting the historical lessons given to crazy pretenders for "world domination"'.*
>
> (*The Defence of Peace and the Struggle Against the Warmongers,* Mikhail Suslov 1949)

During the next four years, under Stalin's wing Suslov's rise in the political firmament was assured, his election to the Presidium of the Supreme Soviet in 1950 followed in 1952 by membership of the Politburo. Stalin's death in 1953 and the arrival of Khrushchev would bring that rise to an abrupt halt, as Suslov fell from favour and was dropped from the Presidium. In 1955 Khrushchev, even before his speech denouncing his predecessor, visited Yugoslavia and declared, '*There are different roads to socialism.*' The assumption might be that as an implied endorsement of Tito's concessions to the free market and an obviously revisionist statement, this would not have gone down well with the Stalinist Suslov.

However, he was by now restored to the Presidium, and would place on record his own criticisms of Stalin and the cult of personality, stating at the 20th Party Conference in February 1956 that they:

> *'...caused considerable harm to both organisational and ideological party work...belittled the role of the masses and the role of the Party, disparaged collective leadership, undermined inner-party democracy, suppressed the activeness of party members, their initiative and enterprise, led to lack of control, irresponsibility, and even arbitrariness in the work of individuals,*

prevented the development of criticism and self-criticism, and gave rise to one-sided and at times mistaken decisions.'

(Serge Petroff, *The Red Eminence: A Biography of Mikhail A. Suslov*)

Endorsing the denunciation of Stalin can be read as Suslov compromising his ideology to maintain his place in the changing climate of Khrushchev's 'thaw', a genuine admission of the fallibility of his late leader and role model, or perhaps both.

A few months later Suslov would become embroiled in another test of Soviet principles, the Hungarian Revolution. In a telegram from Budapest on 27 October 1956 he and Soviet Politburo comrade Mikoyan reported their impression that, '*...as a whole the new government is reliable and in the social sense more authoritative.*

Joseph Stalin and Mikhail Suslov

Comrade [Antal] Apro gave a paper about the military situation in assured tones. He informed everyone, by the way, that in the hospital are about three thousand injured Hungarians, and of those 250 people died. The figure of others killed or wounded is unknown. In connection to the unpeaceful situation in the provinces, comrade Kadar asked the question: can we increase the number of Soviet troops?

We declared that we had reserves, and however many troops were needed we would provide them. The Hungarian comrades were very glad to hear this. (Digital Archive The Wilson Centre)

Khrushchev had been reluctant to intervene, believing that the revolution was not ideologically driven but stemmed from economic discontent. He also referred to the 'real mess' that Britain and France had just got into over Suez, and saw no desire to replicate it. The decision was therefore made to withdraw Soviet troops, and a general declaration on friendship and cooperation between the Soviet Union and other socialist states was issued. Just one day later, however, following further violence and chaos in Budapest, the Presidium thought again and on 4 November Soviet tanks moved in to take control of the city.

Historians are still debating the reasons for the Presidium's sudden change of mind, some citing Hungarian talk of either withdrawing from the Warsaw Pact or becoming non-aligned as the deciding factor. The possibility of the Soviet Union losing a buffer state against NATO would certainly have raised the level of concern in Moscow. *Pravda*'s account, published three days after the invasion, included the following version of events:

'Fascist, Hitlerite, reactionary, counter-revolutionary hooligans financed by the imperialist West took advantage of the unrest to stage a counter-revolution.... Hungarian patriots, with Soviet assistance, smashed the counter-revolution.'

From left to right: Ho Chi Minh, Mikhail Suslov and Leonid Brezhnev on holiday in the Crimea

On the domestic front, by 1959 Suslov was becoming increasingly critical of Khrushchev's drive to remove Stalin's legacy entirely from Soviet discourse, and at the 29th Party Conference he took issue with the leader's latest economic plan, urging a return to first principles: *'Marx and Lenin teach us that communism doesn't appear suddenly, but comes into existence, matures, develop…these social changes will be long, and understandably, cannot end in the course of a seven year period.'*

That year Suslov also visited Britain, and Labour leader Hugh Gaitskill reciprocated with a trip to Moscow. Suslov meanwhile remained consistent in his modified retrospective view of Stalin, claiming that China's Communist leader Mao Zedong displayed the same negative traits in terms of cult of personality. In Moscow, Suslov now became an opposition figure to Khrushchev, who found his own power base compromised in the wake of the Cuban Missile Crisis of 1962. With the arrival of Brezhnev

1 May parade, Baku, 1981

and Kosygin, Suslov was able to strengthen his position within the new collective leadership.

The Brezhnev era was also when the description of 'Chief ideologue of the Communist Party' began to be applied to Suslov, and indeed this was the phrase uppermost in my mind as I made my way to his office that day in 1978. That and '*the longest surviving member of the Politburo, second in the government after the General Secretary from 1957.*' I also reflected that the reputation as chief ideologue may have begun during the Khrushchev era, when it was not difficult to be considered so, considering how poorly educated Khrushchev was compared to Stalin. I knew Suslov was very competent though, and that Stalin had respected him immensely and challenged him in every positive way that he could. Suslov, apart from the cult of personality issue, had always seemed determined to talk positively about Stalin and to follow his ideology.

To reveal what happened the day I was summoned to Suslov's office, I will reprise for the reader a flavour of the encounter as described in my autobiography, *More Than One Life*: No sooner had I shaken hands with Viktor Maksimovich, I could hear Boris Pastukhov saying in a loud clear voice: '*There is a suggestion to appoint Vagif Aliovsat Guseynov, First Secretary of the Azerbaijan Central Committee of the Komsomol, as the Secretary of the Central Committee of the Komsomol.*' I had suspected that this was the reason I had been called. I had first been offered the job a short while ago and had felt honoured – who would not be at the prospect of such a promotion. I was a young journalist, and Baku was quite cosmopolitan in many ways so I would not be entering the larger arena completely unprepared. It could be a good opportunity for me. I had, however, declined the offer.

I was asked to step forward so that everyone could see me, all the members of the Secretariat, the numerous functionaries and invited persons. Silence. Then a rustling of papers along the desks as the Secretaries of the Central Committee scanned the daily documents before them. Chairman Suslov, a tall, slightly bent figure that seemed to hang across the table, to loom indeed over the whole hall, said in a squeaking voice, '*He is a worthy candidate. But it is well known that Comrade Guseynov is not very keen to move to Moscow, isn't that so, Vagif Alivsatovich?*'

Then it was true, one could have no secrets from Mikhail Andreyevich Suslov. His channels of information were clearly well established; he knew every single detail about my previous interviews. Invited to speak, it all came out at once: I lost my father a year ago… not so long ago buried the elder of the family – my wife's father – and now my mother is seriously ill... I am her son and she is my responsibility.... Suslov replied, *'I think the Central Committee of the Communist Party will be able to support the family of the Secretary of the Central Committee of Komsomol.'* The remarks seemed directed at his colleagues rather than at me, and there seemed to be a hint of dry humour, something sardonic in his tone. Suslov had not exactly given me an order, but at the same time it seemed very hard to say no. Maybe I could work something out with my family. Before long, arrangements were made for them and I had moved to Moscow and was Secretary of the Central Committee of Komsomol.

My dealings with Suslov were not to end there. I discovered that he was particularly interested in the Soviet Union's relationship with Yugoslavia. This seemed natural enough considering his enduring loyalty to Stalin's ideals of socialism and the fact that there had been a long diplomatic rift between Moscow and Belgrade. Soon after World War Two, the spirit of fierce independence with which Tito the partisan had fought the Cetniks and Nazis became apparent in his political leadership of the new socialist Federation of Yugoslavia. Whilst declaring his acceptance of the Soviet Union as an example he remained determined to produce his own economic model, and for his country to forge its own future. Stalin was not pleased and he and Tito exchanged a series of vitriolic letters. Stalin remarked, *'I will shake my little finger and Tito will disappear.'* In 1949, Russian and Hungarian forces were on Yugoslavia's northern border. There was no invasion but Stalin's personal displeasure rendered Yugoslavia a pariah state among other socialist countries, which sought to purge suspected 'Titoists.' Stalin also allegedly instigated several assassination attempts against Tito, who threatened in a letter to fight fire with fire: *'Stop sending people to kill me. We've already captured five of them, one of them with a bomb and another with a rifle...If you don't stop...I'll send one to Moscow, and I won't have to send a second.'* (Zhores A. Medvedev, *The Unknown Stalin*)

After some initial disputes and skirmishes over territory, notably Trieste,

Tito's relations with the West, while stopping short of alignment, grew more positive, enabling the Yugoslavian government to obtain US economic aid. Although the regime was repressive, the retention of private ownership in agriculture and heavy industry won further approval from NATO countries, while hardening Stalin's condemnation of Tito as a revisionist. The Soviet Union also perceived a potential strategic threat in Yugoslavia; it had arguably been Churchill's controversial decision in 1943 to switch support away from the Cetniks that had brought Tito to power. The two men had also met and talked in 1944; growth in that rapport might conceivably tip Tito towards joining NATO.

In Baku we enjoyed very good relations with the Bosnia-Herzogovina region of Yugoslavia, and were twinned with Sarajevo, the city in which Archduke Ferdinand had been assassinated in 1914, igniting World War One. Together Baku and Sarajevo ran annual conferences, youth festivals, exhibitions and exchange programmes for students, artists, directors and scientists, and overall had strong cultural, intellectual and sporting links. Now that it was my job to actively maintain and develop these kinds of activities, Suslov expressed a great deal of interest in the Azerbaijan Bosnia-Herzogovina connection.

Thus began for me a series of regular visits to Yugoslavia, spending about eight weeks on each occasion. If there was something very important going on or any issue we could not resolve I would send a telegram for Suslov's attention, and usually receive a reply promptly and in person. Then one day back in Moscow his secretary rang again to summon me. Suslov was very pleasant and referred to a recent telegram I had sent him from Yugoslavia. He said he was very pleased with what my colleagues and I had done in developing Russian ties with Bosnia-Herzegovina youth, and talked of how this could assist the strengthening of cultural relations between the two countries in general. I knew that at the central government level things were still not so good between Moscow and Belgrade. Suslov clearly felt that grassroots work, in other words the dialogue we had been building between the academic, creative and social communities, particularly among the young people, offered a way forward. He therefore asked me to focus on expanding this process throughout Yugoslavia.

During one of the festivals in Bosnia-Herzegovina my colleague in the country, who was a great guy, turned out to be a friend of President Mohammed, and told me I had been invited to the Presidential Palace. I met the President and we had a very pleasant conversation in which he congratulated me on the work. Then to my complete surprise he announced that as a mark of appreciation he would like to present me with the Golden Medal of Tito. He even wrote out a citation on the spot: *'To Vagif Guseynov For Huge Improvement in Relations between the Youth of the Soviet Union and Yugoslavia'.*

Suslov's aim was to bring Yugoslavia to the right side, in other words the Soviet side, rather than see it tilt to the West, towards decadence and capitalism. His efforts to do so were through peaceable means, culture, sport and art, winning the battle of ideas rather than using force, as he had perhaps been obliged to do three decades earlier in Lithuania. When I was visiting Bosnia-Herzegovina around the 1980s the population was 70 per cent Muslim, 20 per cent Catholic and 10 per cent other faiths, living together as neighbours. Suslov would have been optimistic that such harmony would continue and that the people of Yugoslavia would flourish as one within the Soviet family He did not live to see the tragedy of ethnic violence that within just a few years would tear the country apart.

Suslov was once described by the CIA as *'The high priest of communism.'* His political longevity was certainly remarkable: *'With the ease of a charioteer covering dead-laden ground, Suslov survived Stalin's purges and reached the Soviet hierarchy's highest plane of power.' (Harvard Crimson,* 1982)

I would describe Suslov as the epitome of a Soviet leader and a committed Communist. Only after his death did the real de-Stalinisation begin, with the arrival of Gorbachev and everyone saying how awful life under Stalin had been. It all went to pieces. While Suslov was in power he tried to keep it all together – Yugoslavia, the USSR, the whole idea of Communism. A true revolutionary he was also conservative in every way; I remember that even when the temperature was soaring he would be the last to remove his jacket.

LECH WAŁĘSA

In 1980 I returned to Poland as Secretary of the All-Union Lenin Komsomol Central Committee for International Affairs. There had been some dramatic developments in the country since my visit two years earlier, when I had met the man whom, unbeknown to anyone at the time was about to become Pope John Paul II. This appointment had obviously been a huge source of pride for the Polish people. Returning to his homeland in June 1979, the first Catholic pontiff to visit a Communist country, John Paul had been greeted by an estimated 2 million citizens lining the streets of Warsaw and cheering 'Long Live Our Pope'. Speaking to the crowd at an open air mass in Victory Square, he emphasised that his visit was for religious reasons, while adding the hope that it would assist the, *'internal unity of my fellow countrymen and also a further favourable development of relations between the state and the church in my beloved motherland.'*

The relationship perceived to be under strain was perhaps not so much that between church and state, as the Polish government and the people. It was now ten years since the bad harvest and sudden hike in food prices had led to riots in the Baltic cities. Ordering the Polish People's Army and Citizen's Militia to fire on workers apparently returning to their factories had resulted in over forty death and many more injuries. In the aftermath Gierek was appointed as new leader, and meeting workers in Gdansk he apologised for what had happened and pledged political renewal. A further strike by mostly female textile workers broke out six months later in the city of Lodz. The government responded by sending *'sincere workers greetings from comrade Gierek'.* The women replied: *'We have got the greetings, but we have got no money.'* It was this strike that was believed to have forced prices to be lowered and wages increased as promised, and for a while things settled down.

By the mid-seventies, however, with the state no longer able to afford subsidies, the cost of food rose sharply again, with increases of 50 per cent to 100 per cent in staple goods. The resulting strikes of 1976 were more widespread than before, but in some cases more reasoned; workers at the Transformer and Traction Factory in Lodz met with management, urging non-violence and putting the case for parliamentary democracy and free trade unions. Elsewhere people were singing the Internationale and the Polish National Anthem and seizing trainloads of meat. An apparent appeasement by the Prime Minister was followed immediately by a harsh crackdown in which thousands were arrested or sacked. In July Cardinal Wyszinski of the Catholic Church wrote to the government in support of the workers, asking for them to be released and reinstated. (Sources include: Global Non-Violent Action Database)

Among those losing their jobs in 1976 was thirty-three-year-old Lech Wałęsa. A veteran of the 1970 strikes, Wałęsa was already a marked man, his home allegedly bugged and his means of earning a living persistently hampered by his anti-communist views and political activism. Born 29 September 1943 in Popowo, near Włocławek, Poland, Lech had been raised by his mother, his father, a carpenter who had been interned in a labour camp by the Nazis during World War Two, having died at the age of thirty-four. When Lech was nine his mother married her brother-in-law. After leaving school the young man learned the trade of electrician and in 1967 started work at the huge Lenin Shipyard in Gdańsk.

For my visit to Poland in 1980 it was again S. Yakobovsky, my colleague in the country's youth movement, who was my host and guide. It was of course impossible to ignore what was happening in Poland at this time, and the person everyone was talking about was Lech Wałęsa. When Yakobovsky asked if I would like to go and hear him speak, naturally I said yes. As when meeting the former Archbishop of Krakow, later Pope John Paul II, I knew of Wałęsa's anti-Soviet views, but this man clearly had something that drew the Polish people and struck a deep chord in them, and I was fascinated to see for myself what it was. Making our way to the square in Warsaw we found a huge crowd of people all come to hear Wałęsa speak. And speak he did! He was really capturing his audience with his rhetoric, with his sheer charisma. There was a lot of response from the crowd, and you could see, hear and feel them being inspired, uplifted by his words. The impression I got was that here was a man with huge leadership skills and the most tremendous gift for oratory. It was no wonder that the Polish government wasn't happy about him.

Strike at the Vladimir Lenin Shipyard in August 1980

There was no comparable figure in Russia. We had the dissidents of course, and my friends being journalists and writers we were often very critical of the government, but we didn't go on demonstrations. The Soviet system in a number of other countries was however already weakening. The socialist approach simply did not seem capable of solving the problems facing those societies; it could certainly not meet the most fundamental, practical needs of the vast majority of ordinary people. The economic model was doing very badly in comparison to that of the capitalist nations. Socialist beliefs of equal shares were all well and good, but when there was next to nothing for the average citizen those beliefs rang hollow. Opening your fridge day after day and finding nothing to sustain you but a theory of what is right, is hardly going to keep you content with the status quo. One cannot live off ideology and for this reason socialist policies were being challenged. Obviously the issues of censorship and freedom of speech were also very important drivers, but availability of affordable food and other products was a far stronger imperative in calling for change. It must be remembered that there was also now increasing opportunity for comparison; Polish people had been visiting Holland, France, Belgium and other places, where they could walk into shops and find not only goods at reasonable prices but also a wide choice of all sorts of items. After that you could tell them about ideology as much as you liked, but they had seen the reality of life elsewhere, against which their own experience no longer matches up.

Add to this the fact that the curbs on freedom of speech in Poland and other socialist countries were being applied in a really quite stupid way, and you have a recipe for disaster at some point. Certain rules may have originally been invented for a good reason that most people agreed on, but if an idiot is in charge of implementing those rules with a heavy hand, it had a negative effect on everything. Poland and Hungary were the first countries to protest against the lack of free speech, and Lech Wałęsa had already become a figurehead in this growing movement, with a lot of people, including foreign embassies, helping him by providing money and support. With socialism in the doghouse morally, politically and economically, Wałęsa was emerging in the right place at the right time. As is so often seen throughout history, a hero will arise when the need for one becomes urgent enough: 'cometh the hour, cometh the man,' as the saying goes. As the 20th century entered its final quarter, it already looked like Wałęsa might be the man for Poland.

I thought afterwards about the meeting we had witnessed that day, and it seemed very evident to me that people had gone along of their own choosing. Sometimes a gathering can be organised or carefully stage-managed to create an impression for the media, but in those kinds of situation it is hard to muster 500 let alone 1,000 people. That day I would be surprised if there had been less than 20,000 packed into that square in Warsaw, a massive groundswell of popular support. At one point I saw the crowd bearing Wałęsa on its shoulders. Their adulation and respect was nothing if not genuine.

A couple of days later Yakabovsky and I were having a drink in one of the Warsaw bars. We were just about to leave when someone he knew came up to him and said, '*If you want to meet Wałęsa he will be coming here in twenty minutes.*' Having heard the man speak I was certainly interested. Yakobovsky agreed we should stay. Wałęsa duly arrived accompanied by a friend, Yakobovsky and I were introduced and they sat down at our table. Wałęsa spoke excellent Russian with a very good accent so we were able to converse easily. Wałęsa's friend then said he had to be going, but that the rest of us should all stay and talk. Wałęsa cried out in mock alarm, '*No don't leave me, there are two communists here, one Polish, one Russian!*' We all laughed, then Wałęsa said, '*I expect you have been talking about me behind my back here.*' I said, '*No, no, we went to your meeting a couple of days ago, and it was pretty impressive. I was not convinced by your thesis, but I think your oratorical skills are amazing.*' Wałęsa asked, '*Why are you not you in agreement with what I am saying?*' I said, '*Well you have a lot of anti-Soviet and anti-socialist ideas.*' He said, '*You're always in charge of us.*' To this I replied, '*Think about Polish history though, and look at yourselves, it's not really true. It has been hard for anyone to tell you what to do, impossible at times.*'

I conceded his point about Soviet interference. One thing that I thought was very incorrect was not to acknowledge how Russia had helped the Polish people during World War Two. I pointed out that to liberate Poland from the Nazis, 650,000 Russians had died. Wałęsa responded by saying, '*We love the Russian people and Russian culture, its just Communism we are against.*' I said, '*Well then it is important to say so, to make that distinction clear, that the party is one thing, the people are different.*' We had a very lively discussion, and a frank exchange of views, which at the same time was very friendly. Good Polish vodka softened the edges, helping to clarify our ideas and let the conversation flow.

1980 proved to be a pivotal year for Lech Wałęsa, and for Poland. For the first time since World War Two the economy had begun to contract, and overseas debt was approaching $18 billion. With another increase in food prices, the unions, declared illegal and forced to operate covertly, were largely hamstrung. The catalyst for a breakout was coming however. On 7 August, Anna Walentynowicz was alleged to have taken part in union activities and was sacked from her job in the Lenin Shipyard. Anna was just five months away from her retirement. On 14 August her co-workers downed tools in protest, and demanded her re-instatement. It was at this point that Lech Wałęsa, in what would become a symbolic moment in history, climbed the Lenin Shipyard's perimeter fence to join the strikers.

A committee was formed, negotiations with the management took place and three days later an agreement was reached. Like a genie released from a bottle, however, the strikes could not be contained, and when industrial action occurred elsewhere in Gdansk and spread across the country, the various leaders called upon Lech Wałęsa to maintain the shipyard shutdown in solidarity. Wałęsa readily agreed, and now headed up an Inter-Factory Strike Committee that brought together the workers of the Gdańsk, Sopot and Gdynia region. The committee demanded that the right to strike and form free trade unions be recognised in law. It was a bold and unprecedented demand. The fact that on 31 August the Polish deputy premier Mieczysław Jagielski signed an agreement to this effect, points to the seriousness with which the situation, and in particular Wałęsa, were being taken.

Within a matter of weeks the Inter-Factory Strike Committee of Gdansk, Sopot and Gdynia mushroomed into a nationwide federation of over twenty different unions, attracting not only those in factories, but also farmers, bringing the membership to an estimated ten million Polish workers. A new name was chosen for the organisation: Solidarity (Solidarność), and Wałęsa was to be its leader. Over the next few months, under the auspices of the International Labour Organisation, Wałęsa visited Switzerland, Franc, Italy, Sweden and Japan. Probably the most powerful gesture of solidarity

Strike leader Lech Wałęsa stands on a platform at the gates of Lenin shipyard, Gdansk, telling the workers that the strike is now over, 9 September 1980

took place in January 1981, with Wałęsa being received by Pope John Paul II in the Vatican.

The brave new world for Poland's workers was to be short lived, however. In December 1981, little more than a year after Solidarity's formation, Prime Minister Jaruzelski, said to be fearful of a Soviet intervention, declared a state of emergency and the imposition of martial law throughout the country. Land borders and Polish air space were closed, while curfews and censorship restricted freedom of movement and speech. The visible presence of troops on the streets underlined the seriousness of the government's intent. Jaruzelski appeared on national television to announce there was henceforth to be a strict ban on the activities of Solidarity: '*We have been patient, but our patience has run out.*' With Solidarity outlawed

John Paul II visits President of Poland Lech Wałęsa in Warsaw

and most of its leaders arrested, including the founder and figurehead of the movement, Lech Wałęsa, it looked like the honeymoon was over. Yet despite the armoured cars and patrols with riot shields, batons and automatic weapons, many people were more angry than cowed, and crowds gathered in the capital shouting '*Gestapo!*' at the soldiers. Pope John Paul II pleaded that no more blood should be shed, and called for peace.

In November 1982, after being detained for eleven months at a hunting lodge in southeast Poland near the Soviet border, Wałęsa was released. Rumours circulated of pressure from the Catholic Church, allied with Jaruzelski's hope of support in return for freeing the popular leader and allowing a degree of political and economic reform. At the same time it was stressed that Wałęsa's freedom was conditional on him not opposing the government. It was then announced that the Pope would be coming to Poland the following June. John Paul II, however, had stated that he would boycott his homeland while martial law remained in place, which did not happen until July 1983. Three months later came the news that Wałęsa was to receive that year's Nobel Peace Prize.

While the morale of the underground movement was boosted, the state run media expressed criticism of the award, and civil restrictions continued. Fearing that he might not be allowed back into the country, Wałęsa's wife, Danuta went to Oslo to accept the prize on his behalf. Finally however, faced with a deteriorating domestic economy, the soft power of the Catholic Church and the assumption that with Gorbachev now in the Kremlin, Soviet tanks were unlikely to roll into Warsaw, the Polish government was obliged to seek terms with Solidarity. The negotiations were long and fragmented, marred by setbacks and confrontation, and it was not until June 1989 that the first semi-open parliamentary elections were held. The result was a large majority for Solidarity, but Wałęsa refused to enter a coalition with the communists, and decided instead to run for the newly created post of president. The following year saw him succeed, becoming the first freely elected head of state in Poland for sixty-three years.

Lech Wałęsa was clearly born with some remarkable talents. I saw at first hand his gift for oratory, how he was able to hold a huge crowd in thrall with the power of words. A man who eschewed violence, his Catholic faith is said to have been a source of vital inner strength throughout decades of political struggle. His phenomenal rise to fame, as a people's hero and beacon for liberty was an unfolding drama watched by audiences around the world. Great revolutionaries are by definition the ones who bring about change, but do not necessarily make stable leaders in the newly defined status quo.

There is also a tendency to backlash, motivated by personal rivalry, legitimate concerns or both. Criticisms levelled against Wałęsa include an autocratic, abrasive style, a tendency to engender conflict within his own party, and an inability to translate the leadership qualities that created Solidarity into the broader sphere of national government. There were also those who looked down on him; as an electrician with no formal education,

President of Poland Lech Wałęsa and his wife Danuta at the oath ceremony in 1991

they felt he lacked the dignity required of a president. In his favour, overseeing Poland's transition from a communist to a free market economy can not have been easy, but in a media-dominated age he seemed unwilling to present a positive image of himself, refusing to shake the hand of rival Aleksander Kwasniewski after a TV debate, instead offering to shake the former communist leader's leg.

Such public displays of rudeness seemed unlikely to help Wałęsa's popularity, and in the 1995 elections he lost the presidency. After declaring his intention to return to his job as an electrician in Lenin Shipyard, he instead set up the Lech Wałęsa Institute to promote the values of Solidarity, and took to the international lecture circuit to speak about democracy and the impact of an expanded NATO on global security. An attempted comeback with his new Christian Democracy of the Third Polish Republic party in the year 2000 was an utter failure, gaining him little more than one per cent of the vote. Worse still it was his sworn rival Kwasniewski who secured the presidency.

Announcing his retirement from politics, Wałęsa spent more time with the Lech Wałęsa Institute, but in 2006 he abandoned Solidarity in protest at its support for the Law and Justice Party's bid to expose former communist enforcers and secret police.

Pope John Paul II had forgiven the man who had tried to assassinate him. If Lech Wałęsa's rejection of the movement he had created was a refusal to seek revenge, it might suggest that, belying his confrontational persona, as a good Catholic he knew the spiritual as well as practical value of forgiveness.

RICHARD VON WEIZSÄCKER

A busy working life can often make the notion of retirement problematic. When you are no longer gainfully employed what do you do with your time – collect stamps, play cards or sit around drinking vodka? If you are used to being occupied, having challenges, meeting people and meeting deadlines, this sudden idleness can seem like very hard work indeed. You also have decades of accumulated knowledge, which even in today's rapidly changing world can be of value. Sharing experience and staying involved is also good for you and provides personal fulfilment.

It was a combination of these factors I think which attracted people to participate in the Council on Foreign and Defence Policy, a Russian based organisation for the discussion of international issues. Drawing on a worldwide membership the aim was to meet, talk, exchange knowledge and ideas and wherever possible come up with suggestions and recommendations for creating more stable and harmonious relations between countries. Symposia are held throughout the year in various capital cities, and the delegates then convene at an annual conference at which prominent figures from the world of politics are invited to attend. These have included former British premier John Major, Henry Kissinger and Mikhail Gorbachev who was a guest on two occasions.

As a member of the Russian Council on Foreign and Defence Policy I have had the honour of meeting numerous interesting individuals with a wealth of fascinating experience. Their careers and backgrounds are diverse, particularly the more senior members, who have lived through some of the most dramatic and turbulent years of the 20th century. One such person was Richard von Weizsäcker, the former President of West Germany. Almost eighty years of age when I met him, Weizsäcker was born into an upper class German family in 1920. His father being a professional diplomat the young Richard and his sister and two brothers lived for much of the time in Switzerland and Sweden and throughout some of the 1930s were in Berlin. In 1937 as the Nazi Party tightened its hold on West Germany, Richard left for England to read for a Philosophy degree at Balliol College Oxford.

That winter, however, while spending time in Grenoble to improve his French language skills he was called up for service in the German Army. Just over eighteen months later he was ordered to be part of the Blitzkrieg unleashed by Hitler on Poland. This alone would be a formative experience for any nineteen-year-old. Add to this that on the second day of the invasion his brother Heinrich, serving in the same infantry regiment was killed within metres of him, and that Richard remained with the body until the following day in order to bury him, and one has a rare and remarkably poignant story.

It should be stressed for the benefit of anyone that doesn't already know, that Weizsäcker was no Nazi. His regiment the 9th Potsdam was comprised substantially of aristocratic Prussians opposed to Hitler, and Weizsäcker recalls how whilst serving on the Russian front they would take pot shots at a portrait of Hitler. In 1944 it was members of this cohort that tried to assassinate the Führer at his Wolf's Lair HQ. The plot, famously remembered as Operation Valkyrie, failed because an officer had moved the briefcase containing the bomb behind a table leg thus unknowingly lessening the impact of the blast. Valkyrie was one of a string of attempts by high-ranking German officers to remove Hitler and seek peace with the Allies. Weizsäcker had assisted on one occasion by providing a comrade with documents enabling him to travel to a meeting in Berlin, where the Führer was due to inspect some new uniforms. Again chance intervened when an air raid destroyed the uniforms.

For Weizsäcker the remainder of the war was in his own description 'agony', and after being wounded in 1945 he was invalided out of the army and went on to study law, physics and theology. In 1947, his father Ernst's wartime involvement in deporting Jews from France in his capacity as a civil servant came under the spotlight. When Ernst was tried at Nuremberg for alleged war crimes his son assisted the defence lawyers. Ernst was convicted and, after being sentenced to seven years' imprisonment – which Winston Churchill described as a 'deadly error' – was freed in 1950.

Currency reforms by the Allies in 1948 had resulted in a Soviet blockade of the western controlled sectors of Berlin and the subsequent founding of the Federal Republic of Germany in the west and the German Democratic Republic in the East left the Federal Republic's territory within Berlin

One of the not too serious moments is captured during a court recess in the trial of Baron Ernst von Weizsäcker and twenty other former officials of the Nazi government. Here the former State Secretary in the German Foreign Office and last German Ambassador to the Vatican chats with his son Richard, 28, law student and acting as assistant defence counsel for his father

encircled by the GDR. Seventy-eight years after Bismark had forged a cluster of principalities into the modern industrialised German state it was now split in two. In this new paradigm the twenty-nine-year-old Richard Weizsäcker found himself – geographically at least – on the Western side where the Federal Republic's seat of government had been moved to Bonn. For the first ten years people could move relatively freely between East and West but when Ulbricht's Berlin Wall closed down access to the West for East Germans, the sense of a divided people was felt far more keenly, the Wall coming to symbolise a gulf also in ideologies.

Divisions – between people, countries and belief systems – were something that Richard von Weizsäcker would later strive to heal but he did not enter active politics immediately. His personal life and completing his education took first priority and in 1953 he married Marianne von Kretschmann who was twelve years his junior, a move he later described as *'the best and smartest decision of my life.'* They would have four children together. After gaining his doctorate in law in 1955 he took a job with Mannesman, a large German steel company, headed up a bank and sat on the board of a pharmaceutical company. Alongside these commercial interests Weizsäcker maintained a deep involvement with religion as President of the German Evangelical Church from 1964 to 1970. It was during this period that he embarked on one of his first bridge building exercises, writing in support of some other German evangelicals who had advocated that Poland's western border with Germany be the contested Oder-Niesse line. Acceptance of this borderline, a move objected to by many German politicians, was seen by Weizsäcker as an important gesture of reconciliation with Poland and essential to the continuance of peace in Europe.

Weizsäcker had been a member of the Christian Democratic Union Party since 1954 and it seems an indication of the respect attached to him that by 1965 Chancellor Adenauer wrote twice asking if he would stand for election. Wary of any conflict of interest Weizsäcker put the church first and declined. Four years later, however, he entered the Bundestag, beginning the gradual rise

President Reagan stands with Chancellor Helmut Schmidt and Berlin Mayor Richard von Weizsäcker at 'Checkpoint Charlie' at the Berlin Wall, November 1982

to prominence that would include serving as Mayor of West Berlin from 1981 to 1984. Through his role in the church he had already encouraged relations between Christians in East and West Germany and as Mayor, Weizsäcker took the opportunity in 1983 to pay an unprecedented and symbolically important visit to Erich Honecker the leader of East Germany.

Weizsäcker's ascent of the political ladder culminated in his election in 1984 as President of the Federal Republic of West Germany. In his opening speech lay a clear reference to the divided state of Germany: *'Our situation, which differs from that of most other nations, is no reason to deny ourselves a national consciousness. To do so would be unhealthy for ourselves and eerie to our neighbours.'*

The following year coincided with a sensitive landmark in German history, the 40th anniversary of the end of World War Two. How should it be marked? Weizsäcker was in no doubt, his long address to the Bundestag on 8 May, while rejecting the notion of collective guilt was at the same time frank in his admission of the culpability of Germans, whether actively or passively in the Holocaust: '*There were many ways of not burdening one's conscience, of shunning responsibility, looking away, keeping mum…When the unspeakable truth of the Holocaust then became known at the end of the war, all too many of us claimed they had not known anything about it or even suspected anything. Who could remain unsuspecting after the burning of the synagogues, the plundering, the stigmatisation of the Star of David, the deprivation of rights, the ceaseless violation of human dignity?*'

The 1985 speech would be the most famous given by Weizsäcker, and in the same year he travelled to Israel. This was another significant historical act on his part, being the first German premier to visit the country. At Jerusalem's Holocaust Memorial he laid a wreath and was according to the Israeli leader Chaim Herzog, visibly moved: '*Seeing tears in this man's eyes I was struck once again by the extraordinary contradictions of history.*'

Some observers alleged more uncomfortable contradictions, specifically Weizsäcker's legal and moral defence of his father at the Nuremeberg trials in 1947. '*…even as his speeches carefully articulate the distinctions between the guilt of the perpetrators of Nazi crimes and the collective guilt of the German nation, critics charge that von Weizsäcker's own failed effort to come to terms with his family's role in the Nazi regime illustrates the inexorable instinct of people to forget a painful past.*' (Noam S. Cohen, *The Harvard Crimson*, 11 June 1987)

Others felt that the sins of the father to whatever degree proven, should not be visited on the son: '*…the many Jewish leaders who praise the statesman say that such media attention on his father's actions during the war is misplaced when assessing the younger von Weizsäcker's actions. Rather they point out that in an era where president of Austria Kurt Waldheim has covered up his own Nazi past, von Weizsäcker's frankness about his own guilt is practically unique on the world stage, and therefore worthy of honor. "President von Weizsäcker is one of the most courageous, outspoken voices of modern Germany," says*

Abraham H. Foxman, the head of the international affairs commission of B'nai Brith's Anti-Defamation League.' (Ibid)

Weizsäcker had set out his own position in the *New York Times* the year he visited Israel, claiming that as an officer of the Third Reich his father had 'failed', but stressing, *'I really believe that he did not know about the existence of the gas chambers and systematic mass killing. I believe he knew a lot of people were dying, but not how.'*

Meanwhile in Germany the subject most often referred to by visitors tended naturally to be that of the country's political and geographical division. When American leader Ronald Reagan spoke in Berlin in 1987 he quoted his West German counterpart: *'President von Weizsäcker has said, "The German question is open as long as the Brandenburg Gate is closed." Today I say: As long as this gate is closed, as long as this scar of a wall is permitted to stand, it is not the German question alone that remains open, but the question of freedom for all mankind. Yet I do not come here to lament. For I find in Berlin a message of hope, even in the shadow of this wall, a message of triumph.'* (Reagan Library Archives, 1987)

Reagan's message of hope would have resonated with Weizsäcker, who from his own remarks seemed to yearn for the stronger sense of cohesive identity that he had observed in Americans: *'On a visit to the United States to attend the bicentennial independence celebrations, he was struck by "the deep joy and pride" that Americans have for their country.'* (James M. Markham, *New York Times*, 24 May 1984)

But while Weizsäcker lamented what he saw as a lack of this pride and joy in his own country he also praised the humanitarian nature of German society: *'"That would not happen over here," the silver-haired Mayor of West Berlin said, pacing softly in an airy salon of the city's official guest house. "That somewhat unreflecting, instinctual love of your own country – we don't have that here. Even so, this is the most tolerant German state ever, the most tolerant society ever. It's lasted longer than the Weimar Republic and the Nazis combined".'*(Ibid)

Like Reagan he also chose to view the existence of the Berlin Wall in a positive light: '*...it cannot seriously be disputed that 40 years after the war, as a German, I belong as much to the people of East Berlin as to the people of Aachen...somehow the wall, which separates the German people, is very proof that there is a German people. To be a German requires the ability to stand up to these contradictions, despite the fact that they are awkward or difficult.*' For Weizsäcker, acknowledging Germany's past wrongs extended beyond Holocaust victims and the people of Poland. In 1990 during a visit to Britain he attended a service in the bombed out ruins of Coventry Cathedral. In the same year President Vaclev Havel of Czechoslovakia came to Germany and met Weizsäcker in Munich, Weizsäcker reciprocating with a visit to Prague – exactly fifty-one years after Hitler had entered the city as an invader.

Back in Weizsäcker's homeland 1990 was the most dramatic since the end of the war. In East Germany the process of *Die wende* (the turnaround) had begun with the removal of Hungary's border fence with Austria, resulting in thousands of GDR citizens making a circuitous journey into West Germany. The term 'reunification' was at first rejected by the then West German Vice Chancellor Hans Dietrich Genscher in favour of 'German Unity' but the former quickly became the established description of what happened. East Germany abandoned its Warsaw Pact status and instead became a part of the Federal Republic and hence a part of the NATO alliance and the European Union. Weizsäcker's long argued plea on behalf of Poland, recognition of the Oder-Neisse borderline was finally agreed.

Meeting Richard von Weizsäcker in the late 1990s one could quickly sense that here was a thoughtful and very well educated man, of deep religious conviction and with a strong sense of ethics. The conference we had been attending was in the eastern part of Berlin and after the formal events of the day were over I went for a walk with Weizsäcker and a German politician colleague who spoke very good Russian. Our hour and a half stroll through the city was leisurely and relaxed and we talked at length. Weizsäcker was very interested in all aspects of Russian life and culture including the ballet and

Vagif Guseynov with Richard von Weizsäcker

opera, and wanted to know who were the up and coming stars of the Bolshoi.

He also asked me about Putin, the kind of person he was and what people thought of him. He enquired about the Russian economy, and how people were reacting to the Russian leader's policies, what the political weather in Russia in general was like at that time and what books Russian people were reading at the moment. I gave Weizsäcker a copy of my book on Yeltsin and said I hoped he would find it interesting. Knowing that I was from Azerbaijan he then asked about the former Soviet republics, where a good deal of conflict had been breaking out. I promised to send him another of my books, which was all about the Caspian Sea and its surrounding oil reserves.

Weizsäcker was an extremely friendly man and very easy to talk to. He did not mention his days in the Wermacht and though I would have loved to ask about his experiences of that time I did not dare ask. I knew how difficult things were in Germany during this time, because over the 1990s the standard of living had dropped considerably after unification. He said it would take time, perhaps several years to improve health and education services for

German president Richard von Weizsäcker accepts being confirmed in office on 23 May 1989

people throughout the country. Previously he had expressed regret that young people did not seem interested in politics and saw this as a failure of his own generation. Taking the longer view, Weizsäcker's steadfast insistence on the importance of remembering past events, painful and guilt laden as they may be, is surely invaluable for those coming generations if we are to ever to stop the appalling mistakes of history repeating themselves.

If fascism was bred in part out of poverty, making it easier to find scapegoats and persecute them it was vital for future societies to be aware of how this happens. In this respect he was unsparing of his own country's actions and refused any attempts to dilute the scale of the Holocaust by comparison to earlier or later atrocities such as Stalin's purges or the mass killings inflicted by Pol Pot in Cambodia. A *historikreit* (historians' dispute) over the relative size and seriousness of Hitler's 'final solution' had been raging among German writers and academics for some two years when in 1988 Weizsäcker announced that the equivocating must end: *'Auschwitz remains unique,'* he said, *'It was perpetrated by Germans in the name of Germany. This truth is immutable and will not be forgotten.'*

At the same time Weizsäcker felt that the generations growing up since the war whilst being made fully aware of German history should not be burdened by it, for young people, *'cannot profess a guilt of their own for crimes they did not commit.'* Along with an emphasis on speaking the truth about the past Weizsäcker was forward looking in many ways; he was among the first for example to talk about recognising the victim status of homosexuals in the Holocaust. His last book had the intriguing title *German History Goes Forward*, suggesting that the desire for progress be balanced by the salutary of lessons of the past; in short perhaps that tomorrow's history be a much happier story.

With his snowy white hair Richard Weizsäcker seemed to me like a kindly Santa Claus. The soft, polite voice and benevolent demeanour made it hard to imagine that as a young man in 1939 he had rolled into Poland in a tank; or indeed that his countrymen and mine had fought each other to the death in Leningrad, Stalingrad, across the vast steppes of Russia, and in 1945 in the bombed out ruins of the city in which we now stood. Reaching the end of our walk through Berlin we returned to Weizsäcker's residence and as we were saying goodbye he observed that at the end of his life now he was very happy to see that Russians and Germans could have such friendly dialogue.

'Those who close their eyes to the past will remain blind as regards the future.'

Richard von Weizsäcker 15 April 1920–31 January 2015

DMITRY YAZOV

Dmitry Timofeyevich Yazov was Minister of Defence of the USSR from 1987 to 1991. He is sometimes referred to as the last marshal of the Soviet Union, though this somewhat elegiac appellation is probably not one he would have chosen for himself. Had the aims of the State Emergency Committee of August 1991 been achieved the Soviet Union would still be intact, and either Yazov, or more likely his successor would now be heading its armed forces. In fact, as I am writing this twenty-six years after the event there may by now have been two or even three Soviet marshals since Yazov.

In exploring the lives of other high-ranking Soviet citizens featured in this collection, we have discussed what drove the members of the State Emergency Committee to place the leader of the government under house arrest, and attempt to take control of their country. The deteriorating security situation, the compromises to nationalists and ambitious ethnic factions, the economic meltdown and food shortages caused by the oil price slide, opportunism and corruption – all these ingredients had conjoined to create a simmering crisis. Did Yazov and the others simply fear that this crisis was about to boil over into chaos? This was no doubt the overriding factor. There was another aspect too, which especially for the older members of the group must have run very deep: having lived through the existential threat to the Soviet Union it was integral to their identity – in their blood one might say. Some of them had also spilled blood for their country, among them Dmitry Yazov.

Born into a peasant community in the remote district of Omsk in Siberia, Yazov was seventeen when the Nazis invaded his homeland of Mother Russia. Volunteering for the army, he reputedly lied about his age and was signed up to the Moscow Red Banner Infantry School, which in November 1941 had been evacuated to Novosibirsk. From the summer of 1942 he

served at the front line commanding infantry and rifle troops in the defence of Leningrad and the Baltic States, and was wounded in action in the head, face and leg. In 1944 he joined the Communist Party of the Soviet Union.

When the war was over Yazov remained with the army, taking a refresher course for officers and was awarded a gold medal on graduating from the Frunze Military Academy in 1956. Two years later he joined the Leningrad

Military District as a senior officer in charge of Combat Training, followed by appointment as Commander of the 400th Motorised Rifle Regiment and promotion to the rank of Colonel. Amid the huge international tension following the Bay of Pigs landing in Cuba, in September 1962 Yazov's regiment was covertly deployed to the island, remaining there for twelve months on standby to repel any further invasion or threat to the Castro government.

Back in the Soviet Union Yazov moved steadily up the military ladder, and by 1971 was Commander of the Army Corps, with a promotion to Lieutenant General the following year. In 1973 I became First Secretary of the Azerbaijan Komsomol, the Soviet youth organisation, and it was in this capacity that I first met Yazov. Commander Yazov was very keen to engage with the young people who were in or about to enter their three and a half years of military service, and he was quite active in this respect in the Caucasus. He was particularly concerned to promote the recreational side of life in the armed forces – the sports, the outdoor activities, the camaraderie and bonding – making military service a positive and character building experience.

When I moved to Moscow to become Komsomol's Secretary for International Affairs in 1978, I continued to meet with Yazov to discuss issues relating to the army and youth. In 1979, Yazov, now a Colonel General, was put in command of the Central Army Group in Czechoslovakia, and at the end of the following year took over as Commander of the Central Asian Military District.

An event that took place in 1983 would put the whole Soviet military on extra high alert and rack up Cold War tensions once more. On the 1 September a South Korean passenger aircraft en route from New York to Seoul, inexplicably strayed into Soviet airspace. When warning shots from a Soviet Su 15 went unheeded, the craft was deemed to be a spy plane and orders were given to open fire. All 269 passengers and crew were killed. It was said that the South Korean Airlines pilot would have been unaware of the warning shots, and there are theories that the plane was experiencing navigational problems. Yazov was alleged to have asked the US Defence Secretary Frank Carlucci why the Americans had used the plane for espionage; Carlucci was said to be unable to convince him this was not the case. The following year Yazov was posted to the Far East, where he reportedly struck up a friendship with the North Korean leader Kim Il Sung.

Yazov was appointed Minister of Defence in 1987. He was now Frank Carlucci's opposite number, and the following year the two men met in Switzerland to discuss the military situation. High on the agenda was the question of how tragic events like the South Korean airliner shooting might be avoided in future:

> *'Mr. Carlucci and General Yazov, who had met briefly once before when Mr. Carlucci was the national security adviser to President Reagan, did most of the talking themselves as their accompanying aides listened. They covered subjects ranging from military doctrines and the positioning of forces in Europe to arms control, regional issues and the spending constraints on the two military establishments... As he travelled to Bern, Mr. Carlucci said he hoped to begin a broad dialogue on military affairs, and to emphasize steps to prevent hostile incidents between the two superpowers.'*
>
> (*New York Times*, 17 March 1988)

There had been a regrettable incident on the ground too. In March 1985, while photographing a Soviet tank as part of a reciprocal Military Liaison Mission near Ludwigslust, East Germany, US Army Colonel Arthur Nicholson had been shot dead by a Soviet soldier. Like the South Korean Airliner, Nicholson's death had sparked a diplomatic crisis between the Soviet Union and the US. In 1985 it fell to Yazov to try to heal the rift: *'Soviet Defense Minister Dmitri Yazov offered the apology when he met with Defense Secretary Frank Carlucci during the May 29 to June 2 summit in Moscow. "I express my regret over the incident, and I'm sorry that this occurred. This does not promote improved relations. Secretary Carlucci and I have agreed that we will do all we can to prevent these kinds of incidents in the future," Yazov said in a statement.'* (Deseret News, 14 June 1988)

Later that same year Carlucci travelled to the Soviet Union to see Yazov again. Carlucci described their talks as frank, and the itinerary provided by his hosts as comprehensive: *'I think one has to note during the course of this visit the remarkable candour and openness that has characterized not only verbal discussions but our visits to Soviet military installations. No information was withheld from us.'* (*Chicago Tribune*, 3 August 1988)

Carlucci reciprocated by asking Yazov to visit him in the US, an invitation that was accepted.

In 1989 I was appointed Chairman of the Azerbaijani Committee for State Security – the KGB. The new post would bring me into close contact with Yazov, and we would spent long evening discussing the fast-changing geopolitical situation in the Soviet Republics and how Gorbachov was leading the country into the abyss of total chaos and destruction.

In April 1990, Gorbachev awarded Yazov the title of Marshal of the Soviet Union, a gesture that would seem somewhat ironic in the light of what was shortly to occur. Despite a large part of the outside world thinking that everything in the Soviet Union was hunky dory and that everyone was looking forward to a bright future under Gorbachev, the mood was in fact becoming very bleak. Even basic everyday goods like milk, bread and yoghurt were in extremely short supply, and the introduction of ration cards, with a monthly allowance for butter less than during the Great Patriotic War, had pushed people close to tipping point.

A particularly worrying aspect of the shortages was the effect on the military. According to the economist Vasily Selyunin, the army numbered five million but the Soviet Union could only afford to feed around one million. The military was entwined with the economy in other ways:

> *'Yuri Ryzhkov, a member of the Supreme Soviet said that 80 per cent of all machine building in the country is arms-related. Meanwhile draft dodging*

Dmitry Yazov second from right and US Secretary of Defence Frank Carlucci second from left during the visit by an American delegation to the USSR

> *had increased by a factor of twenty-seven in two years, as Soviet troops were brought back from Eastern Europe. General Yazov complained to the Supreme Soviet in July, 'Soon we will have no armed forces', and denounced attempts by the Republics to ensure that their nationals did not serve outside their home territory.'*
>
> (Andy Blunden 1993, *The Collapse of the USSR*, Marxism.org)

Yazov was naturally concerned about the condition of his troops and their ability or otherwise to maintain security; soldiers were demoralized with many lacking even a proper roof over their heads:

> *'The humiliating defeats of the Soviet military in Eastern Europe were creating real alarm and anger in the military. The Red Army soldiers were being bundled on to trains and shipped back to the USSR, to be bivouacked*

in freezing tent cities due to the chronic lack of housing at home.... Gorbachev's glasnost policies had provoked this rebellion, and the mightiest army in the world had to watch impotently as their idols were ridiculed and smashed. Now the Baltic states were demanding independence. Where it was going to end...everyone was asking: Is the military going to allow this to go on? Has Gorbachev gone too far for the "hard liners".' (Ibid)

After his televised 'call for order' in December 1990, Kryuchkov brought in Yazov, Pugo, Yaneyev, Pavlov, Shenin, Boldin and Baklanov, who together formed the State Committee on the State of Emergency. With inflation running at 300 per cent, factory workers' wages not being paid and continuing chaos in the republics, the Committee's aim was to convince Gorbachev that a state of emergency was indeed what was required. Gorbachev, however, demurred.

The referendum among the republics the following year showed a large majority in favour of remaining in the Soviet Union, and that summer the Committee published their manifesto *A Word to the People*, a reasoned as well as impassioned argument against perestroika. It was at this point that Gorbachev held private talks about removing Kryuchkov and some of the other members of the Committee from their posts. Kryuchkov being head of the KGB, Gorbachev's plans did not remain private for long however. Thus followed the events of August 1991: Gorbachev placed under house arrest in the Crimea, his refusal according to his account to sign agreement to a state of emergency, the aborted storming of the White House in Moscow and shortly afterwards the arrest of the conspirators on the charge of treason.

Gorbachev called the incident an attempted coup, but this is not really an accurate description in my view, or that of many others. This had not been an attempt by a small group to seize power for themselves, but a measure of last resort by senior, highly experienced and respected men to secure and save their country. In acting as they did, they also believed with good reason that they had the support of the majority of Soviet citizens. In fact it was this very motive that exonerated them in the courts: the Soviet constitution called for the maintenance of law and order in the Soviet Union, and to prosecute people for supporting that aim would in itself have been unconstitutional.

Former Soviet defence minister Dmitry Yazov (back row centre) who was indicted in the so-called GKCHP State Committee for the State of Emergency case leaving the Russian Supreme Court building

In William Odom's book *The Collapse of the Soviet Military*, the author suggests that when Gorbachev promoted Dmitry Yazov he was only looking for '*careerists who would follow orders, any orders.*' How this description fits a man who, for the sake of his country was prepared to challenge its leader and risk his own life in doing so, is unclear. To the army rank and file, Dmitry Yazov was not some remote, imperious figure, but someone who took a genuine interest in their welfare. Soldiers loved him. Over the many years of my acquaintanceship with Yazov I found him to be a straightforward man of honesty and integrity, who always tried to find the kind thing to say about

Dmitry Yazov (left) Mikhail Gorbachev (centre) and Nikolai Ryzhkov at a military parade marking the 45th anniversary of Victory in 1990

anyone. In all that time I never heard anyone malign him in the slightest way in public or private, which was not true of other high-ranking figures.

What happens in the field of battle always has a political dimension, and whatever the outcome, when people are killed and injured their compatriots on all sides often look for an individual to blame. Yazov was asked whether he felt guilty about what happened in Baku in January 1990. It was a difficult question for a military man by then in his nineties to answer, but Yazov did not refuse:

> *'I obeyed another person's order, now the man who gave the orders denies everything. I still cannot leave the country... I would be arrested, because of the fact that I sent troops, the state of emergency was also announced by me, and I am also accused of the execution of people?...I did not order people to be shot. Neither in Baku nor Vilnius... My position was to protect the country's borders and fight the enemy. I was cheated. I remember, Heydar*

Aliyev once in one of his articles wrote that he would not forgive Gorbachev and Yazov for those events, because we had declared the state of emergency. I believe that I was doing my duty. During a Civil War civilians are always dying. I deployed the army, but that does not mean that I ordered to shoot.'

(*Vestnik Kavkaza*, 20 January 2015)

Vagif Guseynov and Dmitry Yazov in the Czech Republic in 1979

Vagif Guseynov's trip to the Czech Republic in 1979

Vagif Guseynov's meeting Dmitry Yazov again in the Czech Republic in 1980

Baku was not the only flare-up for which Yazoz would later face accusations of a criminal nature. In March 1990, the Lithuanian government had declared itself independent of the Soviet Union, the first of the republics to do so. When Gorbachev demanded a retraction and the Lithuanians refused, he imposed economic sanctions and sent troops to occupy parts of the capital Vilnius. At the beginning of 1991, the military presence was increased, prompting the US to curtail its economic aid to the Soviet Union, much to Gorbachev's ire. Within a few months eleven of the twelve republics had followed suit and declared independence, and by the end of 1991, just a few months after the so-called coup attempt Gorbachev was gone.

For those who had been serving members of the Soviet armed forces, the fall out from these dramatic events was to come years afterwards, when in 2016, Lithuanian prosecutors charged sixty-five former Soviet Army officers, Yazov the most senior among them, with war crimes and crimes against humanity. Yazov, who did not attend the trial, maintained his position that he had never ordered anyone to be shot in Baku or Vilnius.

Perhaps it is only history that can be best qualified to judge men like Yazov. Like so many of his contemporaries he had fought the evil of fascism in the Great Patriotic War, and believed in the communist ideals of equality and fraternity. Seeing those values falling apart at the seams in ethnic slaughter, power-mongering and greed, all he could do was his duty as a Soviet citizen and a soldier.

SHEIKH YAMANI

Sheikh Yamani has been called the terminator of the USSR. How is such a conclusion arrived at? What are the strings and connections, pulleys and levers that lead from the son of a middle class Arab judge with no royal connections, to the cataclysmic breakdown of an entire socialist country and its network of republics, one of the two largest superpowers in the world? The answer is one word: oil.

There are of course more aspects to the story than that, and we will examine them in a moment. But let us look first at the rise of Ahmed Zaki Yamani. Born in Mecca in 1930, Yamani's father and grandfather had both been Grand Muftis, interpreters of Islamic law. Yamani would also study law, first in Cairo then in New York, where he achieved a master's degree in Comparative Jurisprudence, before taking a second master's at Harvard then returning to Saudi Arabia. Taking a job in the Ministry of Finance and to work as a legal adviser on tax and oil matters to King Faisal. Yamani was also writing for the press, and said that one day King Faisal asked to see him; he had been reading the young man's articles, and appeared to like them.

Under the aegis of King Faisal Yamani was soon promoted, and by 1962 had been appointed to the post of Oil Minister. At only thirty-two he was now occupying a key position in the government, but what direction would he now take with his country's most important asset? Following World War One, American and British corporations had been the dominant players in exploiting the Middle East's oil reserves. In 1950, faced with King Abdulaziz's threat to nationalise his country's product, the Arabian American Oil Company agreed to share profits 50/50 with Saudi Arabia. From the early 1960s, the Saudi government began plans for taking further control of the production and marketing of its valuable natural resource. The establishment of a national oil company, Petromin, was followed in

1964 by the opening of the University of Petroleum and Minerals, with the aim of bringing home grown technicians and engineers into the country's oil industry.

In 1960 Saudi Arabia had also become one of the founder members of OPEC – the Organisation of Petroleum Exporting Countries, along with Iran, Iraq, Kuwait and Venezuela. Yamani was careful not to talk of completely nationalising Saudi Arabia's oil, but instead stressed participation, suggesting a willingness to work with other countries rather than against them. The Arab-Israeli war of 1967 would prove a test of this cooperative spirit, with the Middle Eastern producers, angered at what they saw as a defeat inflicted by US support for Israel, pushing to use their oil as political leverage. When trouble flared again in the region in the 1973 Yom Kippur war, America again lent its support to Israel. OPEC's Persian Gulf members took a historic decision to set the price of oil themselves, raising it from $3 to just over $5 per barrel. Saudi Arabia also led an agreement to restrict the oil supply by gradual increments, an additional measure which it was hoped would focus international attention on Arab interests in the conflict. Then on 19 October President Nixon signed off over $2 billion worth of arms to be shipped to Israel. Alarmed by a military aid programme of scale, Saudi Arabia, followed by other OPEC countries announced a ban on all oil exports to the US.

By November OPEC's supply restrictions had been increased to a cut of 25 per cent off normal oil production, cranking up the economic pressure on developed countries around the world. The Japanese government and the European Economic Community urged Israel to pull out of the disputed Arab territories. Meanwhile the Shah of Iran was calling for oil to be raised to $20 per barrel. Yamani felt this was going too far, and agreement was reached on $11.65, though this was still a quadrupling of the price prior to the crisis.

As talks between the Arabs and Israelis progressed, a peace deal was arrived at, and by the spring of 1974 OPEC's oil embargo against America had been lifted. Yamani was now looking to bring the oil price down to more normal levels, though this drew the accusation from some in OPEC that he simply wanted to sell more oil and ramp up Saudi Arabia's share of the market. There was also talk that a lower oil price was a calculated move, designed to remove the incentives for developing alternative fuels, thereby securing the Saudis' long-term economic dominance. Yamani's position was that more affordable oil was better for the world economy as a whole. An educated and thoughtful man, he could also step outside the narrow perspective of vested national interest and see the bigger historical picture, famously remarking that *'the Stone Age did not end for lack of stones, and the Oil Age will not end for lack of oil.'*

Throughout all the drama of the 1973 energy crisis, Sheikh Yamani and King Faisal had maintained a close working relationship in which the King had great respect for his minister, often valuing his opinion over that of more senior figures, including some of the Saudi royal family. The following year, however, brought the kind of drama Yamani would never forget. On the 25 March as he was leading a delegation of visiting Kuwaitis in for a meeting with King Faisal in his office, shots were fired. Yamani was standing next to the King as he was killed, the assassin was his nephew Faisal bin Musad. For Yamani, the moment and the emotion would be indelible:

Saudi Arabian oil minster, Sheikh Yamani, pledges no more cuts for Britain in vital talks with Mr Heath in November 1973

'When I remember how he was shot, how he fell into my arms, and the blood that was everywhere . . . It was 25 years ago, but as I tell the story I cry…the boy wanted to kill me, too.' King Faisal's assassin was subsequently beheaded.

With his friend and mentor King Faisal no longer around, doubts circulated about the future for his protégé. Occupying a favoured position, as well as having become something of an international celebrity, had engendered a degree of envy towards Yamani among the Saudi elite. Faisal's successor King Khalid, however, seemed content with the situation, and it was probably the very fact of Yamani's pivotal position on the world stage – an ambassador for Saudi Arabia and a skilful all round diplomat – that helped him to maintain his place. The second shock was about to occur. Just nine months after the murder of King Faisal, on the 21 December 1975, six armed attackers burst in on a conference in Vienna and took sixty-three people hostage. Among them was a group of eleven OPEC representatives including Yamani. The gang's leader was the notorious Venezuelan terrorist Carlos, otherwise known as 'The Jackal', and the stated aim was the liberation of Palestine. The Jackal's plan was to fly to Iraq with the eleven OPEC ministers and a number of other officials. When they reached Baghdad nine of the ministers would be held as ransom: the remaining two, Iran's Jamshid Amuzegar and Sheikh Yamani were to be summarily executed.

Hostage negotiators organised a plane to take Carlos' men and the hostages out via stops in Algeria and Tripoli. After touching down in Tripoli all but ten of the hostages had been released. In an interview for the BBC some years late, Yamani was asked to describe his most memorable experience in life. Unsurprisingly, it was the events of December 1975 that sprang most vividly to mind:

> *'In Vienna when the Opec conference was invaded by Carlos and his group… he informed me that he had decided to kill me at the end and that I had only two days to live. Then in the afternoon, when they sent their statement to the Austrian Government and they told them: "Unless you announce our*

statements on your radio at four o'clock, at 4.30 we are going to kill Yamani and throw his body into the street." And he came and told me that. They discussed who was going to kill who. They were all ready to kill the Iranian, but they said, "We don't think Yamani deserves to be killed" Carlos said, "But it's part of the plan. He has to be killed. I will kill him." Carlos told me, "I don't want you to think this is against you. We respect you. We like you. This is against your country. If the Austrian Government don't publish our statement by five o'clock, at five-thirty I will kill you."

At four o'clock they did not announce the statements, so he told me: "You have half an hour" I asked him if I could write my will, and I started writing… My feeling was very strange. I never thought I would feel like that. I was not really so scared of death as much those I was leaving behind – as I was concerned about what I hadn't done in my life, and my wife, my children, myy mother, and so on. And at 20 minutes after four he came and touched me, and I looked at him, I looked at my watch, and I told him: "I have 10 more minutes to go." I was negotiating with that. He said: "No, you have more than that because they announced the statements."

Then I realised, number one, that the fear of death might be much greater than when you really face death. And secondly I realised that I have to do what I have to do on a daily basis – I must not delay things. And that is one of the important events in my life.'

From Tripoli the plane returned to Algiers, where Carlos spoke by phone with the Algerian President. A deal of some kind was struck, Carlos and his men walked away, as did all the remaining hostages.

The tussle between OPEC members over where to set the oil price continued throughout the mid seventies, with Saudi Arabia urging restraint and even a six month freeze at one point. In the Middle East another oil crisis was around the corner, when in 1979 a revolution in Iran deposed America's ally the Shah, ending two and a half thousand years of monarchical rule and ushering in an Islamic Republic under the Ayatollah Khomeini. A strike by the country's refinery workers had drastically reduced production, provoking panic buying by oil companies and motorists with memories of the 1973 crisis, and sending the price of crude oil soaring to more than double. As a war with Iraq broke out the following year, Iran's production levels remained unstable, boosting the profits of its OPEC partners still further.

It was only a matter of time before the pendulum would begin to swing back. As early as mid 1981 the media was running headlines about an 'Oil Glut'. The causes were cited as over-capacity through stockpiling after 1979 and a drop in consumption. After the Iranian revolution, to begin with the Saudi Arabian government had followed OPEC's policy of supporting the oil price by regulating production, but on the 13 September 1985, Sheikh Yamani announced an abrupt U-turn. Over the next six months Saudi Arabian oil production was quadrupled, boosting its market share while dramatically forcing down the worldwide oil price.

This brings us to the Soviet Union, which up to this point had been earning substantial revenue from its oil exports. That was about to change. *'After record-breaking prices in the early 1980s, oil prices plummeted in the second half of the decade. Oil was the main export and source of hard currency for the U.S.S.R. Insufficient investment and lack of the modern technology needed to harness hard-to-reach oil fields prevented her from expanding production, however, and in fact Soviet oil production began to decline.'* (Dr. Susmit Kumar)

The crash in prices that occurred in 1986 as a result of the Saudis ramping up production would knock an estimated $20 billion per annum off Soviet annual income. How could the government fill such a huge and sudden shortfall?

One possible solution was to replace the barter trade with the other eastern bloc countries and simply sell them the oil and gas. Going down such a route would mean effectively abandoning the whole socialist ethos of the Soviet Union, and any government leader suggesting the idea would surely be heavily censured if not removed from the Central Committee of the Communist Party. Another way to balance the books might be to save money by cutting food imports. However, to do so to the tune of $20 billion would necessitate universal rationing on a scale not seen since World War Two, a completely unworkable option only likely to lead to anarchy. Swingeing reductions in military spending could likewise free up huge amounts of cash, but at the same time provoke dissent among the army elites in cities supported entirely by the defence industry.

Unwilling to risk any of the above courses of action, the Soviet leadership under Gorbachev decided to borrow money from abroad. Still in possession of a strong credit rating from the good years, it was not difficult to find willing lenders. This policy would however within four years complete the reversal of fortune for the whole Soviet financial system. '*In 1985, oil earnings and net debt were $22 billion and $18 billion, respectively; by 1989, these numbers had become $13 billion and $44 billion, respectively. By 1991, when external debt was $57 billion, creditors (many of whom were major German banks) stopped making loans and started demanding repayments, causing the Soviet economy to collapse.*' (Ibid)

As the credit dried up and loans were called in, the Soviet Union attempted to borrow elsewhere by inviting 300 separate banks to form a consortium. When only five of the institutions agreed, the money that could be raised would be twenty times less than what was required to pay off the debt. The Soviet Union was then told plainly that the amount it was asking for would never be forthcoming from a commercial organisation and advised it instead to seek financial support from Western governments. Such support – reportedly amounting to $100 billion – would inevitably come with a price in terms of political concessions.

Meanwhile, in October 1986, it was announced suddenly that Sheikh Yamani had been dismissed from all his government posts. Yamani apparently first heard the news on the radio. No official explanation was given for the move, though the reasons generally cited are disagreement over oil policy and personal enmity on the part of King Fahd. Yamani retired to his home in Switzerland, his reputation as a sound and respected commentator and adviser to the oil industry undimmed. In 1989 he brought together CEOs, government oil ministers, consumers and OPEC officials in a new London based think tank, the Centre For Global Energy Studies.

Without a doubt, Ahmed Zaki Yamani was the most important player in the world oil market during the 1970s and 1980s. Highly educated and with a cosmopolitan outlook, speaking fluent English and French as well as Arabic, he enjoyed the friendship and full confidence of King Faisal, and those that have met him invariably refer to him as an extraordinary person. A number of economic and political observers and politicians of the time regarded him as the symbol of the oil era. And although on one level he was only a minister, an implementer, the power and influence of King Faisal conferred on him the ability to make decisions that affected many countries. *'For more than two decades, Ahmed Zaki Yamani's commands boosted or battered personal pocketbooks and national economies around the world.'* (Pamela Sherrid, *US News & World Report*, 15 February 1988).

Yet it was not just King Faisal's royal status that rubbed off on Yamani. As the Sheikh himself recalled, Faisal was a king with a difference, unostentatious and thoughtful:

> *'He was modest in a glorious way. He lived in homes that today a middle-class Saudi would not accept. He never took money from the Treasury for himself... He was a reformer...strongly for the education of women. At that time it was forbidden. He used to send girls from his own pocket to study outside the country. One of his achievements was to abolish slavery, and I was an instrument in that. He was a believer in the Arab cause and in Islam without being a fanatic.'*
>
> (Gyles Brandreth, *Farewell to Riches of the Earth*, *Daily Telegraph*, 25 June 2000)

Sheikh Yamani, left, Mr. Belaid Abdesselam, right, share a joke with Britain's Foreign Secretary Sir Alec Douglas Home at London's Foreign Office. The two Arab Oil Ministers were in London to discuss the oil situation

My generation and those before remember only too well the difficulties that led the USSR down the precipitous path to collapse. The blow to the country's budget, in which oil and gas revenues played such a huge role, brought economic then political meltdown. Stir in the deliberate policies of Gorbachev and his team and the lethal cocktail was complete. The story of those years has been told and retold with varying interpretations in countless books and articles, each commentator emphasising a different detail here, another factor there. All try to arrive at some kind of overall definitive explanation of why the Soviet Union came to what was in my view and shared by many, its ignominious end.

Oil, 'black gold', has been an ever-present hand on the steering wheel of modern history, and laid over that hand during a unique period were the skilful fingers of Sheikh Ahmed Zaki Yamani. Over the years I have had the opportunity to converse with the Sheikh on several occasions, and our discussions on the Middle East, the developments in Russia and the world situation in general have always been lively and illuminating. After reading my book *Oil and Geopolitics in the Caspian Region*, which I gave to him as a present, he wrote to me expressing a positive assessment of the work, drawing attention to the relevance of the analysis and the conclusions. Like many other Western politicians, political scientists and journalists, he quite openly and impartially expressed his negative views in relation to Boris Nikolaevich Yeltsin's decision to appoint Vladimir Putin as his successor.

Sheikh Yamani does not drink or gamble. Instead he enjoys time with his family, cooking, collecting old manuscripts, designing his own clothes and making perfume, a traditional Arabic art. In my opinion he has always been a high-class professional, courteous, attentive and a man of dignity. He also gives full credit to people where he believes it is due. As the originator of the North-South dialogue on international diplomacy, he was once at a conference chaired by his good friend Pierre Trudeau and the President of Mexico. At the end of the proceedings he was in no doubt about which of the other delegates he most admired: '*There were twenty-one heads of state and government...only two who did their homework and were shining people, worthy of the highest respect: Indira Gandhi and Margaret Thatcher – the two women! You raise your hat for them and you bow.*' (Ibid)

As far as the future for Saudi Arabia is concerned, he recalls the wise words of his friend King Faisal: '*In one generation we went from riding camels to riding Cadillacs. The way we are wasting money, I fear the next generation will be riding camels again.*' The days when he was on the front cover of newspapers and magazines the world over are long gone. Asked by Gyles Brandreth whether he missed being the centre of so much attention, he replied with characteristic philosophical charm: '*No. Too much light hurts the eyes. If you get away from it and have just enough to see your way you are a happier person.*'

BORIS NIKOLAYEVICH YELTSIN

Yekaterinburg is located in the Ural region of Russia, a sparsely populated, mountainous terrain that stretches from the Arctic Ocean all the way down to the Ural River. Built in 1723 the city has, like many places in Russia had its name changed back and forth during the last hundred years or so. The original name, which it bears again today, was inspired by Catherine, wife of Peter the Great and the monarch who succeeded him. In 1918 Yekaterinburg gained a grislier claim to fame when a group of Bolsheviks, fearful of the approaching Czech legions, took a decision about a certain group of prisoners in their charge; just before dawn in the Ipatiev House, Tsar Nicholas, his wife Alexandra and their five children were shot dead. In 1928 the city they died in was renamed Sverdlovsk in honour of the Communist leader Yakov Sverdlov.

To the east of the city lie the vast empty plains of Siberia, to where Hitler proposed to push the entire Russian population after Operation Barbarossa. As the Russian people fought valiantly to defeat him in that aim, a boy called Boris Nikolayevich Yeltsin, born near Sverdslovsk, was just turning ten years old. His childhood had already experienced a hiatus, between 1934 and 1936, when his father Nikolai had served hard labour in a gulag for anti-Soviet activity. The Yeltsins had now moved to Perm Krai, where Nikolai found intermittent work in the building trade. Boris attended the nearby Pushkin High School, where he enjoyed a range of sports, while his out of school activities included exploring a Red Army base with his friends, where, studying the inner workings of a grenade, he blew off a finger and thumb.

In 1955, Yeltsin left Sverdlovsk's Ural Polytechnic Institute with a degree

in construction and worked his way up to foreman then chief engineer and finally head of the local house-building combine. By 1976 he was the Sverdlovst Oblast Communist Party Committee's first secretary. It was in this capacity that the following year, he was given a simple yet symbolically significant task. The Ipatiev House in which the Romanovs had been executed, had since 1946 been declared a place of historic interest for the Communist Party. Lately, however, it was felt that too many of the visitors having their photograph taken at the site were in fact paying homage to the Tsar and his family. As local party secretary Yeltsin was therefore tasked in 1977 with demolition of the property. Yeltsin's status as a good Communist seemed cemented in 1981, with the award of the Order of Lenin and full membership of the party's Central Committee, and when Gorbachev took power in the Kremlin in 1985 he was called upon to lead the Committee's construction programme, and shortly after was made Mayor of Moscow. It was quite an ascent for an unknown boy from the Urals, but as we know Boris Yeltsin was destined for even higher office.

As mayor, Yeltsin gained popularity with the people by tackling corruption within the party and living in certain respects as an ordinary citizen, often eschewing a chauffeur driven car in favour of travelling by trolleybus. In September 1987, his individuality was displayed in a more serious manner. The trigger was a stern rebuke from Politburo member Yegor Ligachev over Yeltsin's apparently tolerant attitude to a minor public demonstration in the city. Stung by what he saw as unwarranted criticism, Yeltsin wrote promptly to Gorbachev tendering his resignation from the Politburo. It was an unprecedented action in the history of the Soviet Union. When asked by the leader to stay on, he not only claimed Ligachev's attitude made it impossible, but proceeded to question the validity of Gorbachev's own position. Gorbachev now turned on him, and before the party plenum Yeltsin was roundly denounced.

Though now out on a limb, Yeltsin benefited from a growing public disillusionment with Gorbachev, whose attempts to discredit his newfound enemy as simply a drunkard, had limited effect. Over the next three years Yeltsin's popularity steadily increased, reflected in his share of votes in the newly democratic Russia. When the anticipated coup of August 1991 took place, he wisely took the side of law and order against the plotters, famously mounting a tank outside the Russian White House to speak to the people:

'Citizens of Russia: On the night of 18–19 August 1991, the legally

elected president of the country was removed from power. Regardless of the reasons given for his removal, we are dealing with a rightist, reactionary, anti-constitutional coup. Despite all the difficulties and severe trials being experienced by the people, the democratic process in the country is acquiring an increasingly broad sweep and an irreversible character....We appeal to citizens of Russia to give a fitting rebuff to the putschists... Undoubtedly it is essential to give the country's president, Gorbachev, an opportunity to address the people.'

Russians demand to get rid of Yeltsin and his servants

For his magnanimity and insistence on following the rules, Yeltsin was rewarded four months later with the leadership of his country. December 1991 signalled the beginning of the end of the Soviet Union and the birth of the Russian Federation, with Yeltsin as its first president. To say he did not have an easy ride ahead of him would be a major understatement. The process of social and political fragmentation that had been triggered by Gorbachev, both internally and externally, was if anything accelerating.

Yeltsin seemed to think it best to aim for even greater democratisation and liberalisation of the markets, but how fast or slow should it proceed? His advisors were apparently divided on this issue. Yeltsin had to do something drastic, and threw his hat in with those who recommended removing price subsidies. The idea was that this would stimulate market forces and over time improve the economy as a whole. Yeltsin did his best to reassure parliament about the policy: '*Everyone will find life harder for approximately six months, then prices will fall.*'

By 1992 rampant inflation and high interest rates were set to mire Russia in an economic depression. At one point the inflation rate was running at an incredible 2000 per cent and many people found their savings virtually obliterated. Dwindling living standards, shortages in medical services and a growing incidence of crime throughout Russia were all largely blamed on the president. Meanwhile, increasingly high on the foreign agenda was the problem of Chechnya, and by the end of 1994 Yeltsin had ordered an invasion, which would tie up Russian troops in the country for almost two years. Was his motive to restore something of the old sense of the Soviet Union as a cohesive law-enforcing entity for its former republics, or a concession to reactionary elements in Russia? Western observers expressed confusion about Yeltsin: '*...had he become an old-style communist boss, turning his back on the democratic reformers he once championed and throwing in his lot with militarists and ultranationalists? Or was he a befuddled, out-of-touch chief being manipulated, knowingly or unwittingly, by—well, by whom exactly?*' (*Time Magazine*, 16 January 1995)

These uncertainties and instabilities at home and abroad inevitably brought backlash and power struggles within the government, and Yeltsin's position as president could no longer be taken for granted, as a well-supported attempt in March 1993 to impeach him had already demonstrated. Stir in the controversy over the oligarchs, grown rich overnight in what many regarded as effectively a giveaway of Russian state assets, and Yeltsin's opponents had further ammunition with which to attack him.

Boris Yeltsin with Margaret Thatcher at Downing Street. Thatcher remarked during his visit that he was a man we could do business with and they both clearly enjoyed each others' company

1996 brought a presidential election, in which the lines seemed starkly drawn between 'a return to totalitarianism' as Yeltsin's supporters described their Communist challengers' agenda, and continuing the journey towards modernisation and reform. Yeltsin, despite having suffered a number of recent heart attacks, threw himself into the campaign, enlisting the support of his daughter, Tatyana. In the election that June he scraped in with a narrow margin. In November he was in an operating theatre undergoing major heart surgery. He would be in hospital for several months.

For all his seemingly unpredictable behaviour and eccentricity, and amid all the problems that beset him health wise and politically, it seemed like Yeltsin was the cat with nine lives. Prone to frequent hiring and firing of his cabinet staff, he himself had an amazing capacity for survival, and when a further impeachment was attempted in 1999 he emerged apparently unscathed. However, all may not have been as it appeared; the Chechnya problem, one of the reasons cited by those seeking to impeach him, had not gone away, and when it literally blew up again in a series of bombings in Russian cities, it would bring another figure much closer into the political spotlight: Vladimir Putin. As prime minister at the time, Putin responded swiftly to the bombings by ordering an attack on the Chechen capital, thereby initiating a second war, and swiftly afterwards riding into the Kremlin on a wave of Russian patriotism.

This is one interpretation of events of course, and not necessarily the most accurate one. There have also been conspiracy theories about the bombings that prompted the air strike on Grozny. What is known for sure is that Yeltsin left office apparently voluntarily, and was absolved from prosecution. His resignation speech expressed a moving *mea culpa*:

> *'I want to ask for your forgiveness, that many of our dreams didn't come true ...that I didn't justify some of the hopes of those people who believed that with one stroke, one burst, one sign we could jump from the grey, stagnant, totalitarian past to a bright, rich, civilized future. I myself believed this.... in saying farewell, I want to say to every one of you: be happy. You deserve happiness...and peace.'*

Yeltsin drank even more whiskey than vodka. And it was quite true that he drank a lot, like crazy. This is a Russian illness. There were so many talented individuals I have known, lovely, clever people, whom I saw completely destroyed by alcohol – artists, journalists, engineers. Drink is good, its convivial, it binds people together, creates friendship and bonhomie, but you need to know your limits. I must have met Yeltsin a hundred times, and I can't recall many occasions when drink wasn't involved. In my autobiography I wrote about some very close colleagues in the Urals. My colleagues and I from Baku would get together with them about six times a year, either in Sverdlovsk or in Moscow. There were six of us in the group when we visited Sverdslovsk and it just so happened we all clicked, and it was here that I first met Yeltsin. In the Urals, as in Siberia, drink is part of the way of life; some say it's to keep out the cold, but of course that's an excuse.

During one of the first times I was out there, one of the visiting party said quite openly to our assembled hosts, *'It's dreadful that there's so much drinking goes on here – I like a drink myself but my absolute limit is one bottle of vodka.'* Our hosts looked dismayed at this information and drew in their breath. *'Only one bottle, surely not?'* someone replied, *'That's not enough to make it a good night.' 'All right,' my colleague conceded reluctantly, 'maybe two…' 'No – three…!'* came the thunderous reply. This was how the people of the Urals and Siberia would measure their drinking – not in units or glasses per week, but bottles per night. This was the reality. Gorbachev's attempts to restrict the consumption of alcohol in Russia would not have been popular here. The stark fact was though that many people died prematurely as a result of their habit.

We would have wonderful banquets in Sverdlosk, when all the locals drank heavily including Yeltsin. I was a city official in Baku at the time so we had quite a lot in common, he being leader of Sverdlovsk. They were doing well there in manufacturing and heavy engineering, and would ask me to send them consignments of oil, while I would order machinery we needed in Baku. In this way our friendship grew from simple social meetings into a good trading partnership as well.

As time went on Yeltsin and I went our separate ways, but when he became president I sent him a telegram of congratulation, and wished him success in the post. I then called him shortly afterwards and he picked up the phone straight away. A couple of months later I went to Moscow. The Soviet Union was on its way to being destroyed completely; indeed one could already feel the atmosphere changing, as if already the old ideals and ways of life we had taken for granted were slipping away. Economic cooperation among the regions had begun evaporating rapidly.

I was the Chairman of the Azerbaijan Committee for State Security (KGB) by this time, and discussed with Yeltsin the issues that we had in

Baku, and in the country generally. He was always very supportive. On arrival at his office I would ask, '*How many minutes can you give me?*' '*Never mind the minutes,*' was his standard reply. He didn't try to set a limit on meetings; his view was that a conversation must take as long as it takes. Talking to Yeltsin when he was president he was the same, just as I had always known him, warm, friendly and humorous, with no pretensions or ostentation about him. He hadn't changed as a person at all, a very good testimony to his character; an open minded and democratic person.

Then after the regime had changed in Baku and I had been persecuted there, I came to Moscow to see Yeltsin again. It was known that I had no post now and so he offered me a job, to work in his cabinet as administrator of the republics of Baskira and Tatary. Thinking back it was stupid of me not to accept this kind offer, and I should have known better. Hindsight is always very illuminating.

Yeltsin was a very strong personality and he also worked terribly hard. Considering the immense challenges, he dealt as well as anyone might have with the economy I think. He had started out his career overseeing some 18,000 people, and taking on that much responsibility as a young man he must have had to learn things fast; being thrown in at the deep end can be a great teacher, and this experience had taught him above all how to be a good manager. His only problem was the alcohol, over which he seemed to have no control.

Even after I had settled back in Moscow, the Aliyev government in Azerbaijan would give me no peace, and even wanted to extradite me back to the country. Really they disliked the idea of my being in the capital, and close as they saw it to the political elite, they felt that I posed a threat to the established order in Azerbaijan, fearing that, backed by Moscow, I might try to take over there at some point. Such notions were completely unfounded, as I had no intention or desire to get involved in politics, certainly not in Azerbaijan. But Aliyev, grooming his offspring to succeed him, was paranoid and trying to clean out anyone who might conceivably stand in the way of

The National Flag Day was celebrated in St Petersburg on 22 August 2015. Several hundred young people with small red, blue and white flags performed a dance on Palace square in front of Hermitage Museum. Russia's current flag was introduced by President Boris Yeltsin instead of the old Soviet flag and remains one of the few symbols of the new democratic Russia that exists today

this dynastic ambition. He therefore called Yeltsin and requested that I be sent back to Azerbaijan. Yeltsin's reply was unequivocal, and he basically said to Aliyey, what are you trying to do here? He could not touch me, Yeltsin told him, I was a Russian citizen and that was that.

My pursuer was not giving up so easily though. When the request to extradite me was repeated and Yeltsin again said 'no', Aliyvev decided to take matters into his own hands and dispatched members of his private security team to Moscow. I immediately called Yeltsin's private secretary, who in turn sent his security guards to call them off. Yeltsin stayed true to his friends. Our relationship was human, not political.

In public Yeltsin could often, knowingly or unwittingly, play the clown. Shortly after a heart attack in 1996 he was seen dancing crazily at a rock concert, and on another occasion arriving at Shannon Airport for an official visit to Ireland appeared to have fallen asleep on the plane, leaving the welcoming committee standing nonplussed on the tarmac. Everyone talks now about Yeltsin's drinking, and the TV cameras were always looking for the moment when he would once again stumble off a podium, slur his words comically or do something outrageous – 'looking for the strawberry' as they say in Russia. But what is much less remembered is that Yeltsin was a huge democrat and a person of great integrity. Who doesn't have a weakness of some kind? In Yeltsin's case it was alcohol, and he was no hypocrite about it; talking about the economy and vodka, he said the drink had a special place in Russian people's lives, that they enjoyed a nip or two after work – and so he would find it hard to raise the price! The alcohol problem was in large part an inherited one from the region he grew up in. There has even been a study linking the alcohol habits of people born in the Urals, Siberia and other harsh climates to a genetic factor.

About Yeltsin, to sum up I can only say I knew the good side of him. In general he never said no to people – journalists, fellow politicians, citizens – he gave freely of his time and efforts. He never did bad things to people, was never evil or cruel. In August 2007, a few months after his death, what were thought to have been the remains of the Romanovs were unearthed near their place of execution in Sverdlosvsk, now Yekaterinburg, the house that Yeltsin had once been ordered by the Soviet government to destroy. Had he lived to hear of the discovery, one cannot imagine him being unmoved.

Boris Yeltsin remains a controversial figure, and as regards his reputation the jury is still out. Traditionally in Russia from the time of the Tsars, as soon as a leader goes the mud slinging begins. But in Yeltsin's case I don't think this has really happened. The mud was just not there.

Yeltsin monument in Cholpon-Ata, Kyrgyzstan

KIM YONG-NAM

The Korean peninsula, a broad finger of land stretching into the Sea of Japan, is a place of stark contrasts. The north, bordering China and Russia, is largely mountainous, interspersed with arable valleys. The south is relatively warm with plentiful rainfall, while the north is colder. Some may see in this climactic variation a parallel with the societies and political systems of North and South Korea.

For centuries Korea was in essence a single entity, subject to periodic regional conflicts and in ancient times ruled over by a series of dynastic emperors. In more recent years Russia, China and Japan – together with America and the UN – have all played a part in the present day country's political formation. By the middle of the 19th century, sections of the Japanese hierarchy under Emperor Meiji, unhappy about the influence of China in a territory so close to its own waters, were seeking to take control of Korea. Enticed by the promise of raw materials and territorial expansion, there was the added opportunity of gainful occupation and renewed status for the thousands of Samurai warriors left idle by Meiji's modernisation.

Under a good deal of coercion, in 1876 Korea signed a treaty granting trading concessions and the right of habitation to Japanese citizens. Resistance to Japan's commercial takeover persisted throughout Korea, with some elements attempting a Japanese backed coup and others calling on Chinese support against the new interlopers. Competition over Korea brought Japan and China into direct conflict in the First Sino-Japanese War of 1894–5, which left the Chinese humiliated and Japan for the first time the dominant power in East Asia. However, whilst the peace treaty with China stipulated that the 'full and complete independence and autonomy of Korea' should be accepted by both parties, behind the scenes Japan was not relinquishing its hold on the country with ease. The year the war with

China ended, Korea's Queen Min was assassinated, later evidence pointing to a plot by the Japanese Minster to the country. Russia entered the story by providing shelter for the Korean royalty in the Russian diplomatic enclave in Seoul. In 1897, the royal family decided to assert their country's identity with the declaration that it was now an empire.

The thirteen years of the Korean Empire saw a programme of broad modernisation. A standardised system of weights and measures was introduced across the various diverse regions of the county, particularly for land ownership. American companies and Western entrepreneurs and technicians were brought in to install electric lighting, streetcars and telephones, including by 1902 a long distance call facility. Western dress styles, previously derided when the Japanese had adopted them, were also introduced. Meanwhile the Japanese presence remained strong, supported by a significant section of Korean society, and in 1905 a treaty was signed proclaiming the Korean Empire a protectorate of Japan.

Russia had also maintained an interest in Korea. By the end of the 19th century Russian businessmen had already secured stakes in Korean timber and mine workings. The Tsar's fleet had also been spotted in Port Arthur on the Chinese coast. Japan, top dog in the region since its victory over China, now kept an increasingly wary eye on Imperial Russia. Reluctant to test its strength against the Russian military, Japan offered the territory of Manchuria in exchange for exclusive access to Korea. Russia declined, demanding instead that the northern part of Korea remain neutral. Japan responded with a surprise attack on the Russian Navy at anchor in Port Arthur. The ensuing war would result in another victory for the Japanese, bolstering their hegemony in South East Asia. In 1910 they embarked on a full-scale occupation of Korea.

Japan would control Korea for the next thirty-five years. More Japanese merchants and property owners began arriving in the country, buying up further tracts of farmland. Korean tenant farmers were obliged to comply with the Japanese system whereby 50 per cent of their crop yield was surrendered as rent. To pay their families' taxes Korean womenfolk were sent to factories or forced to become prostitutes. Over the next two decades, however, as industrialisation was stepped up, large numbers of the population migrated to the growing cities.

The Japanese invested significantly in the country's infrastructure, building railways and schools, and whilst the production of local newspapers was curbed, to begin with the Japanese and Korean languages were in many areas taught in tandem. Significant numbers of Koreans also migrated to Japan during this period, either voluntarily in search of work or as forced labour. It is also said that recruitment into the Japanese Army was highly sought after by some young Koreans, a number of whom served on the construction of the notorious Burma Railway, guarding Allied prisoners of war, though by 1944, with the tide of World War Two turning against them the Japanese were scouring the country for conscripts. After the horrific *coup de grâce* of Hiroshima and Nagasaki, Korean migrant workers were among the thousands that lay dead across the two cities.

By this time both Soviet and American forces had entered Korea, from the North and South respectively, and an agreement was made to divide the country temporarily at the 38th parallel. A year later the US military administration in the South declared that Koreans who had been obliged to change their names while under Japanese rule could now do so. For many this was not an obvious choice, especially those still living in Japan, who feared being marginalized and hoped to remain there permanently. By 1948, any hope of a reunited country for them to return to had faded: the 38th parallel looked set to remain, a hostile border now between the Republic of Korea in the south and the Democratic People's Republic of Korea in the north.

In 1949, Kim il Sung visited Moscow to seek Stalin's support for a Communist revolution in South Korea. At first Stalin demurred, but in 1950, with Mao Zedong now installed in China and American troops departed from the Korean Peninsula, the idea seemed feasible, providing the Chinese could also guarantee back-up if required. That year Kim il Sung also met with Mao, who like Stalin, was said by some to be unwilling to provoke a war with the US through direct military involvement at this juncture. In dire need of Soviet arms and finance himself, Mao agreed to lend indirect tactical support.

The Soviet Union, which had been supplying arms to North Korea since 1949, now dispatched experienced military advisors. An attack it seemed was not yet a foregone conclusion. In early June 1950, Kim il Sung requested that an election be held throughout the whole of Korea to let the people decide if they wanted a Communist government, and diplomats were sent from the North to seek talks on the issue. Rhee, leader of the Republic of Korea, rejected the offer. Whilst which side fired the first shot remains in dispute, on the 25 June the Korean People's Army crossed the border into South Korea.

The war lasted three years, with troops from twenty-one countries eventually serving in the United Nations force sent to the region from the outset. The largest component at 88 per cent was the US military. The two sides played a deadly game of push me pull you, gaining and losing territory, with Seoul in the South being captured and recaptured four times during the course of the conflict. The North was bombed heavily and dogfights between jet aircraft were seen for the first time.

After the armistice in June 1953, the South Koreans signed a Mutual Defence Treaty with the American government. With the North facing economic ruin after the destruction of its factories and infrastructure, the Soviet Union agreed to waive or cancel outstanding debts and to make a million roubles worth of materials and goods available, while other European socialist countries offered similar help. China also waived debt and dispatched troops to assist in rebuilding work. In terms of social reconstruction, to consolidate the country ideologically an estimated 100,000 were executed in Communist Party purges. This darker side of North Korea seemed to stay dark throughout and beyond the Stalin era. Authors have suggested that in the post-war years to 1987 one million North Koreans died as a result of forced labour.

It has to be said that life was hardly an idyll for South Koreans, particularly in the more immediate aftermath of the war. Under the autocratic rule of President Syngman Rhee communist sympathisers were executed without trial by the thousand. US support for the oppressive regime stirred virulent anti-Americanism among the populace, while mixed race orphans fathered by GIs were shunned.

Deposed by a student uprising in 1960, Rhee was replaced by the equally despotic General Park Chun-hee whose tenure was ended by his assassination in 1979. In an attempt to improve relations with the North, in 2000 President Kim Dae-jung attended a summit meeting in Pyongyang. While Dae-jung was awarded the Nobel Peace Prize *'for his work for democracy and human rights in South Korea and in East Asia in general, and for peace and reconciliation with North Korea in particular,'* North Korea remained isolationist and provocative towards its southern neighbour.

It was in 1986 that I visited North Korea, having just begun working for Shevardnadze as the First Deputy Director of the Directorate of the Diplomatic Corps Servicing (UPDK) at the USSR Ministry for Foreign Affairs. The leader of the country since 1966 to 1994 was Kim Il Sung, who in 1950 had pushed for the invasion of South Korea, leading to the American intervention and the three-year war. Our delegation was given an extended tour. We all knew this was a totalitarian country, but personally I had not expected quite the atmosphere that greeted us. The place had a completely different vibe to anywhere I had been before.

One thing that struck me early on was that every single patch of land seemed to be put to some use or occupied, fenced off and allocated to some person or purpose – there was no waste ground – it was either someone's back yard, or parking space or orchard – this was quite different to other Asian countries where weed infested land quite often just meanders on without division or demarcation. Pyongyang was also extremely clean, as if the roads and pavements were regularly hosed down – perhaps they were – and there was not so much as a matchstick to be seen on the ground let alone an empty can or newspaper. Again this was especially unusual for an Asian country, and by then I had visited a lot of them.

I met the North Korean Minister of Foreign Affairs Kim Yong-nam in his office. It was all very formal and regimented. The Minister asked about our impressions of his country, and expressed his gratitude for the Soviet

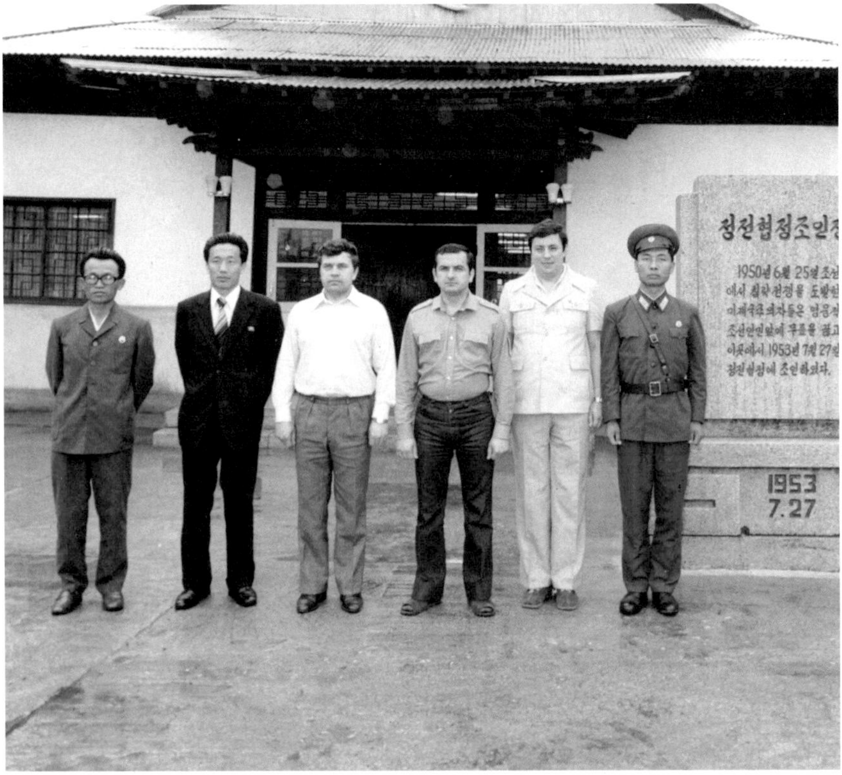
정전협정조인
정전협정에 조인하였다.
1953
7.27

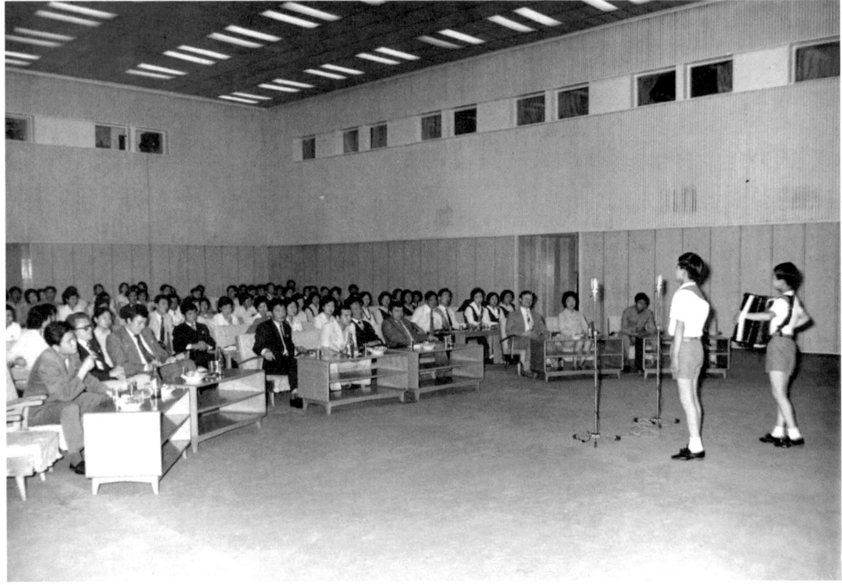

조국해방전쟁 제1계단 개관도

Vagif Guseynov's visit to North Korea in 1986

Meeting at Panmunjom on the North/South Korean border, with the delegation of the Soviet Union

Union's moral and practical support for North Korea. In Baku we had many North Koreans at the oil and gas institute, and they were also very well represented at other Soviet universities, many of them studying medicine. Their very active student community in the Soviet Union included numerous female undergraduates. In numerous Korean historical epics women featured strongly as heroines equal or even superior to men in their martial spirit, hardiness and valour, fighting off foreign invaders from China and Japan.

Another noticeable feature of North Korean society was that everyone seemed to be working, but unlike in Vietnam and Cambodia where people had recently suffered extreme deprivation and conflict, no one in North Korea really smiled in the same way. Whilst nobody was actually hostile or unpleasant, there seemed little in the way of sparkle or spontaneous human warmth. One felt the regime was really taking its toll on people. Was it fear? Probably. They worked hard and they had built a huge strong army, made technical by scientific advances, their public facilities were on the face of it exemplary, but there was this sense of flatness and sterility. Police were everywhere. After a couple of days I almost felt that when I lifted the toilet lid an officer with a large peaked cap would be staring back at me. One could feel the presence of the state intensely. Whatever people had told me about the totalitarian nature of this place was not an exaggeration. Everything was controlled and monitored.

One did get the distinct impression that foreigners and ex-pats could have a pretty good life here, luxurious by local standards, staying largely in separate settlements with their own bars, restaurants and community. One felt that any Americans here would almost certainly feel more comfortable keeping to themselves, for whilst the country used a lot of US products and technology, the North Koreans I spoke to were critical of everything American. For North Koreans this was a divided society in which the party elite lived well. The members of this elite were not hospitable in the sense of inviting us to their homes as people might do in the Soviet Union, that wasn't the practice here. Instead we were taken out – to restaurants, concerts and the opera.

Eating out here was a pleasure. People speak highly of Chinese food but the Korean offerings were superb. Being official visitors maybe my colleagues and I were given above average fare, but it was certainly the best Asian cuisine I have tasted. Grain based dishes and beef are popular, with the plentiful use of ginger, garlic and sesame oil. Dog meat incidentally, often associated with Korea, has I believe gone out of fashion other than for its supposed medicinal benefits. The opera house was full, the performance wonderful, but in the foyer and the auditorium, looking at people's faces and their behaviour again there was this peculiar sense of being somewhere very different. The cinemas showed no foreign films, the programmes consisting mainly of pictures with military and patriotic themes, and the television and press were all state controlled.

Whilst this all sounds very oppressive, on the other hand one didn't see people sleeping on the streets as in most other parts of Asia. Neither was anyone in rags, in fact everyone dressed the same – from the person sweeping the roads to the party officials, they all had the same grey safari suits. There were shops, including clothing stores where one could buy this functional, uniform attire. People were paid a basic salary and in addition received coupons twice a year for shoes, for example, and every two years say three shirts, with a new suit maybe every five years. For those that had dollars to spend, such as the foreign embassy staff, diplomats and overseas representatives, technicians and advisors, there were shops with more choice. North Koreans were not dying of starvation, but neither did they have anything in the way of luxury.

The infrastructure was impressive, the streets wide and well built and there was apparently no accommodation shortage, everyone had a roof over their head. Pyongyang city centre was very modern in appearance with plenty of skyscrapers, block housing and excellent public transport including trams and buses. Cars were less in evidence, and most belonged to party officials and foreigners. The capital city gave the impression of a highly up-to-date society, but there was also something fake about it, the all-round cleanliness adding to the sense of unreality. It seemed like a showpiece for tourists, an exhibition of socialist achievement and efficiency. This concrete landscape was not the norm for 95 per cent of North Koreans, who worked out in the countryside on farms.

Korean civilisation predates the Chinese and the country's early history is extremely interesting, with their art and culture having deep roots. During the Japanese occupation a great many artefacts were plundered and taken to Japan. Through international diplomacy some progress has been made in recovering this heritage, and the museums in Pyongyang contain plenty of fascinating exhibits. The contemporary culture, however, was one of uniformity – in dress, speech, behaviour and attitude. Pictures of the leader were everywhere, again, under the toilet seat seemed the only place you did not see his face. This was the cult of personality in its most all-pervading visual manifestation. Since the 1970s North Korean officials had been issued with a badge bearing a portrait of whichever one of the Kims was in power. If an official was seen outside of his or her home without their badge they risked being accused of committing a symbolic act of disobedience, of being a dissident, inviting imprisonment or worse. All Koreans citizens were expected to have a picture of the leader on display somewhere in their home.

The words of Confucius might once have been the prevailing philosophy in North Korea, but now the official religion was unquestionably based on something called Juche. Kim il Sung's 1955 speech referring to the term, also contained the following: '*To make revolution in Korea we must know Korean history and geography as well as the customs of the Korean people. Only then is it possible to educate our people in a way that suits them and to inspire in them an ardent love for their native place and their motherland.*'

The idea of loving the motherland somehow became equated with loving the Great Leader, who by implication is infallible and beyond criticism. Affirmation of this love is expressed not just through the ubiquitous portraits of the leader but also importantly through public rituals like the Arirang Festival, a celebratory display of gymnastics and artistic performances. Do those taking part put their heart and soul into the event willingly? According to refugees from North Korea the discipline and commitment of the Arirang participants is achieved not by encouragement but fear, beating and scolding people into submission like circus animals.

Three principles of Juche in relation to North Korea's position in the world have been defined as political independence, economic self-sustenance and self-reliance in defence. With regard to self-sustenance, in the decade following my visit, when I had noted that everyone in North Korea seemed adequately fed, the country suffered a severe famine. Partly due to the loss of food support from Russia following the break up of the Soviet Union, at least 500,000 people are said to have died, with some estimates putting the figure closer to a million.

As for the third principle of Juche, to be self-reliant in defence in the post-war world meant for North Korea one thing above all, the development of nuclear weapons, and in 1963 Pyongyang approached Moscow for assistance. The request was refused, and instead the Soviet Union offered to help the country build a nuclear energy programme. China later refused a similar plea for non-peaceable nuclear development input. In January 2007, three months after the North Korean government had announced it had carried out its first nuclear test, the front page of the *Pyongyang Times* bore the following headline: *'Usher in a great heyday of Songun Korea full of confidence in victory!'* Allied to the concept of Juche, Songun is the principle that the military is the first priority of the Korean government, its people and economy. Songun was adopted as a central feature of national identity in 1994, the year of Kim Il Sung's death, also and perhaps no coincidence the start of the calamitous famine. Now the country was proudly claiming to be in possession of nuclear weapons.

Fast-forward ten years to 2017. Kim Il Sung's successor, thirty-three-year-old Kim Jong Un was last year firing missiles over his country's old enemy Japan and engaging in a shouting match with the US President. Like most of us, rather nervously I continue to watch and wait with interest.

'To Rena, with wishes of success and happiness in life! 19.01.77

VITALY ZHOLOBOV

When Alexei Leonov stepped out among the stars in 1965, the second great milestone in space exploration had been reached. The fact that it had again been a Soviet mission was not lost on the Americans. The National Aeronautics and Space Association (NASA) had been far from idle. Founded in 1958, NASA had begun Project Mercury that same year with the intention of being the first to launch a man into space. Their astronaut in waiting was Alan Shepherd, who, when he heard the news of Gagarin's flight in April 1961, was alleged to have slammed his fist down on a table so hard that a colleague feared it would break. Shepherd came a close second just a few weeks later piloting his craft *Freedom 7* on a fifteen-minute sub-orbital flight around the Earth.

The boundaries pushed by Gagarin, Leonov, Tereshkova and the other Soviet cosmonauts throughout the early 1960s had served to galvanise American intent. President John F. Kennedy had initially seemed indifferent to the space race and was put off by the high costs involved. At the beginning of 1961 an ambitious proposal by NASA to vastly outstrip the Soviets by sending an astronaut to the Moon by 1970 was turned down on budgetary grounds. By the spring, as Gagarin's smiling face appeared on billboards and TV screens around the world, Kennedy was having second thoughts. With the US government still smarting from a loss of face over the Bay of Pigs debacle, and now their international rival in that confrontation taking on the universe and winning, the country was in need of a morale boosting and patriotic initiative.

In a Special Message on Urgent National Needs delivered to a joint session of Congress on 25 May 1961, Kennedy appeared to suggest that taking the lead in the space race could also bring victory in the Cold War, '*...if we are to win the battle that is now going on around the world between* *freedom and tyranny, the dramatic achievements in space which occurred in recent weeks should have made clear to us all, as did the Sputnik in 1957, the impact of this adventure on the minds of men everywhere, who are attempting to make a determination of which road they should take... Since early in my term, our efforts in space have been under review. With the advice of the Vice President, who is Chairman of the National Space Council, we have examined where we are strong and where we are not, where we may succeed and where we may not. Now it is time to take longer strides—time for a great new American enterprise...'* Kennedy stressed that upping America's game in space exploration would take several years and a great deal of money – up to $9 billion, a breathtaking sum in the 1960s. But then the destination he had in mind, the plan he rejected only weeks before, was equally breathtaking: '*I believe we should go to the Moon.*'

Kennedy would not live to see his ambition for the American people fulfilled. Among those following events closely on 21 July 1969, as Neil Armstrong emerged from *Apollo* and placed his feet on the surface of the Moon, was Soviet Cosmonaut Vitaly Mikhailovich Zholobov. Born on 18 June 1937 in Staraya Zbur'evka, a village in the Kherson region of Ukraine, Zholobov had studied at the Azerbaijan Institute of Petroleum and Chemistry After graduating in 1959 he served in the Soviet military and trained as a fighter pilot. Post-graduate study followed in the early 1970s, at V. I. Lenin Political-Military Academy.

Although Zholobov had spent time in Azerbaijan I did not have the pleasure of meeting him until later in his career. By that time his achievements had made him a well-known figure in the Soviet Union, indeed around the world. He had been admitted to the hallowed ranks of the Soviet Space Programme's cosmonaut group in 1963, a high achievement in itself, since all incomers are selected from the top aviators, all of them fighter pilots, and on average only six in one hundred go through. In the course of conversation I once asked him how he got into the cosmonaut team; the competition being so intense, was there any special preparation that he undertook for example? His answer surprised me: *'I did not think about becoming a cosmonaut, and I always thought that cosmonauts were people with specialist training, who were being prepared from an early age.'* Referring to Gagarin and the other pioneers of space travel, he said that *'we considered cosmonauts as gods, special people.'* And comparing such remarkable individuals to himself and thinking about what they went through – and more to the point where they went – the god-like status attached to them seemed justified. I had to agree with him. *'Then suddenly in 1963,'* said Zholobov, *'I was asked to join the group of cosmonauts. I passed all the tests and worked in the Cosmonaut Training Centre until 1981.'*

To summarise his career thus was a vast understatement on Zholobov's part, as well as extremely modest. To put his achievements into context we should begin by looking at the Salyut programme. After the Americans became the first to put a man on the Moon, in response to US Skylab programme and to assist in making their own lunar landing at some point, the Soviet Union began work on a series of orbiting space stations. A year in construction, with a length of 14.4 metres and at its widest point a diameter of 4.15 metres, *Salyut 1* was launched on 19 April 1971 from the Baikonur Cosmodrome. Three days later a team of cosmonauts followed on by rocket, *Soyuz 10*, but after encountering difficulties in docking with the space station, returned to Earth. On 6 June, a second crew comprising Georgi Dobrovolski, Vladislav Volkov and Viktor Patsayev was mobilised via *Soyuz 11*, which managed to dock successfully.

Once aboard, the cosmonauts would monitor and test the capabilities of the space station – its control systems, how well it could manoeuvre, its navigational efficiency, speed, and the suitability of its internal facilities and accommodation. In addition to collecting data about the extra-terrestrial environment the crew would conduct studies of the Earth's surface from the perspective of space – their planet's geological formation, geographical features and weather patterns. The effects on the human body of living and working in space for a prolonged period would also be observed and recorded. '*Salyut 1 was equipped to perform a range of scientific experiments, and the spacecraft actually performed well although events surrounding it might suggest otherwise.*' (Robert Christy, *Zarya: Soviet, Russian and International Space Flight*)

Following an electrical fire and other concerns on the station on 29 June, after twenty-three days it was decided that the *Salyut 1* mission should be brought to an end. In that time its cosmonauts had not only achieved the distinction of flying in the first manned space station, but set a new record for the longest period spent in space. The crew returned to *Soyuz 11*, re-entered the Earth's atmosphere and came down 200 kilometres southwest of Kustanai in Kazakhstan. When the capsule was found the hatch was still closed, and on opening it the recovery personnel discovered the crew inside, all three of them dead. An inquest gave the cause of death as asphyxiation due to a faulty valve in the capsule.

Dobrovolski, Volkov and Patsayev did not get the chance to celebrate their record-breaking voyage but their achievement and their names live on. Their sacrifice also paved the way for future comrades to fly in greater safety: '*Members of the Soyuz 11 crew were not wearing space suits. The Soyuz re-design, which followed the Soyuz 11 accident, introduced them for subsequent cosmonaut crews.*' (Ibid)

Following the accident, further missions to *Salyut 1* (which would have included Alexei Leonov) were cancelled and the space station was left to burn out. The next attempt came on 3 April 1973 with the launch of *Salyut 2*. Its undisclosed purpose was to be a military reconnaissance satellite, part of the Almaz programme begun by the Soviet Union in the 1960s. An explosion three days later, however, caused the space station to depressurise. As the structure became strained and began to deteriorate, the loss of the solar panels left *Salyut 2* unable to generate power and by the end of May the debris had fallen into the Pacific Ocean. Its successor, *Salyut 3*, spent six months in space from June 1974, and was again intended to gather military intelligence via, it is believed, a number of on-board cameras trained towards

'To Vagif, son of Aliouset with great respect and appreciation! 18.01.77'

Zholobov arriving at Baku airport in 1977

Earth. *Salyut 4* survived a far longer time in space, from December 1974 until February 1977, among its facilities a running machine to maintain the cosmonauts' fitness while measuring their physical responses.

Meanwhile on 22 June 1976, the launch had already taken place of *Salyut 5*, and cosmonaut Vitaly Zholobov would now be called upon to serve. Zholobov took off on 6 July and docked at the space station one day later. Whilst the military function of the mission again remained under wraps, Zholobov and his comrade, flight engineer Boris Volynov carried out a number of other scientific experiments and observations. Excited schoolchildren were also able to take part in a televised discussion with the cosmonauts as they went about their work far above the Earth – finding out for example about the crystals being grown on board and how being in space affected the fish in an aquarium. All was going smoothly on *Salyut*

'Enjoyed our meeting! All the best wishes in life, Vagif! 23.01.77'

5 until around mid-August when Zholobov began to feel unwell. He and Volynov had noticed a pungent odour, which Zholobov told ground control smelt like that of a toxic propellant. The cause was traced to a fuel leak that had released nitric acid fumes into the living quarters. On the 24 August Zholobov and Volynov returned to Earth.

The television link-up with *Salyut* 5 had brought the work of the cosmonauts into the public eye in a new and more intimate way. Two further crews flew to *Salyut* 5, with a fourth mission being abandoned due to a lack of propellant, and the structure was subsequently de-orbited, burning up on re-entry to the Earth's atmosphere. With specialised spy satellites now taking over the role of military reconnaissance, *Salyuts* 6 and 7, which would be the last in the programme, were used largely for civilian scientific research. Improvements on these stations included a second docking port, enabling unmanned Progress craft to deliver supplies and dispose of waste. A total of sixteen crews worked on *Salyut 6*, the longest for 185 days, with cosmonauts also making extensive space walks of up to two hours duration.

Had Zholobov crewed the final Salyut he would have enjoyed the comfort of a refrigerator, electric stoves and hot running water, along with improved exercise and medical facilities. The last cosmonauts left *Salyut 7* in 1986, transferring equipment to the new Mir space station. The first to be assembled in space, the Mir station was equipped for advanced experiments in a range of sciences, and its facilities designed for long-term human

Vagif Guseynov is greeted by Zholobov in 1978

occupation. Over 1994 and 1995 Soviet cosmonaut Valeri Polyakov spent just under 438 days on board, setting the record for the longest stay in space. Mir, which remained in operation until 2001, was also the first space station to host a civilian, the Japanese television journalist Toyohiro Akiyama, who was given special cosmonaut training for the job. With advertisements for Japanese companies painted on the rocket that carried the journalist, the Soviet Union claimed to have earned several million dollars from the deal, making it the first commercial space flight.

Though *Salyut 7* had been Vitaly Zholobov's first and last voyage into space, his contribution to the Soviet exploration programme had really only just begun at that point. He would also serve extensively in the world of business and public affairs. Resigning from the Soviet military in 1981, between 1983 and 1987 he worked as a Deputy General Director of the scientific organisation Mayak Production Association, and was elected as a Deputy of the Kiev City Council of People's Deputies. In the 1990s he was elected as a full member of the Transport Academy of Ukraine, and from 1993 he was Chairman of the Council of Heroes of the Soviet Union in Kiev. The following year came his election as the Head of Administration of the Kherson Region.

The list of his high-level jobs grows ever more impressive. From June 1996 to February 1997 he held the post of Deputy General Director of the National Space Agency of Ukraine. From 2001 he was President of the Ukrainian Association Slava, and from April 2002 President of the Aerospace Association of Ukraine. Equally praiseworthy are his titles and awards: Hero of Soviet Union, the Order of Lenin, the Order of Merit III Class, the Medal for Merit in Space Exploration and Merited Master of Sport of the USSR. Vitaly is also an Honorary Citizen of Baikonur, Kherson, Kaluga, Prokopyevsk, and Tselinograd.

It was during a visit to Zviozdny Gorodok, also known as Star City, the location of the Yuri Gargarin Cosmonaut Training Centre set up in the 1960s, that I first met Vitaly. As this magical name implies, Star City is a place where Russia's cosmonauts live, work and play. It is a self-contained community with a railway station, houses, shops, post office, schools, sports halls and a cinema. Today the public can visit the Museum of Space Exploration and get a taste of what space feels like in the weightlessness training facility. There is even a statue of Laika the space dog.

In Soviet times Star City was a closely guarded top-secret military enclave, to which few outsiders could gain access. Among those who on occasions could go in, were members of the Central Committee of Komsomol who had been given special permission. As mentioned in the chapter on Leonov, Sergey Pavlov, the First Secretary of Komsomol, and Yuri Gagarin had made this possible by establishing a protocol for conferences and social events to bring cosmonauts and Russian youth together. Nowadays the young people getting the chance to see Star City are not just Russians. The US organisation People to People International sponsored a party of American science students to attend in 1992, which was followed by reciprocal invitations for Star City pupils to visit the States.

After our first meeting, Vitaly and I reunited in Moscow. From that moment on we became good friends and would often get together at our home on Kutuzovsky Prospekt or at his place in Zviozdny Gorodok, where my wife Habiba and I had many other good acquaintances. Then when I returned to Baku I invited Vitaly to come and stay with me there. Everyone welcomed him warmly, and at his old seat of learning, the Azerbaijan Oil and Chemistry Institute, he met the current crop of students and recalled his own time spent studying there. He also looked in on a number of schools in Baku, where staff and pupils alike were thrilled to meet this famous cosmonaut. No doubt some of them had the treasured 1976 postage stamps featuring the portraits of Vitaly and his *Salyut* 5 comrade Boris Volynov in their collections. Vitaly was also well received by Heydar Aliyev, the then first secretary of the Central Committee of the Party of Azerbaijan.

Sociable, laid back and funny, Vitaly is the life and soul of any party, and carries a good store of jokes and anecdotes. More than that he can put them across. Some people deliver even the best joke or story badly, so that you don't know whether to laugh or cry – Vitaly always tells them well, he has that flair. He was very young when he became a cosmonaut, and although about five years older than me he has remained young at heart, which I have observed is fairly typical of cosmonauts. When you have seen what they have seen, I guess you know not to take life too seriously.

That's not to say that Vitaly doesn't take his work extremely seriously. One of the reasons I have not seen as much of him as I would wish in the last couple of years is that he has been based in Siberia at an advanced space research and development centre. Partly for reasons of security his work in this area has in the past been little known about. In the Soviet era in particular, the government did not want the identity of individuals vital to the military and space programmes to be in the public domain lest foreign powers or terrorists try to assassinate or kidnap them. The other reason that people like Vitaly nowadays are much less noticeable is that their roles are by definition behind the scenes. To me he will always be very visible though: among my most treasured possessions is a beautiful photograph of him lifting my daughter off her feet as if to launch her into space. Vitaly has a big, sunny smile on his face, and in the caption underneath he is saying simply: *'Be Happy RENA!'*

AFTERWORD

And so my wanderings through past times and places are now complete. In historical terms it might appear that I have covered only a short distance – a mere fifty years! But within that span life everywhere has changed, in some areas quite profoundly and radically. I am afraid it must also be conceded that, overall, the world has not become more reasonable or kinder. How this affects us, depends on our situation. Our famous writer Yury Trifonov was right when he said that, *'Every man is affected by the reflection of history. It burns with a hot and formidable light for some people, is barely perceptible for others, heats up only slightly, but exists for everyone. History blazes like a vast bonfire and every one of us throws our own firewood into it.'*

I was three years old when World War II ended and twelve when Stalin died in 1953. When Yury Gagarin became the first man in space in 1961, I was still a fairly young lad. Even in 1981, which of us could have imagined that the Soviet Union would disappear forever? Che Guevara considered the deviation of the Soviet economy from Marxist dogma as the sure fire way to the destruction of the USSR, but even he would have been surprised at the speed with which the events unfolded in 1991.

To this day I recall my surprise when Che appeared from the jungle during my trip to Congo. I remember his magnetism, the tone of his voice and how I was stunned to hear about his death in Bolivia several months later. I also recall down to the last detail my unexpected meeting with Archbishop Krakov, who was elected Pope John Paul II shortly afterwards. I remember being struck by his openness and ease of communication, and by his knowledge of classical Russian poetry.

Some of the people in this book I met only once, others became my friends and comrades. There is no doubt that these famous cosmonauts, artists, thinkers, politicians, writers, soldiers and religious leaders, with their diverse talents and characters comprised the spirit and atmosphere of the twentieth century and created its history. Some of them continue their, often selfless, endeavours into the new century.

Our conversation with you dear reader has been about personalities of great magnitude, figures that have dominated their era, and in many cases determined the fates of whole states and millions of people. Everyone has their own version of the past, which also lends a unique value to their vivid recollections – their conversations, dialogues, disputes, pronouncements and judgements. The thirty-nine people here, in their various walks of life, attitudes and opinions, embody all the diversity of the times through which they lived.

There were many other people who left their mark on my life. I did mention Egon Krenz briefly, and now I would like to say a little more about him. A trip I took at the end of 1970s with Egon, leader of the Socialist Youth in Honecker's East Germany, was extremely memorable and instructive. We were travelling on the Baikal-Amur Mainline, the railway that traverses eastern Russia and Siberia. Stopping off along the way in builders' log cabins, Egon and I became friends. Like most German comrades a thoughtful and theoretically literate Marxist, Egon studied the Soviet Union with interest, and saw and understood its problems, and was not perturbed by them in the slightest: '*We have set our sights on a new civilisation, we can't get there without making some mistakes. For we are taking a path into the unknown.*'

By the beginning of the 1980s Egon Krenz was a prominent public figure – intelligent, energetic and insightful. In order to stand out in Honecker's team, which boasted an abundance of bright personalities, you needed to have truly outstanding capabilities. The election of Krenz as Secretary of the Central Committee of the Social Unity Party of Germany, and a member of the Politburo, and his subsequent ascent to the very pinnacle of power of the German socialist state, was perceived as a natural phenomenon. Only the Soviet catastrophe, which plunged the German Democratic Republic likewise into the abyss, interrupted the brilliant career of this extraordinary individual.

Egon Krenz was not the only one to suffer in the political vortex following the collapse of the Soviet Union. In the difficult post-socialist era, when the prosecutions of communists began in Germany, Krenz endured the gruelling and protracted Politburo Process, and spent six years in the notorious Maobit and Pletzsenzee prisons. I was struck by the judicial wording that served as the basis for his eventual release in 2003: *'Owing to the low probability of a repeat crime.'*

Other young leaders appearing in my notebooks – perspicacious, vibrant, modern thinkers – include Ion Traian Tefănescu (Romania), S. Rafael Arube (Cuba), Slabomir Yakubovsky (Poland), Gafurdzhanov (Uzbekistan) and Zakash Kaletdinov (Kazakhstan). Alongside some of these names I have set down detailed records. Take for example Dang Quoc Baoguo – the strong-willed military associate of Le Duan, successor to the legendary comrade and father of Vietnamese socialism Ho Chi Minh. We look on comrade Dang in the same way that as children we admired Alexey Maresyev – the living embodiment of Soviet heroism! Dang commanded a division and became a general after fighting in the jungle for more than twenty years. A merited partisan of Vietnam – this was the deserved leader of Vietnamese youth! Arriving on an official visit to Moscow in 1979, comrade Dang walked in quick time into the conference room of the Central Committee of the All-Union Leninist Young Communist League, laid out maps in military fashion, and explained clearly and precisely the strategy and tactics the Vietnamese youth were using in their continuing transition to peace building.

Returning to the monumental changes that have taken place in Russia and Eastern Europe, here are the prophetic words of my Yugoslavian friend Mohammed Agalich in 1979: *'A dozen years will pass and what we are now discussing on the basis of trust in open discussions – on socio-economic backwardness, the need for pluralism and greater democracy – everybody will discuss this publicly. Actual socialism needs to be revamped, while socialist theory and ideology must be modernised in line with the facts. Communists could incur the same fate as ideologists who lived three hundred to four hundred years ago – they overlooked developments and missed out the transition from a traditional society to a modern one. Then "God died", and hardly anyone paid due attention to this tragic fact. God died. So what, said Europeans, but at least now we have progress, development …'*

And here is an extract from the speech at the Secretariat of the Central Committee of the All-Union Leninist Young Communist League given by the head of the Estonian Komsomol Indrek Toome, discussing worrying tendencies prevalent in the mood of the young: *'We castigate popular culture, deride ubiquitous Americanisation, nevertheless it has swept through Europe and is capturing more and more ground. Pervasive information, ideological and cultural intervention is underway, but we think that this offensive can be withstood by delivering lectures on propaganda.'* In 1988–1990 I. Toome will head the government of a re-born Estonia, be forced to resign by national revolutionaries, and will then go into business, in this endeavour emerging as a modern thinker and a dynamic figure.

So much that Toome and others warned us of, what they feared and dreamed, what they laughed at or grieved over, happened in the space of just a dozen or so years. This demonstrates more than anything else the foresight and professionalism of the leaders of the youth organisations leaders at that time. Idrek Toome is one person I know about, but what happened to others like him during these long and difficult years in the lives of their countries, and where are they now? I hope that they remained true to their convictions and attained the goals that they had set themselves.

The heroes and heroines in this book have helped me to understand that exceptional people spend a large part of their lives working to attain their goals, and that achievement doesn't happen overnight. Through their example, they can also provide convincing answers to some of the most profound questions that life poses for all of us: How should I live? What is the purpose of my existence? What drives me on? Sometimes it is only when we look back, remembering events both large and small, and reflecting on them in our own way that we can know the answers. Only then can we see the wood from the trees, and the firewood that each of us has cast into the vast bonfire of history.

A PORTRAIT OF VAGIF GUSEYNOV

Vagif Guseynov with his extended family

Vagif Guseynov with his with friend and colleague Yuri Poroikov and their wives

GLOSSARY

AVO	Hungarian Secret Police
Bolshevik	Literally 'one of the majority' Bolshevism was the political movement that rose to power under Lenin after the October 1917 Revolution
CIA	Central Intelligence Agency of the United States
CPSU	Communist Party of the Soviet Union
GDR	German Democratic Republic
Great Patriotic War	World War Two as referred to by Russians
Gulags	Labour camps in the Soviet Union
International Pen	Now PEN International, an association of writers that promotes literature and defends freedom of expression
KGB	Soviet secret police and intelligence agency
Komsomol	Soviet Youth organisation affiliated to the CPSU
Kremlin	Literally 'Fortress within a city'. The Russian seat of government. A symbol of the Soviet state and now the Russian parliament, the Kremlin is also one of the largest and most important museums in the country
Kristallnacht	Crystal Night or 'Night of Broken Glass', the mass smashing of Jewish shop windows and synagogues throughout Germany by Nazi paramilitary and civilians during 9 to 10 November 1938
Machiavellian	Scheming, manipulative, from 15th century Florentine political thinker Niccolo Machiavelli, author of The Prince, sometimes called the Bible of realpolitik
Nagorno-Karabakh	Disputed region of Azerbaijan, where armed conflict took place between Armenia and Azerbaijan
NATO	North Atlantic Treaty Organisation
NKVD	People's Commissariat for Internal Affairs: Soviet secret police organisation between 1934 and 1946
Oblast	A term denoting an administrative region, similar to a county or state, used within Russia and parts of the former Soviet Union Star City (Zvyozdny gorodok) Site of Yuri

	Gagarin Cosmonaut Training Centre near Moscow. Set up in the Soviet era, Star City is also a space research facility and community, where cosmonauts work and live with their families
OPEC	Organisation of Petroleum Exporting Countries Order of
Lenin	Highest civilian decoration in Soviet Russia, also awarded for outstanding military service and to individuals that have promoted peace, friendship and cooperation
Politburo	The Soviet Communist Party's supreme policy-making body
Pravda	Literally 'The Truth', from 1918 to 1991 the official newspaper of the Central Committee of the Communist Party
Presidium	Collective Head of State of the Soviet Union
Realpolitik	Coined in the 19th century by Ludwig von Rochau, realpolitik stresses a pragmatic approach to politics, tending to look at what is achievable, rather than at ideology
Red Army	Name for the Bolshevik Army after the October 1917 Revolution, and which in the 1920s became the Soviet Army
Rouble	Currency of the Russian Empire, the Soviet Union and now the Russian Federation
Russian Federation	The official name for Russia since 25 December 1991 NASA America's National Aeronautics and Space Association
SALT	Strategic Arms Limitation Talks/Treaty
Salyut	Literally: 'fireworks' or 'salute'. A series of space stations operated by the Soviet Space Programme from 1971 to 1986
Samizdat	Underground or unofficial publishing during the Soviet era
SFSR	Soviet Federative Socialist Republic
Solidarity	Polish labour movement founded in 1980 by Lech Walesa, and which grew to a membership of 10 million, a third of

	the country's working age population. The first Warsaw Pact trade union not under the control of a communist party
Soyuz	A series of spacecraft launched by the Soviet Space Programme from 1967
Sputnik	The world's first artificial satellite, launched from the Soviet Union 4 October 1957
START	Strategic Arms Reduction Talks/Treaty
Subbotnik	From Russian: суббóта for Saturday – was a day of volunteer unpaid work on weekends following the October Revolution. Initially they were indeed volunteer, but gradually de facto obligatory upon announcement, as people quipped, 'in a voluntary-compulsive way' (в добровольно-принудительном порядке). The Subbotniks were mostly organized for cleaning the streets of garbage, fixing public amenities, collecting recyclable material, and other community services.
TASS	Telegraph Agency of the Soviet Union. Today TASS is the principle Russian news agency and ranked fourth largest in the world
USSR	Union of Soviet Socialist Republics
Warsaw Pact	The Soviet response to NATO, a treaty of friendship, cooperation and mutual defence between eastern European countries, founded in Warsaw, Poland in 1955 with the motto 'Union of Peace and Socialism'
UAE	United Arab Emirates
UNESCO	United Nations Educational, Scientific and Cultural Organisation
Utopia	An ideal society. From the book of 1516 by Thomas More
Yom Kippur	Hebrew for the Day of Atonement, an annual Jewish Holy day involving 25 hours of fasting, prayers and repentance.

INDEX

Page numbers in italics refer to photographs.

H

I

PICTURE CREDITS

The pictures used in this book are from the author's own collection with the exception of the following:

Alamy: pages 10, 19, 22, 36, 47, 55, 88, 112, 115, 116, 119, 121, 126, 130, 135, 139, 149, 153, 155, 157, 171, 179, 181, 183, 189, 195, 197, 201, 203, 205, 208, 235, 237, 245, 247, 249, 268, 273, 275, 276, 283, 287, 293, 295, 312, 319, 344, 348, 353, 355, 359, 379, 394, 398, 403, 405, 419, 420, 422, 434, 437, 441, 443, 444, 449, 451, 457, 459, 461, 465, 469, 473

Getty Images: pages 48, 66, 271

usefulstooges.com/2015: page 61